A SCHOOLWIDE SECONDARY
READING PROGRAM

A SCHOOLWIDE SECONDARY READING PROGRAM: HERE'S HOW

BURT LIEBERT
University of California, Davis

MARJORIE LIEBERT
Sacramento City Unified School District

John Wiley & Sons
New York   Chichester   Brisbane   Toronto

Copyright © 1979, by John Wiley & Sons, Inc.

Library of Congress Cataloging in Publication Data

Liebert, Burt.
    A schoolwide secondary reading program.

    Includes index.
    1.   Reading (Secondary education)
2.   Reading disability.   I.   Liebert, Marjorie,
joint author.   II.   Title.
LB1632.L52   428'.4'0712   78-10904
ISBN 0-471-03549-1

Printed in the United States of America

10 9 8 7 6 5 4 3 2 1

To:

Gary
Cathy
Mark
Nina
Scott
Judy

I should like to thank Cynthia Barnhart for her helpful suggestions for teaching the Let's Read material, Don Greelis for the many projects he has undertaken to help bring this volume to completion, and my wife Margie for her illustrations and for the many ideas she has given me for improving the manuscript.

CONTENTS

A SCHOOLWIDE SECONDARY READING PROGRAM

INCIDENT IN A PUBLIC SCHOOL   "What are the legal qualifications for United States senator?" The teacher's eyes surveyed the room, searching for a volunteer. None surfaced. "Tom Bowman," she called. Tom studied a beetle crawling across the floor and said nothing.

"Tom, can you tell me the qualifications for becoming a United States senator?" Tom's eyes were half closed, but a flush in his cheek revealed that he was not unaware of the question.

"Can you tell me *one* qualification?" A slight movement of the head—barely perceptible—indicated negative. "Well, why not?" Silence, with the color of Tom's cheek increasing.

"Were you unable to study last night? Did you have something more important to do? Is that it?" A light shrug of the shoulders.

"Well, all I can say, young man, is that if you won't even try . . . if you won't even read the assignment . . . I never flunk a student who tries. . . . But . . ." She called on someone else. Yet there is something the teacher did not bother to find out.

You see, Tom Bowman—six feet one-and-a-half inches tall—all conference tackle in his junior year—Tom Bowman, one hundred ninety pounds of well-trained bone and muscle—this young man who now sat with eyes on the floor and lips glued together, wishing he could disappear until the final dismissal bell—this handsome young man had managed to reach the eleventh grade without learning to read.

Well, not exactly. Tom could read—a little. But he had long ago given up trying. Because, for Tom to have ploughed through thirteen pages of social studies, would have taken as much time and energy, word for word, as it took you to plough through the preceding paragraph. And when he finished, he would have come to the same conclusion that I suspect you came to about the value of the paragraph compared to the effort required to read it.

Introduction

Of course, the situation isn't the same. Since this textbook is intended for use by university-educated readers, you must know by now that you are one of the gifted students. You have gone too far in school and read too much to start worrying about whether you know how to read.

So when confronted with a confusing paragraph such as the one on the preceding page, your first reaction is likely to be that something is wrong with the printing, not something wrong with you. You may even have discovered the secret—that the paragraph is printed backwards and can be read easily by holding the book up to a mirror.

But imagine, if you can, that all reading matter looks like this to you. Not just books and magazines and newspapers, but road signs and the labels on cans and boxes. Imagine yourself continually trying to make out, word by word, the contents of print. How much motivation would you have to stay in school? How many of your reading assignments would you try before giving up?

"But," you may justifiably ask, "what has all this to do with me? I am a chemistry teacher, a history teacher, or a teacher of home economics. The reading teacher doesn't teach chemistry, why should I worry about reading?" But there is a difference. One can read well without knowing chemistry or history or any particular academic discipline. But nobody is fully functional in a modern school—or in modern society—without being able to read. Reading is the most basic academic survival skill. This means that your students will be handicapped in your class and elsewhere without it.

We also know that reading disability is a major source of educational frustration. Reading scores correlate highly with academic grades and inversely with discipline problems and dropout rates. In all probability, most of the reluctant students in your class are also reluctant readers. Thus, reading is the key to the learning door.

You and I have been reading so long that we take it for granted, as if anyone can read. But reading requires a complex blend of physical and mental skills. We must distinguish individual letters, making fine discriminations as between o and e, m and n, d and b, b and h, as well as between

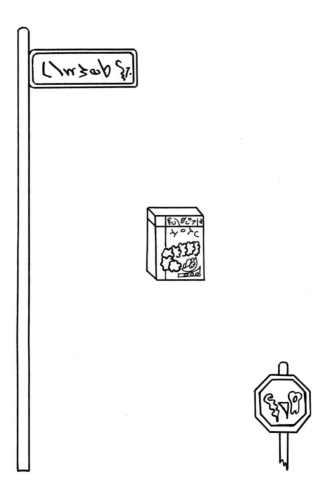

house and *horse, lead* and *led, was* and *saw*. We must train our eyes to go from left to right and from top to bottom and we must train them so that such movements become a habit. We must "crack the code" that is, convert letters into speech. Once the sounds are recognized, we have to make them into words and then into meaning. And we must do all this with lightning rapidity, for two hundred words per minute (or about sixteen letters per second) is not a fast reading rate, except for the most difficult material.

Unlike speech, reading must be taught. Normal human beings learn to speak by listening and imitating, but it is a rare individual who learns to read without going through a systematic course of study. Reading is highly abstract. Letters are abstract symbols for speech sounds, which form words, which are themselves abstract symbols for things and concepts.

Reading involves interpersonal communication—a message must be written and then read by someone else. Reading only happens when two minds mesh. Considering all the complexities, perhaps the real question is not what causes some people to fail to learn to read, but how do so many manage at all?

But why bother the math and music teachers with reading problems? Why not leave the whole business to reading teachers? In many cases, this is exactly what is done. "Remedial readers" are frequently referred to the reading specialist, if the school is fortunate enough to have one, who either works with these students individually or places them in a reading class.

This system has its advantages. It brings the problem reader under the guidance of a trained specialist, who has learned to diagnose reading difficulties and to help students overcome their handicaps. It enables the student to spend part of the school day focusing on reading. In a reading class the students see that others have similar problems, and they do not have to compete with their more advanced peers. Students can get special help where they most need it.

There are also advantages to leaving the remedial reader in the subject classroom. In a science class they read scientific material. In math they read math problems. This is more realistic than the "reading exercises" encountered in special classes—provided the student gets sufficient help from the teacher. Frequently, a student will show considerable "progress" in the reading workshop but, upon returning to class, will regress. This is the result of not learning to cope with the environment and material of the classroom.

Most students are happier doing what their friends are doing—carrying the same books, attending the same classes, talking about the same things. A student selected for special treatment frequently becomes self-conscious. And if the treatment is "remedial," the stigma of being "slow" is often more damaging than the remediation is helpful.

Whether to place a student in a reading class is often a complex problem, involving the extent of the disability, the training and willingness of the classroom teacher to help, the sensitivity of the student to a possible stigma, parental attitudes, and many other factors. In the ideal situation, a reading specialist and a trained subject matter teacher work together towards a common goal.

The person who cannot read a shop manual or a cook book will never make it as mechanic or cook. The student who cannot read the textbook suffers from dependence upon the teacher, a tutor, or *somebody* to help him. Reading is the key to independent learning. And independent learning is what school should be about.

In places this text will appear not to be about reading at all, but about learning in general. This is because reading is not an isolated process. Teaching reading and teaching subject matter cannot be separated. Progress can best be made by involving the entire human organism and its environment. There are no shortcuts. There is no substitute for teaching experience, sensitivity, and know-how. Some of the know-how can be supplied by this book, for we shall discuss ideas and methods. But the teacher remains the key. Knowing methodology is only the first step. Understanding the student is primary. Discovering the source of a learning disability, being sensitive to feelings and attitudes, knowing when to push for greater learning and when to ease the tension are part of a skilled teacher's routine.

Hopefully, the teaching of reading and the teaching of subject matter can be blended. Good teachers have been teaching reading for years, frequently without knowing it.

WADDYA MEAN, READING, I TEACH P.E.

More years ago than I would care to admit, I had a high school chum named Patrick. Patrick's mother was a ballet instructor, and this unique occupation aroused my interest. I attended a number of recitals by various dance studios around the city. My impression is still clear. Even to my youthful, untrained eye, it was obvious that these awkward home-grown Pavlovas were a long way from prima ballerinas. Lack of grace and skill combined with simplistic routines to betray them as products of a small-town dancing class.

All but the students of Patrick's mother. Her performers were an oasis of beauty and charm. So I asked her why, and I shall never forget her reply.

"Most teachers teach dances," she said. "I teach dancing. It's the difference between educated and uneducated instruction." I soon found out what she meant. Most dancing teachers teach routines: "Today we are going to learn a new dance, to the music of . . ."

Patrick's mother began her classes with barre exercises. Then the class worked on individual steps: *Plié* in first, *plié* in third, *plié* in fifth. "Now *tour jeté* across the studio . . . Lead with your wrist! Extend your fingers! Pull with your arms! Come down lightly." Over and over she drilled on each movement, each limb, the inclination of the head.

Her students were continually involved in public performances, and the key to her success was that part of each lesson was devoted to rehearsing the next show. This kept everyone glowing with enthusiasm and eager to work.

Patrick's mother did something else, too. She had a library of books about the dance—beautiful pictures of the great stars, stories of famous ballets, lives of leading dancers and choreographers, and books of criticism and technique. And she was pleased to see these beautiful and expensive books become grimy with use.

Patrick's mother never taught me to dance, but she taught me plenty about education. I learned from her that students need a reason for working, need to use their new abilities. I also learned that ordinary teachers teach little isolated facts or skills, but great teachers teach with scope. Whatever the subject, be it skill development or academic study, there are educated and uneducated approaches. And it seems to me inconceivable that educated instruction in any subject can leave out reading. For despite the elaborate claims of Marshall McLuhan[1] and Company, we have yet to devise a richer, more profound, and more available source of pleasure and profit.

[1]See *The Medium Is the Massage*. New York: Bantam Books, 1967.

CHAPTER 1
Triumph and Torture: The Development of the Art and the Science of Reading Instruction

It is ironic that we have worked so hard at learning how to teach reading, yet we know so little about the subject for sure. Diederich noted that each year more research is done on reading than on any other subject in school—over 1,000 studies annually.[1] We have measured to a hundredth of a second the time it takes the eye to fixate on a portion of print. We have synchronized teaching machines with computers to lay the world of knowledge at the reader's fingertips. We have broken down the reading act into dozens of "substrata factors."[2] Yet, "The Great Debate"[3] concerning how to teach people to read goes on.

Even the terminology we use to talk about reading has yet to be standardized. Inability to learn to read may be called *alexia, dislexia, congenital word blindness,* or *strephosymbolia,* depending on the writer, and an *informal reading inventory,* as we shall see in Chapter 2—means different things to different reading specialists. Nor do we agree on how we wish to define reading. Duffy, Sherman, and Roehler[4] classify definitions of reading into four major categories, noting that our instructional approach springs, at least partly, from our manner of definition:

1. *Reading as a learned system.* Using this approach, the teacher places emphasis on "controlled development of skills in a

[1]Paul B. Diederich, *Research 1960-1970 on Methods and Materials in Reading.* Princeton, N.J.: Educational Testing Service, ERIC Clearinghouse on Tests, Measurement, and Evaluation, ED 072 115, 1973.
[2]See pp. 19–20.
[3]Jeanne S. Chall, *Learning to Read: The Great Debate.* New York: McGraw-Hill Book Company, 1967.
[4]Gerald G. Duffy, George B. Sherman, and Laura R. Roehler, *How to Teach Reading Systematically.* New York: Harper & Row, Publishers, 1977.

structured sequence progressing from the simple to the complex."[5] This teacher would use a basal textbook, phonics, linguistic readers, programmed readers, or a skill building method.

2.   *Reading as language process.* The teacher who follows this concept teaches reading "through shared experiences, discussions, vocabulary expansion, and the reading and writing of child-written stories."[6] This method of instruction if often called *the language experience approach.* The contributions of psycholinguistics to this mode of thinking will be discussed shortly.

3.   *Reading as an interest.* This teacher tends to emphasize "motivation to read through literature appreciation."[6] Good reading material is the basic ingredient of this method. Individualized reading often plays an important role.

4.   *Reading as a cultural phenomenon.* The followers of this definition "emphasize the uniqueness of a child's cultural background by carefully selecting material to enhance that unique aspect."[6] Any approach to teaching reading would fit this pattern, as long as the teacher accepts the student's native dialect and selects reading material that deals with places and concepts that are familiar to the student.

Teachers may use any one or combination of these approaches in a well-rounded reading program.

Many obstacles hinder research in reading, for we cannot manipulate people in a laboratory as we do objects, or even animals. This makes carefully controlled experiments extremely difficult. Some schools, fearful of allowing their students to become "guinea pigs," are reluctant to permit experimentation with classrooms. Also, the human mind is a tremendously complicated mechanism. Even after observing human behavior, we do not necessarily know the motivations behind that behavior.

Another obstacle is the division between educational practitioner and researcher. Despite many notable exceptions, some research is still carried out in universities and other research institutions by people who have little contact with school teaching and are not cognizant of the problems that need to be researched most. And when important findings in reading are brought to light, they are often published in scholarly journals that few

[5]Ibid., p. 4.
[6]Duffy, op. cit., p. 4.

school teachers read. The need is great for more interaction between school and university.

Finally, there may be no answers to some of our most agonizing questions. The human mind and human culture are so complex that findings in one situation may have little or no application in any other.

But if our efforts over the years have yielded little that is definitive and indisputable, we have grown rich in theories. And these have improved the quality of our teaching materials and our instructional methods. Each new bit of research adds to our knowledge, and even though our efforts have yet to solidify, we continue to learn more about the art and the science of reading instruction.

CONTRIBUTIONS OF OTHER DISCIPLINES TO THE TEACHING OF READING

Psychology

Reading specialists have not worked alone. Many other disciplines have contributed information, resources, and methodology to reading improvement. Education and psychology have long been sisters, for it is to the psychologist that the educator owes his awareness of the complex cognitive, sensory, motor, and emotional processes which must be considered if teaching is to be effective.

Much of the terminology of education—stimulus-response, gestalt, operant conditioning—comes from psychology. Such questions as when to start teaching reading, at what age children can deal with certain types of abstractions, and how to use and distribute study time to yield the highest learning curve and the lowest forgetting curve[7] are all psychological-educational questions. So closely intertwined are education and psychology that it is often difficult to classify an individual or a study as clearly belonging to one discipline or the other. It is to this overlap that we owe the term *educational psychology*.

There have been many great milestones in the history of educational psychology. For example, the realization that living beings can be conditioned to behave in certain ways by associating one stimulus with another comes directly from Pavlov's famous salivating dog.[8]

Binet established the concept of the intelligence quotient,[9] later developed by Terman into the famous Stanford—Binet intelligence tests.[10]

[7]Henry E. Garrett, *Great Experiments in Psychology*. New York: Appleton-Century-Crofts, Inc., 1951, Chapter 6.
[8]Ibid., Chapter 1.
[9]Ibid., Chapter 2.
[10]Ibid., p. 223.

Edward L. Thorndike did many pioneering studies in learning, including the effects of feedback on future learning, the role of punishment, and problems of transfer of training. He also contributed much towards the development of mental and educational testing.

Later, the behavior modification theories of B. F. Skinner[11] led to the development of programmed instruction and teaching machines. Jerome Bruner laid the foundation for many of our "new" curricula, particularly in science, and boosted discovery-oriented learning.[12]

Benjamin Bloom,[13] David Krathwohl, and Bertram Masia[14] produced a list of educational objectives that have done much to clarify our goals and increase our insight into the many dimensions of educational growth. These authors divided learning into the cognitive, or thinking skills and the affective, or feeling skills. Their work was later supplemented by Klausmeier and Ripple, who summarized research into psychomotor skills.[15]

Jean Piaget's theory of maturation underlies much in primary education. He claimed that children go through fixed stages of development, and that at each stage they can deal with levels of abstraction previously outside their range. The first of these stages is the *sensorimotor stage* (birth to 18 months), in which the child is unable to deal with any form of symbolism. The *preoperational period* (18 months to 7 or 8 years), marks the beginning of language and other symbolic functions. During the age of *concrete operations* (7 to 11 or 12) the child learns to solve problems by reasoning. He begins to classify and differentiate, and builds concepts of time and physical relationships. Finally, at 11 or 12 years, the person enters the stage of *formal operations,* in which he can deal with principles and other high level abstractions. This theory has enormous implications for the nature of the tasks we can expect school children to perform at any given grade level.[16]

In contrast with the maturation theory of Piaget are the experiential models of Robert Gagné. Gagné claims that children develop increasingly complex learning capacities as the result of previous learning. According to

---

[11]B. F. Skinner, *Science and Human Behavior.* New York: Macmillan Publishing Co., Inc., 1953.

[12]Jerome S. Bruner, *The Process of Education.* Cambridge, Mass.: Harvard University Press, 1960.

[13]Benjamin S. Bloom (ed.), *Taxonomy of Educational Objectives, Handbook I: Cognitive Domain.* Longmans, Green, 1956.

[14]David R. Krathwohl, Benjamin Bloom, and Bertram Masia, *Taxonomy of Educational Objectives, Handbook II: Affective Domain.* New York: David McKay Co., Inc., 1964.

[15]Herbert J. Klausmeier and Richard E. Ripple, *Learning and Human Abilities: Educational Psychology.* 3rd ed. Harper & Row, Publishers, 1971, pp. 102–106.

[16]Jean Piaget, "The Genetic Approach to the Psychology of Thought." *Journal of Educational Psychology,* December 1961, 52, 271–276.

the Gagné model, the school, as the major structured learning situation in the child's life, has much more control over the student's growth than Piaget suggests.[17]

The Gagné theories are especially interesting when coupled with the approach of Jerome Bruner, who claimed that "the foundations of any subject may be taught to anybody at any age in some form."[18] Bruner placed great stress upon teaching not just isolated facts, but the underlying structure of the subject, so that the student may see the entire field in perspective. He also made it clear that instruction must be adapted to the age and intellectual capacity of the student. Where Piaget may have considered certain subject matter beyond the level of third graders, Bruner claimed it is a matter of learning how to put that material into a nine year old's frame of reference. Another interesting aspect of Bruner is his urging teachers to make greater use of intuitive thinking—of allowing students to play their hunches and to skip over time-consuming drill and memorization.[19]

Although he was instrumental in developing new approaches, new materials, and new methods of teaching, he insisted that the most important ingredient in education is a well-trained teacher.[20]

Sociology

In the past two decades teachers have become increasingly aware of the tremendous effects of social factors on school achievement. As the result of both studies of sociologists and recent movements toward social change, such as the women's movement and the turmoil of the sixties, the profession has become aware that "Life Is Fun in a Smiling, Fair-skinned World,"[21] but that many youngsters see school only as a source of frustration and failure.

The Coleman Report[22] emphasized the importance of the home as a determiner of school achievement. Innumerable studies have been made of the effects of parental occupation and attitudes, economic status, use of variant dialects, racial and other ethnic patterns, sex roles, and peer-group

[17]Robert Gagné, *The Conditions of Learning.* New York: Holt, Rinehart and Winston, 1970.
[18]Jerome Bruner, *The Process of Education.* Cambridge, Mass.: Harvard University Press, 1960, p. 12.
[19]Ibid., p. 13.
[20]Ibid., pp. 14–15.
[21]Otto Klineberg, "Life Is Fun in a Smiling, Fair-Skinned World." *Saturday Review,* February 16, 1963, 46, 75–77+.
[22]James S. Coleman, et al., *Equality of Educational Opportunity.* U.S. Department of Health, Education, and Welfare, Office of Education, Superintendent of Documents Catalog No. FS5.23838001, 1966. See especially pp. 296–297.

attitudes. So many studies were made that in the sixties it was said that the average working-class family consists of a father, a mother, 2.6 children, and a sociologist.

Our long overdue realization that school has been essentially a middle-class institution with middle-class values is one of the most significant and productive movements in recent education. As a result, we have looked with new insights on our primary grade basal readers, with their picket fences, dogs named Spot, nicely manicured houses, and nicely manicured children. One result has been a series of "ethnic readers" that are attempting to appeal to a wider divergence of students. In secondary schools, reading material has become more contemporary, more inclined to deal with teen-age situations and problems and less oriented towards classical literature. *Silas Marner* and *Great Expectations* have joined Dick and Jane on the haven't-been-doing-so-well-recently list.

Criticism of the new approach is not difficult. We have little evidence that the ethnic readers have actually improved reading achievement on the primary level, and secondary reading scores on standardized tests have been dropping alarmingly since the mid-sixties.[23] But whether test scores are the only criteria for judging a reading program is an interesting philosophical question. One very encouraging trend in recent years has been a tendency for teachers to be more concerned with the overall well-being of the student—for his self-image, peer relationships, and all-around mental health. This has touched off many debates between educators and parents, legislators, and other educators.

Whether declining scores in secondary reading are the result of less rigid standards in school or of social phenomena outside the school, or whether less rigid school standards are the result of these outside social movements, is as yet uncertain. Opinions concerning reasons for the decline in test scores range from television viewing to parental neglect,[24] to lower standards in school to a change in American birth patterns.[25] Much remains to be done.

Medicine

Because good health is not only important for a good life but can play a role in effective learning, the medical arts, particularly the fields of ophthalmology, optometry, audiology, and neurology, have made many contributions

[23]Annegret Harnischfeger and David Wiley, "Achievement Test Scores Drop. So What?" *Educational Researcher*, March 1976, 5, 5–12.
[24]Ibid., pp. 7–9.
[25]Carol Tavris, "After the Baby Boom . . . The End of the IQ Slump." *Psychology Today*, April 1976, 9, 69–73.

to reading. Unfortunately, there is much to be done before we can diagnose with accuracy the many physical disorders that can affect a student's performance.

Gross vision handicaps can hinder reading, for we cannot read what we cannot see. But even after medical people have diagnosed a vision handicap, we are not sure to what extent it is responsible for reading disability. The human mechanism has a wonderful power of compensation. If one faculty is deficient, we usually learn to overcome the deficiency either by manipulating the environment (such as by wearing glasses or holding a book closer or farther than normal) or by sharpening some other faculty (such as picking up more information by listening). Usually, a "handicapped" person is one whose difficulty is so severe that compensating mechanisms break down, or one who has a multiplicity of difficulties, such as poor vision coupled with low IQ or emotional damage.

Nevertheless, many physical difficulties have been diagnosed and corrected by referring the student for proper medical treatment, and research holds promise of more help in the future. In addition to vision loss, severe hearing loss handicaps the individual by retarding normal language growth. Brain damage can also contribute toward reading dysfunction. These physical difficulties and related perceptual problems will be discussed later.

Linguistics

Although we have evidence of linguistic study dating as far back as 1000 B.C., it is only in comparatively recent times that linguistics has blossomed as an important modern science. In 1786 Sir William Jones noted the similarity between a number of European languages and Sanskrit, an ancient language of India. Since then, linguists have been comparing languages, observing their structures and their evolution, and commenting upon how we shape the language we use, and how it, in turn, shapes us.

It was natural for linguists to become involved in education, particularly those phases of education that deal with language. Later in the chapter we shall discuss the contributions of linguists Charles Carpenter Fries and Carl Lefevre, and the most influential of them all, Leonard Bloomfield. These men looked at current methods of teaching, particularly reading, and concluded that educators lack the profound knowledge of language needed to help young people develop linguistic skills. Although their theories do not always agree, they helped develop the *linguistic readers* that form a major approach to beginning reading instruction, and have introduced a new way of teaching grammar in the schools.[26]

[26]Burt Liebert, *Linguistics and the New English Teacher.* New York: Macmillan Publishing Co., Inc., 1971.

Psycholinguistics

By looking at the "interaction of thought and language,"[27] psycholinguists have given educators valuable insights into perceptual processes and have asked some important questions concerning selection of teaching materials and methods. An early student of perception was M. D. Vernon, who broke the perceptual process into stages by means of a tachistoscope. This is a machine that flashes words, letters, or other forms against a screen for very small fractions of a second. By so doing, he observed what people could perceive first, what comes next, and finally the whole perception.[28]

Admitting that tachistoscopic projection had not been proven to engender the same perceptions as normal seeing, he nevertheless found some consistency in pattern as people had increasingly longer periods to perceive.

The first stage of observation he found to be simply a visual pattern; the object is known to exist as a "something there"[29] awareness. Next, it is seen as an object; "parts of the field stand out slightly but significantly." He called this the stage of *objective reference.*[30] Then comes the stage of *specific object,* in which the object is clearly perceived for what it is. The fourth stage is perhaps the most interesting, for it is here that the object is given a name. It is significant that Vernon recognizes that "there may be a feeling of 'I know what you are' before the actual name is given."[31] He considers language an important ingredient of perception that is not complete until the object is not only identified but at least silently verbalized.

Goodman, et al. combined linguistic information with findings from child development to devise some principles upon which to select reading material for various grade levels.[32] Such information about students as the size of speaking vocabularies, ability to handle abstractions, extent of interests, degree of egocentrism, sex differences, socio-economic factors, and other considerations are discussed in reference to textbook selection.

For example, in looking at syntactic considerations, the authors ask whether reading materials "contain the common syntactical structures of oral language. . . . Strickland found that the most common pattern in basal readers she examined did not occur at all in the speech of children in her

[27]Duffy, Sherman, and Roehler, op. cit., p. 14.
[28]M. D. Vernon, *The Experimental Study of Reading.* New York: Cambridge University Press, 1931, p. 97.
[29]Ibid., p. 98.
[30]Ibid., p. 98.
[31]Ibid., p. 99.
[32]Kenneth S. Goodman, et al., *Choosing Materials to Teach Reading.* Detroit, Mich.: Wayne State University Press, 1966.

study. (This pattern is the 'look, said mother,' or object-verb-subject type.)"
The authors suggest using children's own speech (language experience
approach—see pages 34−36).[33] They question a number of other qualities
of reading texts, including:

> "Is any attempt made to proceed from common to uncommon language
> structures?"
> "Is any attempt made to proceed from simple to complex fillers of the slots
> in language structures?"[34]
> "Is structural and contextual ambiguity avoided?"[35]

These are only a few examples of the types of questions that psycholinguists are asking as they attempt to make textbook material conform to what
we know about language, the child's linguistic development, and the interests and abilities of students.

Semantics

Although semantics is considered by many to be a branch of linguistics,
there are some major differences. The linguist is interested mainly in the
structure of language, that is, how it is pronounced and how its parts fit
together to form phrases and sentences.

Semanticists are concerned with meaning. They want to know what
you meant—what you *really* meant—when you said or wrote what you did.
Words, they are quick to point out, have no meaning. They only have
meaning in your mind and in mine. And whether our attempts to communicate will hit or miss depends largely on how closely the meaning in my
mind resembles the meaning in yours.

For example, if I tell you that X———— is a person of high moral character, you really don't know a thing about X————. What I meant and what
you perceive depend entirely upon our respective concepts of morality. If
those outlooks are different, there will be little or no communication.

Semantics has played a major role in what I call in this volume the
"higher level reading skills," skills that go beyond merely taking words, or
even data, from the page, but involve trying to set up real contact with an
author. This phase of reading instruction is discussed in greater detail in

[33]Ibid., p. 101.
[34]Ibid., p. 103.
[35]Ibid., p. 104.

Chapter 11, using material that has come out of classical semanticists Alfred Korzybski, S. I. Hayakawa, Stuart Chase, and Wendell Johnson.

Literature

Literature has given us one of two major reasons to learn to read—reading for pleasure and reading for information. Although literature falls predominantly into the former, it also contributes much to the latter.

The twin themes of reading for information and reading for enjoyment run throughout this volume. It is important to have a reading specialist work on specific skills when students demonstrate specific deficiencies, but any reading program that does not involve a generous amount of reading of enjoyable literature is pep without purpose.

SOME THEORIES
OF READING

The art and the science of teaching reading does not depend entirely on other disciplines. Quite the contrary, a sizable body of literature has arisen concerning both theory and practice. Before dealing with instructional practices, let us examine some theories of reading and reading disability.

Cerebral Dominance

In 1925 Samuel T. Orton introduced his theory of lack of cerebral dominance as the cause of reading disability. Orton noted that the brain is divided into a right and a left hemisphere, each controlling the functions of the opposite side of the body. For perceptual functions such as reading, while one hemisphere is perceiving what is on the page, the other hemisphere, which is a mirror image of its mate, "sees" the same thing in mirror image. If the image of the subdominant hemisphere is not properly suppressed, the reader may have difficulty distinguishing *d* from *b, p* from *q, was* from *saw,* or *on* from *no,* or may be subject to a host of other confusions, including a tendency to write in mirror images. Orton concluded that reading dysfunction results from failure of the subdominant hemisphere to be properly suppressed.

He suggested the term *strephosymbolia,* from two Greek roots meaning "twist" and "symbol"[36] for this condition.

[36]Samuel T. Orton, "Word Blindness in School Children." *Archives of Neurology and Psychiatry,* November 1925, 14, 581–615, p. 610.

Unlike some of his predecessors, who distinguished between "congenital word blindness" and those who were merely slow in learning,[37] Orton maintained that disabled readers differed in degree of handicap only, not in type.

Although not a reading specialist, he observed more cases of strephosymbolia among students taught to read by whole-word method, and suggested a phonics approach for this type of student. His sample was limited, however, and more evidence is needed.[38]

He recommended reading instruction involving "tracing or writing while reading and sounding and by following the letters with the finger."[39] This is essentially the method used by Grace Fernald, and her success gives credence to the dominance theory.

Fernald

In 1921 Grace Fernald established a clinic for nonreaders at the University of California at Los Angeles. Except during the earliest years, the clinic worked only with students of normal intelligence and extreme reading disability. As a clinical psychologist, Fernald was concerned with the mental stability of her students, and she found that most of these youngsters had begun school happy and well-adjusted.[40]

If her remedial students did not lack intelligence, and if emotional difficulties cannot be charged as a cause, there must be some other factor. A few were spastic or had other discernible difficulties. But many others should have learned to read.

Fernald viewed learning as dependent upon three major perceptors: the visual, seeing the words; the auditory, hearing and saying the words; and the kinesthetic,[41] reacting physically. She criticized the school for overdependence upon visual methods and insufficient use of kinesthetic methods.

The kinesthetic method is not new. From Plato to Montessori, teachers have taught reading and writing by having students trace with finger or

[37]Samuel T. Orton, "An Impediment to Learning to Read—a Neurological Explanation of the Reading Disability." *School and Society*, September 1928, 28, 286–290, p. 286.
[38]Samuel T. Orton, "Specific Reading Disability—Strephosymbolia." *Journal of the American Medical Association*, April 7, 1928, 90, p. 1098.
[39]Samuel T. Orton, "The 'Sight Reading' Method of Teaching Reading as a Source of Reading Disability." *The Journal of Educational Psychology*, February 1929, 20, 135–143, p. 141.
[40]Grace M. Fernald, *Remedial Techniques in Basic School Subjects*. New York: McGraw-Hill Book Company, 1943, p. 8.
[41]Ibid., pp. 25–26.

writing instrument the lines forming letters.[42] But it was Grace Fernald in our own country who pointed out that many students who "should" be able to learn to read but cannot are simply kinesthetic learners who need a different teaching technique.

Beginning with total nonreaders and later with partial readers, she found the following system to work where others had failed: She began by telling her charges that she had a new way of learning words, which she wanted them to try.[43] Then she took them through the following stages of learning:

Stage I: *Tracing.* The word is written for the student, who traces it with the finger, saying it as she does so. This is repeated until she can write the word without tracing. Then the teacher types the word and she reads it from print. This learned word is filed alphabetically in a special box.

Stage II: *Tracing no longer necessary.* After one to eight months, the student no longer need trace a word to learn it. She simply looks at it and writes it. The student begins to read from the words she has written, and can arrange them in stories.

Stage III: *Student can say the word without having it written for him.* At this stage students are encouraged to begin to read from books, not just from their own word stock. They can look at a new word in print, write it in cursive, and usually recognize it after having written it.

Stage IV: *Student can recognize new words from their similarity to previously learned ones.* Now the student can simply be told what the new words are without having to write each one.

Delacato

Also operating on the theory of cerebral dominance is Carl Delacato, but his method of remediation is different from Fernald's. Delacato views cerebral dominance as the final step in the development of the brain—a step that can

---

[42]Ibid., pp. 27–29.
[43]Ibid., p. 33.

only take place after the brain has passed through a series of prior developmental stages. His treatment, therefore, is to retrain the whole being, taking the student through a series of developmental steps reminiscent of a baby's efforts to crawl, to position itself in sleep, and to perform a number of other physical tasks. The object is to develop strong handedness, footedness, and eyedness in an effort to suppress the reversed image of the nondominant cortical hemisphere.[44]

Delacato's methods have been disputed by a number of reading specialists. Harris found that hand dominance develops late in some children (about eleven years of age), so the problem corrects itself without such extensive procedures.[45] Clymer and Robinson also found that many students can be taught to read without establishing dominance.[46]

The Fernald and Delacato methods are only intended for those students who cannot learn by the usual visual and auditory processes. They are to be used only with those who fall seriously behind for no discernible reason.

Substrata Factor Theory

Jack Holmes and Harry Singer have formulated a theory that divides the reading process into 56 factors that account for reading power. Such factors as vocabulary, range of information, and listening comprehension are common to all readers and are necessary for success in reading material on the secondary level. Beyond that, however, "different individuals may perform the same task (reading) with equal success by mobilizing different sets of subabilities; in other words, there is more than one way to solve an intellectual problem."[47]

The factors that account for reading ability are arranged on a three-step hierarchy, with eight abilities listed as primary: vocabulary in isolation, vocabulary in context, visual verbal meaning, tone intensity, verbal analogies, mechanical interest, study planning and deliberation, and auding ability. These primary abilities relate to words and their referents in the real world.

These were analyzed into subsets of secondary factors, including musi-

---

[44]Carl H. Delacato, *Neurological Organization and Reading.* Springfield, Illinois: Charles C Thomas, Publishers, 1966, pp. 25–28.

[45]Albert J. Harris, "Lateral Dominance, Directional Confusion, and Reading Disability." *Journal of Psychology,* October 1957, 44, 283–294.

[46]Theodore Clymer and Helen M. Robinson, "Reading." *Review of Educational Research,* April 1961, 31, 130–144.

[47]Jack A. Holmes and Harry Singer, "Theoretical Models and Trends Toward More Basic Research in Reading." *Review of Educational Research,* April 1964, 34, 127–155.

cal taste, spatial relations, range of information, word sense, reasoning, Latin and Greek roots, literary interest, and school adjustment and morale. At the tertiary level are the factors that support the higher level abilities, including pitch, rhythm, phonetic association, suffixes, spelling, word fluency, and the age of the reader.

The substrata factor theory furnishes an interesting framework for analysis of reading, and may some day contribute insights into teaching techniques. At present, however, it deals only with theoretical aspects.

Synaptic Transmission

More closely related to remediation is the Smith-Carrigan theory.[48] They blame reading failure on chemical imbalance of the nervous system. According to the synaptic transmission theory, fluent reading depends upon proper transmission of perceptions through the synaptic junctions, or points at which the terminals of one neuron touch the cells of another. They claim that the chemical acetylcholine (ACh) "mediates transmission." Then the impulse is removed to clear the nervous system for the next impulse by another chemical, cholinesterase (ChE). Much depends upon the proper balance of these chemicals within the nervous system.

If ACh exceeds ChE "such an individual perceives slowly and is a slow, methodical reader." If ChE exceeds ACh "Such a person should perceive quickly and be a fast, inaccurate reader."[49]

In an experiment with slow readers, they administered Cytomel, Miltown, and gonadotrophic hormone and found some improvement in perceptions.

How wonderful it would be if we could establish a cure for reading dysfunction at the prescription counter! However, their results were mixed and they are still a long way from proving their hypothesis. A year later, Harris strongly attacked the theory.[50]

Reading Rate

In the late 19th century, the Frenchman Émile Javal First noted that the eye does not sweep evenly across the line in reading, but proceeds in little jumps, now known as *saccadic movements*, or *interfixation movements*.

[48]Donald E. P. Smith and Patricia M. Carrigan, *The Nature of Reading Disability*. New York: Harcourt, Brace Jovanovich, 1959.
[49]Ibid., p. 19.
[50]Albert J. Harris, "A Critical Reaction to *the Nature of Reading Disability*." *Journal of Developmental Reading*, Summer, 1960, 3, 238–249.

Between these movements are *fixations,* or intervals during which the eye pauses to "read" a cluster of words.

After Javal, Vernon developed the study of eye movements,[51] and today mechanical equipment is available to "train" the eye in more "efficient" operation. One of the leading exponents of this theory is Evelyn Wood, with the Reading Dynamics Institute Program. Wood claims that Institute graduates can read at rates from 2000 to 20,000 words per minute, a prodigious accomplishment if it can be done without loss of comprehension. The method consists mainly of training the student first to do a prereading to get the general sense of what is about to be read, then to read by making only one fixation per line as the eye moves down the page in a directly vertical movement, and finally, to use certain memory aids.

Although the Wood method is controversial among reading specialists, there is some experimentation to support the theory. Stauffer[52] found that students given a Reading Dynamics course did improve their reading rate for both fiction and nonfiction. Their comprehension was equal to that of a control group which read more slowly in nonfiction, but the control group did better on comprehension of fiction. Stauffer felt that the program had achieved the bulk of its aims. Spache[53] and Taylor[54] also found some advantages in the method, but were much less impressed. Taylor pointed out that the increase in speed he had found with his experiment (about 20%), was not unusual compared with results from other methods.

Today some reading specialists use a number of mechanical devices to diagnose and train readers for increased rate. Among the diagnostic tools are the Ophthalmograph and the Reading Eye,[55] both of which photograph the movements of each eye and record them on film. For training eye movements, there are three major types of devices:

The *tachistoscope* flashes on a screen an image (a word, a number, a series of letters) for a fraction of a second. The reader tries to read from the screen in the short time allowed. The object is to train the eye to read more quickly, to spend less time at each fixation, and to take in more words per fixation.

[51]M. D. Vernon, *The Experimental Study of Reading.* New York: Cambridge University Press, 1931.

[52]Russell G. Stauffer, "Speed Reading and Versatility." *Challenge and Experiment in Reading.* Proceedings of the Seventh Annual Conference of the International Reading Association. Scholastic Magazines, 1962, 7, pp. 201–210.

[53]George D. Spache, "Is This a Breakthrough in Reading?" *Reading Teacher,* January 1962, 15, 258–263.

[54]Stanford E. Taylor, "An Evaluation of Forty-One Trainees Who Had Recently Completed the 'Reading Dynamics' Program" *Problems, Programs, and Projects in College-Adult Reading.* Eleventh Yearbook, National Reading Conference, 1962. pp. 41–56.

[55]See Appendix 1.

The *controlled reader* is similar to a filmstrip projector, but has a timing device that flashes on a screen one line of reading at a time from a series of special filmstrips. Faced with a brief moment to read a line, the reader is forced to read faster. Speed can be increased gradually, as the student's reading skill increases. A series of special training filmstrips can be purchased with the reader.

The *reading pacer* is similar to a controlled reader, but instead of using filmstrips, it contains a rack on which is placed an ordinary book or other reading matter. A beam of light passes down the page, revealing a few lines at a time. This forces the reader to increase reading speed, as the speed of the moving light is increased. This has the advantage of providing practice with regular reading material.

These three machines are available in a variety of models. Prices vary, and a school should carefully weigh the investment in devices against the investment in reading matter, for the price of one controlled reader will buy a lot of books. Evidence concerning the value of these machines is still insufficient. We know that they can increase the reading speed of sufficiently motivated students. But we do not yet know how permanent this increase is, which students are most likely to profit from this type of training, and how to utilize reading hardware for optimal results. See Appendix 1 for a list of sources for reading hardware.

PRECEPT AND PRACTICE: METHODS AND MATERIALS

The age of controversy in reading theories dates from 1955, when Rudolf Flesch's *Why Johnny Can't Read and What You Can Do About It*[56] jolted American parents, teachers, and administrators into a flurry of debate. For Flesch, the problem and the solution could be summed up in one word: *phonics,* or the lack of it. He bitterly attacked the "whole word" method of reading instruction. Professional reaction was less than enthusiastic, for his was a simplistic answer to a complex problem. Nevertheless, Johnny was serialized in newspapers and featured in magazines. *Why Johnny Can't Read* became a best-seller.

Much of Flesch's arguments were based on research showing that current practices did leave something to be desired. A few years later Terman and Walcott[57] reached a similar conclusion. To this day we find ourselves with a multiplicity of theories, research findings, practices, and materials

[56]New York: Harper and Row, Publishers, 1955.
[57]Sibyl Terman and Charles C. Walcott, *Reading: Chaos and Cure.* New York: McGraw-Hill Book Company, 1958.

that are sometimes compatible, more often controversial. And although we are concerned in this volume with helping secondary students in subject classes, some background concerning practices in teaching elementary reading may be helpful in understanding how reading disability develops and how to deal with it.

Basal Readers

Today's basal reading programs have survived countless attacks, both from within the profession and from the popular media. Their persistence is based on the fact that no other approach offers the teacher as complete a program and as much help in teaching. Chall tells of having requested a copy of a basal reading program and having the publisher respond by asking how much storage space she had.[58] Most comprehensive basal programs contain not only the usual two to four readers for each grade level, plus primers and preprimers, but teacher's editions with detailed instructions for teaching every lesson, testing and other diagnostic material, supplementary reading books, phonic supplements, and virtually everything the teacher needs for a complete elementary reading program.

Putting together such a series can run into millions of dollars, and no publisher will risk such an investment without a vigorous promotional campaign, which may also account for the popularity of the basal reader.

In addition to offering the most comprehensive program available, basal readers, with their whole-word approach, offer the beginning reader the immediate reward of being able to read a great many words and sentences quickly. This is a major advantage of the whole-word approach. By learning an entire word at a time, the student quickly builds a stock of instant-recognition words.

Criticisms of the system are numerous, however. One is that the contents are insipid, with characterless Dicks and Janes speaking as no child (or adult) would ever speak (See me run. . . . ride, Spot, ride). They have also been traditionally middle-class, racist, and sexist, picturing mothers baking apple pies and daddies coming home from the office.

In recent years, however, much has been done to correct these defects. The *Bank Street Readers,* the Detroit Public Schools Great Cities School Improvement Program, and the *Chandler Language Experience Readers* were pioneers in picturing children and adults of diverse ethnic groups, and

[58]Jeanne Chall, *Learning to Read: The Great Debate.* New York: McGraw-Hill Book Company, 1967.

most of the more recent basal series have come out with more realistic language and situations.

Another criticism of basal readers springs from the research indicating that phonics is an important ingredient of any reading program. Although most basal programs include a phonics component, the type and amount of instruction in this area are usually inadequate. Chall found the phonics components of basal readers to be poorly coordinated with the rest of the material, as if the authors "do not really seem to expect the pupil to use the letter-sound correspondences taught."[59]

Other criticisms of basal readers include too much stress on pictures, distracting students from the reading task, and too much control of teaching methods by detailed instructions that some teachers follow slavishly. Critics have questioned the need for so many repetitions of each new word as well as the need for such carefully controlled vocabulary.

Phonics

In their very comprehensive survey of reading instruction practices, Austin and Morrison found reading teachers concerned that their charges develop comprehension skills as well as skills in decoding printed words. One of their recommendations was:

> that the emphasis in the beginning and continuing reading programs be placed on the concept that understanding the meaning of the printed passage and not mere word-calling constitutes reading.[60]

Here they articulated the essential reason for reading instruction, for if there is no meeting of the minds between reader and writer, both may as well have forgotten the whole business. Nevertheless, there is considerable evidence that it is necessary for the student to learn to think in terms of sound-letter relationships. A student may amass a large sight recognition word stock quickly using the whole-word approach of the basal reader or other approaches that we will discuss shortly. But unless he can match letters with sounds, he lacks tools with which to attack new and unfamiliar words.

My own experience indicates that some students reach secondary

[59]Ibid., p. 215.
[60]Mary C. Austin and Coleman Morrison, et al., *The First R: The Harvard Report on Reading in Elementary Schools*. New York: Macmillan Publishing Co., Inc., 1963, p. 222.

school with little or no phonic sense. Whether they were never taught phonics or simply failed to learn it when they should have, is difficult to determine. The difficulty for the secondary teacher is that phonics is a very complicated business. Our English language is only partially phonetic. The letter e is pronounced differently in the words *be, set, weigh, the, pie, due, better,* and *rope;* the sound /z/ is spelled differently in *finds, zero, wise, muzzle, prize,* and *girl's.* Teaching phonics thus becomes more complex than many of the enthusiasts claim. In this text we shall deal with phonics by examining the structure of English to determine how that structure can be put to use in reading instruction. Despite efforts to simplify the process, the section on phonics consumes two chapters—the most complex, data-packed chapters in this volume.

This raises the question of whether secondary classroom teachers should be involved in phonics instruction at all, or whether it should be left strictly to the reading specialist. The material is included because not every secondary school is fortunate enough to have a reading specialist. The classroom teacher can, by following the instructions in Chapters 7 and 8, teach reading in a step-by-step course of study. Lacking the time to work with individual students, the teacher can train an aide.

Although there is evidence of superiority of phonics instruction over whole-word methods at the primary level, there is very little reliable research on the subject for older students. We do not know, for example, whether students trained in phonics who test at superior levels at the third grade maintain their superiority throughout their school careers and throughout life. There may be a point at which the groups come together, or at which the lower group surpasses the other. Nor do we know whether phonics instruction at the secondary level is as valid as it was in the early years.

But some things seem evident. First, some knowledge of phonics seems essential if a reader is to attack new words with confidence and skill. Second, complete dependence on phonics will cause a reader to laboriously "sound out" every word. In other words, a good reader recognizes instantly thousands of English words, but can use phonic skills whenever necessary.

Third—and this is vital—in working with secondary students, the key is *motivation.* Many first-graders will be delighted at having learned how to "sound out the letter *m,*" but high schoolers need more enticing bait. These young people can spend their time driving cars, relating to the opposite sex, watching television, or just messing around. If you want them to choose reading, you'd better have something more exciting than just Dick and Jane and phonics workbooks.

Phonic-linguistics

In 1933 American linguist Leonard Bloomfield criticized basal readers, claiming that they "present the graphic forms in a mere hodge-podge, with no rational progression.[61] But he also claimed that current methods of teaching phonics were "complicated by the crassest ignorance of elementary phonetics."[61]

Then in 1961, in collaboration with Clarence Barnhart, Bloomfield brought out his own reading system, an impressive-looking volume entitled *Let's Read*.[62] This system will be examined in greater detail in Chapters 7 and 8, as it is used for phonic instruction in this text. Bloomfield-Barnhart phonics involves first teaching students to read words that follow the most common patterns of the language, only "regular" patterns so students associate every letter with one sound. Later, after the reader has built a stock of instant-recognition words, the "irregular" patterns are introduced.

Today this system has been adopted by those reading texts which come under the heading "linguistic readers." I have used *Let's Read* with secondary nonreaders with some success. Its major disadvantage is that the subject matter has no interest for secondary students, with its early sentences about the *tan van* and the *fat cat,* culminating with the story of Florence and the Picture Country.

Nevertheless, it presents a complete phonics program, step-by-step, in a manner that enables the student to read a complete sentence at the first lesson. And, although it is written essentially for primary school children, there are no pretty pictures to make it look like a "baby book." Quite the contrary, *Let's Read* is a big thick book that looks, from the outside at least, like tough adult reading. It is a book that high school students (if they are not frightened off first) will not be ashamed to be seen carrying around.

The *Let's Read* material is now available in a series of nine short readers with workbook supplements from Clarence L. Barnhart, Inc., publishers. These readers break the material down into easy-to-handle units and offer the teacher additional instructions for using the program.

Structural Linguistics

Within a few years of *Let's Read,* other linguists had entered the reading field, but with less emphasis on phonics and more on structural linguistics— the study of the structure of English words and sentences.

[61]Leonard Bloomfield, *Language.* New York: Henry Holt and Company, 1933, pp. 500–501.
[62]*Let's Read.* Detroit, Mich.: Wayne State University Press, 1961.

Carl Lefevre claimed that understanding the structure of the sentence is the key to fluent reading. He did not present a method of reading instruction, but described in detail what he considered basic knowledge for reading background.[63]

Charles Fries also believed in the need for instruction in linguistics,[64] and followed explanation of his theory with a series of textbooks.[65]

Fries saw reading development in three phases. The first phase is "to *transfer*, from auditory signs for the language signals, which the child has already learned, to visual or graphic signs for the same signals."[66] In professional literature this phase is frequently called *decoding*. The next stage is *cumulative comprehension*, "habits so automatic that the significant identifying features of the graphic shapes themselves sink below the threshold of conscious attention."[67] Here the reader reads well enough to stop concentrating on making out the words, but focuses on content. Finally comes the stage of *vivid imaginative realization*, when "the reading process has become so automatic for the reader that he uses reading equally with or even more fully than the live language of speech in acquiring and assimilating new experience."[68] This is somewhat akin to what we call *involvement reading*—the stage at which what is read becomes part of the mental and emotional makeup of the reader.

i. t. a.

The linguists teach reading by presenting the most common patterns first, then the irregularities when the student is better able to cope with them. Another approach, the *initial teaching alphabet*, was devised by Sir James Pitman, who enlarged the alphabet to 44 characters, each having a special sound of its own. There are no capital letters in **i. t. a.** Capitals are simply lower case letters written larger. Although there is more than one way to spell certain sounds, every character is generally pronounced the same way. Thus the reader is introduced to a purely phonic system. Gradually the **i. t. a.** characters are phased out until the student is reading *traditional orthography* (spelling as we know it).

---

[63]Carl A. Lefevre, *Linguistics and the Teaching Of Reading.* New York: McGraw-Hill Book Company, 1964.

[64]Charles C. Fries, *Linguistics and Reading.* New York: Holt, Rinehart and Winston, 1962.

[65]*Merrill Linguistic Readers.* Columbus, Ohio: Charles E. Merrill Books, Inc., 1966. These readers follow Bloomfield's rules for vocabulary selection and are slightly more appealing to older students.

[66]*Linguistics and Reading,* New York: Irvington Publishers, 1963. p. 188.

[67]Ibid., p. 205.

[68]Ibid., p. 208.

Any English can be written in **i. t. a.,** and Sir James Pitman has generously made it possible for anyone to use his symbols without payment of royalty. Although **i. t. a.** is not the only system of its kind, it has received more coverage than any other, with a number of reading programs available.

In 1967 John Downing announced the results of an extensive study of equated groups using **i. t. a.** and traditional orthography to learn to read.[69] He found the **i. t. a.** group to be superior in every way to the control (traditional orthography) group. By the end of the third year, **i. t. a.** classes were superior in both speed and accuracy. They were also superior in composition and slightly better in spelling. This was particularly true of the superior readers, who far outpaced the best readers in the control group. The slower readers benefited less from **i. t. a.** Only the lowest 10 percent of experimental students were not superior to the control group. Downing concluded that traditional orthography forms a serious block to learning to read, and that students learning **i. t. a.** had a distinct advantage. But at this writing, the use of **i. t. a.** is not widespread in this country.

Printer's characters for **i. t. a.** are available from: Monotype Corporation, 43 Fetter Lane, E. C. 4, England.

Programmed Instruction

In *programmed instruction* the material to be learned is broken into a series of tiny frames. The student responds to each frame in turn, usually by answering a question. If he answers correctly, he is immediately "rewarded" when he checks the correct answer, which is usually found nearby, and he goes on. If he is incorrect, the error is corrected immediately. The course is so structured that mastery of each frame prepares him to undertake the next.

A number of elementary reading textbooks have been structured along programmed principles, including Cynthia Dee Buchanan's *Programmed Reading* (Sullivan Associates) and the Grolier *First Steps in Reading for Meaning.* Current programmed reading texts stress phonic-linguistic teaching, with vocabulary from Bloomfield.

In addition to textbooks, however, programmed instruction materials have been placed on teaching machines that vary in complexity from simple projections to Omar K. Moore's Responsive Environment, in which a giant computer is capable of answering very complex questions with extremely sophisticated data.

Programmed materials have been criticized for reducing teacher con-

[69]John Downing, *The* **i. t. a.** *Symposium.* National Foundation for Educational Research in England and Wales, 1967.

tact, for dull material, and for forcing students through a long and involved learning process.

Their effectiveness has been particularly impressive, however, with slower learners, particularly the mentally retarded. Although teacher manuals advise going through every frame until mastery is achieved, a sensitive teacher may shorten the process by allowing brighter students to skip areas of repetition, provided that the skipped portions do not contain important new material.

Presentation of new material, however, is not the strong point of programmed instruction. Sidney Pressey, the inventor of teaching machines, had serious reservations about their use. He pointed out that because a teaching machine presents one frame at a time, the student cannot go back to reread and cannot look ahead. He, therefore, fails to see the structure of the subject as well as he can in a book which has chapter and topic headings. The same difficulty exists with a programmed text, although to a lesser degree. He therefore suggested that teaching machines be used chiefly for reinforcing previously learned material after an initial presentation by a teacher.[70] Programmed learning seems to be particularly well adapted to material that requires memorization through repetition.

Montessori

In the closing years of the nineteenth century, Maria Montessori, the first woman to be granted a medical degree by an Italian university, did her internship in psychiatry by attempting to educate mentally retarded children in an asylum.[71] Later she was appointed directress of a school for defective children, in which capacity she developed a "method" of education that later was to be used by her and the teachers she trained in a number of schools for slum children. Today her method is used in private Montessori schools throughout the world.

There are three major aspects of the method: First is early childhood education, with schools for children from three to six years old. Reading instruction is largely phonic. It must be remembered, however, that the Italian language for which the system was devised is more phonetic than English.

A second characteristic is a heavy emphasis on individualization. Dr.

[70]Sidney L. Pressey, "Basic Unresolved Teaching-Machine Problems." Theory into Practice. February 1962, 1, 30–37.

[71]Martin Mayer, Introduction to The Montessori Method, by Maria Montessori. Cambridge, Mass.: Robert Bentley, Inc., 1964, p. 25.

Montessori worked one-to-one with children, allowing them considerable freedom of movement while she was working with others. This introduces the third characteristic, an interplay between freedom and discipline. This interplay has led to considerable misunderstanding and controversy over the merits and demerits of the method.

Essentially, Montessori believed in freedom of the child. She criticized the public schools of her time, in which "the children, like butterflies mounted on pins, are fastened each to his place, the desk, spreading the useless wings of barren and meaningless knowledge which they have acquired."[72] She insisted that children be allowed to explore, to make their own mistakes, and to learn from them. Instead of the traditional fastened-down desks of her time, she designed schoolroom furniture that was light and easily carried by children. Her classrooms were connected to open-air spaces, where children can come and go and enjoy the mild Italian climate. Classrooms were decorated with plants and pictures.

"Discipline must come through liberty," she wrote:

> If discipline is founded upon liberty the discipline itself must necessarily be active. We do not consider an individual disciplined only when he has been rendered as artificially silent as a mute and as immovable as a paralytic. He is an individual annihilated, not disciplined.
>
> We call an individual disciplined when he is master of himself, and can, therefore, regulate his own conduct when it shall be necessary to follow some rule of life. Such a concept of active discipline is not easy either to comprehend or to apply. But certainly it contains a great educational principle, very different from the old-time absolute and undiscussed coercion to immobility.[73]

Yet to some, Maria Montessori represents the autocratic teacher. While she believed in freedom to grow and learn, she did not believe in freedom to commit "useless or dangerous acts (which) must be suppressed, destroyed."[74]

The Montessori teacher is expected to guide the child along the road towards self-discipline:

> The first idea that the child must acquire, in order to be actively disciplined, is that of the difference between good and evil; and the task of the educator lies in seeing that the child does not confound good with immobility, and evil with activity, as often happens in the case of the old-time discipline. And all this

[72]Maria Montessori, The Montessori Method. Cambridge, Mass.: Robert Bentley, Inc., 1964, p. 14.
[73]Ibid., p. 86.
[74]Ibid., pp. 87, 88.

*because our aim is to discipline for activity, for work, for good; not for immobil-
ity, not for passivity, not for obedience.*

*A room in which all the children move about usefully, intelligently, and
voluntarily, without committing any rough or rude act, would seem to me a
classroom very well disciplined indeed.*[75]

Thus the Montessori method is not so much a method as a philosophy.
It involves not only reading, but the entire gamut of early childhood education. Some of her concepts, such as nutrition, are obsolete in light of current
knowledge, but the essential message and many of her specially designed
teaching devices, can still be seen in Montessori and other schools.

Individualized Reading

There are many variations of this system, but the essential is that each
student selects what he wishes to read. The teacher may or may not play a
role in influencing the student's selections.

Dillner and Olson see the teacher "(1) carefully guiding students in
their choice of books, (2) developing independent study activities for each
youngster, and (3) developing reading skills through frequent individual
conferences with each youngster. The sequence of skills developed is determined by the youngster's reading needs, which are reflected in his individual conference."[76]

Duffy, Sherman, and Roehler suggest much more latitude be given the
student in selection of reading matter:

1. *Start collecting books. For the average classroom, try to collect
    100 books, which is at least three different books per pupil. If
    there are not enough available in your school, borrow, trade, and
    ask for donations.*

2. *Set up an interesting library area with a rug, pillows, and some
    furniture. Try to arrange the books with the covers facing the
    students.*

3. *Teach your children the "Rule of Thumb." Tell them to select a
    page in the middle of the book and begin reading it silently. Each
    time they miss a word, they should put up a finger. If all of their*

[75]Ibid., p. 93.
[76]Martha H. Dillner and Joanne P. Olson, *Personalizing Instruction in Middle, Junior, and
Senior High Schools.* New York: Macmillan Publishing Co., Inc., 1977, p. 373.

fingers are up before the page is finished, the book is too hard. Older children can just count up to five words missed.

4.   *Teach them to get books quietly.*

5.   *Teach them to get help with a word. They could go to the dictionary, an aide, experience charts, other books that they know, a friend, the buffer, their teacher; or they could try to figure it out from the context, the pictures, or the sounds.*

6.   *Teach them to prepare for a conference with the teacher by:*

a.   *selecting a story*
b.   *reading silently to themselves, or reading aloud to a friend*
c.   *signing up for the conference.*[77]

Individualized instruction makes it possible for every student to read something on his own ability level and areas of interest. It also gives the student some control of her education. For the secondary student these are important motivators.

But an individualized program depends upon the teacher's ability and willingness to provide reading material on a wide variety of topics and reading levels. This, in turn, depends somewhat on budget, on community mores and values, on the teacher's ability to motivate students to read without direct supervision, and on the student's ability to take responsibility.

A major criticism of individualized reading programs is that it is very difficult, if not impossible, for the teacher to provide a systematic program of training in specific reading skills. On the primary level, this usually means systematic phonics, and at this level the argument is strong enough to delay many individualized programs until the intermediate grades. On the secondary level, individualized reading may be supplemented with skill building when the teacher finds it necessary.

Skill Building

Many teachers feel that learning to read is a complex skill that cannot be left to chance. Each facet of the reading process must be carefully monitored by the teacher to be sure there are no learning gaps. There are two major approaches to skill building, systematic and individualized.

[77]Gerald G. Duffy, George B. Sherman, and Laura R. Roehler, *How to Teach Reading Systematically.* New York: Harper & Row, Publishers, 1977, pp. 16, 17.

In the individualized program, each student is tested to determine his areas of strength and weakness, and an individual program to bolster his soft spots is developed by the teacher. In a systematic skills program, the entire class is taken through a prescribed course of study that purports to cover the important skills needed at a particular level. The same materials may be used for either.

One difficulty with skill building is identifying the component reading skills. To a primary teacher, this may be the phonic skills discussed in Chapters 7 and 8 of this text. For secondary instruction, Richard Boning has built a program around eight major comprehension skills:[78]

Working with Sounds	Getting the Facts
Following Directions	Getting the Main Idea
Using the Context	Drawing Conclusions
Locating the Answer	Detecting the Sequence

Walter Pauk has come up with a similar program identifying 10 different skills.[79] Dillner and Olson[80] list 34 reading skills:

1.	Using Illustration Clues	13.	Making Inferences
2.	Using Context Clues	14.	Making Generalizations and Conclusions
3.	Using Phonic Analysis		
4.	Using Structural Analysis	15.	Identifying Tone and Mood
5.	Using Dictionary Skills	16.	Identifying Theme
6.	Expanding Background in Vocabularly	17.	Identifying Characterization
		18.	Identifying Fact, Fiction, and Opinion
7.	Using a Combination of Vocabularly Skills	19.	Identifying Propaganda
8.	Identifying Details	20.	Identifying Author's Purpose
9.	Identifying Main Ideas	21.	Scheduling Time
10.	Identifying Sequence	22.	Setting Purposes
11.	Following Directions	23.	Using a Study Technique
12.	Identifying Cause-Effect Relationships	24.	Using Locational Aids in the Library

[78]*Specific Skills Series*. Baldwin, N.Y.: Barnell Loft, Ltd.
[79]*A Skill at a Time* Series. Providence, R.I.: Jamestown Publishers, 1975.
[80]Dillner and Olson, op. cit., p. 229.

One could go on indefinitely identifying reading skills. But the question is less whether one has the correct or complete list, than of how important it is to do this type of exercise at all. Proponents of the system see reading growth as learning "a skill at a time," but their arguments are based on assumption, not research.

Another important question concerns transfer. A student may become quite proficient at "Getting The Main Idea" in the Barnell—Loft reader, but see no connection when he picks up a book, a magazine, or a newspaper. If transfer of a specific skill is to be made, for most students the teacher will have to make it by bridging the gap with the student and by showing him how to apply the skills learned in drill books to other reading situations.

Language Experience

There is considerable evidence of the existence of a general linguistic ability. Reading, writing, speaking, spelling, listening, and vocabulary seem to be closely interrelated, and improvement in one area can result in improvement in others.[81] This knowledge, combined with the search for more motivating methods of instruction, has given rise to the *language experience process*, which uses the student's own experiences and his own words to teach reading, writing, spelling, and other language skills.

One approach is to have the student dictate to the teacher a story or an experience, which the teacher writes for the student to read back. The student, having just said the words, can usually read them, learning them in the process. A list is kept of the words that the student has thus learned and the list is frequently reviewed by pulling out the words from a file. The

---

[81]Arthur N. Applebee, "Writing and Reading." *Journal of Reading,* March 1977, 20, 534—537. Applebee summarizes research on this subject.

student may read the words singly in review or the teacher or student may arrange them in phrases or sentences.

Spache and Spache suggest a five-step method, involving: (1) encouraging students to share their ideas and experiences orally, (2) helping students summarize these thoughts and discoveries, (3) writing these thoughts on paper as the student dictates, (4) encouraging students to read and discuss their work with others in the class, and (5) adding to this program skill development in word choice, sentence structure, and the sounds of letters and words.[82]

Teacher and student may become involved in a conversation, which is written or typed by the teacher. Or the student may dictate a story or relate an experience, which the teacher transcribes. Students may work in small groups, reading their compositions to each other, or they may take turns reading to the entire class or to the teacher only. Proponents of this approach, such as Roach Van Allen[83] and James Moffett[84], suggest a wide range of language activities, including many varieties of discussion and dramatization.

I have found the language-experience approach to be one of the most useful in working with secondary remedial readers. Because it involves the student's personal thoughts and feelings and his own organic language, it has motivational value that no other technique can match. A reason for this is suggested by Newton, who claims that "The heart of adultness is independence and self-direction."[85] For this reason, elementary skill building frequently breaks down. The teen-ager is striving for adulthood, and may become bored or resentful of methods that signify childhood. A description of one approach to teaching nonreaders in the secondary school is found on pp. 156–158. The "active learning" situations described in Chapter 4, which embody the whole concept of the turned-on classroom, make use of the language experience approach.

Although I consider language experience a vital component of a secondary school remedial reading program, it has limitations. To begin with,

[82]George D. Spache and Evelyn B. Spache, *Reading in the Elementary School.* 3rd ed., Boston: Allyn and Bacon, Inc., 1973, p. 245.

[83]Roach Van Allen, *Language Experiences in Communication.* Boston: Houghton Mifflin Company, 1976.

[84]James Moffett and Betty Jane Wagner, *Student-Centered Language Arts and Reading K-13: A Handbook For Teachers.* 2nd ed., Boston: Houghton Mifflin Company, 1976. See also the 1973 edition, which is less theoretical and more methodological: James Moffett, *A Student-Centered Language Arts Curriculum, Grades K-13: a Handbook for Teachers.* Boston: Houghton Mifflin Company, 1973.

[85]Eunice Shaed Newton, "Andragogy: Understanding the Adult as a Learner." *Journal of Reading,* February 1977, 20, 361–363.

there is no provision for systematic diagnosis and teaching of reading skills. The theory is that once students get turned on to reading, writing, and otherwise using their language, specific skills will develop naturally. This seems to be true for some students, particularly the bright ones, but those who need remediation may also need more specific types of skill building. The teacher's dilemma is that sometimes the student finds such skill building dull and eventually loses interest. Other students may obediently do skill exercises for years but not really develop skills, only the ability to do exercises (see p. 34). The dictation program in Chapter 6 is effective in helping nonreading students get going. But if these students lack phonic skills, I supplement this approach with a systematic phonics text, such as *Let's Read*, alternating between phonics and language experience.

Another limitation is seen in the difference between the organic language of the student and the language of the textbooks with which he must cope. Young people's speaking and writing vocabularies are not equal to those of their history, science, or math texts, and if all their reading is limited to their own expressions, they may not learn to cope with adult material. Spache and Spache suggest that language experience teaching be confined to primary grades for this reason.[86]

However, a truly comprehensive language experience approach in the secondary school involves far more than writing simple little sentences and stories as the student dictates. It begins there, if that is all the student is capable of doing, and goes to the active learning situations of Chapter 4, which call for research skills to prepare complex reports on subjects of special interest, or gets as close to that as the student is capable.

A third criticism of the language experience approach involves the purpose of learning to read, which is to communicate with a writer. If the student is too involved in reading only his own thoughts, he may find that reading someone else's writing is a new and difficult experience. That is why language experience must progress beyond the narrow dimensions from which it begins. It is the starter on the engine. It gets the student going. But once his engine is turning over, it is necessary to give it the gas—to broaden the program, to have the student read what his classmates have written, then simple reading material, and finally, the adult literature and textbooks that are vital to secondary school survival.

[86]Spache and Spache, op. cit., p. 181.

CHAPTER 2
Say "Ah"
A Diagnostic Method

The "Incident in a Public School" is fiction. Yet, in a larger sense, it is also true. Such incidents are routine. Yet they needn't be, because "there is something the teacher did not bother to find out." By means of a simple test of reading ability, she could have found out at the beginning of the term who is capable of reading the textbook with ease and accuracy. With that knowledge she could design an appropriate program.

STANDARDIZED TESTS

There are many types of reading tests, but all can be classified into two main categories: *standardized tests* and *informal inventories*. Standardized tests are developed over a long period of time by reading specialists. They are carefully composed and field-tested. The final test is administered to an extensive sampling of students, preferably over a large geographic area, and the results are carefully recorded and analyzed. From thousands of test scores, national norms are derived, so that any student taking the test can see how he compares with his peers. Many of these tests have been revised and refined over a period of years.

Most commonly, test results are expressed as a "grade level." For example, a score of 9.2 on a standardized test means that this student is reading on an average level for the second month of the ninth year of school. A student who makes this score in the seventh grade is an accelerated reader, while the same score by a twelfth grader indicates disability. Standardized tests may also be scored in percentiles so that a student may be rated by how he or she would place in comparison with a hundred typical students in that grade level. A percentile score of 62 means that in a typical group of 100 peers, 61 students will be below and 38 above him.

Dozens of standardized reading tests are available for purchase from publishers. Most of them contain a number of forms for various grade levels. A short list of standardized reading tests will be found in Appendix 2. A comprehensive bibliography of such tests is Oscar Buros' *Reading Tests and Reviews*[1].

The Gates—MacGinitie is a fairly representative standardized reading test. It comes in 10 forms, from Primary A for first grade to Survey F for high schools. Each form has, in addition to the test booklet, a *Teacher's Manual*, with directions for administering; and a *Technical Manual*, with information such as the makeup of the test, how the norms were established, and relationships between scores on this test and scores on other tests. There are also scoring keys and class record sheets. Both hand-scoring and machine-scoring sheets are available, and the desired form should be specified in ordering. Samples of questions from the various Gates—MacGinitie reading tests are shown in Figures 2—A, 2—B, and 2—C. Note that some, but not all, tests have questions of graded difficulty.

Reading tests are informative, although subject to all the pitfalls and inaccuracies of testing. No test is perfect, despite the painstaking care with which the good ones are composed, tested, revised, tested again, and finally, after years of research, marketed. A low score on a test may be the result of a stomachache, a crisis in the home, or a feeling of indifference. When the results of a reading test alone are used for purposes of placement in "reading groups", the results are often harmful. Test results must always be checked against subsequent performance by the student, and adjustments made in his placement if they seem warranted. Nevertheless, standardized tests are widely used throughout the school system, and when properly used, are useful and reasonably accurate instruments.

The Reading Expectancy Level

Even if an accurate grade level score can be established, that score only tells how the student compares with others at the same grade level. It says little about whether the student is reading at, above, or below what may be reasonably expected on the basis of age, grade placement, life experience, and IQ. A more realistic picture may be the *reading expectancy level*, computed by grade placement and IQ. This is, at best, only a very rough instrument, for there is no conclusive evidence of a direct mathematical relationship between reading capacity and IQ. We do know, however, that as IQ increases, so does the potential for reading. On this basis we can use IQ as at least an approximate measure of reading level expectancy.

Before we do, however, it would be well to clarify our definition of IQ.

[1]Highland Park, N.J.: Gryphon Press, 1972. Buros not only lists dozens of available tests, but gives publisher, price, the various forms of each test, and critical reviews. Similar information is found in Buros' *Mental Measurements Yearbooks*.

```
┌─────────────────────────────┐ ┌──────────────────────┐
│      Speed and Accuracy      │ │      Vocabulary      │
│                              │ │                      │
│ START                        │ │ 1. flexible          │
│                              │ │    A  safe           │
│ 1. In the game of Jai Alai,  │ │    B  easily bent    │
│ players, using curved        │ │    C  worthless      │
│ cestas, hurl a ball at speeds│ │    D  full of holes  │
│ up to 150 m.p.h. and catch   │ │    E  brittle        │
│ it on the first bounce. The  │ │                      │
│ game is extremely            │ │                      │
│   A      B      C      D     │ │ 2. mourn             │
│  easy relaxing slow   fast   │ │    F  arise          │
│                              │ │    G  adorn          │
│ 2. Photosynthesis is the     │ │    H  drift          │
│ process by which plants con- │ │    I  grieve         │
│ vert sunlight and carbon     │ │    J  praise         │
│ dioxide into starches and    │ │        • • •         │
│ oxygen. This process occurs  │ │                      │
│ in                           │ │ 49. apprehensive     │
│   E      F      G      H     │ │    A  understanding  │
│ carbon animals plants starches│ │   B  waning         │
│         • • •                │ │    C  fearful        │
│ 35. Both clocks and calendars│ │    D  demonstrative  │
│ are used to keep track of    │ │    E  rubbery        │
│ time. The units measured by  │ │                      │
│ clocks are arbitrary, but the│ │ 50. allusion         │
│ units measured by a calendar │ │    F  revery         │
│ are                          │ │    G  image          │
│   A       B       C      D   │ │    H  impermanence   │
│ reversible longer invented natural│ │ I  reference      │
│                              │ │    J  falsehood      │
│ 36. Medieval craft guilds did│ │                      │
│ not negotiate with employers │ │              STOP    │
│ as modern unions do. They set│ │   CHECK YOUR WORK    │
│ standards for their trade.   │ └──────────────────────┘
│ One of their functions was to│
│   E      F       G      H    │
│ strike bargain regulate picket│
│                      STOP    │
└─────────────────────────────┘
```

FIGURE 2-A   Gates-MacGinitie Reading Tests, Survey F, Form 2M, sample questions. (From Columbia University, 1965.)

At one time IQ was considered an absolute capacity, as if it were measuring only an innate and finite amount of mentality. This is the "empty bucket" approach, that is, thinking of the brain as a bucket, capable of being filled with only so much and no more. Some people were thought to have larger buckets than others, and there was nothing anybody could do about it.

There is considerable evidence, however, that a person's IQ is also subject to environmental influences. There are too many examples of IQs changing—in some cases being deliberately changed—to accept the inevitability of IQ as a permanent, limiting factor. IQ scores have also been found to reflect the cultural biases of the tester, with low income youngsters, particularly those of racial minorities, having a distinct disadvantage.

Speed and Accuracy

1. In the United States we use dollars, in France they use francs, in Italy they use lire, in Mexico they use pesos. Which country issues lire?

Mexico	Italy	United States	France

2. In 1620 the Speedwell and the Mayflower sailed for the New World. The Speedwell was forced to return to England. The ship reaching America was the

Speedwell	New World	Mayflower	Pilgrim

35. The kangaroo usually does not attack other animals. It prefers to use its speed to avoid trouble. It can and will fight strongly if need be. It is

wary	helpless	slow	vicious

36. Whales rise to the top of the water to breathe, or "blow." Then they may "sound," or plunge far below the surface. When a whale sounds, it is

resting	diving	grunting	blowing

STOP

Vocabulary

1. rescue
remember
reduce
mistake
save
charge

2. illegal
forbidden
distressing
enormous
loyal
cheap

49. vestigial
remnantal
feminine
shining
sordid
novel

50. ostentatious
showy
bony
fat
wise
experimental

STOP
CHECK YOUR WORK

Comprehension

Sea lion pups play in much the same way as dog pups do, except that, when they are older, they like to play under ___1___, which ___2___ pups do not like to do.

1. sky	trees	tents	water	fire

2. fish	drowns	sea lion	play	dog

The archaeologist tries to add to our knowledge of ancient peoples. He must often dig down through layers of earth and debris to ___3___ relics of an ancient civilization. By digging carefully, he hopes not to miss or ___4___ valuable evidence.

3. discard	waste	impossible	uncover	dirt

4. make	destroy	discover	understand	search

When Austria ruled Switzerland, it is said that Gessler, a tyrannical Austrian, set a hat on top of a pole in a Swiss village. He then ordered the Swiss to bow to this hat, a ___50___ of Austria. William Tell, a skilled archer, ___51___ to bow. Gessler ___52___ him, under penalty of death, to shoot an apple from the head of his son. William did this but never bowed to the hat.

50. flag	ruler	time	symbol	village

51. wanted	rejected	tried	refused	decided

52. begged	determined	shot	cheered	forced

STOP
CHECK YOUR WORK

FIGURE 2-B   Gates-MacGinitie Reading Tests, Survey E, Form 1, Grades 7 through 9, sample questions. (From Columbia University, 1965.)

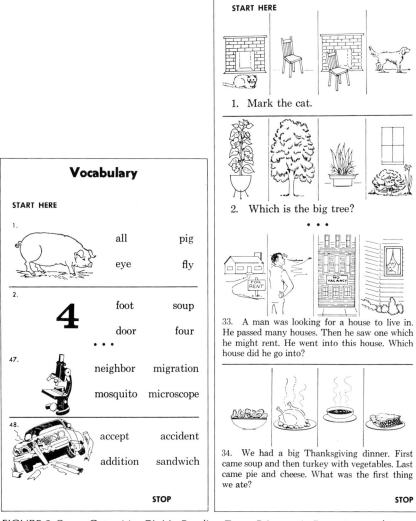

Vocabulary

START HERE

1.

all	pig
eye	fly

2.

4

foot	soup
door	four

• • •

47.

neighbor	migration
mosquito	microscope

48.

accept	accident
addition	sandwich

STOP

Comprehension

START HERE

1. Mark the cat.

2. Which is the big tree?

• • •

33. A man was looking for a house to live in. He passed many houses. Then he saw one which he might rent. He went into this house. Which house did he go into?

34. We had a big Thanksgiving dinner. First came soup and then turkey with vegetables. Last came pie and cheese. What was the first thing we ate?

STOP

FIGURE 2-C   Gates-MacGinitie Reading Tests, Primary A, Form 1, sample questions. (From Columbia University, 1965.)

Yet the IQ score does indicate reading ability and success in school. The most obvious explanation seems to be that the cultural biases of the IQ test are also those of the school, so that a student who is having learning difficulties will also have difficulty taking the IQ test. IQ tests correlate highly with school achievement, and the so-called "culture-free" tests, designed to eliminate culture as a factor, show a lower correlation with success in school.

If, then, we think of IQ as the *current capacity to do schoolwork,* we have some idea of what we are measuring. We measure in an IQ test the student's total inherited intelligence, life experiences, language development, intellectual maturity, attitudes, feelings, and state of health. And if we think of IQ in terms of all the things that go into it, we have a rather accurate measure of what we might reasonably expect of a student.

Returning to reading, if we consider the reading expectancy level as that which the student should be doing on the basis of grade in school and IQ, we can use the formula:

$$\frac{\text{grade placement} \times \text{IQ}}{100} = \text{reading expectancy level}$$

Example (Bob):

$$\underset{9.2}{\text{grade placement}} \times \underset{80}{\text{IQ}} = \frac{736}{100} = 7.36$$

This means that Bob, in the second month of the ninth grade, might be expected to read at the seventh grade level. If he reads at the 8.3 level, for example, he is not really a retarded reader but is actually doing slightly better than might be expected. Carol, in the same grade with an IQ of 130 making the same reading score is an underachiever:

$$\frac{9.2 \times 130}{100} = 11.96 = \text{reading expectancy level}$$

This score can be inaccurately low if the student makes a low score on the intelligence test because of reading disability.

The Reading Achievement Ratio

The reading achievement ratio may be calculated once we obtain a student's reading expectancy level. Harold was given, along with his classmates, the Gates–MacGinitie reading test at the beginning of the eighth grade. He scored 9.6, putting him over a year and a half ahead of his class. But with an IQ of 140, he has a reading expectancy level of

$$\frac{8.0 \times 140}{100} = 1120 = \frac{11.2}{100}$$

Using the formula:

$$\frac{\text{reading score}}{\text{reading expectancy level}} = \text{reading achievement ratio}$$

$$\frac{9.6}{11.2} = .86$$

Therefore, Harold is reading only 86 percent of expectancy, even though he is above grade level. This indicates that there are bright youngsters in the public schools who are not reading at capability, but are not considered problems because they are keeping up with or exceeding their classmates. It bears repetition that both the reading expectancy level and the reading achievement ratio are only approximate, but they remind the teacher that IQ is an important factor in reading progress.

INFORMAL TESTS

An informal inventory is a teacher-made test, usually designed for a particular purpose. Zintz[2], Kennedy[3], and Karlin[4] describe a procedure somewhat as follows: Take any set of graded readers[5] and select the volume you would estimate to be about one year below your student's reading level. That is, if you would guess that your student is reading at high fifth grade level, select the reader for high fourth grade. Have him read a selection and answer questions. If he cannot read it with reasonable speed and comprehension, try the next lower volume. If he reads easily, try the next higher. Continue up

[2]Miles V. Zintz, *The Reading Process.* Dubuque, Iowa: William C. Brown Company, 1972. pp. 52–53.
[3]Eddie C. Kennedy, *Classroom Approaches to Remedial Reading.* Itasca, Ill.: F. E. Peacock Publishers, Inc., 1971, pp. 24–25.
[4]Robert Karlin, *Teaching Reading in High School.* 2nd ed., Indianapolis: The Bobbs-Merrill Company, Inc., 1972, pp. 94–101.
[5]*Readers Digest Skill Builders* is a good example. Pleasantville, N.Y.: Readers Digest Association, Inc. There is also an informal reading inventory that provides both silent and oral reading forms on pp. 495–520 of: Martha H. Dillner and Joanne P. Olson, *Personalizing Reading Instruction in Middle, Junior,* and *Senior High Schools.* New York: Macmillan Publishing Co., Inc., 1977.

or down the set of readers until you find the highest level at which the student can read easily. Consider this the student's reading level. Reasonable speed and comprehension are, of course, subjective, but they usually mean ability to read about 95 percent of the words and answer from 70 to 80 percent of the comprehension questions, depending on difficulty.

But this type of inventory, like the standardized test, still has not told you what most classroom teachers need to know: Can the student do the required reading for a particular course? A more direct and more helpful device for the classroom teacher is the *specific reading inventory,* an informal, teacher-made test. Like the standardized test, the specific inventory is subject to all the inaccuracies of testing, plus the additional hazard of an instrument that is put together quickly. But the specific inventory can be constructed to measure exactly what the teacher wishes to measure and can be administered in comparatively little time without the purchase of additional material. With a bit of practice a teacher can become quite effective in using specific reading inventories to diagnose, in advance, the capacity of the class and of each individual to handle the reading requirements of the course.

Administering the Specific Reading Inventory

Select a passage of about five hundred words from the textbook or other reading material you plan to use. Try to find a piece that has internal unity. Have the students read the selection silently in class. As they read, watch for clues to reading difficulties: lip movement, squinting, frowning, or restlessness—which indicate difficulty with the printed page. Holding the book too close or too far away may signal vision problems. A student who looks away from the material frequently is probably having difficulty concentrating. Also watch for the student who reacts with hostility or rebelliousness. A more complete description of symptoms of reading disorders will be found on pp. 55 to 63.

After the students have read the passage, pass out a sheet of questions. Do this immediately, with no discussion of the content. Include the following:

VOCABULARY QUESTIONS   These are designed to see if the student understood *specific words* in the selection. They may be multiple choice:

A *mendicant* is a:

    A doctor
    B beggar
    C place where women are not allowed
    D man who fixes things

They may be taken from the story:

When Joe *mesmerized*	A	helped her
Sally he:	B	admired her
	C	hypnotized her
	D	made her unhappy

Or they may take any form you feel appropriate. In writing your vocabulary list, do not neglect those words that are not directly related to the lesson. They can be just as difficult to read, and you need to measure their readability also. For example, an auto mechanics manual may state:

The viscosity of oil decreases with the temperature of the engine.

Viscosity is sure to make the vocabulary list, as it is central to the lesson. But if the student is tripped up by *temperature,* you want to know that too.

FACT QUESTIONS   These are designed to see if the student is getting information from reading:

Marie Antoinette was:	A	A queen of France, wife of Louis XVI
	B	A campaigner for women's rights
	C	A wealthy woman who hated Napoleon
	D	The first great woman scientist

CONCEPT QUESTIONS   These test whether the student understands ideas, issues, and implications. They may deal with the author's opinions, relationships with other concepts, or any of the higher level reading skills. For example:

The theory of the indestructibility of matter means that if you burn 100 pounds of wood down to 5 pounds of ashes:

	A	Important chemical changes have taken place in the wood.
	B	The earth and its atmosphere are now 95 pounds lighter.
	C	The other 95 pounds must be *somewhere,* even if in another form.
	D	5 pounds may be considered the *pure* weight of the wood.

Take care not to make the test questions more difficult to read than the text, or you may receive inaccurately low scores. In composing the reading inventory, think carefully about which reading skills are important. In a biology assignment you may be concerned with students' ability to read such words as *deciduous* and *cotyledon*. In history you may wonder if the class is sufficiently familiar with the period of Henry VIII to understand the subsequent struggle between Queen Elizabeth and Mary, Queen of Scots. An English teacher may be concerned with students' capacities to think symbolically before exposing them to stories by Joseph Conrad. Thus the nature of the reading task largely determines the approach to the inventory.

PROCEDURE   After the students have read the story, allow them to use their books to answer the questions. This is a test of reading, not memory. Allow a sufficient but not excessive amount of time. Of course, if you wish to test for speed of reading, you may shorten the time, or record the number of minutes it took each student to read the material. But at this stage you are more likely to be interested in whether the student can perform the task *at all*, regardless of the time it takes. After the papers have been collected and checked, and scores computed, the students can be ranked in order on a chart, such as the one in Table 2−1.

The table tells you that this is a very heterogeneous class, ranging from 18 to 94 points. Either there were more possible points on the vocabulary section and fewest on the concept part (which is frequently the case), or most of the students had more trouble with *meaning* than with words. This is also common. Table 2−1 reveals that at least three students, and possibly four more, are likely to have serious reading difficulties. Only six understand the concepts, and these are not necessarily the top readers in vocabularly and data gathering. Finally, Table 2−1 shows an approximate correlation between vocabulary and data gathering but less relationship with concept development.

On the basis of the data given, students may be classified as:

Independent readers: Those who can read and understand the material with little difficulty.

Instructional readers: Those who can read and understand the material if given some help.

Frustration readers: Those for whom the reading is so frustrating that trying to read is more damaging than helpful.

TABLE 2-1

CLASS SCORES ON SPECIFIC READING INVENTORY

STUDENT	TOTAL POINTS	VOCABULARY	DATA	CONCEPTS
1	18	9	7	2
2	19	6	10	3
3	26	8	8	10
4	34	20	10	4
5	34	22	8	4
6	36	20	16	0
7	36	14	14	8
8	43	21	10	12
9	48	28	8	12
10	48	22	23	3
11	49	16	16	17
12	56	34	16	6
13	58	34	19	5
14	61	30	28	3
15	63	30	22	11
16	65	25	23	17
17	69	25	18	26
18	70	32	14	24
19	70	32	25	13
20	76	32	31	13
21	79	35	30	14
22	82	34	27	21
23	88	31	38	19
24	90	40	35	15
25	91	40	37	14
26	94	38	40	16

Specific methods of working with each type of reader will be discussed in the following chapters. The designations independent, instructional, and frustration reader are only approximate. Students do not group themselves into neat little categories, but along a continuum, with a complex and frequently bewildering array of abilities and limitations. These categories can be used only in reference to *some specific material*. An individual may read one book on the independent level and another at the frustration level. We are all frustration readers, faced with sufficiently esoteric or technical material, and all but a few secondary students can read something independently. Thus we do not say that X—— is a frustration reader, but that he or she *reads a particular work* at the frustration level. This is important, because most of

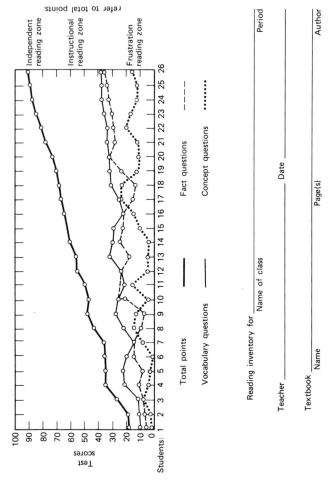

FIGURE 2-D   *An informal reading inventory.* This figure gives the same information as on p. 47. The heavy black line represents total scores for each of the 26 students; the thin black line, vocabulary scores; the dashed line, fact scores; and the dotted line, concept scores. There are no lines separating independent, instructional, and frustration reading zones, indicating that the classifications are difficult to define, and at best somewhat arbitrary.

the instructional techniques in this volume are aimed at building confidence and motivation by *helping students read at the independent level.*

Specific reading inventory data may be more vividly expressed by means of a graph, as illustrated in Figure 2-D.

Note that there are no lines separating independent, instructional, and

48

frustration reading zones. This indicates that the classifications are difficult to define and at best somewhat arbitrary.

SAMPLE SPECIFIC READING INVENTORY (BASED ON *INCIDENT IN A PUBLIC SCHOOL*)

Answer the following questions according to the information in the reading assignment.

In giving directions, stress that all answers refer to the reading material.

1. *Legal qualifications* for United States Senator are:
   - (a) The promises he made during the campaign.
   - (b) Requirements such as age, residence, and so forth, that must be met before he can be a senator.
   - (c) His education and experience.
   - (d) His salary and other benefits.

   Tests background knowledge. Reader must differentiate "qualifications" from "legal qualifications."

2. A *volunteer* is somebody who does something:
   - (a) Without being paid for it.
   - (b) Without enjoying it.
   - (c) Without being called upon.
   - (d) Without learning from it.

3. To *surface* is to:
   - (a) Fail to see the inner meaning.
   - (b) Remain at the top.
   - (c) Make oneself seen.
   - (d) Write on.

   The words in 2 and 3 have particular meanings in this passage.

4. When something is *barely perceptible,* it
   - (a) Can hardly be noticed.

(b) Can be heard easily.

(c) Can make little difference.

(d) Cannot help very much.

5. When Tom *indicated negative,* he:

(a) Let it be known without speaking that the answer was *yes.*

(b) Let it be known without speaking that the answer was *no.*

(c) Told the teacher the answer was *yes.*

(d) Told the teacher the answer was *no.*

A B from C D differentiate *indicated;* A from B or C from D differentiate *negative.*

6. The *dismissal bell* signals:

(a) Time to start working.

(b) Time to stop working and pass in all papers.

(c) Time to discuss what has just been read.

(d) Time to leave class.

7. If Tom had *ploughed* through, he would have been:

(a) Farming.

(b) Reading with difficulty.

(c) Reading with ease.

(d) Writing with ease.

Requires ability to understand a word with a nonstandard meaning.

8. The *preceding* paragraph is the one:

(a) Just before.

(b) Just after.

(c) Easiest to read.

(d) Most difficult to read.

9. Tom Bowman weighed:

(a) 160.

(b) 170.

(c) 180.

(d) 190.

9, 10, and 11 are simple data questions.

10. When the teacher called on him, Tom:
    (a) Answered the question.
    (b) Tried to show off in front of the class.
    (c) Was rude to the teacher.
    (d) Looked at the floor.

11. After calling on Tom, the teacher:
    (a) Called on someone else.
    (b) Answered the question herself.
    (c) Was pleased with Tom's answer.
    (d) Realized that Tom had more important things to do than read the assignment.

12. The teacher was angry mainly because: Requires some elementary interpretation.
    (a) Tom had not tried to read the assignment.
    (b) Tom knew the answer but refused to say it in class.
    (c) Another student was disturbing the class.
    (d) Tom was an athlete, and she disliked athletes.

13. The teacher could have taken the trouble to find out that: Slightly more complex.
    (a) Tom really did not know as much as he seemed to.
    (b) Tom could not read well enough to read the lesson.
    (c) Tom was very interested in beetles.
    (d) Tom was named all-conference tackle in his junior year.

14. The significance of *Incident In A Public School* is that:

   (a) Although Tom Bowman was an excellent athlete, he could not read, even though he was in the eleventh grade.

   (b) Tom's superior accomplishments disproved the myth that athletes are poor readers.

   (c) It's disgraceful the way kids go through school these days without learning to read.

   (d) Many teachers do not realize that some secondary students cannot read the textbooks.

This is the ultimate question: Did the reader get the message?

This inventory is short, as the passage contains only about 300 words. Although such a short test must be considered tentative until checked against the student's subsequent performance, it can give a rough idea how well the student reads. Questions one through eight are vocabulary, testing both reading ability and comprehension. They do not tell you whether the student knows the word in conversation but is unable to read it, or does not know the meaning of the word. Questions nine through fourteen begin with simple data and become increasingly complex and conceptual.

Variations on a theme: Further Explorations with Reading Inventories

To complete the specific reading inventory successfully, students must perform a complex task: They must read the passage unassisted and come to terms with its meaning. Then they must read the questions, formulate the answers, and express these answers in writing. A breakdown at any point in this process can result in a low score, and the teacher has no way of determining where the breakdown occurred. To analyze the results more carefully, let us consider administering similar reading inventories but in different forms. We can call the test as described above, Form A:

Form A.   Students read the passage.
             Students answer the questions on paper.

Form B.   Teacher reads the passage and the questions aloud.
             Students answer questions on paper.

If you administer Forms A and B, using similar passages from the same text and asking equated sets of questions, you have a comparison between scores made by students after *they read* and after they *hear it read.* A significantly higher score on Form B indicates that the student has a reading problem, that he may learn more through inputs other than reading. In addition to needing special help in the classroom, as described in subsequent chapters, these students should be referred to the reading specialist for assistance. Students who do about as well when read to indicate that their problem is not essentially reading, but lack of comprehension, lack of experiential background and vocabulary development, low IQ, or a number of other possibilities, including indifference to the whole process.

More information can be obtained by administering a similar test in other forms:

Form C   Student reads the passage.
            Student answers the questions orally.

Form D   Teacher reads the passage and the questions aloud.
            Student answers the questions orally.

Forms C and D factor out the writing process. If scores on these tests show dramatic improvement over those on A and B, you have a strong indication that the problem is getting something down on paper. To some students, even the simple task of selecting the correct answer from a multiple-choice quiz introduces the trauma of "taking a written test."

Oral questions (Forms C and D) have to be administered individually and privately. Frequently, the teacher has the difficult—in some schools, impossible—task of finding time when both student and teacher are free. Perhaps a counselor, reading specialist, teacher aide, secretary, or administrator will be willing to administer the test before or after school or during the student's study period. Although this eliminates personal contact during which the teacher can get to know the student's attitudes, abilities, and limitations, it may be the only available option.

A testing program as extensive as this has some built-in dangers. Too much testing can turn students off and cause them to stop trying, not only on the inventories but in the class in general. If possible, the reading inventories should be part of the lesson. After administering, discuss the questions so that the class does not get the feeling they are being continually tested. One approach might be to administer Forms A and B to the entire class, and then select those who have low scores to give Forms C and D, to see if it could be the writing that is giving them difficulty.

Some possible results, and what they may indicate, are shown in Table 2-2.

Not all profiles will turn out as nice and neat as the ones above in Table 2−2. Some will show data much more contradictory and difficult to analyze.

The scores on any measuring instrument can be influenced by:

Physical or mental health. A low score on a particular day may result from nothing more than stomach cramps or a fight with parents or friend.

Lack of motivation. Many students simply do not *care* what score they make. Why should they?

Rebelliousness. Any number of hostile attitudes can cause a student to work below capacity.

Inaccuracy of instrument. A specific inventory has been put together quickly. One form may be more difficult than another; therefore, the teacher must compare total scores of the class on each form, as well as a student's scores on the various forms.

Once more it must be stressed that all test scores, whether from standardized or informal instruments, must be considered only *tentative indicators.* They alert the teacher to possible problem areas but must always be verified on the basis of subsequent performance.

Even if we can assume that the evaluation accurately reflects the student's ability at the time of testing, there is little guarantee that the situation will continue. Growth and change are intrinsic in the human condition, particularly with developing youngsters. A testing program, therefore, gives only a quick, rough estimate of human ability. It may or may not be accurate, and the data may or may not be lasting. The best measure of student reading ability, or almost any student ability, is teacher judgment. If the results of a test say one thing, and a trained, sensitive teacher, after careful,

TABLE 2-2

FORM A	FORM B	FORM C	FORM D	IT MAY INDICATE:
High	High	High	High	Independent reader
Low	High	Low	High	Reading problem Auditory learner
Low	Low	High	High	Writing problem
Low	Low	Low	Low	IQ low Poor language development Experiential limitations Emotional problem Physical problem Counterproductive attitude
High	Low	High	Low	Not auditory learner Learns more easily by reading
High	High	Low	Low	Not orally articulate

(Header spanning FORM A–FORM D: **IF STUDENT SCORES:**)

extended observation, says something else, I will usually go along with the teacher. But "careful, extended observation" is not to be confused with making assumptions: "Tom didn't do his homework because he is just plain lazy."

SYMPTOMS OF READING DISABILITY

Indications of reading disorders are many and varied, and the classroom teacher can hardly be expected to be an expert. But a teacher can learn to watch for certain signs of learning and reading difficulty. The following are warnings of a possible problem, but are in no way conclusive. When a cluster of symptoms are noticed, however, the teacher may wish to refer the student for special attention.

Poor Health

Poor health has not been conclusively established as a cause of reading disorder, although it can cause a student to be excessively tired, listless, sleepy, or cranky. Professional diagnosis can only be made by a physician, but sometimes the symptoms are obvious. Watch those who breathe loudly, laboriously, or with mouth open, or who complain of chronic headache, stomachache, earache, or other health problems. Do not pressure these students to achieve, for it may be nearly impossible. They should be referred to the school health officer, counselor, or administrator, and ultimately to the parents. Indigent students, who are usually beset with health problems, may be eligible for public assistance. These may have to be taken for treatment by the proper school official.

Low IQ

Low IQ students tend to be dull and passive, lacking interest, curiosity, enthusiasm, and sense of humor. They usually have a short attention span, and quickly forget what they have learned. Their school performance is poor all-around, although they may have a strong area, such as music or home economics. They are frequently small for their age, and health problems are common. Frequent absence may result from illness or apathy. They may have unquestioned opinions, which are likely to be based on traditional mores, values, and beliefs. Behavior is frequently juvenile, in extreme cases infantile. Social adjustments are poor, and they may be withdrawn from their peers or easily badgered into a fight or argument.

They may be more interested in manipulative activities—industrial arts or leather-craft—than in academic studies, although it is a mistake to assume that this is always the case. They tend to have a poor sense of time and space, and may not be able to tell you whether Christopher Columbus came before George Washington or if St. Louis is on the way to San Francisco.

Their ambitions and desires seldom reach great heights, and they are satisfied by comparatively simple achievements, finding security and comfort in workbook exercises that require a minimum of creativity or problem solving. Lengthy or complicated assignments can produce anxiety, frustration, or boredom. In class they may exhibit restlessness and fidgeting but are more likely to slump into their desks and not be noticed. They read slowly and may look away frequently. Speech in class may be muttered.

Spelling and handwriting are usually poor, speaking and writing vocabularies, use of modifiers and complex sentence structures, and power of articulation limited. These students have difficulty conceptualizing and seeing new relationships. For example, after "learning" that 60 percent of 100 = 60, and 30 percent of 100 = 30, they may still lack the insight to tell you that 10 percent of 100 = 10. Such skills as summarizing and picking out the important points from a passage are generally lacking; and when confronted with new reading words they have no way to figure them out.

As long as IQ remains low, achievement is in proportion. If the student is making even minimal progress in your class and seems contented, he should probably remain. Check the file for test scores and discuss with your school counselor. If the disability is severe enough, he may be better off in a special class for the mentally handicapped. Many reading teachers will not take a student unless his reading achievement ratio is below .80, for even with expert help, learning will be minimal.

Hyperactivity

Hyperactive children are compulsive movers, and literally cannot sit still a minute. They are in their seats one moment and up the next. Lecture and discipline do no good and may only add guilt to other problems, for they have little self-control. Fortunately, most children outgrow hyperactivity before they reach secondary school, but when such cases do appear, the school health officer should be alerted. Hyperactivity may be difficult to distinguish from lack of self discipline. A physician is needed to diagnose and treat a hyperactive child.

Neurological Disorder (Brain Damage)

See pp. 16–17. Neurological disorder may be present even in very bright youngsters. These are the most difficult to diagnose, unless the condition is severe. Most common symptoms are reversals. Often there is confusion between left and right. Refer such cases to the reading specialist and school health officer.

Emotional Damage

Hostile students are seldom difficult to spot, as they tend to carry their problems on their sleeves. They are generally antagonistic, rebellious, and easily upset. The slightest incident can cause a flare-up at the teacher or a fellow student, and they are often involved in fights and arguments. These unhappy youngsters are seldom interested in learning. They do not work well with others and may belittle their fellow students or the teacher while boasting about their own prowess. They usually sit in the back of the room and are restless, fidgety, and uncooperative. They give up easily and may not try at all.

Such students tend to drive their teachers up the wall, for we deal with the hostility, which we can see, rather than the cause, which we seldom know. Nor do we usually know whether the best treatment would be tender loving care or a verbal punch in the mouth. But if we knew the enormous troubles faced by some of our youth, much of our counterhostility would dissipate.

Not all emotionally damaged students exhibit such overt symptoms. Sullen or defeated ones may sit in the back of the room and never be noticed. They may appear dull or uninterested in class, and unable or unwilling to respond when called upon. These students are sometimes easily embarrassed. A minor upset can be a catastrophe. They will seldom try anything unfamiliar. Because they are not trouble makers, they usually get no help. But this attitude frequently leads to reading and other learning problems.

Some youngsters come to school so starved for attention or affection that they are continually vying for the attention of the teacher and their peers. They may be victims of hard-working, inattentive, or emotionally damaged parents. The teacher should try to find some time to give these students the approval and attention they need, difficult as this is in a busy classroom.

The emotionally damaged student may need an outlet for his energies. I have seen major personality and attitude changes take place when a student "found himself" in journalism, drama, music, art, athletics, industrial arts, clubs, or school political or social life. And it's amazing what can happen when a student acquires a girl friend or boy friend.

The severely disturbed youngster has little chance for success in school. Under pressure to perform, he responds by sinking deeper into emotionalism. Such students are very difficult to work with under ordinary classroom conditions. They should be made to feel that the teacher is sincerely interested in them, that they are part of their peer group. Acceptance is very important, not just meaningless flattery, but genuine acceptance for their own real worth. They must feel secure in the classroom, that they will not be called upon to do what is beyond them or embarrassed before their friends. They need to experience success and the joy of accomplishment, even when they are resisting accomplishing anything. To do all this while at the same time being firm in not allowing this student to destroy the learning situation of the others can be done. All it requires is a master teacher, a hero, and a saint.

Serious cases of emotional disturbance should be discussed with the school counselor or psychologist. Some schools have special classes for the emotionally disturbed.

Poor Motor Skills

Poor physical coordination is frequently a symptom of other problems, such as low IQ, orthopedic impairment, or neurological handicap. It may result in reading retardation. Such students tend to be awkward of movement, often hitting themselves getting in and out of desks or performing other motor tasks. They are sometimes hyperactive and restless. Their walk is awkward, and they are uncoordinated in athletics. They usually have barely readable or unreadable handwriting, and reading is slow and word-by-word. They sometimes skip words as they read, sometimes whole lines. Such cases, particularly when accompanied by other disorders, should be referred to the school health officer.

Hearing Loss

Although the direct effect of hearing loss on reading is not yet clear, the educational and social losses that result from isolation can affect reading. Hard-of-hearing students may be spotted by failure to respond when they are not looking at the speaker. In severe cases, pronunciation, enunciation, or tone of voice may be unnatural. They may hold the mouth open for breathing or listening, and ask to have things repeated. They may complain of headaches, frequent colds, sinusitis, discharges of the ear, or strange noises. Sometimes they give up trying and appear lazy or listless, or lost in daydreams. Others may ask to change seats, either to get closer to the action or to put the stronger ear in a favorable position. A student with one deficient ear may turn it toward the speaker, if the defect is slight, and away from the speaker, if it is severe. I have seen students do this without knowing they have a hearing problem. Ask the school health officer if the student has had an audiometer test recently, and if not, try to arrange it. Sometimes the condition can be corrected with a hearing aid, and if the money is not available from the family, the student may be eligible for public assistance. Check with the school counselor or county welfare or public health office. Even after receiving a hearing aid, the student may have to adjust emotionally or mechanically to its use. Meanwhile, place the student in the best hearing position, or allow him to place himself.

Vision Loss

Students with vision problems may hold their book at an unusual angle, or too near or too far from their eyes, or frequently adjust the distance. They usually read slowly, sometimes squinting or frowning, showing signs of restlessness or physical or emotional strain. Reading may cause their eyes to become bloodshot or to tear, itch, or sting. They may blink or rub their eyes while or after reading. They may complain that the words look fuzzy or double. They may read large print considerably better. Reading may cause them to be excessively tired or irritable. Handwriting may be poor, although poor handwriting may be caused by a number of other problems, including an attempt (conscious or otherwise) to disguise poor spelling. They may need glasses. Check with the school health officer about testing and possible public assistance. Request that diagnostic vision tests be made at reading distance, not at 20 feet, as frequently happens in vision testing. Allow students to work in short spurts, with rest periods or physical activity between. Looking at faraway objects or shifting the eyes is restful. Place the class so that students are not looking into glaring light. Allow students with vision loss to shift position.

Speech Disorders

Speech disorders can affect a student's linguistic development and self-concept, hence reading progress. The symptoms, if severe, are obvious, including stuttering, cleft palate and other physical deformities, a foreign accent or unusual dialect, or sloppy speech habits. Although speech and reading handicaps frequently go together, this is not always the case. I believe a major determinant is the student's self-concept.

Carefully observe students who resist talking, who move their heads in an unusual manner when talking, who have unnatural vocal qualities, who hesitate before speaking, or who speak unusually loudly or softly. Unless another cause is obvious, these students' hearing should be checked. Some will have difficulty only with particular vocal sounds. Such cases should be referred to the speech therapist or school health officer. Except for accent or

THE BORN LOSER   **by Art Sansom**

Copyright © , 1976, the Newspaper Enterprise Association.

dialect problems, be very cautious about trying to correct speech disorders. One cause of stuttering is thought to be an attempt to correct minor and temporary speech problems.

Poor Reading Habits

Students with no physical or emotional disabilities may develop poor reading habits for no reason you can discern. Symptoms include lip movement while reading silently, restlessness, yawning, or looking away during reading, and slow, word-by-word reading. The poor reader seldom reads voluntarily, either silently or aloud, and when called upon to read aloud may refuse, try to beg off, or mutter his words. He is a poor speller, and generally does much better with oral language than written. His school work improves when it does not involve reading. The average or bright student with poor reading habits is the one most likely to profit from the help of a reading specialist.

Lack of Phonics

Some people have a natural sense of phonics, but every normal person can learn enough phonics to serve her reading needs. Students who lack training in phonics have difficulty with new words. They substitute words that have no phonic resemblance. These may be synonyms, such as *car* for *automobile,* or reasonable but wrong guesses, such as *cat* for *dog,* or *big* for *little.* Or they may make completely wild and unrelated guesses. These readers may sound out part of a word but not the rest, so that *sometimes* becomes *something.* You can often literally see these youngsters laboring over a word, particularly if they have learned the sounds but not learned to blend them. Thus *school* is read: s—k—uh—s—k—u—uh—l—s—k—u—l. A student who lacks phonic skills can benefit from the services of a reading specialist.

WHERE DO WE
GO FROM HERE?

Having conducted a testing program, standardized or informal, and having observed the class long enough to pick out those with symptoms of reading disability, the teacher is faced with decisions. Should the deficient student remain in a regular class or be placed in a special program for the mentally retarded, physically handicapped, or emotionally disturbed? Should the teacher attempt to help the student with the reading problem or defer to the reading specialist? Is the intervention of a school counselor or health officer warranted?

In cases of severe impairment the need for special help is obvious, but these students are usually channeled into special programs instead of the regular class. Classroom teachers are more likely to be faced with borderline cases, and these are not easy to decide.

The primary question is, *What is the prognosis for success and happiness, if the student remains in your class?* I have seen two types of extremism operate, both detrimental to the student. Some teachers become so emotionally tied to their students that they have a difficult time giving up any of them, or even sharing them with a specialist. Although this often reveals a dedicated teacher, it can hamper the student who needs individualized, specialized attention. On the other hand, the teacher who sloughs off every problem student not only overburdens the special programs but takes the student out of his peer environment, where he operates most effectively.

But there are guidelines. First is the degree of reading retardation. If you can calculate his reading achievement ratio at .80 or higher, there are probably more severe cases demanding the attention of the reading specialist. But most important is whether the student can do the work required for your class, including the reading. If he finds the situation more frustrating than educational, it is better to relieve him. This depends on how much time you are willing and able to devote to the techniques that will be explained in the following chapters. Many teachers are strongly oriented toward the bright student, others to the underdog. Whichever is the case, the teacher should know himself and bring all his resources and those of the school to bear on the problem.

Also to be considered are the size of the class, and whether its structure permits the kind of special help needed, as well as the type of relationship the student has to the teacher and to his peers in the class. Remember to consider the prognosis for success *and happiness*. Little will be accomplished by turning out a student who is knowledgeable but miserable, although the two do not necessarily go together.

You may, of course, retain a student but find after a few weeks that he is not getting along well. If at that time a change seems justified, it is not too late. Conversely, a student may be taken out of a classroom and returned when appropriate.

Another consideration is the availability of special services. Most schools have reading specialists, counselors, administrators, and health officers, all willing and able to assist. But they may be so overburdened that they cannot adequately help everyone in need. Special classes may have a waiting list, or be too large, or not suited to the needs of your student. For example, a borderline IQ may be thrown into a program with severely retarded students, and this could be disastrous. Frequently, the teacher, having established a warm, trusting relationship, is in the best position to help. There is a trend to place all but the most severely handicapped students in regular classrooms rather than special programs, so they can learn to adjust to the real world.

A good diagnostic program combines standardized testing, informal reading inventories, and extended observation in the classroom. Supportive personnel can be called upon for consultation. But careful consideration of each student's need is as much a function of the teacher as instruction in subject matter, and is likely to have a greater impact on the student's life. If the teacher is not familiar with the problem of the handicapped reader, "Incidents in a Public School" can be a common and disastrous result.

CHAPTER 3
The Dark at the End of the Tunnel: Sources of Reading Disability

If your class is typical, your diagnostic program will reveal that in your classroom you have students doing the required reading at independent, instructional, and frustration levels. But to diagnose is not to remedy, and we have much to do. Unfortunately, reading retardation is the result of one or a combination of causes, and unless the causes are considered, haphazard attempts at remediation are like trying to cure measles with a makeup kit.

Let us examine the many reasons why some students fail to keep up in reading. These are diverse and complex, and in a single chapter we can deal with them in only the most casual manner. Once we understand the difficulties that lie in the way of normal reading development, however, we may see in the causes the germ of a solution.

PERSONAL DIFFICULTIES

Reading difficulties have their roots in three main areas: the physical and psychological limitations of the student, social conditions that prevent the individual from realizing full potential, and faulty educational practices. The first category was discussed in the previous chapter; therefore, it requires only a brief summary here.

Vision Loss

Hyperopia (farsightedness) causes difficulty seeing close objects, such as reading material, but can be corrected with glasses. The Snellen Chart test, administered at 20 feet, tells little about vision at reading distance. It is unfortunate that this procedure is standard in many schools, when a vision screening at reading distance would be more useful. Close vision tests, such as the Jaeger and Lebensohn, are available from optical supply houses listed in the yellow pages of any big city telephone directory. (See Figure 3−A.) Other vision difficulties include *astigmatism* (blurred vision), *heterophoria* (poor focus), and *esotropia* (crossed eyes). These may or may not impair reading, depending upon severity and how well the individual can adjust. At one time faulty eye movement was considered a vision defect, but evidence suggests that this is a thinking function. Nevertheless, many school reading programs continue to use machines to "train" the eye in efficient reading movement, although the value of such machines is still uncertain. (See p. 20)

Hearing Loss

It is self-evident that vision defects handicap the reader, but it is perhaps less obvious that hearing loss is likewise handicapping, and in the long run may be more so. Consider the blind. From the moment they enter our presence, with dark glasses and cane, we are aware of their handicap. We tend to show them every consideration, helping whenever appropriate. Our taxes provide braille books at considerable expense. The deaf and hard-of-hearing are not so visible. Few of us realize their intense isolation. We live in a language-centered social order, and the great bulk of our interpersonal communication is by speech. And as we shall see later, reading development is highly dependent upon the individual's social, intellectual, and linguistic development, as well as total life experience. The person with hearing loss misses much of the social interaction necessary for normal development.

Hearing aids are not worn by everyone who needs them, either for financial or social reasons or lack of awareness of the need. Hearing aid manufacturers who stress in their advertising that their product is not noticeable, are doing their clients a disservice by keeping alive the stigma attached to wearing a hearing aid. We have come to accept wearing glasses as normal, but too many of us are still self-conscious about hearing aids.

Although some hearing and visual difficulties are physical, many perceptual problems (failure to properly distinguish between letters, words, or sounds) are cultural and economic. For example, children who grow up in homes in which there is little reading matter or where there is little conversation may come to school underdeveloped in language perception, although their eyes and ears may be normal and perceptions adequate in areas other than language.

Neurological Disorders (Brain Damage)

The brain is a complex and delicate mechanism. With over 10 billion cells, many of its parts are specialized in function. Brain damage can stem from

Near V. E. %: 5
Jaeger 14

man oxen

24 Point

25 37 84 90

Acuity: Approx. 0.12 (20/170)
Sight-saving texts.

OXXO OXXX

Near V. E. %: 10
Jaeger 12

raw see van

18 Point

90 89 76 60 54

Acuity: Approx. 0.15 (20/130)
Books, children 7-8 yrs.

XOXXX OXOOO

Near V. E. %: 15
Jaeger 10

noon even mew

14 Point

38 72 80 93 54 60 76

Acuity: Approx. 0.2 (20/100)
Books, children 8-9 yrs.

XXOX XXXX OOOX

Near V. E. %: 20
Jaeger 8

war use worm eve
avenue ransom err

12 Point

40 53 82 64 79 60 47
809 423 657 980 765

Acuity: Approx. 0.25 (20/80)
Books, children 9-12 yrs.

XOOX OOOXO OOXXX
remo romero suma

Near V. E. %: 30
Jaeger 7

scum crease nervous
cocoon cannon saucer

10 Point

98 67 45 34 23 50 86 73 98
456 309 582 740 605 182 765

Acuity: Approx. 0.28 (20/70)
Adult textbooks.

XOOO OXXO OXXX XXXX
saca zarco cascarron

Near V. E. %: 40
Jaeger 6

arrow scour noose razor
zone reverence sorceress

9 Point

35 98 20 82 47 30 74 73 42 65 27
740 203 965 423 807 203 460 244

Acuity: Approx. 0.3 (20/65)
Magazines.

XXXO OOXX OXOOX XOXOX
remanso semana asma

Near V. E. %: 50
Jaeger 5

amaze wares curve scarce
snooze caress sewer wax

8 Point

82 34 65 90 58 83 67 46 98 65 42 54
426 397 564 752 205 350 575 369 246

Acuity: Approx. 0.4 (20/50)
Newspaper text

OXXO OOOO XOXX XXXX OOOX
remesa suave arrancar

Near V. E. %: 90
Jaeger 3

comma worse reason measure vase
census arrears recover crane now

6 Point

75 23 68 90 44 63 40 53 82 64 79 00 47 35
890 375 204 534 626 987 654 932 246 479 268

Acuity: Approx. 0.5 (20/40)
Telephone directory.

XOXX OOXO OXXO OXOO XXOX OOOO
resaca carecer crecer sazonar

Near V. E. %: 95
Jaeger 2

success numerous assurance consume
cocoa convex morocco uncommon err

5 Point

56 87 92 30 47 62 45 27 98 80 46 25 43 85
209 354 872 405 625 829 204 350 575 482 657

Acuity: Approx. 0.6 (20/30)
Want ads.

XOXX OOOX OOXO OOXXX XOXO XXOX OXOO
sesos sucesor vaso zamarra azar

Near V. E. %: 100
Jaeger 1

occurrence nevermore successor romance worm
crazy arson crew amorous scow aroma samovar

4 Point

72 55 40 58 36 58 60 65 50 57 98 46
284 454 306 905 593 460 744 829 360

Acuity: Approx. 0.8 (20/25)
Small bibles.

XXXOX XXOOX OOXXO XOXOX OOOXO XOXX
comarcano rosca serrano amanecer

Comparable:
Jaeger 1 +

3 Point

Acuity: Approx. 1.0 (20/20)
Mailorder catalogues.

XOXXO XXOOX OOOOO OXXOO XXOOX XXXXO OXOOXX
serrano avance zorro cansano canutro

Letter height—
0.3493 mm.

2 Point

Acuity: Approx. 1.5 (20/13)
Photo-reduction.

FIGURE 3-A   Lebensohn reading distance vision testing chart, 1935, available from optical supply houses.

such commonplace experiences as birth trauma or high fever. When severe, it can result in a serious handicap (cerebral palsy). But far more common is minimal brain damage, producing an individual who functions normally until faced with a complex task, such as reading. When brain damage is severe enough to constitute a learning problem, the classroom teacher can refer the student for expert assistance of a reading or speech therapist, or in extreme cases a physician. See also the cerebral dominance theory, pp. 16–17.

Hyperactivity and Poor Motor Skills

Learning and reading difficulties can be caused by hyperactivity and poor motor skills. Even if these conditions are outgrown before secondary school age, they may have left the student educationally retarded.

Maturation

There is some evidence that physical and mental maturity can affect reading and that slow developers may fall behind. Although by high school most young people are sufficiently mature to read on their grade level, this may be a problem mainly in junior high schools. Evidence is not conclusive, however.[1]

Sex

In this country there are about four boys with reading disability for every girl.[2] This may be the result of cultural conditioning among males. School may be seen as an essentially feminine institution, with emphasis on sitting down, being quiet, and studying from books. The slower maturation rate of boys may also be a factor.

General Health

Karlin points out that "While no direct relationship appears to exist between reading failure and general physical condition, some evidence supports the conclusion that the presence of poor health can interfere with learning to

[1]Robert Karlin, *Teaching Reading in High School,* 2nd ed., Indianapolis: The Bobbs-Merrill Co., Inc., 1972, p. 30.
[2]Ibid., p. 31.

read."[3] Next time you have a toothache or stomachache, try cramming for a test. Then try to imagine what it would be like to have a chronic problem—never to feel right because of allergic respiratory difficulties, or to have painful infected ears that have gone unattended for years.

In the past, reading specialists looked largely to physical difficulties as the source of reading loss, but recent research indicates that this is less often the problem than was previously thought. Nevertheless, teachers need to be aware of the symptoms discussed in these first two chapters, not to diagnose or treat physical conditions, but to describe the symptoms observed to the reading specialist, school health officer, counselor, or administrator. Parents should be informed so they can have the condition checked by a physician.

If parents refuse to take action, public assistance may be available. Meanwhile, you can help, possibly by moving the student to a better position for seeing or hearing, giving whatever special aid your busy schedule permits, and using the methods discussed in the following chapters.

Emotional Damage

Although reading specialists may have overemphasized physical conditions in the past, we probably underrated the impact of psychological difficulties. It is difficult to assess the role of emotional disturbance in reading disability, partly because teachers do not have the tools for clinical analysis, and partly because it is hard to tell the chicken from the egg. That is, to what extent is reading disability the result and to what extent is it the cause of emotional disturbance? We do know, however, that they go together. Gates estimated that 75 percent of students demonstrating severe reading retardation show personality maladjustment.[4] Harris placed the figure at close to 100 percent, ". . . and the per cent in which the emotional difficulties are thought by the staff to have had a causal relationship to the reading problem runs over 50 percent."[5]

Fear, hostility, boredom, and insecurity make concentration on schoolwork difficult. Emotional problems may spring from tensions at home, difficulties with the law, social entanglements, racial tensions, school itself, or a wide variety of sources. But whatever the origin, the school frequently becomes the object of aggressive action, simply because the student cannot effectively fight back against parents, police, or peers.

[3]Ibid., p. 30.
[4]Arthur I. Gates, "The Role of Personality Maladjustment in Reading Disability." *Journal of Genetic Psychology*, 59, 77–83, 1941.
[5]Albert J. Harris. *How to Increase Reading Ability.* New York: David McKay Co., Inc., 1961, p. 264.

Even if the student's fears or hostilities do not appear well grounded, they must be recognized. Reading teachers only frustrate themselves and their students trying to teach those who are so emotionally knotted up that learning is minimal, perhaps impossible. It is more effective to deal with the emotional difficulty first. Although teachers should not dabble in amateur psychoanalysis, they can begin by gaining the student's confidence.

This does not imply abandoning the effort to teach. Emotional disorders may spring from the student's own self-hatred or contempt, based partly or wholly on dissatisfaction with school progress. In some cases, a good "tough" teacher may help by insisting on quality work, finding many ways to say, "You can do it!" until the student does it. Result: a new self-image. Working with such a student may call for a more personal approach, demonstrating that you do care—and care enough to take the time. It requires a sensitive teacher, one who knows when to give in and when to be firm. And it demands the creation of a classroom atmosphere of acceptance, curiosity, and the satisfaction of accomplishment.

Sometimes, to create that atmosphere, a teacher must depart from traditional school values. I recently attended a parent meeting in which I heard the teacher explain to the parents how much difficulty he was having getting the students to express themselves in an open, honest, articulate manner. He concluded sadly that today youngsters do not seem to trust adults, especially authority figures. Yet a few minutes later that same teacher observed that if he had accomplished nothing else this year, he had managed to "clean up" (those were his words) at least in his classroom, some of the "disgraceful language" that had crept into youngsters' vocabularies. Apparently, he could not see the contradiction between working for open, honest, cooperation and imposing taboos on people's speech.

Ego Deflation

We are all victims (or beneficiaries) of the self-fulfilling prophecy. Once a student becomes convinced that he cannot perform a task, such as learning to read, or that he is stupid, he will expend a great deal of energy proving it. The "I'm not OK" syndrome is one of the most defeating and frustrating in education.[6]

Many youngsters start school with defeat built in. Children from pov-

[6]An excellent explanation of the self-fulfilling prophecy is Thomas Harris's *I'm OK—You're OK*. New York: Harper & Row, Publishers, 1967.

FIGURE 3-B   The failure syndrome is easy to set in motion but difficult to erase.

erty areas learn very early who's who. Children with domineering, critical parents or brilliant parents or siblings may have gross fears of inadequacy.

The failure syndrome is not only common, it is difficult to deal with. People do not like to admit, even to themselves, that they have a low self-image, that they do not try because of fear of failure. They will make up all kinds of excuses and do the most illogical things to cover their feelings of inadequacy. Frequently the teacher writes off the student as lazy. Feelings of inadequacy can cause a student to become a discipline problem.

It is important that the experiences of ego-deflated students be success-ful. But success must be real, not lavish praise for an obviously poor perfor-mance. Most adolescents are too sophisticated to be taken in. They must feel genuine growth. This involves careful planning of lessons they can cope with but which do not appear to them juvenile. Once achievement, however small, can be seen by the student, then praise goes a long way. Fortunately, more and more teachers are becoming aware of this, and there is a decreas-ing tendency to reward only the outstanding, to measure achievement only in terms of grades, and to require students to cope with subject matter and reading material that are beyond their interests or capacities.

Low IQ

Too many students have been classified as mentally retarded on the basis of an IQ test alone. If the tester had taken a moment to talk with the subject, or better yet, to observe him with his friends, he would have seen an enthusiasm, an animation, a sense of humor that clearly indicated something other than low IQ. Dozens of factors, from membership in a racial minority or low income family to hearing or vision difficulties can cause a bright student to score low on an IQ test. Fortunately, the IQ test is losing favor as a single reliable measure of human capacity. See pp. 38–42.

BOOBY TRAPS:
SOCIOLOGICAL FACTORS

Physical and psychological difficulties do not just happen; they are caused. And to deal with remedies, one must first look at causes.

Poverty

Of all the undesirable social phenomena, the dubious honor of first place goes to poverty. It is true that we find brilliant scholars among the lowest income families, and some very poor students in the upper middle class. But *statistically*, there is a high correlation between income and success in school.[7]

In the Peace Corps, one of the major thrusts of a corp person's training is "cross-cultural," an attempt to understand the life style and philosophical patterns of the host country. Yet few of us realize how different are the patterns that exist within our own borders. Teachers also need a "Peace Corps"-type cross-cultural training program to cope with all their students.

The difficulty is that after well over a decade of "compensatory education," in which a multiplicity of experimental projects were attempted to aid disadvantaged students, and even after a considerable number of studies of the effectiveness of these programs, little real headway has been made in educating the children of poverty more effectively. Nor have the many studies of the subject produced definitive answers. There are, however, a number of theories.

[7]A number of studies to support this are cited by Edith H. Grotberg, "Learning Disabilities and Remediation in Disadvantaged Children." *Review of Educational Research*, December 1965, 35, 413–425.

HEREDITY   Arthur Jensen, leading exponent of the heredity theory, sees individuals falling to the bottom of the ladder because they were born with less intelligence. Particularly, Jensen sees race as a factor. This theory has never found wide support, partly because it is difficult, in this egalitarian society, to accept all the political, economic, and educational implications of racial superiority. But there are also solid, scholarly reasons for nonacceptance of the Jensen theory, for his data and his methods have been criticized.

ENVIRONMENT   Most remedial efforts in recent years have been based on the environmentalist theory, which lists a complex of factors to account for educational handicap.

Homes

Usually, the lower the income, the smaller the house.[8] The result is more crowding, more noise, more confusion, as people rub against each other physically, emotionally, and vocally.

How does one adapt to living under crowded conditions? According to Cynthia Deutsch, one way is to learn to "tune out" undesirable or irrelevant noise, zeroing in on just that which one wants to hear.[9] This skill is frequently carried into the classroom: "I told them three times to put their names in the upper right-hand corner of their papers," complains the teacher bitterly, "and half the papers came in with no name at all." It's like a radio station with nobody tuned in.

Ausubel found poverty homes somewhat austere, with fewer books, art works, manipulative toys, and other artifacts of verbal or numerical significance so that children come to school lacking skill-building experience.[10]

These children are also less likely to have gone to the zoo or summer camp or other parts of the country or to foreign countries—in short, to be lacking in experiential background. Or, if they have traveled, they lack the verbal skills to make it a learning experience. I have observed migrant children, including teen-agers, who travel frequently but have little geographical perspective on where they have been and who cannot trace their own route from, say, Texas to California, on a map. To such children, school

[8]*Housing Characteristics by Household Composition.* U.S. Department of Commerce, Bureau of the Census, 1970 Census of Housing, Table A–3, pp. 21–23.
[9]Cynthia P. Deutsch, "Auditory Discrimination and Learning: Social Factors." *Merrill-Palmer Quarterly of Behavior and Development,* July 1964, 10, 280.
[10]David Ausubel, "How Reversible Are the Cognitive and Motivational Effects of Cultural Deprivation? Implications for Teaching the Culturally Deprived Child." *Urban Education,* Summer 1964, p. 23.

textbooks often make little sense, with their references to Henry VIII, the Suez Canal, ecology, or a camel caravan.

The middle class child is more likely to encounter reading in the home. Daddy arrives in the evening and grabs the newspaper. Older sister is reading *Gone with the Wind*. Mama devours a magazine, and older brother sneaks *Playboy* under the covers. It all carries a subtle message: There must be something to this reading business if older people read when they could be playing. By the time middle class Jimmy gets to school, he knows what he is there for. And he has been so tantalized by being read to, by looking at beautifully illustrated children's books, and by seeing others read, he is eager to get on with it. To Poverty's Child, reading may be a strange and useless business.

Life Style

In middle class life, everything is a preparation for something else. We work hard in school so we can do well in high school, then work twice as hard in high school so we can get into college. There we work three times harder than ever for a teaching credential. But once on the job, we find ourselves going back to school, piling up units to attain a higher salary, perhaps an advanced degree or an administrative position, and eventually working toward retirement.

But in the ghetto or in the barrio, there is not much to work for. Jobs are scarce and largely temporary. Nothing leads to anything. There is little hope, little future. The result is a philosophy that emphasizes living for today rather than tomorrow, enjoying the moment and worrying about the future as it comes.[11] School is the essence of delayed gratification. We work hard in school so that some day . . . But if one's life style does not involve the future. . . ?

Adult-Child Relationships

Although there is disagreement concerning whether the children of the working class actually receive less verbal stimulation from their parents and other adults than do middle class children, there seems to be evidence that middle class parents' conversations are more likely to contain references to the broad range of topics that will become part of the school experience.

"What's inflation?" the child asks after hearing a discussion of the

---

[11]For a sensitive and penetrating study of life in the lowest economic brackets, see Jules Henry, "Hope, Delusion, and Organization: Some Problems in the Motivation of Low Achievers." *The Low Achiever in Mathematics*, U.S. Department of Health, Education, and Welfare, Office of Education Bulletin OE–29061, 1965, No. 31, pp. 7–16.

news, and a new word, a new concept, is added to her vocabularly. She is also becoming familiar with language *patterns* and with hearing complex and compound sentences, modifying words and phrases, and a variety of prepositions, interjections, and conjunctions. All this is subconsciously teaching her to understand and use language—a skill that will serve her well when she begins to read.

Nutrition and General Health

Poor nutrition is not uncommon among low income families. There is considerable evidence that lack of protein can inhibit mental growth, particularly during the prenatal period, and that this tendency is not reversible. This indicates that untold thousands of low income youth are unable to cope with school because they lack the high protein diet of the middle class.

The problem is further complicated by the lack of adequate medical and dental care. In low income neighborhoods, illness is common and money for doctors is scarce. Many middle class Americans are under the impression that the poor are given excellent medical care at taxpayers' expense, but that is because they have never been poor. The legacy of poverty is a high incidence of uncorrected vision problems, hearing problems, digestive problems, and a host of illnesses that frequently add up to never having a full day of really feeling good. And we wonder why such students cannot work up enthusiasm for learning to read!

Philosophy of Life

In an area where jobs are temporary, money is scarce, and nobody is getting anywhere because there is nowhere to go, the life style of the individual is built around day-to-day living. Ambitions are often minimal ("I work at a gas station"), or unrealistic ("I haven't decided whether to be a model or an airline flight attendant"). Ideals are related to glamor and fame. Intellectual values take a back seat. A pragmatic approach to living leaves little room to learn about the Civil War or sentence diagramming. Such students need concrete, demonstrable experiences that have a "payoff," rather than abstract exercises.

CULTURAL DIFFERENCE   Advocates of the cultural difference theory see certain students struggling in school because the culture of the school is different from that into which they were born. Schools are essentially middle class institutions. Most teachers never question the intrinsic value of learning or the worth of economic advancement. But in this multiethnic nation, not all the objectives, assumptions, and living patterns of the middle class are embraced by low income families.

According to Joan Baratz, Roger Shuy, William Labov, William Stewart, and other advocates of the cultural difference theory,[12] poverty children are not particularly *less* advanced, they simply belong to another culture. They see language as one of the chief barriers to school progress, particularly for those black students who speak the dialect of the ghetto. They point out that many of the linguistic patterns of standard English are foreign to black children and to others whose native dialect is nonstandard. The difficulty is not so much with pronunciation, as it is with syntax. For example, a black child who pronounces *pin* and *pen* alike[13] is simply doing the same thing his white friends do with *to, too,* and *two.* This is not a reading problem, unless the teacher attempts to correct the student and, in the process, only confuses her. But when that same child sees *I asked if he did it,* there can be a problem because, in that child's native dialect, the expression would be *I ask did he do it.*[14] This syntactic switch means that she must literally learn a new dialect while *simultaneously* learning to read. Learning to read is complicated enough.

Some have suggested that we teach black children to read with materials written in black vernacular. This would do for black children what i.t.a. has done for the white middle class.

The advantages of such a system are clear. It would simplify the reading process by making the language familiar to the readers. It may build the self-worth of the children by giving acceptance to their own language, instead of implying or stating outright that in order to be educated, they must learn the language of the middle class.

But there are powerful arguments against this idea. I doubt the validity of the argument that this would impair the development of standard speech in black children, for we have evidence that learning to read one language or dialect does not, in any way, inhibit learning another.

But a body of black dialect literature is not presently available, particularly carefully graded readers. Also, not every black child speaks the dialect, and each child would have to be carefully tested to determine his language preference, then segregated into classrooms or reading groups. In the Southeast, for example, there is less difference between black and white speech than in the northern cities.

I also believe that the greatest objection to the system would come from the black community itself, which would see such a move as a condescension, an attempt to "talk down" to black children.

---

[12]A good summation of this theory can be found in Joan C. Baratz and Roger W. Shuy, Eds., *Teaching Black Children to Read.* Center for Applied Linguistics, 1969.
[13]Ibid., p. 97.
[14]Ibid., p. 100.

At least on the secondary level I doubt that standard speech is as much of an obstacle as some linguists believe. If I say to you, "She come home every day," you may not award me any prizes for grammar, but you understand what I mean. And by the time most black children reach secondary school, they have heard enough standard English to know what it means, even if the syntax is a bit strange.

Weighing the difficulties involved in using black dialect readers in the primary grades against the possible advantages, it would seem to me that the idea would not be worth trying unless the community supports the effort. I would be even less inclined to attempt it with secondary school students.

In working with low income youngsters, I suggest an activity-centered approach, involving the hands and body as well as the mind. Some methods of doing this will be discussed in the next chapter. Do not be shocked if this student has never heard of Thomas Jefferson, Bangladesh, or the Equal Rights Amendment. Whenever possible, begin with something familiar, but take advantage of every opportunity to expand into new ideas, new concepts, new data:

> Yesterday we discussed the proposal to build a drag strip on the edge of town. You also heard the other proposal–to build a bicycle path system. You were told that the county has money for one or the other but not both. Do you know who will decide which project will be funded and which will not? The county Board of Supervisors. Do you know who these people are and how they got to be supervisors? Chapter Eight discusses county governments. Next week we can take a trip to sit in on the supervisors' meeting to hear them discuss this question, and I've arranged for you to meet some of them afterwards. You can tell them how you feel about. . . .

Capitalize on every opportunity to build language skills, for this is the most serious educational deficiency of the low income student. Take time to introduce new words—defining them, pronouncing them several times, teaching the spelling and usage.

Try to get the students to read, write, and discuss new ideas, even if these exercises are short and simple. Do not hesitate to read to the class, especially if you read well orally, or use the tape recorder as we shall suggest in Chapter 4. Accept oral work where necessary but also encourage use of written language. Always begin at the student's level, even if you think he should be further along: 6×8 comes before 643×879, regardless of where the student *ought* to be.

This does not mean that the teacher should accept work that does not represent the best a student can do at the time, or that when teacher and student are working on the same level, they should stay there. Once 6×8 is learned, go on from there. Let the student know that he is capable of growth, and he will grow. The good teacher accepts human limitations but is death on laziness, although distinguishing one from the other is not always easy.

Most important, take time to develop a relationship with these youngsters. Let them know you really are interested in their entire welfare—not just their progress in your class, but how they think and what they feel. Low income youngsters are more difficult to reach. But once they are reached, they give the teacher a feeling of being needed, being wanted, and of making a difference in their lives. And this is what teaching is about.

The Children of Woodstock

Educational problems are by no means confined to poverty students. Recent social movements among middle class youth have caused many to react to school in ways traditionally associated with low income culture. Although the turbulence of recent youth movements, with antiwar demonstrations, demands for educational reform, and stress on individuality, has certainly run its course, I see a strong residual effect among many young people.

It has frequently been said that we value most that which we lack and that which we struggle to attain. Since this is the case, it is easy to see why the Depression Generation placed so much stress on economics. Getting a good job, establishing a sound business, providing the greatest possible measure of security for oneself and one's family became the goal—almost an obsession—with those who grew up during the difficult thirties. But their children, reared in the affluent fifties and sixties, satiated with material things, went off in search of other values.

The result is that among a portion of today's youth, there remains a tendency to rebel against the work ethic, to place greater stress on living for the here and now and less on delaying gratification while preparing for the "future." There is also a still-active rebellion against destruction of the environment and less tendency to see as right and good busy little factories across the nation gobbling up resources and spewing out manufactured products at ever increasing rates.

I believe there is a new freedom, a rebellion against conformity, a tendency to "do your thing," and let others do theirs. This freedom has been applied to everything from traditional dress codes to methods of earning a living. I am talking about only a portion of today's middle class youth. Reactions to the turbulent sixties have varied. Many young people have become more conservative. But those students who no longer assume that the end-all of happiness and virtue is a steady job and a house in the suburbs are naturally going to place less emphasis on school, the traditional road to "success." If, for them, the work ethic is losing out, if consumption of goods and services is no longer the primary goal, if the very morality of our production system is in doubt, then school and everything it has traditionally stood for is also in question. To many youngsters, busily "doing their thing" and trying to find out just what their thing is, school has simply lost its clout.

Many schools have responded to the needs of these middle class rebels by initiating an "alternative program." These programs range from good to mediocre and may point the way to education of the future. In the better projects, students are studying subjects never seen before in secondary schools, are exploring occupational skills and opportunities, examining their innermost feelings, and designing and personalizing their educations. I am convinced that if schools are to serve the needs of these youngsters, they must initiate many new, innovative, and creative activities.

Racial Tensions

Since the Supreme Court decision of 1954 that outlawed school segregation, and to some extent even before that, civil rights has been a major social movement in America. Increasingly, Americans have been forced to recognize the unfair manner in which minority groups have been treated. Also, members of minority groups are refusing to accept second class social and economic status. Under the leadership of the late Martin Luther King, Caesar Chavez, and many others, America's Blacks, Chicanos, Asians, and Native Americans have become increasingly vocal.

The effect on the schools has been enormous. We have many new programs in ethnic studies, bilingual education, remedial reading, and a host of areas designed to compensate for the disadvantages of poverty. But we also face militance and deep feelings of resentment and rejection of anything that is done by a "honky" school system.

Many schools have been caught in the web of hostility built up by generations of injustice and have been unable to deal with it, despite numerous special programs. In some inner-city schools the situation is literally out of control and will require bold and creative solutions.

AS WE SOW

Much has been written in criticism of the public schools in recent years, some of it, I believe, unfair because the schools have been victims of the social conditions we have just discussed. Yet the critics are not entirely wrong, for despite progress in recent years, in many cases the schools are still turning students off to learning. So much has already been written on this subject that I hesitate to add more. Yet no discussion of the causes of reading difficulties would be complete without some attempt at self-appraisal.

Fortunately, many of the educational practices discussed in the next few pages are being dealt with in many schools throughout the country. Teachers, administrators, boards of education, and legislators are proposing, discussing, and implementing. But the time lag between recognition of a need and implementation of the improvement is often distressing. Following are some of the practices that I believe remain a source of educational frustration, including reading inhibition.

Compulsory Attendance

Many human beings do not take well to being regimented. There is, of course, an ease, as well as a comfort and security in having someone else do one's thinking. Yet, for years compulsory education has been challenged by some of the nation's outstanding thinkers, such as Paul Goodman[15], Edgar Friedenberg[16], and Ivan Illich[17], to mention just a few. We offer our youth almost no opportunity to participate in decisions concerning their education. We tell them they must not only attend school, they must attend *this* school, must arrive no later than 8:00 A.M., must take three years of English, two years of math, a year of science, or whatever local or state boards or legislators dictate. Students have very little choice of teacher, classes, books, teaching methods, rules and regulations, or selection of who is to make the rules.

But I do not see the dissolution of compulsory attendance on the immediate horizon. Adult society does not want teen-agers glutting the job market and "messing around," although I doubt that that would happen. I believe that if compulsory attendance were abolished beyond the eighth grade, there would be just about as many students in school as we have now. Many who complain bitterly about having to attend school would go on attending, even if given the chance to drop out. School is, after all, a place to find friends. It offers a variety of social and athletic events, as well as some interesting classes. And there is still a residual faith that school somehow offers the keys to the economic kingdom. Perhaps there would be more "stop-outs" who would take a semester or a year to change the scene, then return, more mature and more highly motivated.

Faced with the prospect of losing students, the public schools would become more responsive to student needs. The net result would be more, not less, learning.

[15]See Paul Goodman, *Community of Scholars.* New York: Random House, 1962; *Compulsory Miseducation in the United States.* Horizon Press, 1964; and other works by this author.
[16]See Edgar Friedenberg, *The Vanishing Adolescent.* Boston: Beacon Press, 1967.
[17]See Ivan Illich, *Deschooling Society.* New York: Harper & Row, Publishers, 1971.

Preoccupation with Control

Not only are students forced to attend school and follow the exacting demands of schedules, courses, and requirements, but they may be subjected to regulations about everything from when they may drink water to how they may dress and wear their hair. Such rules have nothing to do with education. I still remember, although it was years ago, the first time a high school girl asked me for permission to go to the bathroom. It suddenly struck me how thoroughly we regulate everything from their thinking to their digestive processes. I have seen teachers, especially in junior high schools, say to their class, "It's almost time for the bell. Put your work away and sit with your hands folded until the bell rings. Nobody is going to lunch until you are all completely quiet and sitting with your hands folded on your desks."

Some students find it comforting never to have to make a decision, to be told where to be every moment of the school day and what to do when they get there. While such tactics comfort the insecure and the mentally lazy, they hardly produce intelligent, creative, turned-on citizens. And they hardly encourage wide reading. Considerable progress has been made in recent years in eliminating irrelevant dress codes and relaxing many unnecessary regulations. Unfortunately, such progress is far from universal.

Physical Appearance of Schools

Many school buildings and grounds are depressing. Older schools are frequently run-down and drab. Even newer schools, brightly lighted and clean, with nicely manicured lawns and generous window space, are sterile, with little, if any, decoration or softness to relieve the monotony. Current trends toward carpeted floors and student lounges show promise for the future. In the following chapter we shall discuss some things a teacher can do to make his own classroom—and possibly the school—more comfortable, more stimulating, and more functional.

Grades and Credits

The only area in which I can see the justification for issuing a degree is vocational education. If I am going to yank out your appendix, repair your television set, advise you about legal matters, or build a bridge over which you travel, you have the right to know that I have a pretty good idea just what I am doing. But what does a high school diploma mean?

Actually, credits and degrees really measure time. Some students learn

more in a semester than others do in their whole secondary experience. Some are better educated at high school entrance than others are at graduation. Yet in most schools, all students are put through the same routine, as if the human brain were some sort of apple pie that can be brought to full flavor by putting in the right combination of ingredients.

The Specter of Fear

The result of the system of grades and credits, combined with concentration on control, has been increased fear and insecurity. Our competitive system breeds fear of failure, fear of punishment, fear of ridicule, fear of nonacceptance, fear of isolation by exclusion. In a system that ought to be devoting itself largely to combating the fears and insecurities that plague the human condition, we are instead often increasing them. A grade of "C," except to a student who habitually makes little more than "D's" and "F's," is clearly a sign of failure, despite the teacher's protest that it represents "average" work. In a system that ought to devote itself largely to helping people learn to live together in peace and cooperation, we stress competition. From the athletic field to the report card, from tryouts for the school play to a place on the school newspaper, we are forever teaching youngsters not to explore themselves, not to work in harmony, but to "get ahead" by beating out the next student.

But, you may argue, this is realistic. This is training students for life. Up to a point, it is true. I believe that we must encourage excellence by rewarding it, but I also believe that involving everyone who wishes to be involved in an intramural athletic program is more important than a winning varsity team; that the experience of being in the school band is more important than bringing home a "superior" at the local music festival. I believe in allowing *each student to work to the best of his own ability;* but in any high school rally, it is evident that the real action is in cheering for the outstanding performers. The progeny of competition are callousness of the winners, ego deflation of the less gifted, and an increase in tension and insecurity.

The Turned-Off Curriculum

In the early grades, school tends to deal with reality. Language skills—reading, writing, spelling—are important, and so are addition, subtraction, multiplication, and division, along with fractions, decimals, and percentages. These are the survival stuff of our culture, and they rightly form the essence of primary school education. Of course, in a world in which many Blacks and Whites have almost stopped trying to communicate, as have many rich and poor, young and old, college-educated and working class, the skills of human understanding and human communication may be just as basic as the three R's. Yet they are mysteriously absent from most elementary school education. Once a student gets beyond primary level, his education becomes less meaningful.

In a world preparing to atom bomb itself to bits, populate itself into starvation, exhaust its energy supply, and pollute itself into extinction, we set our youth to working out such problems as:

Underline the subject of each of the following sentences once and the predicate twice, and tell whether the complement is a predicate nominative or a predicate adjective.

While the nation is failing miserably to eliminate poverty amidst affluence, as crime and venereal disease are reaching epidemic proportions, young people are preparing for adulthood by working out such issues as:

Explain why two triangles, ABC and DEF, are congruent if angle A is congruent with angle D, angle B is congruent with angle E, and line segment BC is congruent with line segment EF.

This should not detract from the legitimate study of language, mathematics, or any area of academic interest. Linguists and mathematicians, and scholars in every field, have made valuable contributions to the quality of life. But allowing students to explore their own interests is worlds away from *requiring* a host of traditional subjects for which they see little use. Frequently, we teach in a mythological framework: *Mathematics develops the mind,* we tell our students, and *the study of grammar will improve your English,* although we can cite little evidence that either is true.

The situation was pretty well summarized by a high school student in a class discussion I recently experienced. Eddie is tall, athletic, very good-looking, very bright, very angry, and very black. And he leaned back in his chair with an eye-closing smile and told the visiting professor the facts of life: "Shoot, Man," he commenced, "why do we have to go to high school anyway? Once we get past the third or fourth grade, they ain't nuthin' school has to teach us that we gotta know." Eddie's vision, of course, was limited.

He had no idea of the heights he could reach with first class education. But his remarks clearly typified the unfortunate concept too many students have of school because his school experience was not an opportunity to explore, but rather a distasteful need to check off requirements.

The Sedentary Approach

There is probably no worse way to become a curious, intellectual person than to spend too much time sitting down. Most real learning contains an element of experiencing, of doing, of getting physically and emotionally, as well as intellectually involved. Of course, there is a place for sitdown book-and-paper-and-pencil learning. But such learning is like chalk talks to an athletic team. When certain information has to be made clear, coach and team trek into the classroom for a chalk talk. Then back to the field for scrimmage, for you can't learn to play football in a classroom. Nor can you become intellectually curious, turned on to living, growing, developing.

This may seem an odd claim for a textbook on teaching reading. But that is only so if we accept an obsolete school tradition. This tradition puts learning backwards. We say to our students, *First learn the fundamentals. Then you will learn to apply them.* We begin with drills and exercises so we can get to the good stuff later. The trouble is, we never get to the good stuff. Because who cares about learning chemistry or history or French, unless there is a goal for which that knowledge is needed? The goal, of course, must be in the mind and heart of the *student,* not just the teacher. With no goal in mind, the student resists learning, and we spin out our lives diagramming sentences, bisecting parallel lines, and wondering what's the matter with kids, anyway, don't they ever want to learn and amount to something? Real education involves *participation.* In the next chapter we shall make some suggestions for turning the process around—for starting with the good stuff, then coming back to the classroom when lack of knowledge or skill frustrates our efforts.

Fragmentation of Learning

In the Middle Ages scholastic knowledge was so limited it was generally believed that one could become "educated" simply by mastering certain standard bits of information. This information was organized into seven major disciplines—grammar, rhetoric, logic, mathematics, music, astronomy, and theology. There was no thought to expanding knowledge because it was believed that all knowledge was known, that the answers to

all questions could be found by close scrutiny of the scriptures or the works of Aristotle.

The outgrowth of this is that we still fragment knowledge into "subjects." So ingrained is the concept of the subject that we think of ourselves as science teachers, English teachers, or teachers of industrial arts. Our teacher training programs follow the pattern, as specified by various state legislatures as well as by the universities and colleges that require a "major" in some field commonly taught in secondary schools. Contrast this to a remark recently made to me by an English industrial arts teacher: "I decided to switch to teaching woodshop because I found I could reach the kids better when we were working with our hands."

This is not to imply that we do not need the kinds of specialized competences now found among secondary school teachers. Quite the contrary. But the continual fragmentation of learning into traditional "subjects" encourages a parochial kind of thinking that limits the horizons of teachers and students alike. We fail to grapple with realities because we are afraid somebody will ask, "But what does this have to do with chemistry?" That everything doesn't always have to do with chemistry seldom occurs to teacher or student because the class is labeled *Chemistry 1*.

My sad experience has been that many high school students will sit endlessly filling in blanks, making choices between *sit* and *set* or *lie* and *lay*, because they have been conditioned to think of this as English. But they continue to talk and write their language as if English in school and *English* as a means of communication had little to do with each other. After what I thought were some of my most thought-provoking and stimulating classes, one or two of the more rigid students usually asked when we would get back to English. In short, these students felt most secure when they were doing rote exercises of little value and were least secure when learning was at its most fruitful level. We cannot blame the students. They are products of the turned-off curriculum.

As a matter of fact, I think it a reasonable assumption that much of the same subject matter stereotype is at work at this moment. The standard question for students to ask at this point is, *"But what does this have to do with reading?''* as if reading could be taught apart from all the considerations examined in this chapter. This tendency to teach reading as a subject can result in failure. It is more effective to integrate the teaching of reading with the rest of education and to integrate education with the whole process of living and growing.

But what can I do about all this? is a more fruitful question. The school teacher, or even the school system, cannot wipe out poverty. It cannot, single-handed, alter social trends. Nor can the school system, through other than painfully slow evolution, deal with its sometimes ineffective methods. For just as the student is the captive of the mandatory school system, the school system is the captive of the legislators, boards of education, taxpayers, and parents who are still beset with the misconceptions, prejudices, and fears that have spawned so many harmful practices.

But there is much that can be done. Teachers can learn to diagnose and compensate for many of the physical and emotional ills that block student learning. We can understand the poverty culture and we can *fill in* many of the reading readiness experiences that our students lack. We can recognize social movements, such as youth culture and civil rights, and find in them the sources of motivation so desperately needed. And we can also examine our own educational practices with a view to the most effective, most satisfying, and most growth-producing experience.

CHAPTER 4
The Turned-On Classroom

A dramatic stillness came over the room as the teacher walked in. The seventh graders sensed that something was up. In his hand Mr. Logan carried a large paper bag.

"I'd like to show you something interesting," Mr. Logan began after a pause. "I was walking down by the river recently, when I tripped over something sticking out of the ground. Looking back, I thought at first it was a stone. But it didn't quite look like a stone. Too square at the top, too artificial, as if a tool had shaped it. So I examined it carefully, but I couldn't tell much. Only a corner was sticking up, and it was covered with dirt. I went home for a spade. I carefully dug up the—thing—and it turned out to be—well—it looked like—of course, I had to wash it off—but when I had cleaned it up, it looked like—"

Mr. Logan was good at this, building the suspense. Tommy had already leaned over Melvin's desk and asked, "Is he kidding?" It was hard to tell with Mr. Logan. His face was serious, but his eyes had a sparkle. . . .

Finally, it was time. Slowly, Mr. Logan pulled it out of the bag. It was flat and rectangular and covered with markings.

"You all know," he continued, "that less than 200 years ago Indians lived along the river bank, and lots of their stuff has been found there."

"Wow! could it be Indian writing?"

"Well, what do you think?"

"How should I know?"

"It isn't as difficult as you think," said Mr. Logan. "Let's see if we can figure out if it's authentic Indian writing." Everyone studied the tablet with great interest and no small amount of frustration.

"I don't get it."

"I bet it's fake."

"I bet it ain't."

"Wait a minute," said the teacher. "How do we go about finding out things?"

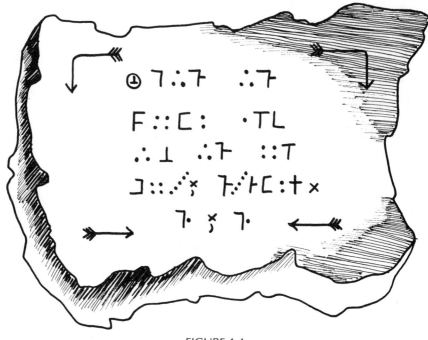

FIGURE 4-A

"We ask questions."

"Look at the thing. What are the obvious questions to ask?"

"What is it?"

"That's too general. Narrow it down."

"What are those funny markings?"

"That's better. You're looking for clues."

"Is it some kind of writing?"

"Great! It could be."

"I don't get it."

"Well, if it isn't language, what other possibilities are there?" There was a pause. "Why not form a hypothesis."

"What's that?"

"A hypothesis is a theory. It's a guess—but usually a guess based either on evidence or reasoning."

"I form the hypothesis that the marks are writing," came from the back of the room.

"O.K. Now test your hypothesis," suggested Mr. Logan.

"How do you do that?"

"Go ahead as if you are right and see if it works. For example, ask yourself if the marks have any characteristics of writing."

"They go across the page like writing."

"Maybe they go downward."

"Chinese writing goes downward."

"It's got separations—like words."

"And some of the marks are repeated—like letters."

"But even if we decide it's language, we don't know which language."

"Yes we do," interrupted Mr. Logan. "At least you can *find out.*"

"How?"

"Look for clues you know about—like English clues or non-English clues."

And so it went. Little by little the class began to "crack the code." A big breakthrough was the suggestion that the dots could be vowels and the lines consonants. The single dot at the end of the first line (if it is English) could only be *a* or *i*. One, two, three, four, five dots—five vowels. Maybe it goes alphabetically: one dot for *a,* two for *e,* and so forth. Mr. Logan told them nothing but offered lots of ideas about how to look for things. He showed the class how to ask questions *methodically;* to form hypotheses, to test them, discard them if they don't seem to be working and follow them up if they do; to *listen* to each other and pick up someone else's clues—in short, to behave *scientifically,* to solve a problem intelligently. It took most of the period, but the class finally figured out that the tablet said:

This is a Joke and it is on You, Sucker. Ha, Ha.

Mr. Logan had two major objectives in this lesson. He was beginning the study of English grammar and he wanted the students to realize that language is a series of rules, that the most basic rules are those which native speakers of the language know somewhat intuitively, although they may never have thought about or verbalized them. So he asked the class to list all the things they had to know about language to solve the mystery and come to the conclusion that this tablet was definitely not an Indian artifact. Everyone was surprised at the length of the list. It included:

What We Had To Know About English To Crack The Code

English is composed of words, which have meaning.

These words must be arranged in certain ways in order to "make sense."

The words can be written as well as spoken.

Written words are composed of letters, which have no meaning but more or less symbolize sounds.

The letters come in alphabetical order, from A to Z.

The same letters are repeated in different combinations to form many different words.

There are two kinds of letters—consonants and vowels.

The vowels, in alphabetical order, are A, E, I, O, and U.

The consonants, in order, are B, C, D, F, G, H, J, K, L, M, N, P, Q, R, S, T, V, W, X, Y, and Z.

English is read across the page from left to right in rows from top to bottom.

There is a standard spelling for each word.

The words on the tablet are spelled: T—h—i—s i—s a j—o—k—e a—n—d i—t i—s o—n y—o—u s—u—c—k—e—r h—a h—a.

Each of the above words either has a meaning or performs a particular function in the utterance. Each meaning or function had to be known by the students.

The only single-letter words in English are *a* and *i*.

There are certain common short words, such as *is* and *it*.

In addition to letters, English has punctuation.

Combinations of words that make sense (sentences) begin with a capital letter and end with a period.

A comma indicates a pause.

The symbol ⟫——⟶ is not part of the language!

Mr. Logan's second objective was more subtle. He wanted his students to experience the *thinking* skills discussed previously: to observe, to form and test hypotheses, to listen to each other, and to go about problem solving in a methodical, scientific fashion.

Discovery Methods: Freedom to Learn

This type of teaching is called the *discovery*,[1] or *inductive* method. It consists of encouraging the class to discover for themselves, rather than to memorize predigested data from a text. So well did Mr. Logan do this job that the students even discovered that the consonants as well as the vowels were coded in alphabetical order, as in Figure 4-B.

Thus by careful analysis, the code was cracked and the tablet was exposed as a fraud. But more important, the students had been curious and excited. *Finding out* became a challenge. In meeting that challenge, they not only had an adventure in learning, but also managed to get much closer to the educational process than data-based classrooms ever get—they were learning to observe, to listen, to put together evidence. They were learning how to learn.

Discovery learning comes in many forms, but they all stem from the same basic principles:

1. It is more interesting to discover something than to be told.

2. The increased interest results in increased learning. Discovery teaching is slow. Frequently, the teacher can "cover" an area in a few minutes, while the discovery method may take all period—or a week. But when the teacher covers an area, there is no guarantee that the students are also covering it. That students may have "learned" something well enough to quote it back on a test is no proof that they understand what they are quoting or that they can apply their knowledge to a life situation. (Remember the student who wrote at five in the afternoon: "Dear Teacher, I wrote 'I

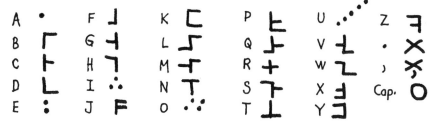

FIGURE 4-B

[1]Some of the theory behind discovery learning is laid out in Jerome Bruner, *The Process of Education.* Cambridge, Mass.: Harvard University Press, 1966. A good text on methodology is Bryon G. Massialas and Jack Zevin, *Creative Encounters in the Classroom.* New York: John Wiley & Sons, Inc., 1967.

have gone' a thousand times like you said, and have went home.") Even if the material is understood well enough to apply it, the teacher still has no proof that it will be remembered long enough to make the experience worthwhile.

3. Most important, discovery learning puts the emphasis where it belongs—on learning how to ask questions intelligently, how to research, how to form and test hypotheses. In the twentieth century, we have accumulated so much knowledge that no one person can acquire more than an insignificant fraction of the total. Today's education should concern itself with learning how to find out, as well as learning how to use knowledge with wisdom and skill.

Consider: You are driving a car, and you come to a deep gorge. A thousand feet below, sharp rocks beckon menacingly. Two parallel bridges span the gorge. The first bridge was designed by a brilliant engineer. At engineering school he memorized vast quantities of data and could often repeat long sections of the textbook, word for word. He designed this bridge, filling in the specifications for every pier, every truss, every cable, from his memory of engineering data. The other bridge was designed by an engineer of less prodigious memory. In school he had only been an average student. Therefore, when he came to this job, he looked up every specification to determine the correct metallic content for each piece, the proper height and thickness, carefully researching each item for tensile strength and endurance. You are now about to drive the first automobile over the gorge. Which bridge will you choose?

Yet data memorization remains the mainstay of the classroom.

In its simplest form, discovery teaching consists merely of not committing the cardinal sin of teaching, which is to tell them what you should have asked them. I see it committed by teachers and textbooks: "There were five main reasons for the war between the states. They are

1.   . . . .

2.   . . . .

3.   . . . .

4.   . . . .

5.   . . . . ''

Thus the student can get through the test with the least amount of effort and the least amount of learning. Even if he can parrot back the five reasons perfectly, there is no cause to assume he has any real understanding of the economic, political, psychological and philosophical differences between two segments of the country that ultimately led to war. *After reading this material, try to figure out the major causes underlying the Civil War* would be a more discovery-oriented approach.

In its more elaborate forms, discovery teaching can involve setting up specific teaching situations, such as the "Indian" clay tablet that was designed to catch the students' attention, to involve them in a problem-solving situation, and, ultimately, to help them come to some new insight or to compile new data. Sometimes the teacher is used as a source of data, with students permitted to ask questions (somewhat like the game of Twenty Questions), until the desired response is evoked. Sometimes the library is the source of data, sometimes selected material; and sometimes students are asked to make observations on the school campus, around the home, or in the community. Some discovery teaching is directed toward specific answers (as with the clay tablet, the class realizing that it was a fake). Sometimes there are a number of possible answers. (Who, for example, can say for sure which were THE causes of the Civil War?) Sometimes, the major value of a discovery lesson is the realization that there is no one valid answer, but many ramifications of a complex problem: *Should the United States build a dam across the X River? Should the team use a zone or a man-to-man defense?*

Discovery learning, like any other teaching method, is as good as the teacher. I have sat in on discovery classes that were superficial and futile, with students uttering clichés as if they were dropping gems of wisdom. I have also seen discovery teaching that challenges students and teacher to new intellectual breakthroughs, with all opinions based on carefully documented data or personal observation.

This is not to say that the lecture and the textbook have no place. They are still the most efficient method of imparting quantities of information. But they only work when the students are tuned in. It's the chalk talk again—a useful technique, but hardly a single method of building a fine athletic team—or a fine math or science team.

But what has all this to do with reading? It has to do with *creating a learning situation,* as does everything in this chapter. Without the learning situation, very little will happen, including reading progress. It has to do with starting with the "good stuff"—using our curiosity, getting involved in *doing,* creating a situation in which the students will *want* to read, either for pure enjoyment or because they need information.

Readiness

Most primary teachers are very conscious of reading readiness, the physical and psychological growth that facilitates reading. Very few secondary teachers are aware that readiness is just as important on their level. Readiness must be considered in relation to some particular reading situation. A student may be "ready" to read a general science textbook but not ready to read Chemstudy. Failure to recognize this basic fact is a continual cause of frustration, discouragement, and failure in school. Readiness for reading, at any stage of an individual's life, can be related to four major factors—language development, intellectual growth, emotional status, and experiential background.

LANGUAGE DEVELOPMENT   Learning language is a slow, gradual, and under best circumstances, a lifetime process. From the first baby words to the technical vocabulary, the accumulation of language should never stop. There is also a sequence: The earliest language experiences involve hearing and learning to understand words. Only after a substantial amount of hearing does the individual develop speech; only after considerable experience with oral language is a person ready for the written word. Thus reading is the third process to develop, and a good reading background is important in the development of composition skills.

At any stage of language development, a person's oral vocabulary will exceed his written vocabulary. You need some general idea of what an elephant is before you can read the word with comprehension. Recognition vocabulary will exceed usage vocabulary. This is why students who do not have a background of being read to or are not involved in adult conversations, or students who come from homes in which a foreign language is spoken, are more likely to have reading problems. These youngsters may be able to converse or to read simple material, but they lack the vocabulary and the language control to cope with the variety of textbooks presented to them in school. The most effective reading instruction for them may be the development of oral language, and it is to that end that many of the techniques in this volume are directed.

INTELLECTUAL GROWTH   Along with language development goes intellectual development, the ability to abstract, to memorize, to understand complexities, to appreciate humor, and to reason. To offer *Hamlet* to students who cannot conceptualize that literary themes transcend barriers of time, place, and language is an exercise in futility. To offer a student something *slightly* beyond his current intellectual capacity is to challenge him to expand his horizons. But to offer something that is completely out of range is only to frustrate and discourage. Another important phase of intellectual status is a healthy curiosity, which motivates the student to find out.

EXPERIENTIAL BACKGROUND   Middle class children who have been to the zoo dozens of times usually gobble up animal books, while their less affluent friends may have no reaction to a rhinoceros, never having seen or heard of one. The more a person has traveled, worked, and experienced of life, the more he brings to his reading. Experience is self-perpetuating. As one experiences, he becomes hungry for more.

This includes vicarious experiences such as watching television, listening to conversation, going to the theatre, and reading. The nonreader frequently is the victim of never having stepped on the experience merry-go-round. His life has been so full of nothing doing, that when confronted with a book, anything that does not concern his age group, his race, his economic bracket, his neighborhood is completely out of his experience. Such an individual seldom finds anything "interesting" to read. He finds school irrelevant because he cannot visualize any possible use for history or math or English. He needs to develop imagination, sense of humor, and a grasp of the environment and how to relate to it, but he resists such efforts because he cannot see beyond his immediate neighborhood, current vocational goals, and present life style. He is Eddie of the previous chapter—trapped in the ghetto and working after school in a grocery store. Eddie sees no reason to improve his reading because he cannot see beyond his current situation. How can he understand the possibility that he might some day pioneer in brain surgery, discover a new source of energy, or write the great American epic?

EMOTIONAL STATUS   Reading is intimately tied to students' desire to read, their curiosity, and their quest for knowledge and experience. It is fruitless to push reading on a student who is consumed with insecurity, hostility, or self-doubt. Concentrated effort should be made to deal with the emotional factors, meanwhile exposing the student to a tempting array of reading material. A sensitive teacher watches for signs that indicate readiness, such as the student's voluntarily picking up reading matter and looking through it or asking questions about where to look for information.

Kennedy[2] deals with these same factors, likening the reading process to a tree, in which the foundation or a nourishing soil is the reader's *linguistic*

[2]Eddie C. Kennedy, *Methods in Teaching Developmental Reading*. Itasca, Ill.: F. E. Peacock Publishers, Inc., 1974. pp. 6–7.

and intellectual development, along with his *maturity.* The trunk is the student's *background of experiences,* both direct and vicarious. From these come the branches and leaves of the reading tree, consisting of word *recognition, comprehension,* and utilization of what is read.

Duffy and Sherman[3] identify four reading skills: *word identification, comprehension, efficient study* (including study techniques and reading rate), and *literary skills* (including interpretation of literary devices and higher level thinking).

SETTING THE STAGE
—BUILDING A
LEARNING ENVIRONMENT

If I were asked to design an environment in which human learning and growth were to be kept to a minimum, I would have a place withdrawn from society—away from the streets, the factories, the stores, the homes—a place that is out of the action. I would enclose it with four walls and a roof, that those who dwell within would be unaware of the magnificence of nature.

Having thus isolated my subjects from both natural and human activity, I would further isolate them from each other by placing them in an unnatural and uncommunicative arrangement. One way would be to face everyone in the same direction, so they cannot look at each other, cannot communicate, cannot learn from each other. I would encase the decor in sterile symbols of institutionalism—rectangular walls and ceilings, walls covered with maps, charts, printed rules and directions; look-alike furniture; glaring lights. Animals, comfortable furniture, and music would be strictly forbidden. Finally, I would permeate the atmosphere with a series of rules designed to carry out the theme of isolation and disinterest. Human interaction would be called "talking without permission," and working cooperatively would be "cheating."

This view of the classroom is admittedly lopsided. The classroom does have its value. By deliberately filtering out extraneous influences, the classroom achieves *focus.* Eyes are focused on the teacher, the chalkboard, the textbook. A classroom is a great place for a quick retreat for a specific purpose. For example, your activity has been frustrated by lack of knowledge or skill. So back to the classroom—focused, concentrated learning—zero in on the problem—practice—exercises—textbooks—discussion. Then back to work on the project, this time with more profound understanding,

---

[3]Gerald G. Duffy and George B. Sherman, *Systematic Reading Instruction,* 2nd ed. New York: Harper & Row, Publishers, 1977, p. 4.

additional data, finer skills. But on a continual basis, hour after hour, week after week, year after year—many classrooms are hospital-sterile.

But it is this classroom that the teacher is given; the problem is moving from sterility to stimulation. A few suggestions follow.

Furniture

On two occasions when I organized "experimental" schools, we wrote articles for the local newspapers about our program, stating that we would appreciate donations of old couches, chairs, rugs or carpeting, lamps, and other household furniture. The response in both cases was generous. Out went the cold, hard, restrictive desks. (We saved a few for a "study corner.") In came comfortable, sprawly, homey furniture. Kids love to sprawl. Their young bodies need to fidget, and they need something to fidget in. Clip boards for writing on took the place of desk tops.

Floors

Many newer schools are being built with carpeting. The new commercial carpets of synthetic fiber and level piles are no more expensive and as easy to maintain as hard-surfaced floors. They are far more attractive and much less noisy, and they are great for sitting on. But if the school cannot put in carpeting, you can probably get bits and pieces donated, either through the aforementioned newspaper article or by going to carpet houses and asking for leftovers. Sew or tape (duct tape at hardware stores) these scraps together, either using a random pattern or making an art project out of designing and putting it together.

In addition to carpeting, floors can be laced with sit-on-me cushions, sewn together with strong but attractive fabric remnants, and stuffed with shredded foam or styrofoam balls. Bean bag chairs are even better, if budgets allow. For a great variety of creative do-it-yourself projects in the classroom, see *Farallones Scrapbook*.[4]

Walls

Chalkboards are handy sometimes, but they are also symbols of in-stitutionalism. Student work, exhibits of all kinds, art, posters, book jackets, tool boards, anything that will catch the imagination of young people can go

[4]New York: Random House, 1971.

on a wall. Wall shelving is important, and sheets of building board[5] covered with fabric make inexpensive bulletin boards. "Clotheslines" of wire running from wall to wall are great for exhibiting student work. Attach papers with clothes pins or paper clips.

Partitions and Elevations

Real learning often involves having more than one activity at the same time, and sometimes it is advantageous to partition the classroom into areas. See *Farallones Scrapbook* for ideas for creating special "areas" within the room. Partitions can take the same treatment as walls, being handy for bookcases or other exhibits.

Light

The "good" school lighting, so popular today, may be medically OK for the eyes, (although recent evidence indicates that fluorescent lighting may be harmful to some students). The same benefit can be achieved, however, in a softer, more inviting manner with individual lamps that students can turn on and off. A variety of effects can be achieved by placing donated lamps around the room—on tables, floors, desks, low partitions—wherever they are most likely to be needed. Try using colored light, interesting effects, and concentrated light to spot areas for reading and writing.

Stuff

Most of the great teachers I know are incorrigible pack rats. They are the scourge of doctor and dentist offices, for they cannot read a magazine without ripping off an article or two "for the file." They can never be trusted with money at flea markets, for half the stuff they see gives them a new teaching idea. And they are continually pestering their principal for a new filing cabinet or storage cupboard. You can recognize their classrooms the minute you walk in, and their students may complain occasionally of overwork but never of boredom.

A classroom can become a place where every kid walks in and says "Wow!" Books are as important as ever, but so are phonograph records, tape recorders and tapes, science equipment, tools, collections of all kinds,

---

[5]Such trade name products as Celotex and Simpson Board are cheaper than cork. Sound deadening board is still cheaper but must be covered with cloth.

displays, art work, student work—anything that will seduce the student into asking, "What's that—how does it work?"

I still remember the "nature study" room of my elementary school— and I remember precious little else of that long-ago experience. But that room was a veritable museum—collections of everything you can imagine from butterflies, moths, insects, stuffed animals, dried leaves and flowers, to samples of grains, pictures of people from all over the world, tree bark, rocks and minerals. Every wall was festooned with the glorious variety of nature. Everything elicited an endless array of questions: "What's the name of that animal? Why do butterflies have pretty colors? How come leaves die in winter?" Motivation? No problem! But why limit creative classrooms to the elementary school?

For several years I mounted an electric "question board" at the front of my classroom (Figure 4—C). This is a board with holders for mounting 3 x 5-inch cards arranged in two rows. In one row the teacher places the question cards and, in the other, the answer cards. When students plug one wire into a question and the other wire into the correct answer, a light goes on and a bell rings. If a question is connected to the wrong answer, nothing happens. The question cards can be changed regularly. I found that many students who were turned off to conventional tests and exercises would rush to the question board every day to ring the bell. The question board can be

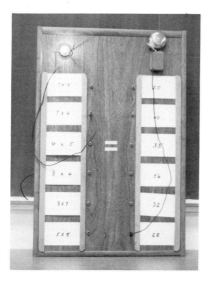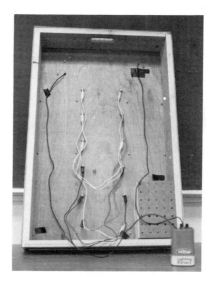

FIGURE 4-C   Left, question and answer card arrangement on the question board; right, the back, showing electric wiring.

made in any size or shape, with any number of questions and answers, and as simple or fancy as budget permits. From these illustrations and diagrams, the board can be made by any shop teacher or by a talented student.

EXPLANATION OF WIRING   The current for the question-board comes out of the battery and goes to the light (rear of board), then comes out of the light and goes to one of the loose-hanging banana plugs (front of board). The teacher connects each numbered question jack with the letter jack containing the correct answer to that question (rear), using alligator clips connected by wires. These connections should be changed frequently so that students cannot memorize the question-answer pattern. Another loose-hanging banana plug is connected to the bell. These two loose-hanging banana plugs are the only wiring on the front of the board. The power leaves the bell and goes to the other terminal of the battery.

When the student connects one banana plug with a question and the other with the correct response, the circuit is completed, the bell rings, and the light comes on. If the light is disconnected or the globe burns out, the board will not work. (See Figure 4—D.)

The approximate cost of the question board is

1 bell	$3.00
1 light socket	1.00
1 light globe	.40
12 jacks	3.60
2 banana plugs	.80
6 pairs alligator clips	3.60
wood	2.00
Total	$14.40

A simplified form of the question board is shown in Figure 4—E.

SETTING THE TONE
—BUILDING A
LEARNING ATMOSPHERE

The prerequisite for healthy growth is an attitude of acceptance—the teacher accepts the student just as he is, youthful inadequacies included, and shares in the student's discovery of self and the environment. The student knows he is accepted by the teacher and by his peers. In such an atmosphere the

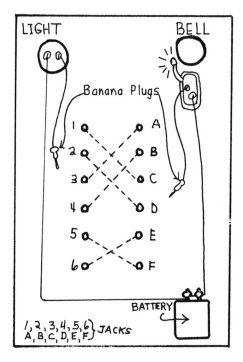

FIGURE 4-D   Diagram of wiring for the Liebert question board.

student feels free to express himself, free to inquire, free to experiment. He knows he can make a mistake without serious penalty and can try new things without fear of ridicule.

Such an atmosphere does not come easily. Although disciplined learning and high quality work are not necessarily related to repressive rules for control, the two are often confused. Many students, used to being told exactly what to do each hour of the school day, will have difficulty responding to the freedom of a maximum-learning classroom. Such students will have to be taught to work independently, to trust, to feel secure, and to be guided by their own natural curiosity. Such a classroom requires a sensitive teacher, secure enough to permit true freedom of inquiry, whether that inquiry concerns controversial political matters, sexual mores, or the policies and procedures of the school itself.[6]

[6]An outstanding volume on the creation of a growth-producing classroom is *Perceiving, Behaving, Becoming,* Yearbook 1962, Washington, D.C.: Association for Supervision and Curriculum Development, National Education Association, 1962.

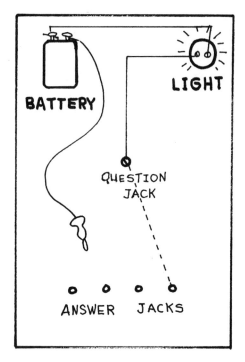

FIGURE 4-E   A simplified form of the Liebert question board that eliminates the buzzer and has space for only one question with four possible answers.

INDIVIDUALIZED INSTRUCTION, OPEN CLASSROOMS, AND WHOOPS! THERE'S A HUMAN BEING IN THAT DESK

In recent years educators have become increasingly concerned with the individuality of the student. Yet the requirement-centered curriculum, state or district-adopted textbooks, and uniform assignments urge us to act as if children were manufactured on a production line, identical in characteristics, having uniform needs, desires, talents, limitations, and interests.

But new methods are emerging. Popular in elementary schools but less frequent on the secondary level is the technique described by Herbert Kohl in *The Open Classroom.*[7] In this volume Mr. Kohl makes an excellent case for the need for a more flexible system, but, unfortunately, gives us little

[7]New York: Random House, 1969.

methodology to guide us.[8] The essence of the open classroom is simply that not every student has to be doing the same thing at the same time. I have visited classrooms that were virtual anthills of activity. John may be sprawled out on the floor, lost in the story of *Johnny Tremain,* while Sally catches up on her geography. Jimmie and Tom are measuring the room with a flexible tape, calculating its area and volume in square and cubic feet. The stranger walking into the room may believe that nothing educational is happening, with such diverse activities going on, even some students "wasting" their time chatting. But the most rigid, structured classrooms come equipped with a generous measure of wasted time.

Breaking away from traditional methods is difficult. But the open classroom is available to any teacher with the imagination and courage to try. Unfortunately, we have few secondary school models to follow, and little in the literature that is specific enough to guide the teacher of mathematics, English, or history. Some schools are initiating "alternative," or "school-within-a-school" programs, using open classrooms with varying degrees of success. The best of these seem to be the ones in which the teachers bring in a lot of stimulating ideas and insist on high quality effort.

One suggestion may serve as a starting point. To experiment with the open class, the teacher can divide the room into "areas," each equipped for a specific purpose. These areas may include:

1.   *Reading area,* a place with comfortable chairs, reading lamps, and a room library. In place of or in addition to the single textbook, students may choose from a wide variety of related reading. They may make individual reports based on their findings, discuss what they have read with the teacher or the class, or simply read for interest and pleasure. This variety of reading matter enables students to find something closer to their individual interest and reading level. (see appendix 4.)

2.   *Listening area,* equipped with turntables and tape recorders, record collection and tapes. This area is particularly valuable to students with reading difficulties, for they may get information from prerecorded tapes that they are unable to get from books. In

[8]A more methodological approach is provided by Don M. Beach in *Reaching Teenagers: Learning Centers for the Secondary Classroom.* Santa Monica, Calif.: Goodyear Publishing Company, 1977. See also Martha H. Dillner and Joanne P. Olson, *Personalizing Reading Instruction in Middle, Junior, and Senior High Schools.* New York: Macmillan Publishing Co., Inc., 1977, Chapters 7 and 8.

a later chapter we shall discuss in more detail the use of recorded tapes in lieu of textbooks for students with reading difficulties.

3.   *Viewing area,* where students have access to pictures, films, filmstrips, and a wide variety of related artifacts.

4.   *Arts and crafts area,* with hard surfaced floor, cupboards filled with paper, paints, brushes, glue, old picture magazines, and a variety of material useful for creative work with the hands. Here students can make models, pictures, collages, mobiles or geometric forms.

5.   *Discussion area,* having a table and chairs for sitting in small groups to hear reports and conduct discussions.

6.   *Publication area,* headquarters for the class publishing enterprises, which may be a class newspaper that circulates to parents or friends, a literary magazine, a report to the community on the subject under study, or any type of publication appropriate to the purpose of the class. We will discuss publications in greater detail in the next section.

7.   *Research area* may consist of a small reference library in the room, or may be the reference section of the school or public library. A good library is a valuable extension of every classroom.

These are only seven of many possible "areas" into which the room can be divided. But the divisions need not be rigid. Perhaps a working definition of *area* should be in terms of activities appropriate to the class. In other words, the same space may serve a variety of purposes, and partitions may be put up, taken down, or moved around as needs dictate. The object of the open classroom is to provide a living-working environment, where students may pursue a variety of activities and find the needed equipment and materials.

Let the World Shine In

Once the classroom has been transformed from a lifeless row of desks to a workshop, the next step is to conquer the isolation in which the typical school exists. Every community is equipped with tremendous learning potential—but students are too busy doing their lessons to take advantage of it. Why not bring the world into the classroom? The local baker, the farmer, the policeman, the fireman, the social worker, the architect, the grandmother, the college student—all these and many more have something to share with young people, and my experience has been that with a proper invitation very few will refuse.

The Universe as Classroom

Not only can the community come into the classroom, but the classroom need not confine itself to four walls. The baker is an interesting person; so is his shop. But too many "field trips" are conducted in the passive, show-and-tell manner of the classroom. Secondary students are beyond that. A visit to a hospital could be an exercise in futility. Try a *working* day—bringing patients their food, books, and magazines, reading to children and the elderly, wheeling wheel chairs, playing cards or checkers, or just talking with those lonely, frightened, forgotten souls who populate our hospitals, nursing homes, and children's homes. Many a reluctant reader can be motivated to read, if offered the opportunity for public service and personal contact. Not only are medical and nursing centers excellent sources for field study, so are the local bicycle and motorcycle shops, the newspaper office, and the community theatre.

ACTIVE AND PASSIVE LEARNING: DIRT UNDER THE FINGERNAILS

In the traditional classroom, the teacher does most of the work—plans the course of study, makes assignments, collects papers, gives tests, assigns grades. For this reason, the teacher also does most of the learning. My university students frequently tell me how much they learn during their student teaching experience. They learn so much because they have changed roles from the student busy fulfilling someone else's requirements, to a responsible adult with a challenging job. Granted, it would not be possible without their prior academic preparation. But something happens when they switch to the other side of the teacher's desk. Yet it seldom occurs to these young teachers (or to veteran teachers either) that the way to increase student learning is to switch roles from passive child-learner (student) to active adult-learner (worker). How do we transform a classroom from passive to active? The most difficult part is to overcome our own inertia, our tendency to think of school only in terms of our own experience with it—to teach, in other words, as we were taught. But the teacher who has the courage and the imagination, can discover a whole new world of teaching and learning.

Once we have overcome our own fears, our own uncertainty, we have next to overcome those same emotional blocks in others. School administrators and parents are often fearful to try something different. Many students have been so conditioned to think of school as daily drudgery, that real life in the classroom may produce, from the more timid ones, the plaintive cry of "But when are we going to do math?" But if you can help them through these early rough weeks, ultimately they will come to recognize how much math will be needed to complete their "project," perhaps along with generous amounts of English, social studies, and industrial arts.

Any attempt to list a series of active learning projects is but an introduction. Your own ideas will fit your unique pattern of talents and training, and be more appropriate for your subject and your students. But here are a few starters:

Each One Teach One: The Learner as Teacher

We have considerable evidence that teachers learn more than their students. We also have evidence that students frequently learn more from their peers than from adult teachers.[9] Put these together and turn your students into teachers. There are a number of ways to do this. The class may be divided into two groups, each group a "specialist" in some phase of the work. The teacher teaches "group A" the daily unit, then another unit to "group B." Finally, the groups get together, with each student assigned an "intergroup tutor" and an "intergroup pupil."

This breaks the class period into four sessions:

I.   Group A works with the teacher.
        Group B has open classroom.

II.   Group A has open classroom.
        Group B works with the teacher.

III.   Group A tutors group B.

IV.   Group B tutors group A.

[9]The results of a number of interesting tutorial projects were reported by Turee Olsen in *The Reading Teacher*, February 1974, 27, 506–508.

If this seems to produce a chopped-up period, you can alternate teaching in groups one day, tutoring the next. My own experience has been that breaking the period into segments is usually helpful, that one or two concentrated sessions accomplishes more than a dragged-out period, particularly in junior high schools, with the short attention span of the early teenager. But you will have to experiment with a number of tutoring systems and schedules to find which ones best suit your subject and style. There are many variations of the tutoring project, some of which we shall discuss in a later chapter.

Publish Your Own: The Learner as Author

Special programs can be organized to study a community problem. Students could be apprenticed to local planning commissions to look at community development. Why not build a curriculum around an in-depth inquiry into a single question, such as *why is crime?* Students could read Ramsey Clark's *Crime in America,*[10] along with the works of other criminologists. They could look into the psychology and sociology of crime, using such classics as the *Report of the National Advisory Commission on Civil Disorders* (The Kerner Report).[11] Next come interviews with local law enforcement officers, judges, criminal lawyers, probation and juvenile officers, convicts and exconvicts. This could be followed by a detailed study of the community, local economic and social conditions, interviewing people—community leaders, housewives, other teen-agers, and the man-on-the-street. The group could then assemble their findings into a *Report to the Community,* with copies sent to the City Council, civic leaders, legislators, and public libraries.

Similar projects could study methods of conserving energy, transportation, recreation, special problems of minority groups, or children, or teen-agers—the possibilities are endless. Think of the real knowledge needed to tackle such projects, the skills to be developed, the research and writing experience, and the satisfaction of a job well done.

This is just a sample of the infinite variety of publications that could come out of an active classroom. Literary magazines covering the poetry, prose, and dramatic creations of the class;[12] a class newspaper; scientific reports on such topics as the merits and demerits of nuclear power plants,

[10]New York: New York Times Company, 1968.
[11]New York: Simon & Schuster, Inc., 1970.
[12]See Joan and Carroll Harrington, "The Book Factory: a Children's Publishing Company." *The California Reader,* May–June, 1977, 10, 5.

steam generating plants, or hydro-electric plants; a pamphlet on the history of the community and its contributions to the nation; an analysis of local pollution problems, including air, water, and solid waste, with suggested solutions; a booklet entitled *Our Town* (or whatever you want to call it) giving the community's vital statistics, social services such as hospitals, a list of where-to-find-help-if, theatres, interesting places to take out-of-town guests, restaurants, hotels, shopping, and a street map. Few small communities have such a booklet, and in the larger cities, the directory could cover a single neighborhood.

If the school cannot finance free distribution of the publication to students, parents, and libraries, selling the finished product inexpensively can recover the cost of paper, stencils, and possibly bindings. Becoming the author of something that somebody reads is a giant step from turning in a report or a composition that merely attempts to psyche out the teacher. If these studies seem overly adult for your students, stick to topics of more immediate concern. How about a series of booklets entitled *Teenagers Speak: Teenagers Speak to Their Parents, to Their Teachers, to the Chief of Police, to the City Council,* or even the boys speak to the girls or the girls to the boys.[13]

Civic Action: The Learner as Prime Mover

Suppose that some of the students have observed that a nearby vacant lot has become a rubbish heap, with piles of junk and mosquito-breeding mud puddles. They have also observed that the nearest public park is miles away. How do you go about turning a dream into a reality? Seven students decide to make this their project, and they comprise the "park committee."

First stop is the city (or county) clerk's office. Who owns the lot? How do you look up such information in the public records? How much would it cost the city to purchase the property? The local assessor is consulted for a lesson in real estate appraisal.

Then comes a survey of the neighborhood. Armed with a form to fill out, the committee rings doorbells. *Do you feel the need for a park in this neighborhood? Is there a better place than Lot X? What facilities would you like to see installed? Would you be willing to have your tax money go into such a project?* The survey not only gives the committee the information they need, it begins to achieve support for the project. People have now heard about the park, discussed it, offered suggestions.

[13]Susan Warfield has listed a number of commercial outlets that publish student work. See "Publishing Outlets for Student Writing." *Journal of Reading,* March 1976, 19, 472–474.

Next, see a landscape architect who has offered to help design the park. After that comes a contractor who has volunteered to teach the committee how to estimate costs. Then the landscape architect, the contractor, a civil engineer, and four other citizens are invited to form a neighborhood committee to help design the park.

After weeks of research, debate, and calculation a plan is agreed upon and cost estimates readied. A *Report of the Citizens' Committee for a Public Park* is prepared, and a spot reserved for its presentation at the next City Council meeting. Win or lose, think of the social studies involved in learning the realities of the political-economic system, the psychology involved in presenting the plan to the public and to officials, the design of a beautiful and lasting park, the math needed for cost estimates, and the English that goes into writing and presenting the report. Compare with taking a test on the legal qualifications for United States senator.

There is not a city or county government that could not be profitably approached with an idea, a board of education or school administration that could not profit from active involvement of students in educational policies and practices, or a student council that does not need counseling. Nor are state and federal officials, despite their geographic distance, immune from the need for contact with young constituents. Letters, if not visiting delegations, are still the major link between office holders and the electorate. Students need to learn not only that they *can* influence the system, but *how* to do so—how to prepare an influential brief and how to present it in the most favorable light. Too often, young people are led to believe they cannot influence the system because when they have tried, they have done such an inadequate job of presenting their case that they naturally were not taken seriously.

The Recycling Center: The Learner as Ecologist

If the community or neighborhood does not have a recycling center—or even if it does—this is an excellent school project. Recycling centers need not be merely parking lots where people dump cans, bottles, and newspapers. They can be centers for the study of the area's ecology and action programs to improve it. Currently, recycling centers do not really recycle anything. They simply make material available for recycling. What happens after all the stuff leaves the center is generally a mystery.

There are many questions a student ecologist can ask: Is the recycling center worthwhile, in terms of resources saved versus resources expended to transport the raw material first to the center in private cars and then by truck to industrial establishments? Or would the community be better off using its solid waste, as some communities have, to fill in swamps or build up hills for parks? How helpful would it be to require all containers to be the reusable, deposit type? What types of packaging material are least destructive to the ecology—aluminum cans, steel cans, glass, paper, or plastic? All these and many more questions can turn a routine science class into an adventure.

The Clinic: The Learner as Health Worker

Moving from the physical to the biological sciences, the class could combine the study of physiology with active service in the school or community clinic. Along with fundamentals of anatomy can go essentials of emergency medical treatment, hygiene, public health, sanitation, and nutrition. Students can volunteer to help in community clinics, writing pamphlets or teaching classes to help less educated citizens learn about good eating habits, child care, and domestic hygiene. They could accompany the deputies from the Department of Health as they inspect restaurants and other establishments.

A productive field for the school clinic, one which would not border on practicing medicine without a license, would be *holistic health*. This involves teaching people to lead more healthful life styles, including more wholesome habits of eating, working, and recreation, as well as forming more salutary attitudes. A lot of good literature is available on the subject. A beginning would be *Mind As Healer Mind as Slayer*.[14]

Enterprises: The Learner as Businessman

Students can be encouraged to begin their own business enterprises, possibly a store to sell student art work, craft items, sewing, industrial arts— anything the students can produce for sale. Or open one classroom for a coffee house featuring homemade punch and pastries, plus cokes and the usual items. This room could function as lounge and snack bar, and may become the only place where students and staff can meet informally. Evenings, it may become a teen center, or showplace for student talent, such as rock bands looking for a tryout, musical and other entertainment, dramatic skits, parties, and a host of special events. The students who operate the coffee house can be involved in everything from cooking and serving food to sweeping the floor, ordering supplies, and keeping the books. What a valuable adjunct such an enterprise could become for a Commercial Depart-

[14]by Kenneth R. Pelletier. Delacorte Press, Distributed by Dial Press, New York, 1977.

ment, Home Economics Department, for mathematics, music and drama, crafts and industrial arts.

My student teachers and I recently launched a project in a local high school designed to integrate school with the world of work and business. It operates somewhat as follows:[15] Every student who wishes may purchase one "share" of "stock" for $1. Students may participate with or without purchasing shares. The money will be invested in fund-raising projects to generate capital, which student groups can borrow to initiate "businesses." Under consideration as money-making companies are an arts and crafts sales and rental service, duplicating service for teachers, a bakery, a coffeehouse-teen center-game room, a bicycle repair and sales shop, tropical fish breeding and sales, a store to sell student-made items, and an organic minifarm. A great deal of hard work and research will be necessary to make a reality of these proposals.

The Broadcast: The Learner as Showman

Why not rig up part of the classroom on occasion as a broadcasting studio, beaming a regular (probably weekly or perhaps even daily) "radio" program to the rest of the school via the public address system. Or the programs could be tape-recorded for broadcast later. Programs could include interviews with students, staff, or outside guests; news; musical or dramatic shows; or discussions of topics of interest. If the school district or county office has a television camera, the broadcasts can be enhanced considerably, although the addition of the visual factor involves a more complex performance.

Such productions need not be limited to closed-circuit operations. Local radio or television stations may offer public service or sponsored time to the high school broadcasters.

Why not build a unit around taking an outing, such as a bike hike, or camping trip. Almost every discipline in the curriculum can be utilized:

Geography	Select the site or plan the route.
Home economics:	Plan a nutritionally balanced diet.
Math:	Do complete cost breakdown for your group (maybe four to six to a group) including food, transportation, equipment, and so forth.

[15] With students making decisions, the initial proposal may, of course, undergo any number of changes.

English: Read the guidebooks. Write a pamphlet about the
                         trip such as a guidebook for others, or articles
                         about your experience for the local newspaper.

Social studies: In retrospect discuss the informal power structure
                         of the group. Who were the decision makers, and
                         who were the followers?

This is the merest sampling of ideas. Many other projects will originate
with the class itself. Of course, there is very little really new in all this. It has
been suggested and described by educators from before John Dewey to Ivan
Illich. Active education is not unknown in practice, although unfortunately
rare among the rows of desks.

At this point, having beaten the drum for active learning, we need a
word of caution. The active learning project is a springboard, not a replacement for disciplined learning. Effective learning frequently involves direct

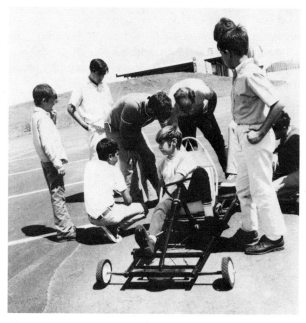

FIGURE 4-F   Junior high school students at the Experimental School of the University of California at Davis
complete a class in go-cart building.

teaching. This means that if you want to develop good readers, extensive reading and reading instruction are vital. A student who is to develop writing skills will need to do a lot of writing with help from the teacher. The same holds true for math skills, physical education, home economics, industrial arts, or knowledge of history, science, or Spanish. But a steady diet of lesson learning is boring, frustrating, and self-defeating because many students simply turn off the whole process. Also, the older the students, and the brighter the students, the more frustrated and bored they will be unless their instruction is generously sprinkled with interesting and creative activities.

After a decade in the late sixties and early seventies in which American education sought creativity, relevance, and freedom, we are now in a period of reaction. This reaction frequently means "back to the basics." The movement does have some validity, for in our eagerness to free the student from "irrelevance," we tended to neglect basic skills, as indicated by dropping scores on such standardized tests as the Scholastic Aptitude Test and the College Entrance Examination Board Tests of Basic Skills. High schools and colleges are now "tightening" their requirements, usually by requiring more courses in basic skills at the expense of electives.

But adding an English class is not the only method of upgrading students' language skills. One can teach reading in an agriculture class, if the teacher thinks it important, by maintaining a classroom library of material appropriate to the subject, and by encouraging, helping, and even requiring students to read. One can teach math in home economics, if the teacher thinks it important, by having students calculate household budgets, figure costs of yardage and various recipes, or by performing other arithmetic processes. What you label the course is less important than what the teacher considers valuable.

A teacher who decides to adopt an active learning approach should know in advance that this method, as any other, has its difficulties and limitations. It is more difficult for the teacher, who cannot simply follow a textbook or the district course of study. There is no carefully worked out sequence of learning, with every lesson carefully designed to filter out the extraneous and the overly difficult. Frequently, the knowledge or skills required for a particular chore may be beyond the students' ability levels, requiring much help from the teacher. Some activities may not be challenging enough. Projects can be useless and superficial, as lacking in learning and as passive as the textbook.

The key to a successful project lies in careful planning. It is here that a good teacher will be most deeply involved. It is the teacher who must fill in the details that make the difference between superficiality and depth: What should be read to get background information? What is to be written, what is to be done, what is to be made? Who must be interviewed, what questions asked or answered, what observations must be made, what reports submitted? Throughout the project, from planning to summation, the teacher's presence is felt—suggesting, questioning, challenging, teaching the students how to plan and execute the project.

It is on this vital point that I have seen many programs fall. Once a project is launched, many teachers sit back and let the students "learn by doing." But faced with a task that is beyond them, and without sufficient help, students become frustrated and give up. Or they complete the task in a sloppy, superficial manner and come out with no new understanding or skills.

Frequently, an effective approach would involve a *team* of teachers, each contributing his own knowledge and skills. The science and social studies teachers might pool their talents to sponsor a student committee reporting to the Board of Education the need for an outdoor education center. Or the journalism and foreign language teachers might jointly sponsor a bilingual newspaper. Perhaps the home economics and commercial teachers could turn the teachers' lunch room into a restaurant, with tablecloths and sit-down service. Frequently, community resource people can profitably be added to such teams. Active education does not require extra financing, only extra measures of courage, imagination, and determination.

Mindful of the difficulties and limitations, we also recognize some powerful values of active learning. The method provides an interesting approach to classroom organization. Both the "track" system and heterogeneous grouping have many obvious pitfalls—as long as we assume that everyone must be doing the same thing at the same time. But once we break into active learning groups, each individual may contribute something. Leaders come to the fore; organizers organize; brilliant students assume the most challenging tasks, and the less gifted contribute according to their ability. Within a heterogeneous classroom can be found a variety of students with a variety of interests and abilities, each participating in whatever assignment is appropriate for him.

Students in an active learning classroom have the opportunity for both independent study and team work. They may participate in a group project or go off as individuals. More important, students can follow their own interests, choosing from a wide variety of proposals, or they can submit a proposal of their own.

Most important, young people can become involved in doing something *real,* not just completing assignments to please a teacher. Becoming part of the adult community is important to teenagers, but we frustrate their ambition by nailing them to a desk six hours a day. Then we wonder why motivation and discipline are such overwhelming problems in school, and why they read so poorly.

A number of years ago an ingenious Japanese music teacher named Sinichi Suzuki realized that learning the complexities of a spoken language is a prodigious mental feat, accomplished with no real guidance from adults—just imitation.[16] He decided that if young children can learn language by imitation, they can learn to play the violin the same way. So he devised a new method of teaching music, doing away with learning notes, playing scales, and practicing long, dreary exercises. Only after students have learned to enjoy playing music by imitating what they hear on records does he show them notes and let them learn the 'fundamentals."

The dramatic results—Suzuki's students have won praise from professional musicians—have profound implications for education. Can we be sure of our most cherished beliefs about learning? Is it really necessary for students to spend hours playing scales to learn to play the violin? Must students do calisthenics in physical education to achieve strong, healthy bodies and skills in sports? Is it necessary to know a transitive from an intransitive verb to read and write well? How much of the "fundamentals" that we teach in school is really necessary, or even helpful, and how much is actually harmful because it turns students off to learning?

I doubt that Suzuki would claim that one can become a concert violinist without learning to read music. But how many youngsters with violins under their chins will ever become concert musicians anyway? How many are denied the joy of music in their lives because they were bored by the tediousness of the whole business?

And how many have turned away from learning because schools make it unnecessarily tedious? Maybe we could all take a page from Suzuki—first get kids involved in doing. Make it fun and get the student hooked. Then pick up details as the student feels frustrated by lack of knowledge or skill.

Earlier in the chapter we described reading readiness as dependent upon the emotional, linguistic, intellectual, and experiential development of the individual. This is where the active learning classroom directly relates to reading, for it is in the active involvement in life that the individual grows, experiences, and develops.

There is no shortage of creative and interesting methods of building a stimulating learning environment. This has been only a quick look at a few.

[16]N. H. Pronko, "On Learning to Play the Violin at the Age of Four Without Tears." *Psychology Today*, May 1969, 2, 52–53.

Vol. I

P. 1

Dixon Soccer Team	Equipos de Futbol
The Dixon Soccer teams have been doing well for the last four weeks. The intermediates won two games, lost one, tied one and the Jr. team won three, lost one, and they're in third place. R.V.	Los equipos de fútbol de Dixon siguen jugando bien por las últimas cuatro semanas. Los intermedios han ganado dos juegos, han perdido uno, y empataron uno. El equipo juvenil ha perdido uno, ha ganado tres, y están en el tercer lugar. R.V.

FIGURE 4-G   Seventh graders in a cross-cultural education program at the University of California at Davis for the Dixon Public Schools publish a bilingual newspaper, *Chango Chatter*.

```
Dixon High School                              Nonprofit
455 East A Street                              Bulk Rate
Dixon, California  95620                       U.S. Postage Pd
Telephone 916 678-2391                         Dixon, CA. 95620


Dixon High School      Noticias Importantes    W.M. O'Neill, Principal
                                               C.D. Ary, Vice Principal


Queridos Padres:

      Están cordialmente invitados a asistir a nuestra escuela secundaria el
jueves 2 de abril para participar en la observancia anual del mes dedicado a
las escuelas públicas. Despúes de las introducciones preliminares, ustedes
tendrán la oportunidad de observar instruccion en varios salones de clase, y
hablar informalmente con los maestros o observar las exhibiciones.

      Algunas de estas actividades serán: ciencias y matematicas, inglés,
instrucción especial educativa, una lección en taquigrafia, una lectura en
ciencias sociales, idiomas y educación bilingüe, pasaje de modas presentado
por la clase de economía doméstica, artes y bellas artes.

      Esperamos colaborar con su presencia.

      El lugar: Dixon High Little Theatre.

      La Fecha: martes, 2 de abril, 1974, a las 19:30 horas p.m.

                              Sinceramente


                              Wesley M. O'Neill
                              Director
                              Dixon High School
```

FIGURE 4-H   Dixon High School Spanish for Spanish speakers students translate the school bulletins and send them to Spanish-speaking parents as part of the bilingual education program of the University of California at Davis.

Such important techniques as simulation games,[17] role playing, [18] and contract learning,[19] have been crowded out by lack of space.

[17]Simulations are highly developed in the social studies, which lends itself to such methods. It teaches concepts by putting students into imaginary but true-to-life situations. Simulation materials are available commercially from a number of publishers. For a good introduction, including bibliographies of published material, see Alice Kaplan Gordon, *Games for Growth*.

Beginning with Chapter 5, we shall discuss specific methods of working with students at various reading levels. But to work with the reading problem without working with the readiness problem and without creating a healthy, active learning classroom, is like treating a victim of malnutrition with medicine instead of food.

Palo Alto, Calif.: Science Research Associates, 1970; William A. Nesbitt, *Simulation Games for the Social Studies Classroom*. New York: The Foreign Policy Association, 2nd ed., New York: Thomas Y. Crowell Co., 1971.

[18]Role-playing utilizes improvised dramas to achieve understanding and empathy. Some models are found in Fannie R. Shaftel, *Role-Playing for Social Values: Decision Making in the Social Studies*. New York: Prentice-Hall, Inc., 1967. See also pp. 258–260.

[19]I have seen two types of contract programs. Teacher-designed contracts are written in advance by the teacher, who prepares dozens, perhaps hundreds, of suggested activities. These may be as simple as read a book, article, or chapter and then answer certain questions. Or they may be more elaborate, involving library research, writing a paper, building something, or interviewing people. The students browse through the file of contracts and select one of interest. These are sometimes called Learning Activity Packets, or LAPS. Student-designed contracts are written by students, usually in collaboration with the teacher, and are tailored to meet the individual interests and abilities of the student. Upon completion of either type of contract, the student receives a grade and a prearranged amount of credit.

CHAPTER 5
The Silent Majority: An Action Plan for Instructional Readers

The dismissal bell galvanized the class into action. Eyes opened and books closed, and there was the usual rush for the door. "For tomorrow . . ." The teacher's voice could be heard trilling sharply above the stampeding feet. "For tomorrow, read pp. 75–87 and answer the first eight questions on pp. 87 and 88." The first third of the class had already made a clean escape through the door; the next third were close enough to claim they hadn't heard. But the last third were trapped and would have to do the homework.

Granted, this example is somewhat extreme. But it is hardly an exaggeration of some I have seen. And when, on the following day, the teacher became angry at the many students who had come back without their homework, my sympathies were with the students. For a teacher demonstrates, by actions if not words, just how important an assignment really is.

MAKING THE ASSIGNMENT

Motivation

We can all work up a lot more enthusiasm for a job when we see some purpose for doing it. In the active learning classroom students share in selecting the task, and some motivation is built in. Nevertheless, a good teacher is aware of the need to keep enthusiasm at a continuously high pitch. And in a teacher-centered class the need to motivate is even more acute. Therefore, in making an assignment, you might consider three motivators: a *hooker*, a *connection,* and an *objective.* Here are a few suggestions.

119

THE HOOKER

Imagine that last night you rolled three straight sevens. What are the chances of doing that again without loaded dice?

(Introduction to probabilities.)

Holding a tetherball by the cord, the teacher swung it around in circles over his head, asking:

Why is a tetherball like a man-made satellite–and also like the moon and the Earth?

(Introduction to inertia and centrifugal force.)

What do you think of gals who sometimes kill and eat their husbands as soon as they have mated?

(Introduction to entomology—the widow spiders.)

THE CONNECTION

Yesterday's speaker said that the United States should recognize Spanish as well as English as a national language. Does he have any basis for his claim?

(The Mexican War and subsequent land cession.)

At last night's Student Council meeting, it was decided that the theme of the Senior Prom would be the Arabian Nights. What are some of the Arabian Nights stories? Where did they come from? Who wrote them? What kinds of decorations would be appropriate for the prom? Let's read some stories from The Arabian Nights.

THE OBJECTIVE

Before we present our proposal to the Board of Education, we should know if any other schools in the country have done anything similar. Let's go to the public library and research this topic so our presentation will be more nearly complete. I suggest you begin with a journal called Education Index, which lists . . .

After doing tomorrow's assignments we should be able to figure exactly how much something costs, including finance charges. We can figure the rate we are paying for credit, so if we buy a car or a motorcycle, a new dress or a stereo set. . . .

Sometimes a longer discussion or a prereading activity is appropriate:

Tonight after dinner try to notice what time the moon comes up. Do the same on Saturday and Sunday nights. Monday, we'll read about the movements of the solar system and why the sun and moon do not come up at the same time every day.

Timing

A well-made assignment is incorporated into the lesson, not tacked on to the end. Today's lesson flows naturally into tomorrow's. Time is built into the lesson plan for explanations and questions. If possible, time is allowed to do some, if not all, of the assignment with the teacher present to help.

Clarity

All directions are precise and clear. What is to be read? Written? Made? Done? Are you assigning specific pages in a particular book, or questions to be researched in the library? Is anyone supposed to be interviewed or any place visited? Or is the student supposed to use his judgment and imagination about sources of information?

Deadlines

Exactly when is this assignment due? Specify date and time. Is there any flexibility in this deadline?

GETTING THE HORSE IN FRONT OF THE CART: AFTER YOU, MY DEAR STUDY GUIDE

Establishing an active learning classroom is a good beginning for any teaching program, but to improve the reading skills of secondary students, it is only the prerequisite. After taking the informal reading inventory discussed in Chapter 2, we divided the students into three groups:

1.   *Independent readers,* who can read and understand the textbook with little or no help.

2.   *Instructional readers,* who can read the textbook, provided they are given additional help, presumably from the teacher.

3.   *Frustration readers,* whose reading ability is so far below the textbook's requirements that to try to read at all is more damaging than beneficial because of the frustration encountered.

This does not imply, of course, that all students fall into neat little categories, but for instructional purposes, we can discuss techniques of working with students who are at approximately each level.

People can read with enjoyment and comprehension, even if occasionally they come across words they do not know or concepts they do not understand, or do not understand with depth. But as the number of unfamiliar words and concepts increases, comprehension decreases and frustration rises. Students reading at the instructional level are those who are missing enough words and concepts to make reading difficult and comprehension limited. They are not totally lost, however, and can best be helped before they read by raising their reading level for that selection from instructional to independent. This can usually be accomplished by incorporating a *study guide* into the assignment. In using the study guide, the teacher predicts where students are likely to have problems and works on those problems before they are encountered in the reading.

The study guide reverses the usual order of classroom procedure. The normal order is: read, then recite. With the study guide, the recitation comes first to make the reading faster. Of course, there may be another recitation after the students have read the material. But the pre- and postreading recitations have different purposes. The postreading recitation is to deepen the students' perceptions. The prereading study guide increases the students' knowledge; it is not discovery-oriented, but information imparting; not intended to challenge the student, but to simplify the reading task. The study guide may consist of:

Vocabulary List

Teach students to use the proper terminology, not *that thing* or *those guys*. There are many techniques for teaching vocabulary. The teacher may select the most appropriate method or combination:

Say the word. Recognition of a word is largely based on having heard it many times. After numerous repetitions the students should say it, to get the feel of the word on the tongue as well as the ear.

Note syllabication and stress. Although I believe syllabication is overused in some classrooms, there is a value in breaking up a long word into simple syllables that can be handled one at a time. Students should pronounce, read, and write the word, using syllabication at the beginning if necessary, but ultimately taking the word as a whole.

After the students have written the word, have them check their spelling. This makes the word less vague.

Discuss meaning *in the specific context.* For *grain elevator,* DON'T say:

An elevator is a device for raising and lowering people and things.

This is not very helpful. Better to establish:

Grain elevators are warehouses where grain is stored.

This description will not, in itself, teach the word *elevator,* but at this stage, it is more important to help the student understand what he is reading.

Then, if time permits, discuss related meanings:

These are called elevators because usually the grain is first raised to the top of the warehouse and then dumped. It's like the elevator of a building, except instead of raising people, it raises grain.

Ask for synonyms and perhaps antonyms. Help the class understand that a synonym for *elevator* is *lift* (usually British), but a synonym for *grain elevator* is *warehouse.* Do not forget to check out *grain.* Don't assume. Ask for examples of grains.

Use the word in sentences. First the teacher, then the students compose original sentences.

Note the morphological structure of the word (See Chapter 8): elev—at(e)—or, as well as *elevate, elevates, elevated, elevating,* and *elevator* (person who elevates).

Use visual aids. Locate on map or chart, point out in diagram, picture, or model, bring in artifact, or give demonstration. Have students draw pictures or make up jokes about the word:

Joe died of inversion. *He got stuck head first in a mud puddle.*

NAMES   Pay special attention to names, particularly if they are hard to pronounce or have some significance:

Afghanistan is a kingdom in southern Asia (Pronounce carefully; have the students pronounce.). Here it is on the map (locate), bordered by Russia on the north, Pakistan on the south and east, and Iran on the west.

Make whatever connections are necessary:

Gloucester (pronounced with two syllables /'glos tr/) is a region in southern England, similar to one of our states. In this play (Shakespeare's Richard III) Richard is the Duke, or ruler, of Gloucester. That is why he is sometimes called Richard, *sometimes* Duke of Gloucester, *or just* Gloucester, *or* My Lord of

Gloucester, *or* Brother Gloucester. *The same word can be applied to the region as well as the man, although the region may also be* Gloucestershire.

As in the specific reading inventory, do not neglect nontechnical words (those not immediately related to the lesson, but still likely to present a reading problem. See p. 45.)

ABBREVIATIONS AND ACRONYMS   Do not assume that students can translate *lb, yd, doz, gal, ibid, viz, OE, Ariz, syn, Au, Ag, NATO, UNESCO,* or *NOW.* Refer students to the glossary, the *Periodic Table of the Elements* in the chemistry book, the *List of Abbreviations* in the dictionary, or any special references available, to help them get used to using these aids. If such help is not available in the text, include potential hot spots in the study guide.

PHRASES   Sometimes phrases must be considered as a whole. *Gross national product* may be composed of three easily read, easily understood words, but full comprehension is not possible unless the student knows what the whole phrase means.

SYMBOLS   Introduce new symbols and review those that have not been used consistently in the recent past. Do not assume students know the meaning of $=, \mathrm{ɔ:}, \sqrt{}, \#, >, <, \pi, \neq,$ or even %.

Charts, Graphs, and Maps

These may be a source of concentrated information, or they may be unreadable, depending upon the reader. Many students are unable to deal with symbolic language without explanation.

> *Does this graph deal with time, people, products, or baseball scores? What do the vertical and horizontal designations mean? How much or how many does each square represent?*

If students cannot answer these questions, explain.

Which lines on the map are roads, which are railroads, which are rivers? What does the green area signify, as opposed to the brown? Does the map show population of cities, and which are state capitals and county seats? How do you compute road or direct mileage? Students should understand that there are dozens of *kinds* of maps for showing specific information, such as climate, elevation, farm products, population distribution, topography, soil conditions, roads, political boundaries, and many other features. Point out that a good map has a *key*, usually located in a lower corner, that unlocks the data.

Illustrations and Cartoons, with Captions

Pictures serve not only to motivate, but to enhance the information and the emotional response of the reader. Yet many students either ignore this valuable assistance or stare blankly and receive little enrichment. Cartoons need particular attention. The political cartoon requires the ability to think symbolically. The cartoon shown on p. 126 (Figure 5−A) must be seen as social commentary, not humor. The reader should comprehend the *personification* (see p. 270) of the city as a little man, boxed in by nearly insurmountable difficulties, crying "Help!" We realize that "city" stands for no particular place but American cities in general. We cannot assume, however, that our students will understand all that.

Background Information

Students frequently need information before they can read with comprehension:

> In this chapter you will see references to anemia. This is a deficiency of hemoglobin, the material that gives blood its red color. People with anemia are usually pale from lack of hemoglobin. Because hemoglobin carries oxygen to the body and helps rid the body of wastes, people who are anemic tend to be listless and dull.

Do not assume the class remembers what came before in the course. Frequent reminders and summaries are helpful:

> Last week we studied the Reconstruction, that period in American history after the Civil War when . . . In this assignment we shall look at the Postreconstruction Period. . . .

Culture-Bound Allusions

These are references to things that are only known if they are part of the individual's culture or his personal realm of experience. *But Venus must have smiled upon the happy couple* means nothing to a student who does not know that Venus was the goddess of love and patroness of lovers. Students should understand that the writer does not necessarily believe in Greek pantheism, but is merely indulging in a poetic manner of saying the lovers were lucky.

HERBLOCK'S CARTOON

"Help!"

FIGURE 5-A   In Stephen B. Jones and Marion Fisher Murphy, *Geography and World Affairs,* 3rd. ed. Skokie, Ill.: Rand McNally & Company, 1971, p. 134. From The Herblock Gallery, New York: Simon & Schuster, Inc., 1968.

Concepts

Concepts and vocabulary often involve the same word, but concept development frequently encompasses, in addition to learning the word, a greater depth of understanding. Define the concept:

> Symbiosis *is a process by which two dissimilar organisms live together and mutually benefit from the presence of the other.*

Give examples: Exhibit a lichen and explain the symbiosis of fungi and algae. Try a picturesque example: *a boy and a girl holding hands.*

Connect, if possible, with other concepts in the course:

> *We have already looked at parasitic and saprophytic relationships. Symbiotic relationships are a third type.*

GENERAL ORIENTATION.   What problem(s) must be solved in this reading assignment, what question(s) answered or discussed, or new material understood? Attention should be called to hidden meanings or implications likely to be missed:

> *In this play Mr. Antrobus is the father. But on another level, what does Mr. Antrobus symbolize? What does Sabina mean when she says, "We came through the depression by the skin of our teeth"?*[1] *Who came through?*

(Although the purpose of study guides is to give information rather than ask questions, it is sometimes sufficient to direct the students' attention to certain important concepts by asking stimulating questions.)

Reading Style

Few secondary students (or adults either) know how to pace themselves in reading—how to judge which material to skim, which to read with care; when to take copious notes, when to read for enjoyment; how to look for specific information; how to use tables, charts, and other instructional aids. *Topic headings* provide important structural clues to tell the reader which are the main sections of the work, and which topics are subsumed under other topics. Students should understand that most textbooks contain a hierarchy of topic headings, from chapter titles to the smallest boldface or italicized type.

Many of our common connecting words tend to be glossed over. *And, but,* and *or* do not mean the same thing; neither do *however, nevertheless,* and *moreover.* Boldfaced type and italics also have a mission. Sometimes even phrases, such as *in spite of* and *because of,* need pointing out. I have

[1] *The Skin of Our Teeth,* by Thornton Wilder. Act I.

seen students come out confused about which event the author said came first, which was the cause and which the effect. In Chapter 10 we will discuss reading styles in greater depth. Ultimately, the mature reader learns to adopt a reading style appropriate to the material. The immature reader needs, however, to begin by learning that there are different styles:

> I suggest you skim lightly over the first section, noting the general differences between nourishing and inadequate eating habits. Then on Page 86 you'll begin the section on nutrition. Read this carefully. Note the different classes of foods and the contribution each food group makes toward health. Check the nutrition chart on page 89. Tomorrow when you buy your lunch, ask yourself how many items from the nutrition chart you are getting.

Instructions such as these are for students who have not learned to pace their reading. Your ultimate goal is to develop a reader who can make such decisions for himself.

SAMPLE STUDY GUIDES

THE NOTORIOUS JUMPING FROG OF CALAVERAS COUNTY[2]

(Because of its length, the story has not been included. However, it is available in many anthologies of short stories and works of Mark Twain. This guide is considerably longer than the usual recommended length, largely because of the list of vernacular terms. Once the students catch on to the dialect, the remaining material will require very little study. This piece is typical of those that appear frequently in secondary English programs, despite some very difficult reading.)

The story is told in the everyday language of an uneducated Californian of about a hundred years ago. Language common to a particular time and place is called *vernacular,* and the wild tale is a *yarn.* Don't worry about whether the story seems logical or possible. It isn't intended to be. Just enjoy the rich humor of a clever schemer who is beaten at his own tricks.

Vocabulary

notorious	Famous, usually for something bad.
Calaveras	/kalə 'verəs/ County in California, famous during the gold rush.
garrulous	Talkative.
In compliance with a request	In order to do what was asked.
Leonidas	/lā o 'nē dəs/.
I hereunto append the result	To *append* is to add, or attach. He means he is now adding, or telling, the story.

[2]Based on work by Mary Ellen Daly.

myth	Something that is not true. He suspects there is no such man as Leonidas W. Smiley.
conjectured	Imagined—made up.
infamous	Famous for doing bad things.
exasperating reminiscence	Very bad story. Mark Twain continually pokes fun at his own yarn by letting the narrator, who tells the story, refer to Wheeler's tale of the frog as a terrible, unbelievable story.
tranquil countenance	Peaceful expression.
Angel's Camp	Where the story took place. Angel's Camp (What a beautiful name for a place where so much devilishness is found) can still be seen in Calaveras County, California. Because of this famous story, the residents still hold a jumping frog contest every spring.
interminable narrative	Never-ending story.
transcendent genius in finesse	Very intelligent men. Wheeler admired the cleverness with which each tried to cheat the other.
flume	Channel for carrying water, presumably for use in the gold mines.
Rev. Leonidas W. H'm, Reverend Le———	He tries to remember, thinks out loud about the name, stops, starts again, and gives up. Then he decides to tell about Jim Smiley.
exhorter	One who exhorts, or urges people. In this case, a preacher.
asthma	/ 'az mə/ An illness that makes one gasp for breath.
distemper	An animal disease.
consumption	Tuberculosis, a sickness causing shortness of breath.
cavorting and straddling up	Humorous description of the way the horse ran—legs flying in all directions, panting and gasping, but going very fast.
fo'castle	/ 'fōk sl/ Compartment on a boat, usually where the sailors live.
nap of the neck	(usually spelled nape) The fleshy part at the back of an animal's neck.
buttonholed me	Caught me, made me listen.
afflicted	Having severe trouble, here used humorously about the lack of a tail.

Many of the words and phrases in this story are distortions that result from the speaker's vernacular. You may recognize them more easily if you say them aloud.

recollect	Remember.
warn't	Weren't or wasn't.
curiousest	Most curious.
no solit'ry thing	Not a solitary (single) thing.
ary	Any.
resk	Risk.
cipher it down	Decipher it, figure it out.
ornery	From *ordinary*, in this case good-for-nothing.
j'int	Joint.
rat-tarriers	Terrier dogs.
ketched	caught.
cal'lated	Calculated, decided.
Dan'l	Daniel.
strong suit	Special skill—from the card game bridge.

There are also a number of other slang expressions:

You'd find him flush or you'd find him busted.	If he won he'd be rich, if he lost he'd be broke.
lay for	Wait for.
bully-rag him	Get the better of him.
shucked out	Beaten up.
a piece	A short distance.
fall to	Begin.
Dan'l give a heave, and hysted up his shoulders—so—like a Frenchman.	Daniel pulled up his shoulders, trying to hop. "Like a Frenchman" is Twain's joke about the gestures of the French people.
What that frog throwed off for	Why the frog didn't jump as usual.

Note that this is a story within a story, that is, Twain begins in the barroom, then has one of the characters, Simon Wheeler, tell the main story. This gives the yarn a setting and flavor—the decaying, rotting old mining camp, the feeling that Jim Smiley, in spite of his cleverness, was spiritually rotten.

Here is a very different type of study guide.[3] The teacher found that his students were having little trouble reading the words of the text, even getting the data. But they were skimming over the significance of the material. So he devised a series of questions to ask during the prereading discussion period along with a series of directions for careful reading. These are designed to

[3]Based on work by Doug Kline.

focus the students' attention on the material. Note how the new vocabulary words are worked into the discussion.

EXPLORING THE UNIVERSE[4]

Could there be life on other planets in our solar system?

Assuming you don't have a space ship, how would you go about finding out?

The first part of the chapter tells you how scientists look for answers to such questions. Keep in mind that we do not really know the answers, but we have some very important clues.

For example, what might you think if you looked through a telescope at Mars and found patches of green? (Remember what we learned earlier about chlorophyll in plants, but be careful—there's more to it than that.)

In this chapter we shall learn about *infrared light,* a red light that our eyes cannot see. But infrared light tells us some important things. Notice, as you read, what we learn from it.

A *spectroscope* is a gadget that breaks light into its parts, so we can see each color. Can you imagine how a spectroscope can be used to determine if there is life on some planet?

Suppose you wanted to find out if a planet contained animals and not just plants? What would you look for? What do animals need that plants do not?

Look at the picture on p. 77 and notice what it tells you about plant life on Mars.

The gases that surround some planets, such as the air we breathe, are called its *atmosphere.* What do you suppose the Earth would be like if it had no atmosphere?

That being true, what clues concerning life do we find in a planet's atmosphere?

Do you know why the temperature inside a greenhouse is higher than it is outside?

When the text discusses the *greenhouse effect* it refers to anything that allows more heat to enter than it allows to leave, causing the temperature to rise. Notice in the reading what this tells us about a planet's atmosphere.

Do you think people could live on Venus?

As you read, list the evidence that human beings:

Could live on Venus without space suits.
Could live on Venus only with space suits.
Could not live on Venus even with space suits.

How would you like to be the astronaut who goes to Venus some day to bring back the answers to all these questions?

Do you think it important to keep spending time and money to answer questions such as these?

[4]From: MacCracken, et al., *Basic Life Science.* Singer Science Series, L. W. Singer, School Division. New York: Random House, 1964, Chapter 5.

Gary Grout, a music teacher, found that his choral students were not getting meaning from the unusual syntax and archaic words of some of their songs. This was interfering with interpretation, so he wrote paraphrases to simplify the meaning and included other information on his study guide:

GOD OF COMFORT, GOD OF COURAGE

Instructions

⁊	Breathe here.
⌒	Do not breathe here.
*	See pronunciation guide.
<u>word</u>	*See vocabulary list.*

Pronunciation Guide

comfort	chum-<u>fohrt</u>
courage	cuh-<u>redge</u>
though	<u>thow</u>

Vocabulary List

doth	does
nourish	feed
steadfast	constant, not changing
undergirded	strengthened, held up from below
thee	you (objective form)

Original	Paraphrase
God of com-fort,* God of cour-age,* ⁊	God: You make us
pre-sent help in	brave and always
time of need,	give us comfort
Who the faint-ing	and help when we
soul <u>doth</u>	need it. You feed
<u>nour-ish.</u> ⁊	our souls when
Make us strong in	they are fainting
faith and deed. ⁊	from hunger.
Though* the	Please strengthen

moun-tains shake
and crumble ⌢
In the might-y
crash-ing of the
sea, ⸙
Keep us <u>stead-fast</u>,
keep us humble, ⸙
<u>Un-der-girded</u>,
Lord, by <u>thee</u>. ⸙

our faith and help
us to humbly do
the right thing—no
matter how bad
things get.

The study guide alone is useful only for students in the instructional zone, those who can almost, but not quite, handle the reading independently. If a student would ordinarily encounter 20 new words within the reading assignment, and the study guide deals with 14 of them, you reduce this list to 6, a tolerable level that raises him from the instructional to the independent level, *for that assignment.* But if he has 50 or 100 new words to cope with, the study guide becomes hopeless. It hardly pays to spend 3 days preparing to read for 20 minutes. Such students are in the frustration zone, and they are to be handled by other means, to be discussed in the following chapters.

PRESENTING THE STUDY GUIDE

There are many methods of presenting the study guide to the class. The teacher may discuss the material orally. It can be put on duplicated sheets and passed out, with or without accompanying discussion. The teacher may utilize the chalkboard or a transparent projector.[5] The study guide may be read into a tape recorder, and the tapes played over a speaker for the entire class. Or the tapes may be played through a listening post for a smaller group,[6] or ear phones for individuals.

The study guide may be presented to the entire class, if necessary. But more frequently, some students will be able to read independently while others use a study guide. In an open classroom there is ample opportunity to divide into groups, so that each student can work on his own level.

Another technique is to have the entire class skim the lesson (See p. 263). Next, the teacher gives the study guide a quick oral skimming with the class. Then each student decides where to begin. Some go to work immediately on the reading, others work with the teacher on the study guide,

---

[5]A transparent projector throws an image on a large viewing screen. The teacher can write the study guide on a sheet of transparent plastic and project a large image for the entire class.

[6]A listening post is a box containing a number of ear phones plugged into a tape recorder or record player. It enables a small group of students to listen to a recording.

while a third group may listen to a tape recorder and a prerecorded study guide.

The study guide can be incorporated into the daily lesson as part of the process of making an assignment. An alternative would be to set up the study guide on paper or tape in one section of the classroom, where students could utilize part of the class period or any free time they might have before, during, or after school to come in and work on the guide. The teacher or an aide, hopefully, would be available for help. A variation of the study guide, to be read *while* the student is doing the assignment instead of before, is discussed by Daniel Tutolo.[7]

As with the informal reading inventory, the nature of the study guide will vary with the material and the students. If you think the major reading problem is likely to be vocabulary, that is what the study guide stresses. But if major problems exist in concept understanding or culture-bound allusions, a different type of study guide will naturally emerge. In some cases, time permitting, the teacher may want to prepare more than one study guide for different groups of students, with different degrees of comprehensiveness or different emphases.

A good teacher may utilize a *variety* of techniques, frequently in combination, to adapt to the needs of students. This is the key to the problem. Many secondary teachers plan their programs around a textbook, a course of study, or their own college majors. Their methods are those that were practiced on them as students. But for a truly effective program, knowing our subject and knowing teaching methodology are only first steps. It is important to know how to develop and administer a study guide. It takes experience and sensitivity to know when a guide is needed, with whom, and how extensive it should be. In short, don't forget to plug the student into the system.

[7]Daniel J. Tutolo, "The Study Guide—Types, Purpose, and Value." *Journal of Reading,* March 1977, 20, 503–507.

CHAPTER 6
The Forgotten Ones: An Action Plan for Frustration Readers

GENERAL SUGGESTIONS

For the student who experiences serious reading difficulty, the study guide is not sufficient. Other, more involving methods are needed. First, let us consider some general suggestions.

Academic assignments should be short term, with the end always in sight. Reluctant readers tend to have short attention spans, intensified by repeated frustration and failure. The need is for immediate payoff—the satisfaction of accomplishment NOW. Long term academic goals—for this student—can be useless and futile. An assignment due a week from Monday will probably be begun, if not long forgotten by then, a week from Sunday. An assignment due in twenty minutes has a much better chance.

Assignments must have meaning for the student, not just for the teacher. This in no way implies that the student may be allowed to do as he pleases, but that it is the responsibility of the teacher to find a responsive note within the student. A student may, for example, recognize the need to improve his reading but lack the self-discipline to do the job. In this case the teacher may need firmness and determination to see to it that the student learns. Suppose, on the other hand, the student actually believes that he can "make it" without learning to read, that he is going to be a mechanic and work with his hands. The teacher would do better to let the student experience the frustration of being unable to read directions for doing a tune-up, then teach him to read the manual. Once he has done this, he may be better able to see the value of reading other things as well.

Bright, college bound youngsters expect a teacher to know the subject and be able to teach. They are likely to respect knowledge and intellectual leadership. Reluctant readers, I find, are more interested in the teacher *as a human being* and in how they and the teacher relate. *The teacher likes me* gets better results than *he sure knows his math.*

Fortunately, much of the professional distance between teachers and students is breaking down. I find in recent years that teachers are increasingly warm, friendly, and human—and less defensive. More and more teachers are conducting new experimental programs in building human relationships, taking their students on camping trips and other field experiences, even opening their homes for class parties. This is one of the healthiest, most encouraging trends in education. The traditional warning that "teachers must not get too close" has a surface validity, for it is quite possible for a teacher to reduce effectiveness by appearing juvenile in the eyes of students. Teacher effectiveness can also be destroyed by remoteness, however. The impersonal teacher, tied to a book and a course of study, is particularly unable to reach the reluctant reader. Contrary to popular belief, dignity and distance are not necessarily handmaidens. There is no conflict between being mature and dignified, and being friendly and warm also. The teacher who would work with the reluctant reader must rate high in both.

SPECIFIC METHODS

Alternative Textbooks

If a student is unable to read a text, even with the help of a study guide, it is better to look for a simpler text. Unfortunately, they are not always easy to find. Lower level (elementary grade) textbooks appear juvenile, reminding the reluctant reader of his deficiencies. Most books that are mature in format and interest level are also difficult to read.

Much depends on whether the teacher is committed to a particular course of study, for the selection may be widened tremendously by adopting trade books as well as texts. Much beautiful reading by leading writers and layout artists becomes available to the school that is not restricted to books on an approved list. See Appendix 4.

I believe many teachers try too hard to push students into reading challenging material. My experience has been that easy reading builds speed, fluency, comprehension, enjoyment of reading, and self-confidence. Once students enjoy reading and believe they are good readers, they gravitate to more challenging material. Frustration reading can produce the opposite effect. Dolch[1] also found that we learn more from easy books than from hard ones. He claims it is the *reaction to reading* that counts, not the struggle. This does not mean that students should not ultimately be encouraged

[1]Edward William Dolch, *Problems in Reading.* Champaign, Ill.: The Garrard Press, 1948, p. 3

towards deeper, more meaningful reading, only that many teachers push too hard, too fast. Reading should involve pleasure as well as challenge.

ENGLISH   There are unlimited quantities of good material for reluctant readers. Many literature programs have an additional "track two" series with a lower reading level. There are also many "high-interest, low reading level" series books, with stories ranging from second or third grade reading, as well as special, simplified editions of popular stories. English classes can also use anything published in the English language, from trade books in literature to special interest materials of all sorts. I have found *The Guinness Book of World Records* very popular with boys, despite its high reading level, presumably because of the high interest material and the shortness of its articles. The Department of Motor Vehicles study book for driver's license test is a good reader for students getting ready for the big event. Despite recent trends downgrading traditional sex roles, shop manuals of all kinds are popular with boys, and beauty aids and romance stories in books and magazines with girls.[2]

SOCIAL STUDIES   More and more programs are coming out in short paperback pamphlets with easier reading and less abstruse subject matter. This is particularly true in the ethnic studies. Additionally, a good social studies program can include historical novels and films, biography, and many excellent trade books on topics of social concern.

SCIENCE   Science textbooks have been getting better—more interesting, more discovery-oriented, more concerned with things to *do*. There are also hundreds of excellent trade books, from the very simple, but by no means juvenile, *First Books* series[3] to the beautifully illustrated *Life* books.[4]

FOREIGN LANGUAGE   One of the difficulties with learning a foreign language is that the student is always reading at frustration level. There is so much emphasis on learning new words, new idioms and new grammatical structures that the student cannot enjoy *reading*. Try the study guide before the student reads a new lesson, introducing new words, new idioms, and new grammar, so that when he does read, he can read faster and with less

---

[2]Daniel Fader and Elton McNeil's *Hooked on Books*. New York: Berkley Publishing Corporation is a must, especially for English teachers. This little paperback has nearly revolutionized the teaching of English in the last decade, and has profound implications for other subjects.
[3]Franklin Watts, Inc.
[4]Life Nature Library, Time, Inc.

effort. Look for the most interesting literature the students can handle—short bits of poetry and prose that are high in humor or story value.

MATHEMATICS   This is one of the few areas in which reluctant readers tend to function somewhat close to normal. Obviously, it is one of the least dependent upon verbal skills, but even math texts contain explanations and word problems. The difficulty in math is terminology, which cannot be sidestepped by purchasing simpler texts. *Logarithms* and *vectors, sines* and *cosines* are either dealt with or not dealt with. Most math teachers report best results either by placing students in programs that do not require such difficult reading and profound concept development, or by making very heavy use of study guides to teach the terminology. Another interesting approach is the SEED math program (Special Education for the Educationally Disadvantaged). SEED math teachers teach advanced concepts to elementary school children in low income areas. But they do it by an oral approach based upon teacher-student dialogue. Some writing is done, but it is mainly chalkboard work with mathematical symbols and numbers rather than words. Bill Johntz, founder of the program, claims that the key to its phenomenal success is his method of discovery teaching.

OTHER SUBJECTS   Much excellent material is available in industrial arts (plans for projects, manuals for tools and machines, do-it-yourself books and magazines of many kinds); home economics (cook books, patterns, books on home decoration and beauty aids, and texts on family planning and interpersonal relations); physical education (rules of games, sports stories, biographies of players, information about interschool and professional athletics); geography (beautifully illustrated travel books available free from travel agents); and many other areas.

In this publication-happy society, there is a wealth of free and inexpensive reading matter available to the teacher with the patience and persistence to scrounge. For years I gathered advertising pamphlets from new car agencies when the new models came out (usually in September). Other manufacturers similarly produce colorful and interesting material. I have used Sears Roebuck and Montgomery Ward catalogs, supplied free, for lessons in consumer economics and using indexes, and to get young people to read.

The United States Printing Office in Washington, D.C. issues thousands of booklets annually on a tremendous variety of topics. Every federal agency spews out its share of documents, and a catalog of available material can be had from any large reference library or from your congressional representative. Many state and local agencies are also prolific publishers.

Often "salvage" stores—Salvation Army, Goodwill Industries, and others—have large selections of inexpensive old magazines. Credit unions, banks, and savings and loan offices have excellent publications on consumer economics. Doctors frequently have material on health and hygiene.

The 4-H Club has booklets on animal raising, home decoration, cooking, nutrition, mechanics, auto repair, sewing, bicycling, recreation, budgeting, and dozens of other topics. These books are well written, with a careful eye to readers of limited stature. The county agricultural agent, who is also a source of much good reading, can direct you to the 4-H office. Teachers might consider the formation of a 4-H Club within the school if there is not already one. 4-H activities can be a turn-on for students, who can gain access to excellent free reading matter.

Obviously, the teacher must select carefully from among the deluge of publications available, finding what is relevant and not loaded with propaganda. A well-equipped classroom could include as part of the room library, a selection of pamphlets, some on display and others classified by topic and filed for easy access. Into this file can also go clippings from newspapers and magazines. I usually xerox newspaper articles, because newsprint yellows with time. Except for syndicated items, newspapers are not copyrighted, hence duplicating them is legal.

Lou Burmeister suggests a method by which students may be stimulated to read supplementary material: The teacher collects a number of books related to the subject, then writes one-sentence descriptions of each book. The sentences are short, interesting, and designed to whet the student's appetite. These descriptions may be posted in the reading area or duplicated and given to each student. Burmeister provides a sample reading list based on history, World War II Period:

QUESTIONNAIRE—WORLD WAR II (HISTORY)[5]

Name_____

Would you like to read a book or article about (circle Yes or No):

1. Yes-No: Norwegian children who helped smuggle millions of dollars out of Norway to America to keep it from their German captors? (*Snow Treasure*)

2. Yes-No: a Jewish girl who spent several years in an attic room in Amsterdam to escape the Nazis? (*Anne Frank: Diary of a Young Girl*)

[5]Lou E. Burmeister, *Reading Strategies for Secondary School Teachers.* Reading, Mass.: Addison-Wesley Publishing Co., 1974, p. 63.

3. Yes-No: a hunchback who sailed the British Channel to rescue stranded soldiers in Dunkirk who were being forced into the sea by the Nazis? (*Snow Goose*)

4. Yes-No: five men who lived through the atomic attack on Hiroshima and tell their story? (*Hiroshima*)

5. Yes-No: a Japanese girl who saw her mother die in the atomic attack on Hiroshima and later fell in love with an American soldier—her dilemma? (*Flowers of Hiroshima*)

40. Yes-No: a possibly true account of attempted surrender by the Japanese before the dropping of the atom bomb? ("Was it the Deadliest Error of Our Time?")

Rewrites

Frequently, when a diligent search fails to turn up satisfactory material on the proper reading level, the teacher may wish to rewrite available texts, simplifying and shortening. This involves a lot of work, particularly for a busy teacher, but material, once rewritten, can be valuable and permanent. Perhaps talented aides can be found to help rewrite. A few such projects each year, and soon the teacher has a useful stock-in-trade. These rewrites can be duplicated on a ditto, mimeograph, or Xerox. If long passages are rewritten from copyrighted material (If it is copyrighted, it must say so on the reverse of the title page.), it would be worthwhile to write the publisher for permission to do so. Teachers with writing talents might send the publishers samples of their rewrites with a view towards selling for publication. There is a need for good educational material written for reluctant readers.

However, rewrites should be used with discretion. They are useful for enabling reluctant readers to cope with difficult material, but can become a crutch for good readers. In a recent study, high ability readers reported greater enjoyment from original works of literature than from rewrites. They also read the originals more rapidly. Average and lower ability students preferred the rewrites and read them more rapidly.[6]

[6]T. Stevenson Hansell, "Readability, Syntactic Transformations, and Generative Semantics." *Journal of Reading*, April 1976, 19, 557−562.

CALCULATING READABILITY

Thus far, we have discussed "simpler" reading material as if it were self-evident what constitutes reading difficulty. In broad general terms, anyone can distinguish very difficult from very simple reading material, but how do we know which can be considered "third grade" reading level, which sixth, which tenth, and so forth? A number of reading specialists have worked out formulas for computing these factors. Some of these formulas tend to be technical and, at best, approximate, for a multiplicity of items influence readability. Some formulas are not consistent, even with each other, and are of value mainly to reading specialists. The classroom teacher can, however, compute reading difficulty with sufficient accuracy to select appropriate reading matter and to simplify the material on hand.

Let us begin by examining the first four paragraphs of O. Henry's short story, *The Cop and the Anthem*.

THE COP AND THE ANTHEM

by O. Henry

On his bench in Madison Square Soapy moved uneasily. When wild geese honk high of nights, and when women without sealskin coats grow kind to their husbands, and when Soapy moves uneasily on his bench in the park, you may know that winter is near at hand.

A dead leaf fell in Soapy's lap. That was Jack Frost's card. Jack is kind to the regular denizens of Madison Square, and gives fair warning of his annual call. At the corners of the four streets he hands his pasteboard to the North Wind, footman of the mansion of All Outdoors, so that the inhabitants thereof may make ready.

Soapy's mind became cognizant of the fact that the time had come for him to resolve himself into a singular Committee of Ways and Means to provide against the coming rigor. And therefore he moved uneasily on his bench.

The hibernatorial ambitions of Soapy were not of the highest. In them there were no considerations of Mediterranean cruises, of soporific Southern skies or drifting in the Vesuvian Bay. Three months on the Island was what his soul craved. Three months of assured board and bed and congenial company, safe from Boreas and bluecoats, seemed to Soapy the essence of things desirable.

This is the start of an absolutely delicious story, but unfortunately O. Henry's writing style makes it unavailable to all but the best secondary school readers. Now let us look at the same material, rewritten.

THE COP AND THE ANTHEM
by O. Henry

Soapy moved uneasily on his park bench. When wild geese fly south, and when Soapy moves uneasily on his park bench, winter is coming.

A dead leaf fell on Soapy's lap. He knew he would have to find a place to stay for the winter. New York was too cold to spend winters in the park.

Soapy didn't ask much. He wasn't thinking of plush vacations in warmer climates. Soapy just wanted to spend the winter in jail. In jail it was warm. He would be fed. He would be with his friends. A ninety day term would get him out by spring.

What has happened to this story in the simplification process? Admittedly it has lost much of its pizzaz. No one can pretend that this rewritten version can compare with O. Henry's delightful word choice and richness of imagery. But if the entire story were rewritten, its essential humor—the frustration of this poor bum trying so hard to get into jail, and the ironic turn of events at the end—all this remains. But now it is accessible, even to the reluctant readers. To be specific, here are some of the things that happened in this brief excerpt:

COMPENDIUM OF SIMPLIFICATION TECHNIQUES

from The Cop and the Anthem

I.   Larger printing and spacing, (Use pica or primary typewriter.) This is a two-edged sword, as some students will feel it is juvenile.

II.   Shorter total length: 103 words versus 208.

III.   Shorter sentences: Average 8.5 words versus 17.

IV.   Simple vocabulary:

    A.   Fewer two-syllable words: 18 versus 33
    B.   Fewer three-syllable or more words: 2 versus 20.
    C.   Fewer uncommon words: *denizens* (2 per 1,000,000)[7], *footman* (4

---

[7]The numbers refer to the ratings of these words on the Thorndike-Lorge word scale. See: Edward Thorndike and Irving Lorge, *The Teacher's Word Book of 30,000 Words*. New York: Bureau of Publications, Teachers College, Columbia University, 1944.

per 1,000,000), *pasteboard* (1 per 1,000,000), and *soporific* (8 per 18,000,000).

V. Conventional sentence construction (see sentence No. 2): "On his bench in Madison Square, Soapy moved uneasily." → "Soapy moved uneasily on his park bench." (Modifier of predicate placed within predicate.)

VI. Simple expression of ideas: "hibernatorial ambitions" → "Soapy didn't ask much."

VII. Reduction or elimination of:

A. *Subordinate clauses* (except sentence No. 2): ". . . so that the inhabitants thereof may make ready."
B. *Culture-bound allusions*: Madison Square, Jack Frost, Committee of Ways and Means, Boreas, The Island.
C. *Implied Meanings*: ". . . when women without sealskin coats grow kind to their husbands . . ."
D. *High level abstractions*: "When wild geese honk high . . ."
E. *Digressions from the main plot line*: "At the corners of the four streets he hands his pasteboard to the North Wind . . ."
F. *Imagery*: "That was Jack Frost's card."

VIII. *Tells the reader what the original implies*: "A 90-day term would get him out by spring."

There are other factors, not illustrated in this example, involved in reading difficulty, such as compound sentences:

Harry struck out, but Bill saved the day with a home run.

or plays on words:

They say that miniskirts make women look shorter. But they also make men look longer.

Out of this mass of data it is possible for the teacher to derive a simple mathematical formula for testing readability. Two factors are of such outstanding importance that a formula based upon them alone will produce a readability index sufficiently accurate for the classroom teacher's purpose. These factors are *vocabulary* and *sentence length*.

Vocabulary is the obvious and most important one. Some words are used more frequently, hence recognized more easily. Some words contain uncommon combinations of letters or confusing similarities with some other words (thorough—through, tired—tried, diary—dairy). But one factor that is simple to compute and reliable enough for our purpose is length. The longer the word, the more difficult, roughly, it is to read. Length also correlates somewhat inversely with frequency, as our commonest words tend to be short.

After vocabulary, the next most important factor is sentence length. You and I, college educated readers, can cut our way through a William Faulkner-type page-and-a-half sentence and follow the intricacies of his thoughts and feelings. But many read so slowly that by the time they get to the predicate of a long sentence they have forgotten the subject, or by the time they pick their way through a series of modifying phrases and clauses, they cannot focus on the meaning of the main clause. Therefore, although the content of a sentence is important, a rough index can be derived simply by combining average sentence length with vocabulary.

Therefore, to compute the readability of written matter, select a passage that seems typical of the entire work. (If time is available and you wish a more accurate assessment, select three passages from various parts of the book and take their average.) Count the words in this passage. Count all words, including a, to, an, the, and so forth. Count hyphenated words as two words. Count numerals as single words, regardless of length, unless the numeral is divided into separate units of meaning. Thus, July 4, 1776 would be 3 words, but telephone 767-8900 would be 2. Abbreviations count as if they were written out, and symbols and sets of initials count as single words. Thus UNICEF is 1 word, and A. J. Thompson & Co. is 4. From 400 to 500 words will give a reasonable sampling.

Count the number of sentences in the passage. Flesch gives instructions for counting sentences:[8]

> In counting sentences, count as a sentence each unit of thought that is grammatically independent of another sentence or clause, if its end is marked by a period, question mark, exclamation point, semicolon or colon. Incomplete sentences or sentence fragments are also to be counted as sentences. For example, count as two sentences: What did the minister talk about? Sin. Count as two sentences: The Lord is my shepherd; I shall not want. Count as three sentences: There are two arguments against this plan: 1. It is too expensive. 2. It is impractical. Count as two sentences: Result: Nobody came. But count as one sentence only: He registered, but he did not vote. (Two independent clauses, combined into a compound sentence with only a comma.) Count as one sentence: There were three people present: Mary, Robert, and John. (The words after the colon are not a separate unit of thought.) Count as one sentence: This project is supposed to: (a) provide training; (b) stimulate suggestions. (No part of this is an independent clause. Count such material as one sentence even if it is paragraphed.)

[8]Rudolf Flesch, How to Test Readability. New York: Harper & Row, Publishers, 1951, p. 3.

In dialogue, count the words he said *or other speech tags as part of the quoted sentence to which they are attached. For example, count as one sentence:* He said: "I have to go." *Count also as one sentence:* "That's all very well," he replied, showing clearly that he didn't believe a word of what we said.

Divide the number of sentences into the number of words to compute the *average sentence length:*

$$\frac{\text{number of words}}{\text{number of sentences}} = \text{average sentence length}$$

Then count the number of two-syllable words, counting repetitions of the same word as half. Multiply by 20, and divide this by the total number of words to get the *two-syllable index:*

$$\frac{\text{number of two-syllable words} \times 20}{\text{number of words}} = \text{two syllable index}$$

Finally, count the number of words of three or more syllables, counting repetitions of the same word as half. Multiply by 300 and divide this by the total number of words to get the *three-syllable index:*

$$\frac{\text{number of three or more syllable words} \times 300}{\text{number of words}} = \text{three syllable index}$$

Then add the totals for the *readability* score (See Figure VI-A). For example, the computation of the two passages from O. Henry is shown in Table 6-1.

TABLE 6-1

	ORIGINAL		REWRITE	
Total number of words:	208		103	
Number of sentences:	12		12	
Average sentence length:	17.33	17.33	8.58	8.58
Number of two-syllable words:	33½		13½	
× 20 ÷ number of words:	3.22	3.22	2.62	2.62
Number of three or more syllable words:	20½		2½	
× 300 ÷ number of words:	29.57	29.57	7.28	7.28
		50.12		18.48

Evaluator   Date

Readability index

Title   Page

Author   Subject

Publisher   Date of publication

Average sentence length [   ]   Intended grade level [   ]
Two syllable index   [   ]   Reading level   [   ]
Three syllable index   [   ]
Readability index   [   ]

FIGURE 6-A   The readability index form.

By use of this readability score alone you can compare a number of works you are considering for class use, as long as you realize that this is just an approximation. Some readability features are difficult to assess, such as degree of abstraction, the writer's skill in clarity of expression, the use of topic headings and other comprehension clues, and the familiarity of the reader with the topic. Even type features can make a difference.[9] Other factors can motivate the student to *want* to read, and motivation is a powerful force (although it does have its limits). Burmeister lists other considerations in determining readability.[10]

> How are paragraphs organized? What types of headings does the author use? (Has the reader formed the habit of studying headings?) What kinds of illustrations, if any, are used? Do they add to, or subtract from, the intended meanings? (Does the reader notice illustrations?) What kind and size print is used? (Is it appropriate to the reader?) Is the paper slick or dull? Is the book hardcover or paperback? (Which does the reader prefer?)
>
> All of these factors affect the difficulty of printed materials. In most cases, there is a definite interaction between factors found in written materials and factors found within the person who is reading.

[9]See: M. D. Vernon, *The Experimental Study of Reading*. New York: Cambridge University Press, 1931, Chapter 7.
[10]Lou E. Burmeister, op cit., p. 27

We have already discussed the *Guiness Book of World Records,* with its interesting subject matter coupled with intriguing pictures and short write-ups. Usually, I find that a generous sprinkling of dramatic illustrations can be very seductive, although there is also something compelling about the paperback pocketsize format. I have had students refuse to read *The Red Pony* or *The Pearl* in an anthology, then purchase it in paperback and read it.

A hot rodder may read directions for installing a new set of shocks that any test will show him "unable" to read. That is why a specific reading inventory is usually the most useful assessment for the classroom teacher. But the readability formula furnishes a quick estimate of how the class will do with the book.

Keeping in mind that readability formulas give only an approximate idea, they can give us a reasonably good basis on which to compare the reading levels of two or more works. In so doing, we are not measuring absolutes, but are looking at relationships. Given three textbooks on food and nutrition, for example, the formula can tell you which one is most likely to be readable by the greatest number of students.

To assign a reading "grade level" to a book is more difficult. Just what constitutes fifth grade, or eighth grade, reading? Literature on the subject is inconsistent. A recent study concluded that most American secondary students are reading "below grade level." But how can you establish the authenticity of a grade level if most students are reading below it? An examination of secondary textbooks reveals little consistency in reading levels.

Therefore, to say that a readability score of 30 equals a grade level of *X* is somewhat hazardous. On the other hand, the problem of textbook selection and the delicate task of matching a particular reader or group of readers with a particular book remains. We need some quantifying basis upon which to classify written material. after an extensive examination of graded textbooks, I suggest the scale listed in Table 6−2.

SEDUCTION IS THE BETTER PART OF SALESMANSHIP

In addition to selecting the right book to fit the ability and interests of each student, there are many things the teacher can do to arouse curiosity in books. One is to display them properly. I usually see books stacked in rows, as on a library shelf. But this shows only the most unattractive part of the book. Book publishers spend thousands of dollars annually to design and print attractive covers. Use them. Put books out on tables or lean them against surfaces with the cover showing. In our experimental school I found

TABLE 6-2

READABILITY SCORE	GRADE LEVEL
0–9	1
10–14	2
15–19	3
20–23	4
24–27	5
28–31	6
32–35	7
36–38	8
39–41	9
42–44	10
45–47	11
48+	12

that books left lying carelessly on the floor were often picked up and looked at first. Cardboard display racks can usually be had for the asking from book dealers, who get them from publishers to display their wares, then throw them away when the next shipment comes in. By cutting out some partitions, you can convert them for use with larger books. See Figure 6-B.

Also shown is a display rack made entirely from throw-away parts by Don Greelis in the Davis Senior High school shops. Don rummaged the junk pile at the auto shop, finding an old hub, which he used for the base; a drive shaft, which he welded to the hub for a center pole; and a larger drive shaft, which fits over the first. He welded a cap on the larger drive shaft so it fits over the smaller and turns. The wire baskets for holding books (given to me by Tower Books, Sacramento) were welded to the outer drive shaft. Then he made the wooden racks from scraps pulled from the woodshop scrap box. The only material we bought was a can of black spray paint. Any industrial arts teacher or talented I. A. student should be able to make you one from the illustration, with an infinite variety of sizes and shapes to meet your needs.

Things can be done to the books themselves to provide eye-catching novelty, once you realize that books are wonderful but hardly sacred. They can be covered, cut, written on, glued, taken apart, and put together differently. Here are just a few ideas:

Cover books with some unusual material, such as cloth, leatherette, or ⅛'' plywood.

Have students illustrate books, and use the products for covers, gluing

FIGURE 6-B   A book display rack.

on with rubber cement so the paper will not wrinkle. Cover this, if possible, with clear Contact, available in most dime stores or wallpaper shops.

Or use all the illustrations submitted, inserting them in the book at appropriate places.

Write captions or comments in the margins.

Take apart, insert the pages into sections cut out of larger sheets, perhaps with blank pages interspaced. Staple groups of pages together for easier handling and put into an illustated folder, or insert into a loose-leaf binder. Invite students to make comments or draw illustrations as they read.

Spray with scents, available from craft shops.

Take the pages apart and put together in the form of an accordian or a scroll.

Wherever space permits, cut pages into interesting shapes.

Tape Recordings

For students who did well on the oral but poorly on the reading forms of the specific reading inventory, rewritten versions of the text may be too simple in content, even if appropriate for their reading ability. There are also students who cannot read even the simpler material. Such students may do better with tape recorded editions of the text, prepared by the teacher or teacher's aide, and kept on file, carefully labeled, in the listening center. Students may hear the lesson over earphones while the others are reading. Simplified versions may be recorded, if necessary, as well as the original. Notes and explanations as well as the study guide may be included on the tape.

A novel twist in tape recording was introduced by William Bell. On the tape he portrayed a student wrestling with his "alter ego," which tried to get him to watch television instead of doing his homework. Each time the alter ego interrupted with an "I don't get it" remark, the student had to explain it to him. This resulted in an interesting, humorous, and effective study guide. The same dramatization could represent a conversation between two friends or a student explaining his homework to a parent.

Of course, if the teacher can read the material to the students, a more effective learning situation will result. A tape recorder is a poor second to direct teacher-student interaction. But it is one answer for the teacher who asks: "How can I take care of all those students at once?"

Fernald, however, cautions against reading to students who are involved in remediation, and this would undoubtedly apply to tape recordings:[11]

> It should be noted here that the children are never read to. They must do all their own reading. Most of them have been read to, in the attempt to get information to them or to compensate for their inability to read, until they expect someone to read anything that seems difficult. While the remedial work is being done, we even insist that no one shall read to the child at home. After the child has developed normal reading skill, there is no objection to having anyone who can get him to listen read to him.

[11]Grace M. Fernald, *Remedial Techniques in Basic School Subjects*. New York: McGraw-Hill Book Company, 1943, p. 52.

Her point is well taken. Students must not get into the habit of thinking that they can always get somebody to do their reading for them. This may be why some are unable to read. I suggest reading to students here because they are not in a clinical situation, but are forced to cope with a demanding and multifaceted curriculum. Listening is a temporary method of getting information for some, and a motivator for others. Sooner or later, however, the student must be told to read for himself, and the sensitive teacher observes when the student has acquired enough skill and confidence for that demand to be effective.

Tutorial Program

In Chapter 4 we discussed a plan for dividing the class into groups that would tutor each other. Many youngsters will learn more as tutors than they will as students. Many will learn more from peer tutors than from teachers.

Volunteer tutors can also be recruited from the community. These volunteers can read to students, answer their questions, go over study guides, prepare tapes, and write simplified reading matter. They can be from parent groups, service clubs, the local college or university, or from within the school. Use the "Future Teachers" club if students develop a stigma about being tutored by their peers: "We're giving them an opportunity to practice teaching." If there is no such group in your school, organize one and arrange for the tutors to get credit for tutoring.

There are many other methods of operating tutorial projects. The entire class may be divided into "interest groups" of from one to six students, each group under the tutelage of a teaching assistant. The teacher would work intensively with the teaching assistants as well as alternating time with each group.

Perhaps only a few students will need special help, in which case they may be assigned to tutors. Singling out a few for tutoring can create an atmosphere of special privilege (which may be an ego-restorer, or create a destructive atmosphere of the "dumb" student needing special help). At times I have recruited sisters or brothers, parents, even girl friends to help a particular individual outside of class time.

Another approach to tutoring is to ask your students to volunteer to go into the nearest elementary school to tutor younger children. This must be arranged between the school administrations. It is an excellent way to get reluctant readers to read material on their own reading level in science, math, social studies, literature and other subjects without the usual stigma. It is also a good way to get reluctant readers interested in learning—by putting them on the side of the teachers instead of the students.

READING TIME   If an elementary school is not available, or even if it is, set up a project to have your students read to youngsters. Most public libraries have a "story time," and most librarians would welcome the help. Or work through churches, convalescent homes, hospitals, and youth clubs. Or even visit homes. Discuss with your students the importance of being read to, so they will realize the value of their services. This is another method of getting students to read low level material without stigma. You can give them easy reading children's books and teach them to "read aloud to children," using emphasis, dramatic pauses, and periodic eye contact.

STUDY CENTERS   In many communities study centers are available where your students can tutor or read to youngsters. If not, you can set up your own. For minority pupils, contact the local Urban League (Black), Concilio (Chicano), or Asian-American Concern. Or see your local Community Services Council or Human Relations Committee.

One important ingredient of a good tutorial program is the teacher working closely with the tutors, whether these be his own students or outside volunteers. Some tutors will be quite competent and know just what to do. But many will need lots of help, material, ideas, and supervision.

THE HARD-CORE—DECODING

Decoding is the primary level of reading. It involves "cracking the code"—translating written symbols into speech. The reader matches letters with sounds, building sounds into words and words into meaningful utterances.

Simplification techniques are useful for students who are below the instructional reading level of your text, but who can read simple material. Fortunately, there are not many total nonreaders in secondary schools, but when they are encountered, they are a very difficult problem. The teacher frequently has to decide whether to not require reading, but to use tapes or tutors to read the lesson to the nonreader, or to attempt to teach the student to read. This latter course is difficult and time-consuming, but with study and practice the classroom teacher can learn to teach reading.

This may be done by the teacher personally, but more likely the teacher will train tutors or aides to work with individuals. First, however, a word of caution. There are some types of nonreaders with whom the classroom teacher should be extremely cautious about attempting to teach decoding, and in many cases not attempt it at all.

THE LOW IQ STUDENT   As discussed in Chapter 3, too many students have been classified as low in IQ, or retarded, as the result of a test score, a language deficiency, or an emotional problem. Many a student so classified has been saved by alert and sensitive teachers who noted other symptoms of intelligence (see pp. 38–42) and worked with the student until good things happened. But if a student really does have a low IQ, and if this is the reason for failure to learn, then capacity for learning is limited. Concentrated work in reading can be frustrating to student and teacher alike. If attempted at all, reading instruction must be very low key, relaxed, unhurried, non-competitive, ungraded, and if possible, fun. Few teachers have this kind of time to devote to one student. Not all tutors have the understanding, the skills, or the patience, but some can be trained, using the techniques in the balance of this and the next two chapters.

THE HOSTILE-RELUCTANT STUDENT   Many young people are so filled with resentment that they are too emotional to focus on school. Thus they have never learned to read, and do not intend to learn. Such a one may secretly yearn to read, but be unable at this point to invest the confidence in any teacher. You may, of course, become the one adult in his life that he does trust and like. In that case, you may be the one adult who can teach him to read. But otherwise, if you do not deal effectively with the hostility first, you may end up increasing it.

THE DEFEATED STUDENT   Years of perpetual failure leave the young-ster convinced she cannot learn to read. To protect her self-image from continual erosion, she eventually gives up. It is very difficult to break through the defenses of such students and get them to risk further humilia-tion. Pressure to perform often results in further withdrawal.

THE SEVERELY HANDICAPPED STUDENT   The severely handicapped student has probably been removed from your classroom, but current trend is to return students to regular classes if they can possibly cope with the situation. In such a case, or if you suspect a student has a hearing or vision loss, neurological handicap, or orthopedic impairment severe enough to cause dyslexia, the classroom teacher should work closely with a reading specialist. (See Chapter 3.)

In addition to identifying and referring problem students to a reading specialist, the classroom teacher may also work on *reading readiness* by attempting to raise the IQ through exposure to rich and varied experiences, by reducing hostility with a warm, trusting, and nonthreatening classroom atmosphere, by placing the student in room positions to see or hear better, and by building the student's ego through success experiences and recogni-tion. Much can be accomplished by softening the pressure to perform by establishing a feeling of noncompetition and cooperation. When substantial progress has been achieved in these areas, *then* begin teaching reading.

In the balance of this and in the next three chapters, we shall discuss seven types of decoding "clues" by which readers identify new words. Each approach has a value as a method of teaching reading, as well as limitations. These are: *configuration, sight word, context, phonology, morphology, syllabication,* and *dictionary.*

Configuration Clues

Configuration clues are based on word shapes. The reader associates words with the overall letter pattern:

house   mother   say   pizza   wish   young

Certain letters or combinations of letters may stand out, such as the double *z* in *pizza.* This method is very limited, used mainly by beginners and by very slow readers. Although evidence concerning use of configuration clues is inconclusive, readers who consistently confuse such words as *house* and *horse, say* and *may,* or *hit* and *hid* may be overly dependent on configuration. In the early stages, it is well to point out the shapes of letters—which ones extend above the line (ascenders), and which ones go below (descenders). Some preliminary word distinctions may thus be made, but configuration as a teaching tool is more valuable to distinguish letters. Differentiations such as *n* and *h, b* and *d,* or *b* and *p* may be handled by configuration. Teachers can work out their own way of describing those letters that stick up, hang down, or point this way or that. Spache suggests the use of certain memory devices, such as identifying *dog* by the curly tail at the end, or *look* by the two eyes in the middle.[12]

Sight Vocabulary

Sight vocabulary involves recognizing the "whole word." It is sometimes called "look-say," since the reader simply looks at the word and says it from recognition. It is frequently employed as the first approach to teaching reading because most students learning sight vocabulary can build up a large stock of words in a short time. Sight vocabulary teaching recognizes that good readers read whole words, actually whole phrases, at a time, that ultimately, good reading depends upon having a huge inventory of instant-recognition words. But *total* dependence upon sight vocabulary does not

[12]George D. Spache, *Toward Better Reading.* Champaign, Ill.: Garrard Publishing Company, 1963, p. 235.

give the reader the tools for recognizing new and unfamiliar words. Therefore, other, more analytic (phonic) methods are also needed. Conversely, the reader who becomes over-dependent upon phonics to read everything cannot progress beyond the slow, painful, letter-by-letter and word-by-word method of the poor reader. See p. 24. Often the elementary reading teacher begins reading with sight vocabulary, then introduces phonic analysis as a tool for decoding the new and unfamiliar.

The secondary teacher can use a number of sources for selecting words for teaching sight recognition. One is a basal reading series, which has the advantage of (1) carefully controlled vocabulary, (2) words selected for progressive difficulty, and (3) all new words repeated frequently. Unfortunately, the stories are juvenile and insulting to a secondary school student. For many students, already struggling to maintain a semblance of ego in the face of continual scholastic disaster, such a reading program would be unthinkable.

A sight list can also be built around the textbook and the course vocabulary. This material may be interesting. It can help the student feel that he is on a level with his peers, but it may be beyond the ability of the nonreader. You can hardly expect him to get *numerator* and *denominator* if he is having trouble with *of* and *from*.

A third alternative is to bring in any book, magazine, pamphlet, clipping—anything the student is interested in learning or reading. An automobile buff may work on *The First Book of Automobiles* and actually learn the vocabulary which is "too hard" for him. If necessary, break up this material, word for word, and teach each word as a unit. Write the words on flash cards (Be sure your printing resembles the type in the book.) and let him practice with you or an aide or take the cards home to work by himself or with a tutor. Then—and this is extremely important—arrange the words into phrases and sentences and have him read for *meaning*. Do not just have him read aloud. You may, for example, arrange the words into a sentence:

The piston is attached to a rod.

Instead of asking the student to read aloud, ask questions:

What is attached to a rod?

You may or may not want to continue questioning, depending upon the answer you get.

Do not worry about "covering the material." If a reluctant reader in a general science class only learns the principle of the internal combustion engine, this is more valuable than trudging his way through a text that only teaches him to hate both science and reading. If he improves his reading, building a sight vocabulary of a few dozen words, this is even more valuable. And if he builds his self-confidence by enjoying some small measure of success, you will be one of the few great teachers in his life.

A fourth clue is found in *Teacher,* Sylvia Ashton-Warner's beautiful description of her method of teaching reading to Maori children in New Zealand. The author describes the first words she uses in reading instruction and the importance of letting them spring from within the reader:[13]

> *First words must mean something to a child.*
>
> *First words must have intense meaning for a child. They must be part of his being.*
>
> *How much hangs on the love of reading, the instinctive inclination to hold a book! Instinctive. That's what it must be. The reaching out for a book needs to become an organic action, which can happen at this yet formative age. Pleasant words won't do. Respectable words won't do. They must be words organically tied up, organically born from the dynamic life itself. They must be words that are already part of the child's being.*

Sylvia Ashton-Warner wrote this about working with small children. But how do you transfer her "organic vocabulary" for use with American secondary school students? Throughout this volume we have discussed the need to base education on the thoughts, the feelings, and the interests of the student, rather than on a preconceived course of study, particularly for the reluctant reader. But for the true nonreader, where do you start? The chances of finding something on his interest level but also within his reading capacity are slim.

One technique is as follows: sit down with a typewriter in front of you, paper inserted ready for action. Begin a conversation with your pupil. Talk about something real. Suppose it goes like this:

Teacher: Hi, Tom. I saw you at the game last night. What'd you think about that last-minute touchdown?

Tom: Aw—O.K., I guess.

At this point the teacher types: *Aw—O.K., I guess.* Type it exactly as it is said. Do not "correct" anything, but use standard spelling. Pull the paper out of the typewriter immediately and give it to Tom. Ask him to read what you have written. Almost everyone, including total nonreaders will be able to. Only in the most extreme cases will the teacher have to help, and then it may be an emotional or attitudinal problem. But if the student seems willing to try, then begin by teaching him to read the words he has just spoken.

---

[13]Sylvia Ashton-Warner, *Teacher.* New York: Bantam Books, 1963, p. 30.

Because he has used them in conversation, they are no doubt familiar and part of his "organic" vocabulary. After the reading, quickly put the paper back and continue:

Teacher: I was afraid we'd really get clobbered because they were so much heavier. But we seemed faster. Some of those end runs were pretty exciting.

Tom: We'd a did better passing.

Now type that: *We'd a did better passing.* Type it exactly—no cheating. After Tom has read this bit, focus his attention on what he has done. Ask questions:

"*Point to the word* passing."
"*How do you spell* did?"
"*What is* this *word?*"

In a few minutes you can have half a page of typing which Tom has read. Give him the page and congratulate him on beginning to learn to read. Point out that there are about twenty words which he can read now by sight. If he'll keep working on these words—and add a few more each day—he'll be surprised how soon he'll be reading. For reinforcement, write the words—or if he can, have him write the words—each on a separate 3 x 5 index card. Then he can drill himself or have somebody drill him on the words separately. He can match the individual words with the written page, arrange the cards in proper sequence, or compose new sentences.

Each day a new conversation, a few new words added to the pile. Soon he can "write" with his word cards. But be careful not to get so involved in reading words that Tom forgets to read meaning. Continually ask questions that will challenge him to discover what the words collectively mean. Gradually expand from brief "one liners" to more extensive utterances. The goal is to get Tom to tell, and ultimately to write, about himself, expanding his range to paragraphs and finally stories and essays. But the essence of the method is to have Tom read only his own words, which express his thoughts, his feelings, and his experiences. This is the "language experience" approach discussed on pp. 34–36.

Why can nonreaders often read what they have just said? They can usually read *their own organic vocabulary,* the words they use to express their own thoughts. Also, having just said the words, they are working largely from memory. By giving Tom something he can do, you give him a success experience. Even if he is just saying the words from memory, he *feels* he is reading. And having read the words once, he has a better than average chance of retaining them, particularly if you continue to reinforce them with subsequent drill.

After a while, start typing in some of *your* dialogue for him to read. Later he may want to do the typing. Encourage this, even if you have to spell every word for him.

Gradually—very slowly—start to wean the student away from the organic sentences, first by rearranging the words into new sentences, then little by little having him point out words, then phrases, then sentences in printed material. Bridging the gap from reading one's own words to reading those of another is important, for the real reason for learning to read is to communicate with a writer. Thus the dictation approach is only a starter—a motivator and an initial skill and confidence builder. It may be months before you get away from the typewriter, and more months to get through the weaning process. Do not be impatient. Tom has gone many years without learning to read, and if you can get him started after all his repeated failures, you're performing miracles. Anyone for a miracle?

Context Clues

O Romeo, Romeo! Wherefore art thou Romeo?

You have just read the most misunderstood line in all English literature. I have yet to find a group, including graduate classes in English and drama, in which the majority did not interpret that line to mean *Where are you, Romeo?* But there is no comma before *Romeo* to indicate a noun of address. And read the rest of the line:

> **Deny thy father, and refuse thy name;**
> **Or, if thou wilt not, be but sworn my love,**
> **And I'll no longer be a Capulet.**

Does Juliet seem to be asking *where?* Let's continue:

> **'Tis but thy name that is my enemy;**
> **Thou art thyself though, not a Montague. . . .**

As one reads, it becomes clearer that this speech is not about *where,* but about *who,* or more specifically, about *names.*

> **What's in a name? That which we call a rose**
> **By any other name would smell as sweet;**

If we fail to pick up on such obvious clues, we have not been trained to examine *content*—to read the whole passage and to make an educated guess about the meaning of a new word or a complex phrase. In the line from *Romeo and Juliet,* the key word is *wherefore,* which means not where, but *why.* So we find that Juliet is not asking where Romeo is, but why, having fallen madly, hopelessly in love—why of all the nice young men in Verona—why did it turn out to be Romeo, the son of the family's deadly enemy! So now we have added a new word to our vocabulary—*wherefore,* which means *why.*

If we can teach our students to pick up on context clues, they will not only add new words to their reading, speaking, and recognition vocabularies, but save themselves many hours of trudging off to the dictionary. In the example above, the clue to the word *wherefore* was in the general meaning of the passage. But there are other types of context clues:

Built-in explanation:
The Rolling Stones played a *medley* of their most popular songs.

Synonym or antonym:
Accept the fact that she's a *diurnal,* and you're a nocturnal.[14]

Metaphor (A figure of speech in which a word or phrase carries an implied comparison with something else) (See also p. 270).
He is a *disaster* trying to happen.

Simile (A metaphor in which the comparison is specified by words such as *like* or *as*) (See also p. 270).
His ego *expanded* like a balloon.

Appositive: (A noun or noun phrase which follows another noun or noun phrase and carries the same meaning).
He is a *hypocrite,* one who preaches love and practices hate.

Contrast:
This time we hired a little old lady. The more *voluptuous* types had been distracting the boys around the office.

Situation or mood:
The ghostly figure started forward, and we *recoiled* in horror.

[14]Thanks to Ann Landers.

Humor:

The thing about this ending that makes us even madder,
It's a test of the *endurance* of the music lover's bladder.[15]

Summary statement:

It was, in short, complete *devastation.*

Following is a suggestion for introducing the class to context clues as a decoding method. Its object is to convince students that educated guesses can be made with no prior knowledge about the meaning of a new word. First, have the class read the following exercise:

As we entered the park, we noticed that the glubug was so tame it came right up to us and begged for a handout. It would hold up its little gahuten for us to fill, and if we failed to deliver a morsel mahali, it would proceed to climb into our pockets, back packs, or any likely looking hiding place.

If the search yielded results she would whompf the stolen morsel down with great relish. But if she failed to uncover anything edible she would lose all interest in us and klankel away, utterly geshmecken.

Then, ask questions:

Write an essay about the glubug. Tell everything you know, but be sure you say nothing you cannot justify on the basis of the above.

What goes gahuten mean?

Select the best synonym for mahali:

tasty	*running*	*small animal*
quickly	*meat*	*broad-leaf plant*

What part of speech is whompf?

Does klankel have a plural form? A past tense form?

List three synonyms for geshmecken.

After the questions have been answered, ask: How did you figure out the answers? How did you know the meanings of words that do not even exist? This can lead quite naturally into a discussion of context.

Additional material for developing skill in reading context clues can be composed from text passages or other written material:

The world of microorganisms is inhabited by creatures that are invisible to the eye.[16]

---

[15]Alan Sherman Record: *Variations on How Dry I Am.*

[16]From Biological Sciences Curriculum Study. *Biological Science: An Inquiry into Life,* 3rd ed., New York: Harcourt, Brace, Jovanovich, Inc., 1973, p. 452.

What does *inhabited* mean? Any explanation that means *composed of* or *populated by* is acceptable. Even logical guesses, such as *infected by* are acceptable. These latter indicate the limitations as well as the value of context clues.

Or try leaving out a key word and having students fill it in:

> *Biologists began to* _____ *this world only after the microscope had been invented.*[16a]

The word is *explore,* but any logical answer, including *observe, understand, appreciate,* and so forth, indicates the student is getting the idea.

As Gray observed, "Context clues are perhaps the most important single aid to word perception."[17] We not only determine new words by context, but we are able to read rapidly because the context carries us along. It also enables us to tell the difference between such words as:

> This is my *last* class today.
> How long will these shoes *last?*
> The cobbler has leather but no *last* has he.
>
> *Lead* on, and I shall follow.
> This gasoline contains *lead.*

Secondary textbooks are full of passages that can expand the students' knowledge and vocabularies through context clues:

> *This setup can be used to measure the rate of respiration for a small organism. Remember that during respiration an organism uses up oxygen and gives off carbon dioxide.*[18]

Many of the junior high school students for whom this text was written may not know that *respiration* is simply a fancy word for *breathing.* But they may know that breathing involves using up oxygen and giving off carbon dioxide. Or they may know what respiration is—may recognize it and even use it orally—but not identify it in written form. Or it may work the other way. They may have no trouble with *respiration* but be stumped by *carbon dioxide, organism,* or even *oxygen.* In any event, the close interrelationship of these words can be a giveaway, once the student is trained to think in terms of content. Much of this training consists of having the teacher ask the right questions:

[16a]From Biological Sciences Curriculum Study. Op. cit.

[17]William S. Gray, *On Their Own in Reading.* Glenview, Ill.: Scott Foresman and Company, 1960, p. 25.

[18]Gary D. Day, et al. *You and the Environment: An Investigative Approach.* Boston: Houghton Mifflin Company, 1976, p. 78.

Student: What does this word mean?

Teacher: Take a good look at the sentence. What happens during the process?

Student: (*reading*) The organism uses up oxygen and gives off carbon dioxide.

Teacher: Right. Can you think of anything you and I do that uses up oxygen and gives off carbon dioxide?

Student: Well—we breathe.

Teacher: Right again. So it's just a five dollar word for _____?

Student: Breathing!

Teacher: Very good. You're learning to use context clues. Now can you pronounce it?

Student: Ah – Res—res—

Teacher: Respiration.

Student: Respiration.

Teacher: Good. Say it a couple of more times.

Student: Respiration. Respiration.

Teacher: Here's a piece of scratch paper. See if you can write it without looking. Watch your spelling.

Thus far we have examined three methods of decoding new words: configuration, sight vocabularly, and context. These approaches are somewhat intuitive, that is, the student recognizes new words largely by prior knowledge or an educated guess. In the next two chapters we shall examine the more analytical, systematic approaches to word attack.

CHAPTER 7
The Systems of Language
Phonics I—The Sounds of People

There are few areas in education on which so many unqualified opinions have been lavished as on the subject of phonics. Since Rudolf Flesh's *Why Johnny Can't Read*[1] shocked American parents into believing that failure to teach phonics was the great crime of a hopelessly "Progressive" school system, much criticism has been heaped upon reading programs. Although some criticism is valid, much of it is simplistic.

An effective reading program utilizes many instructional methods, partly because each has its own particular usefulness and also because different students learn differently. Some are intuitive, and learn quickly by whole word; others are more analytical, and depend largely on phonics. Good readers tend to use the whole word method and fall back upon phonics for decoding new words.

Phonics is a method of teaching the reader to analyze written matter into constituent parts, then to synthesize the parts into words and utterances. It involves far more than "sounding it out," as we shall presently discover.

LANGUAGE SYSTEMS

Languages do not develop at random, but tend to follow patterns, or *systems*. These patterns are sometimes inconsistent and confusing because people do not speak or write in precise mathematical fashion. Nevertheless, each language system has a framework, and in order to communicate, we can only be inconsistent within the limits of that framework. For example, English has a *syntactic*, or grammatical framework that dictates a rather rigid word order for sentences. Certain deviations are permissible within the language, but others are not. The general rule in sentence construction, for example, is that

[1]New York: Harper & Row, Publishers, 1955.

in English the subject comes before the predicate. But witness the well-known poem:

Ooey Gooey was a worm,	(Subject first.)
A little worm was he.	(Predicate first.)
He sat upon the railroad track;	(Subject first.)
The train he did not see.	(Predicate first.)
Ooey Gooey!	(Sentence has neither subject nor predicate.)

On the other hand, one could not say:

Was Ooey Gooey worm a.[2]

The same is true of other systems. In the *graphemic,* or written system, one can make a capital *A* like this **A** , like this **ꓤ**, or like this *a*, but not like this **ᐊ**. In the *orthographic* (spelling) system, one can spell *color c o l o r,* as preferred in the United States, or *c o l o u r,* as preferred in England, but never **I r u o c o.**

In addition to the above-mentioned syntactic, graphemic and orthographic systems, English consists of the *phonemic,* or sound system; the *morphemic,* or meaning system; and the *syllabic,* or articulation system. Teaching to read by phonics involves teaching the student to decode the symbols of the graphemic system into those of the phonemic and to a lesser extent the morphemic and the syllabic systems; in short, how writing is decoded into speech.

The teacher of phonics should know considerably more about language systems than is necessary for the student. One can drive an automobile quite well knowing very little about the workings of the internal combustion engine. But the mechanic needs to understand each engine part and how it functions. For example, one of the basic rules of phonics is that in most three-letter, consonant-vowel-consonant words, the vowel carries the *short* sound:

fat   tap   mil   dot   rip

but when a final *e* is added, the first vowel becomes long and the *e* silent:

fate tape mile dote ripe

To teach these words, it is usually not necessary to go into definitions of long-short vowels. It is enough to tell the student that *f a t* spells *fat,* and

---

[2]An asterisk is used by linguists to indicate that the utterance as written is not one that would be used by a native speaker of that language.

when you add a final e, the e is silent and the word becomes *fate*. (Final e makes the other vowel say its name.) For most students, this is sufficient. Occasionally, however, you will encounter someone who will have difficulty with such incomplete information, who learns faster and retains longer when he has a principle to hang on to. For such a student, you may need to give more information. Many students will discover principles for themselves, so that after learning a great many consonant-vowel-consonant words, they will intuitively make the bridge from *tub* to *tube*. It is when the student is not making the transfers that the teacher has to supply information. This is frequently the case with deficient readers.

LET'S READ

For years phonics was taught by what Lyman Hunt describes as the *Letter-Sound-Blend* method.[3] This means that the student was trained to look at the letter or group of letters and attach the appropriate sound, repeat the process for all the letters in the word, and finally blend together the whole cluster. This system is still experiencing widespread usage, and is not without merit. However, the Bloomfield–Barnhart system pioneers what Hunt calls the *Letter-Sound-Relationship* method. Words are arranged so the most common patterns of the language are encountered first. The student, seeing the same letters take the same pronunciation over and over, learns, or rather absorbs, phonic principles inductively, without having to be taught. These common patterns are called the *regular* spellings. After introducing all the regular spellings, the student learns the irregularities. But by then, the reader has a large instant-recognition vocabulary and is able to cope with more difficult words, having built up self-confidence. This suggests that there is a definite sequence that should be followed in teaching a student to read, and this sequence concerns teaching the most common patterns of the language first. Karlin[4] calls this the *family* method, as distinguished from what he refers to as the *synthetic* system. He also discusses a third approach, the *analytic*, in which "The learner is taught to take down words and make appropriate substitutions in them to form the new word." For example:

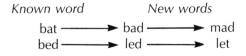

	Known word		New words	
	bat	⟶	bad ⟶	mad
	bed	⟶	led ⟶	let

[3]Lyman Hunt, "The Right Questions About Phonics." *Education*, May 1962, 82, 540–544.
[4]Robert Karlin, *Teaching Reading in High School.* 2nd ed., Indianapolis: The Bobbs-Merrill Co., Inc., 1972, pp. 124–125.

The first step in learning to read, say Bloomfield and Barnhart is to learn to speak the language. This seems basic, but I am convinced that one of the major reasons some students have difficulty reading is that we give them textbooks filled with words that are not part of their speaking, that is, their organic vocabulary. We cannot read an unfamiliar word. It makes no sense. We may guess, based on context or phonics, but we must learn the word before we can read it.

A good example is the word *top*, which appears in many reading primers, alongside a picture of a children's toy. But how many children today play with tops or know what a top is? Even in my day, they were passé. In the higher grades, the problem is compounded for those students whose vocabularies are inadequate to cope with the demands of textbooks in science, mathematics, social studies, literature, and the many other subjects. This is why conversation is an important reading readiness exercise, building as it does the growing person's vocabulary, knowledge, and concepts. Just listening to a teacher, another student, or even a tape recorder is good preparation for reading.

The second step is learning the alphabet—first being able to recognize and name all the capitals, then the lower case letters. They claim that this should be mastered before attempting to read. The advice is sound for the bright young preschoolers for whom the system was originally devised (Bloomfield's adopted children), but many remedial readers have difficulty learning the alphabet. There are so many different characters that the whole process becomes confusing.

I have frequently had better success with this type of remedial reader by teaching the alphabet as needed. I show the student the word *man*, for example, and teach three letters: *m-a-n*. Next, I add the letter *c* and teach *can*, then *f* for *fan*, and so forth. This gives the letters meaning, some connection with real speech, and helps the student feel he is reading, rather than remaining hopelessly hung up on learning the alphabet.

The final readiness experience is making left-to-right and top-to-bottom patterns habitual. *Let's Read* includes exercises designed to train the eye in these directions. My own experience has been that this is not a major problem for most older readers, and that the best left-to-right training is reading.

The content of *Let's Read* is hardly likely to stimulate anyone to explore the exciting world of reading. Bloomfield claims that this is not important because the student is focused on learning to read and not on content. I doubt that this is true even for the bright young children for whom his system was devised, and it is less true for older students, turned-off students, and for the boys who constitute the bulk of our remedial problems. Therefore, I suggest that the teacher not rely on this system alone, but alternate it with other, more motivating methods, such as the organic approach described on pp. 156 and 157, reading to students, and using tape recorders and other high-interest material.

Now let us examine the first lesson in *Let's Read* (Figure 7-A).

can Dan fan man Nan pan ran tan an
ban van

a can a fan a pan a man a van
a tan van a tan fan

Dan ran. Nan ran.
Van ran. A man ran.

Nan can fan Dan.
Can Dan fan Nan?
Dan can fan Nan.
Nan, fan Dan.
Dan, fan Nan.

Dan ran a van.
Dan ran a tan van.
A man ran a tan van.

FIGURE 7-A   Lesson 1 from *Let's Read*. (Wayne State University Press, 1961.)

There is only 1 vowel on the page, the *a*, but there are 10 consonants. This is consistent with a very important principle of phonic instruction: *teach the consonants first, then the vowels.* Consonants are relatively regular and easy to learn. Most of the trouble is with the vowels. Most students can learn the sounds of all the consonants in the alphabet in the time it takes to learn only a couple of vowel sounds.

With only one exception, all the letters are pronounced exactly the same way every time. This is the key to the *Let's Read* system. The student is not confused by learning the sound of *g* in *go* (hard *g*) and then encountering *general* (soft *g*). He associates each letter with a single sound, with enough repetitions to learn the association.

The exception is the one-letter word *a*, which has two possible pronunciations. In isolation, most speakers pronounce this word with the "long" sound, as in *say*. But in ordinary speech, it may come out with the "schwa" sound, as in *afford*. (The terms *schwa* and *long vowel* will be explained shortly.)

In teaching *Let's Read* to a nonreader, it might be worthwhile to reproduce each of the words and phrases on the page on a separate flash card, being careful to make your letters resemble those on the printed page. Show the student each word, one at a time, and if he cannot read it immediately, tell him the word. Spell it for him and have him spell it and pronounce it several times before going on to the next word.

When enough flash cards have been collected, arrange them to form sentences, or have the student do so. Encourage silly sentences, such as *I am a tan van,* or *A hat can pat a fat cat,* as long as they are structured grammatically.

Next, introduce the single word *a* as a separate lesson. Point out that this word is pronounced differently from all the other *a's* on the list. Accept whichever pronunciation comes naturally to the student. There is no "preferred" pronunciation. Concentrate on the reading problem, and don't get sidetracked by irrelevancies such as pronunciation, which can lead to more reading problems by making the process unnecessarily difficult and progress slow.

However, the pronunciation problem may intrude upon the lesson in spite of your efforts to keep it out. For example, a student may say something like, "But I don't pronounce the *e* in *get* the same as in *yes*." He will probably be right, and have a good sense of phonetics, if he can distinguish /get/ from his pronunciation—/git/. When this happens, I would explain that English is spoken many different ways by different people, and this is just one example. It is impossible to produce an extensive list of English words that everyone pronounces alike. Keep the explanation short, matter-of-fact, honest, and nonthreatening. Admit freely that this is one example of English irregular spelling, and one reason why it is a difficult language to learn to read. Be particularly careful not to state or imply that any pronunciation is better than any other. Keep the discussion simple and concentrate on learning to read.

The second vowel, *i*, is not found until Lesson 9. By then, the student has encountered all the regular consonants except *k* and *z*. *Q* and *x* are not included in the list of regular consonants because they merely repeat sounds that are also spelled with other, more common letters. Their use early in the process would be confusing. The letter *c* is included because, even though it also repeats sounds of other letters (*k* and *s*), it is used so frequently in English that it must be introduced early to spell many common words. But it always has the sound of /k/ (hard c), and that is why the letter *k* is not introduced early. The letter z has not been introduced because so far all words are monosyllabic with three or fewer letters, and there are few such common words in English beginning with z.

The letter k is introduced in Lesson 10. At this point, it would be worthwhile to tell the student that we now have two letters that are pronounced /k/, but point out that in spelling, k and c cannot substitute for each other.

The introduction of the letter z in Lesson 15 completes the list of regular consonants, with only two vowels—a and i. The balance of Part I is devoted to introducing the other three short vowels—u as in bus, e as in bet, o as in cot.

Special attention should be called to the schwa sound, spelled here with a u (fun, but, us, cub), but spelled phonetically with the symbol /ə/ on the chart on p. 178. This is the central vowel sound of the English language (See vowel positions, p. 182) but has no single spelling. It can be spelled with u as in must, e (the), o (son), i (sir), a (China), or with diphthongs in words such as mountain or young.

At the end of the section is a set of tests, which include a number of nonsense syllables, designed to see if the student has caught on to the phonic principles involved, or if he is sight reading whole words.

If the student can pronounce the words in the tests with minimal help, particularly if he can pronounce the nonsense syllables, it would be a reasonable assumption that he has learned that much of the phonic system. This is the essence of the Let's Read method. The student learns to make sound-letter relationships not just by being told, but by seeing the same combinations over and over.

But if the student is having difficulty at this point, especially if she is unable to pronounce the nonsense syllables, it might be well to introduce the first formal lessons in phonics, explaining the principle of sound-letter relationships, going back over preceding lessons to point out that every letter is always pronounced the same way, and doing more drill work to help form the proper associations.

LANGUAGE AND SYSTEMS

Thus far we have been able to discuss vowels and consonants, long and short sounds, and other linguistic terminology because most educated speakers of English have at least a general idea of what we are talking about. But a professional needs more profound knowledge. Let us, therefore, take a brief look at the systems that compose our language.

The Written System

The written, or *graphemic*, system is *alphabetic*. The characters, or letters stand for *sounds,* as opposed to those of most Oriental languages, which stand for words. Thus the Chinese or Japanese speaker must learn several thousand characters to read and write his language, whereas the English speaker need only learn 26. The third type of writing is hieroglyphic, or picture writing, in which the characters resemble, in stylized form, the word or concept depicted. But while English writing is alphabetic (based on sound), it is only partially *phonetic*. This means that there is only an approximate relationship between letters and sounds, that one letter may represent more than one sound, and a sound may be written different ways. This inconsistency is the main reason why English speaking school children have more difficulty learning to read and write their language than German or Spanish speakers, whose language is more phonetic.

The English alphabet is *sequential*. Each letter is assigned a first, second, third, and so forth, place from a to z. This makes it easy to index lists of things, such as names in a telephone directory or words in a dictionary. Learning this sequence is basic to being able to use almost any kind of reference tool.

Of the 26 letters, 5 (a — e — i — o — u) are considered *vowels,* and 21 (b — c — d — f — g — h — j — k — l — m — n — p — q — r — s — t — v — w — x — y — z) are *consonants*. The difference between consonant and vowel in the written system is somewhat arbitrary, although based roughly on the sound system. We shall discuss consonants and vowels when we look at language sounds.

This written system is comparatively simple. We have described its most important characteristics in a few paragraphs and merely summarized and classified information which you, as literate English speakers, already know. The phonic difficulty your students experience is not, therefore, in learning the written system so much as coping with letter-sound relationships, trying to decipher words such as *through* and *threw* or *cough* and *tough*.

The Sound System

The sound, or *phonemic*, system is more complex. The science of phonology is the study of speech sounds. The phonetician divides the sound system of language into its simplest units, called *phonemes*. The phoneme is the smallest sound unit of the language. It cannot be subdivided and the native speaker of a language can distinguish it from other phonemes. In writing, phonemes are enclosed in slashes (//) to indicate that they stand for sounds, not letters. To clarify still further, letters and words are frequently written in italics (underlined in typing. *A* and *a* refer to the first *letter* of the written alphabet. But /a/ refers to the middle *sound* (phoneme) in the word *cat*.

Phonology consists of *phonetics* and *phonemics*. Although these two terms are frequently confused, they do not mean the same. Phonetics is the study of human vocal sounds—how they are produced, their infinite variations, and what they sound like. Phonemics is the study of the sound system of language, as used by a native speaker of that language. In other words, vocal sounds *as they exist,* and *as they are perceived in the mind of the speaker* are not the same.

To illustrate this, consider the sound /p/ in *pill* and *spill*. Are they the same? Hold a sheet of notebook paper with the top edge between thumb and one finger, the rest of the paper hanging loosely in front of your face, with the bottom edge about an inch from your lips. Say *pill*. Note the little puff of air that moves the paper on /p/. Now say *spill*. Note that the paper does not move as much. That little puff of air with *pill* is called *aspiration*. Now ask a sampling of English speakers if the letter *p* has the same sound in *pill* and *spill*. I have yet to find one with no linguistic training who did not say yes. Thus /p/ is a single phoneme in English, because English speakers do not recognize the difference between aspirated and unaspirated sounds. But in phonetics, /p/ would be distinguished from /p^h/.

At birth, we were capable of learning to recognize and produce an infinite variety of speech sounds. But as we grew, we began to hear and imitate the language around us. That language made use of only a few of the many possible vocal sounds. These were the sounds we learned to recognize and reproduce. Unconsciously, we began to think of them as *the* sounds of language, until today we have difficulty recognizing any others. When we hear speakers of certain unfamiliar languages, those languages may sound jumbled to us because they use sounds that our ears have not learned to distinguish.

Even within our own language, we only learn to recognize those sounds that we use to distinguish one word from another. We can tell the difference, for example, between /p/ and /b/, although these sounds are very similar, because we must distinguish between such words as *pill* and *bill* or *mop* and *mob*. But there are no words in English that are distinguished by whether they are aspirated.

Another interesting example is the contrast between *gear* and *gore*. Almost any English speaker with no training in phonetics, will tell you that the initial sounds of these two words, represented in both cases by *g*, are identical. But if you listen carefully as you say them, you can hear a difference. The second sound in gear is long e /ē/, while the second sound of gore is /ȯ/. The English consonant /g/ is conditioned by the succeeding phoneme, that is, the tongue gets "set" to make the next sound. Thus the tongue is brought forward on gear, because /ē/ is a frontal vowel and back on gore, because /ȯ/ is produced at the rear of the vowel area. But English speakers do not hear the difference because there are no English words that are differentiated on the basis of front or back /g/.

We also have little difficulty distinguishing between the unvoiced sound /s/ and voiced /z/. We have such word pairs as ice and eyes, zeal and seal. But had we been brought up to speak Spanish, we would find it very difficult to hear and produce the sound /z/, because it is not used in Spanish. Thus when the teacher explains to the class the difference between the sounds of the letters s and z, many Spanish speakers are lost. To them the teacher seems to say: "The letter s is pronounced /s/, but the letter z is pronounced /s/." These same students tend to substitute /ē/ for /i/. And if you consider the many linguistic differences between English and other languages, it seems a wonder that so many non-native speakers learn to read English.

This is why an understanding of phonetics and phonemics is important to teachers. Frequently, we and our students are simply not communicating—literally speaking different languages. Even native speakers can have the identical trouble when the student and his teacher (or the writer of his reading textbook) speak different dialects. We have noted the student who says /git/ for get, and then is taught to read get along with bed, men, and yes. If these dialectal differences crop up frequently enough, the student may become so confused that he may decide reading is not for him.

In most cases, pronunciation will offer no problem. The student may be aware of his dialect ("I jist talk sloppy," said a student to me recently), or he may not have a sensitive enough ear to distinguish sounds. Or he may simply make allowances for English inconsistencies.

But when students are confused, reading problems can result. The first step towards solution, of course, is to recognize the problem—that different students hear different sounds. Next, the teacher must rid himself of the tendency to be continually "correcting" pronunciation, and to zero in on the problem of reading. The teacher must be able to explain, when necessary, about dialectal differences and the approximate nature of the sound-letter relationships in English. Also, the sensitive teacher learns to listen to the student, learns to hear differences in pronunciation, and learns to tell when these differences are causing reading problems.

Finally, the teacher has to decide what kind of help the student needs.

As long as the reading problem is critical, concentrate on it. But when the student has made substantial progress in word-attack—when she can say the words and sentences and score reasonably well in comprehension—if she still has a problem of a foreign accent, you might slowly begin a program of ear training. This consists largely of devising special exercises around her particular problem. You may, for example, have her say:

sheep	*cheap*	Note that the sounds under study are placed in the
shoes	*choose*	*initial position* in the word. This should always be
shore	*chore*	done first, as it is there that the sound gets its shar-
share	*chair*	pest focus.

After that, use the same sound in the *final position*.

wish	*witch*	These drills are not to be undertaken (except or-
wash	*watch*	ally) until the student has a good enough com-
mush	*much*	mand of phonics and reading to read the words.
mash	*match*	

The third stage of pronunciation drill is to use the sounds in *medial position*.

washing	*watching*	
mashed	*matched*	Ultimately, the student will have to use the words
mushy	*much more*	in sentences. This is more difficult than pronounc-
wisher	*witch-like*	ing lists of words:

Did you choose your shoes?
This cereal is much more mushy than that one.

Do not spend too long on this type of exercise. A few minutes daily is more effective than long, drawn-out sessions. Do not get discouraged if these exercises do not seem to be yielding results. One of the most difficult changes for a human being to make is speech. To learn a new speech pattern usually involves day-after-day, week-after-week of listening while the ear tries to compensate for years of being deprived of that sound, of hearing it over and over until it gradually begins to take form in the mind and upon the tongue.

If a student does not want to drop an accent (and I believe many people, proud of their ethnic origin, consciously or unconsciously use an accent as an identity symbol), there is little the teacher can do. But if a student wishes to acquire a more nearly standard pronunciation, and if both student and teacher are willing to put forth the effort, and if the teacher understands something of the science of phonology, the results can be rewarding.

The type of exercise suggested previously may also be used with students who have other kinds of auditory discrimination difficulties, such as confusion of /m/ and /n/ or /f/ and /v/. (See p. 177.) Sometimes the problem is less of oral than of visual discrimination, that is, failure to distinguish such letters as *b* and *d* or *p* and *q*. As you listen to students read, be alert for consistent patterns of confusion. You may wish to devise special drills to help overcome a specific difficulty. Follow the general pattern of going from initial to final to medial positions, and finally to sentences:

bear	*pear*	*cub*	*cup*	*dribble*	*pebble*
bay	*pay*	*mob*	*mop*	*symbol*	*simple*
bet	*pet*	*slab*	*slap*	*robber*	*wrapper*
bit	*pit*	*web*	*whip*	*throbbing*	*tapping*

Bob's pup barked at Pete and Ben.

Note that this exercise begins with minimal pairs (words that differ in only one phoneme) and gradually introduces more complex differences, until in the sentence the reader is challenged by capital as well as lower case letters. If you cannot build the entire exercise with appropriate words, mix with nonsense syllables, but tell the student you are doing so:

>   *bot   pot   tub ˃ tup   hipple   hibble*

The Organs of Speech

Human speech occurs when a column of air is exhaled through the lungs, traveling up through a passage called the *larynx,* in which the *vocal cords* are located, then through another passage called the *pharynx,* and finally out through the *oral* and *nasal cavities.* If the vocal cords are relaxed and spread apart, there is no sound, as when we are not speaking. But to add speech, we put a tension on these cords so the air is restricted as it passes through. If the tension is slight, the friction of air passing through this restriction produces a hissing sound, as when we whisper. This is called *voiceless* speech. But if the tension is increased, the cords vibrate, producing sound as the strings of a violin do. This is *voiced* speech. Some English sounds are voiced, others are voiceless.

Figure 7–B shows a membrane separating the oral and nasal cavities. As illustrated, the *velic* at the end of this membrane is open to allow most of the air to enter and resonate in the nasal chamber. It is in this manner that the *nasal* sounds /m n ŋ/ are produced. But if this passage is closed, all the air enters the oral cavity. There the airstream is constricted at some point and in a particular manner. It is the place and manner of constriction that largely determines which particular sound will be produced. Other factors also are involved, such as whether the jaw is closed or open. In the illustration the jaw is almost closed.

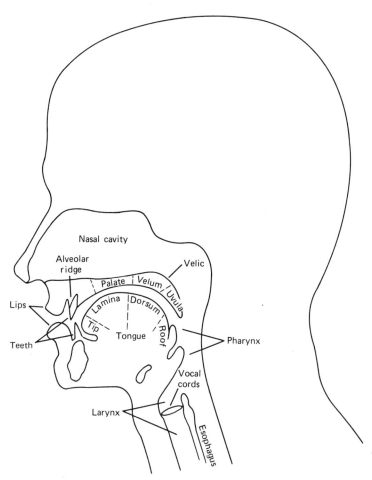

FIGURE 7-B   Major speech articulators (From Burt Liebert, *Linguis-tics and the New English Teacher,* New York: Macmillan Publishing Co., Inc., 1971.)

The Phonetic Alphabet

It is difficult to discuss speech sounds in writing. Sound must be heard to be conceptualized. To overcome this difficulty, linguists have devised various *phonetic alphabets.*[5] Not all phonetic alphabets are alike, and this is a source of confusion, but the principle behind all of them is the same, to

[5]see pp. 177 and 178.

establish a system in which each symbol corresponds to a particular phoneme. Dictionaries use phonetic alphabets to indicate pronunciation. To use this information, however, it is necessary to identify the sound of each phonetic symbol. This text, therefore, includes the phonetic alphabets of two dictionaries that are commonly found in secondary school classrooms, the *Thorndike—Barnhart Advanced Dictionary*, Second Edition, and *Webster's New Collegiate Dictionary*. These are shown on pp. 177 and 178. The two systems are, for the most part, similar, with many symbols taken directly from the graphemic alphabet. Only two consonant phonemes are different. *Thorndike-Barnhart* uses /ng/ to represent the final phoneme in words such as *sing* and *song; Webster* uses /ŋ/. Also, the voiced sound of *th* in *there* is represented by /FH/ in *Thorndike—Barnhart,* but is /th̲/ in *Webster.* In the vowel system, there are a number of differences.

In any phonetic system, each symbol always represents the same phoneme, although there may be more than one way to represent some phonemes. For example, the final phoneme of *threw* can be spelled either as a consonant /w/ or as a vowel /ü/.

Phonemic Classification

The 40 phonemes of the English language shown on pp. 177 and 178 may be classified a number of ways. First, we show 24 *consonants* and 16 *vowels*. Vowels are produced with the jaw comparatively open and the tongue low, so that air flows with little restriction through the oral cavity. The positions of the tongue, jaw, and lips determine which particular vowel is being formed. The 24 consonants are produced with the tongue higher, the jaw less open, and the air flow more severely restricted in the oral cavity.

Most of the consonant symbols of the phonetic alphabet correspond with those of the graphemic (conventional) alphabet. However, the letters *c, q,* and *x* represent sounds made by other letters and hence are not needed for phonetic writing. On the other hand, the letter *n* has two pronunciations—/n/ as in *sin,* and /ŋ/ as in *sink.* Thus *n* requires two phonetic symbols to express its two pronunciations.

There are also some phonemes that do not have a letter in the orthographic system and are represented by two symbols. Two letters used to represent a single phoneme is called a *digraph*. These include /th/, /th̲/, /sh/ and /zh/. To write these phonemes with two phonetic symbols is something less than scientific, for they are not really combinations of these two sounds at all, but completely separate phonemes. Most linguists use other symbols to represent them, such as /ʃ/ for /sh/ and /ʒ/ for /zh/. Dictionaries use digraphs because that is the way English readers are used to seeing them.

TABLE 7-1

THE ENGLISH CONSONANT SYSTEM

TYPE	COMMON SPELLINGS	THORNDIKE–BARNHART	WEBSTER
Stops	pie, rope, supper	p	p
	bit, bribe, robber	b	b
	tie, rote, butter, slipped, doubt, caught	t	t
	die, rode, paddle, rubbed	d	d
	kit, like, cane, lick, quit, ache, talk school	k	k
	gain, beggar, rogue	g	g
Nasals	main, summer, come, dumb, calm, autumn	m	m
	no, scene, winner, know, gnaw, John	n	n
	song, sink	ng	ŋ
Continuants	fine, wife, cuff, phone, tough	f	f
	vain, save, of	v	v
	sane, rinse, essay, cent, mice, scene cat's, cats'	s	s
	zoo, size, muzzle, boys, boy's, boys', rise, says	z	z
	thin	th	th
	then, bathe	ŦH	th
	sure, shy, attention, permission, special, machine, ocean, anxious	sh	sh
	loge, seizure, Jacques, vision, measure	zh	zh
	lie, role, roll	l	l
	rain, rare, hurry, rhythm, wreck	r	r
Semivowels	hail, whose	h	h
	yet, onion	y	y
	wail, what	w	w
Blends	jig, gentle, ridge, gorge, soldier	j	j
	chick, itch, nature, question	ch	ch

Source: Based on Burt Liebert, *Linguistics and the New English Teacher.* New York: Macmillan Publishing Co., Inc., 1971, p. 79.

TABLE 7-2

THE ENGLISH VOWEL SYSTEM

TYPE	COMMON SPELLINGS	THORNDIKE–BARNHART	WEBSTER
Short vowels	sat, laugh	a	a
	bit, build, busy, pretty, hymn, sieve,	i	i
	the sun, son, young, mountain,	ə or u	ə
	leopard, bury, set, head, said, friend,	e	e
	any, guess		
	got, father, heart, guard	o or ä	ȧ or ä
Long vowels	be, bee, beat, field, receive, people,	ē	ē
	key, gasoline		
	gauge, obey, vein, cave, bait, way, weigh	ā	ā
	steak		
	soul, no, know, boat, hoe, sew, beau,	ō	ō
	though		
	bite, buy, high, pie, by, guide	ī	ī
	youth, cue, use, few, beautiful, view	ū	yü
Other vowels	wolf, took, pull, could	u	u
	boy, join	oi	oi
	fruit, rule, true, to, too, two, chew,	ü	ü
	through, shoe, soup		
	broad, hall, bore, haunt, awful, fought,	ô	o
	awe, board, caught		
	house, brown, bough, hour	ou	au
	term, learn, bird, urge	ər	ər

Source: Ibid, p. 80.

Teaching students to recognize and read digraphs is an important part of teaching phonics.

The phonemes /j/ and /ch/ are in a class by themselves, called *affricates.* They are really *consonant blends,* that is, combinations of two consonant phonemes that come together without an intervening vowel. The phoneme /j/ consists of /d/ + /zh/, and /ch/ is really /t/ + /sh/. However, in normal speech they are blended and come out sounding like single phonemes. Hence they are given separate symbols. Some linguists write these phonemes as blends (/tʃ/), others as single phonemes (/č/). For our discussion, however, it is simpler to use only one system. Therefore, in this text all phonetic symbols are taken from Webster. It isn't important whether these two phonemes are called blends or affricates, as they can be recognized regardless of how they are spelled, and the sounds can be explained when students have difficulty.

VOICED AND VOICELESS   In addition to consonant and vowel, phonemes can be classified as *voiced* or *voiceless,* depending upon whether they are produced with or without vibration in the larynx. All vowels and consonants /b d g m n ŋ v z th zh l r y w j/ are voiced. Voiceless consonants are /p t k f s th sh h ch/. English contains a number of "pairs" of phonemes, which are identical in every way except that one member of the pair is voiced and the other is voiceless. These pairs are:

Voiced	Voiceless
/b/	/p/
/d/	/t/
/g/	/k/
/v/	/f/
/z/	/s/
/th/	/th/
/zh/	/sh/
/j/	/ch/

Sometimes beginning readers, particularly those who speak another language natively, will confuse a voiced or unvoiced phoneme with the other member of the pair. We have noted the case of the Spanish speakers, who tend to substitute /s/ for /z/.

Here are two ways to test a phoneme for voicing: One way is to place the hand on the larynx (Adam's apple) and say the phoneme aloud. If the phoneme is voiced, the vibration in the vocal cords can be felt with the hand. Another method is to place one's hands tightly over the ears and say the phoneme aloud. The vibrations emanating from voiced phonemes are clearly audible.

TYPE OF ACTION   Another method of classifying phonemes is the type of action. Vowels may be used *short* or *long*. Short vowels consist of only one phoneme. See chart below. Long vowels are not necessarily longer in duration, but are really *vowel blends,* or *diphthongs.* A diphthong consists of two vowel phonemes coming together without an intervening consonant. The diphthong /ē/, for example really consists of /i/ + /y/; but in normal speech, these are blended so closely that they come out sounding like a single phoneme. English long vowels and their equivalents are as follows:

/ē/	= /i/	+ /y/	This list shows eight long vowels. How-
/ā/	= /e/	+ /y/	ever, the first five are generally considered
/ō/	= /ə/	+ /ü/	the common long vowels. They are the
/ī/	= /à/	+ /y/	sounds that "name" the five vowel letters
/yu/	= /y/	+ /ü/	of the graphemic system.
/oi/	= /ò/	+ /y/	
/aù/	= /à/	+ /ü/	
/ər/	= /ə/	+ /r/	

Words such as *bread, laugh,* and *guard* contain diphthongs in the written system (*ea, au,* and *ua*), but not in the spoken system because each of the two combinations of vowel letters is pronounced as a single short vowel phoneme.

There are two major types of consonants, *stops* and *continuants.* Stops are produced by a single brief puff of air. A stop, sometimes called a *plosive,* cannot be continued. As indicated on page 177, there are only six English stops.

Continuants are made by friction as the air is restricted somewhere in the oral cavity. These phonemes can be continued until the speaker runs out of breath. A singer who "holds" a note must be voicing a vowel or one of the continuants.

Nasals and semivowels are really continuants, but with special qual-ities. Nasals are made with the velic open so that much of the air resonates in the nasal cavity. Semivowels result from the lack of a dividing line between consonant and vowel, that is, from no definite plane located where one can say that everything below this is a vowel, everything above is a consonant. The tongue can assume an infinite variety of positions, and some are in-between consonant and vowel, hence are called semivowels. Semivowels can be used either as consonants or vowels. For example, *y* is a vowel in *fly* and a consonant in *you.* Some English phonemes are spelled with a vowel in some words, a consonant in others, as in *joy* and *voice, twin* and *quit, shy* and *die,* and *saw* and *bought.* In phonetic spelling, either the consonant or vowel symbol can be used. Some linguists also classify /r/ as a semivowel.

The blends, or affricates, are particularly interesting because each consists of a stop (/d/ and /t/), plus a continuant, (/zh/ and /sh/). I have found that it simplifies the reading problem for most students to consider them single phonemes.

POINT OF ARTICULATION   Another method of classification of phonemes is the point of articulation. This refers to the point in the oral cavity where the greatest restriction of the air flow takes place, and is largely responsible for determining which phoneme is produced. Page 175 reveals a number of points along the oral cavity at which the air flow can be restricted by the lips, teeth, tongue, and roof of the mouth. These points of restriction are listed in Table 7−3. Affricates begin at the front of the alveolar ridge, near the teeth. During production, the tongue moves slightly backwards towards the hard palate.

All vowels are produced in the palatal-velar area. Linguists classify vowels according to whether they are produced with the tongue high or low, or at the front or back of the palatal-velar area. Tongue positions for the major English vowels are illustrated in Figure 7−C. Short vowels are depicted by dots, and long vowels with arrows, indicating the direction of tongue movement during the duration of the blend.

The reading teacher should understand the sound system of the language to help his charges decode the written system into the spoken system

TABLE 7-3

Name	Place	Phonemes
Bilabial	Two lips	/p b m w/
Labio-dental	Lower lip against upper teeth	/f v/
Dental and alveolar	Tongue against teeth and/or alveolar ridge	/t d n l r th th s z sh zh j ch/
Palatal	Tongue against the hard palate	/y/
Velar	Tongue against the velum, or soft palate	/k g ŋ/
Glottal, or pharyngeal	Pharynx	/h/

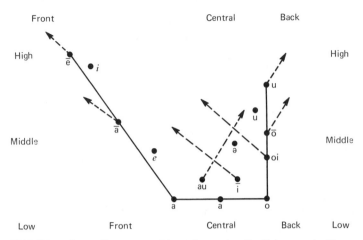

FIGURE 7-C   Tongue positions for major English vowels (From Burt Liebert, *Linguistics and the New English Teacher,* New York: Macmillan Publishing Co., Inc., 1971.)

and to diagnose some of the difficulties that youngsters frequently experience. Most important, teachers must sort out in their own minds the difference between written and spoken symbols. The letter e, for example, is the fifth symbol of the *written* system. It has a variety of pronunciations. But the symbol /e/ belongs to the sound system of the language, and is spelled e in *met,* ea in *lead* (the metal), *ai* in *said,* and *ie* in *friend.*

I have heard teachers talk about "the sound of e." This is confusing to a student. Always *pronounce* sounds and *name* letters, and make it clear that the two systems are different, although they have enough correspondence to be confusing.

Let's Read Again

Reading material in Part I of *Let's Read* is confined mainly to the common consonant-short vowel-consonant pattern. Part II introduces the first consonant blends (two or more consonants coming together without an intervening vowel: *sled, snag, skin.* This is a very important phase of the program, since many students have difficulty blending. It may require a considerable amount of work. In the new soft cover series this is handled very well, with all of Book Four devoted to consonant blends.

Part I also introduces us to the five short vowel (*a e i o u*) and nineteen consonant letters (b c d f g h j k l m n p r s t v w y z). Part II, however, begins by introducing the "plural suffix of nouns." This represents a shift of systems, and the text does not explain this. The plural suffix is not a phoneme, but part of another language system, the *morphological,* or *meaning* system. Before proceeding, let us devote our next chapter to a brief introduction to English morphology.

CHAPTER 8
The Systems of Language
Phonics II—The Meaning of People

Speech sounds are only the tools by which we achieve the real purpose of language—communication. We speak and listen, read and write, to exchange information, ideas, thoughts, and feelings. Hence in addition to a sound system, language needs some way of organizing units of meaning into utterances that carry a message. This is called the *morphological system* of the language.

The English morphological system consists of three subsystems, each involving different types of *morphemes*. A morpheme is the smallest unit of meaning in the language, and words are composed of one or more morphemes. The subsystems of English morphology are: 1) the inflectional system, morphemes that give words such qualities as number and tense; 2) the *distributional system,* which determines whether a word is noun, verb, or adjective; and 3) the *lexical system,* which adds to or otherwise changes the meanings of words. As speakers of English, we are already familiar with these systems, for we cannot use our language without them. But in the course of teaching reading, we are frequently called upon to diagnose a difficulty or make an explanation. This may require a conscious understanding of language.

THE INFLECTIONAL SYSTEM

Lesson 51 of *Let's Read* introduces the reader to the plural suffix of nouns (cap → caps) and the third person singular present tense suffix of verbs (I bat→ Dan bats). These are not new sound-letter relationships, because we have already learned to associate s with /s/. They are units of the inflectional system of English. English is not a highly inflected language. Its inflectional morphemes can be reduced to a scant ten, compared with hundreds in some other languages. However, the inflections we do have are very important.

Except for a few irregular forms, English inflections are *suffixed* (added at the end) to the *stem* (uninflected form) of the word. Following are the inflectional morphemes of English:

1. The Plural Noun

The plural noun changes nouns from singular to plural. It has three pronunciations:

/s/ after singular nouns that end in unvoiced phonemes / p t k f th/: ship→ships, book→books, graph→graphs, length→lengths, mat→ mats

/z/ after voiced phonemes /b d g m n ŋ v th l r y w/ and all vowels: girl→girls, picture→pictures, bag→bags, papa→papas

/iz/ after the phonemes /s z sh zh j ch/: glass→glasses, quiz→quizzes, wish→wishes, garage→garages, judge→judges, church→churches

The pronunciation of the plural suffix of nouns is conditioned by the *pronunciation,* not the spelling, of the final phoneme of the stem. This is logical. If we are voicing the final phoneme of the singular (stem) form, it is easier to pronounce the voiced suffix /z/ than to stop our vocal cords from vibrating (wall→walls). But if we are pronouncing a final unvoiced phoneme, it is simpler to follow it with the unvoiced /s/ (cup→cups). The phonemes /s z sh zh j ch/ are called *sibilant* sounds (/s/-like). Two consecutive sibilants sound awkward in English, so to make these words plural, we insert the vowel /i/ before the /z/ (dish→dishes).

In teaching the plural suffix, the reading teacher should know that there are three possible pronunciations, although at this point (Lesson 51), Bloomfield is careful to use only unvoiced final phonemes to keep the pronunciation of the letter *s* consistent (/s/). In teaching plurals, as well as other inflections with varying pronunciations, do not emphasize differences, since English speakers usually shift pronunciation intuitively. But be careful not to state or imply to the student that plurals are always pronounced /s/, just because they are spelled *s* or *es*. Otherwise, you may have problems to untangle later.

There are, of course, many irregular plural nouns, such as leaf→leaves, sheep→sheep, mouse→mice, ox→oxen, phenomenon→phenomena, nucleus→nuclei, datum→data, and woman→women. Lesson 51 of *Let's Read* is not concerned with these, however.

2. The Possessive Noun

The possessive noun declares ownership. It is pronounced exactly as the plural noun, but is spelled *'s*, except for nouns that end with sibilant phonemes, which are usually spelled with apostrophe only. But regardless of spelling, the pronunciation is conditioned along the same principles as the plural noun, so that *Pete's* is pronounced /pēts/, *Bill's* is /bilz/, and *James'* is /jāmziz/. Sometimes however, in the case of sibilant endings, we leave off the final syllable and simply say /jāmz/ for *James'*.

Because of the similarity in pronunciation, these two inflectional phonemes are very confusing. Even educated English speakers frequently use apostrophes for plural forms, as many frustrated English teachers know. To complicate matters, English *does* use the apostrophe for plural forms under certain circumstances, such as with numbers and symbols:

There are three sevens in my telephone number.

There are three 7's in my telephone number.

Mississippi is spelled with four s's and four i's.

Yes, it's a very confusing language, and many people have difficulty learning to read. One problem in teaching language is a tendency to confuse *letters* with *phonemes* and *phonemes* with *morphemes*. The result is that, frequently, we see a letter *s* and add an apostrophe, without quite knowing why and without being able to sort out the plural from the possessive. Apostrophies seldom present difficulties for the reader, but occasionally you may have to explain the difference between the plural and the possessive. The greater problem is in writing, and many students need help with apostrophies.

Because of inflectional endings, every noun can be written in four forms: the stem (singular form), the plural, the possessive, and the plural-possessive. Below is a table of noun forms for a regular noun, *boy,* and an irregular noun, *child*:

stem	*boy*	*child*
plural	*boys*	*children*
possessive	*boy's*	*child's*
plural-possessive	*boys'*	*children's*

Note that in the regular noun (boy), the plural, the possessive, and the plural-possessive are pronounced exactly alike but are spelled differently, while the irregular forms (child) are all pronounced differently.

3. Third Person Singular Present Tense Verb

The third person singular present tense verb is the only verb conjugation in English. All forms of the English present tense verb are alike except the third person (person or thing spoken about) singular. Thus we say *I go—you go—he goes.* He (or she, or John, or the little dog) also *sees, finds, wishes, creeps, eats, runs,* and does many things ending with the letter *s.* This only happens in the present tense. Past tense verbs do not change in the third person: *I ran—you ran—he also ran.* Third person singular present tense inflectional morphemes are pronounced exactly as noun plurals and possessives—the same /s~z~iz/ pronunciation, and conditioned exactly the same way—by whether the preceding phoneme is voiced, unvoiced, or sibilant. This is the phoneme that *Let's Read* introduces (*gets, limps, helps*)—along with the plural noun (*desks, tents, cats*)—in Lesson 51. Because of the similarities in spelling and pronunciation, there is some possibility of confusion, although I have found that this is minimal, since nouns are seldom misread for verbs.

But the plot thickens in Lesson 52 when *Let's Read* adds the possessive noun suffix. We have one verb and two noun inflections introduced in two lessons, all three pronounced exactly alike, spelled somewhat similarly *but having vastly different meanings.* Further, Lesson 52 introduces two contractions, both spelled with *s.* They are the unstressed forms of *is: Nat's* (Nat is), and *us: let's* (let us). These contractions are not morphemes, but are merely abbreviated ways of writing and speaking. They are, however, written and pronounced exactly as the possessive noun (*'s*). Unstressed *is,* is pronounced /s~z~iz/, and is conditioned on the same principle as the inflections. *Let's* is pronounced /s/. Only the unvoiced form /s/ appears in this lesson.

Thus in two lessons the reader is introduced to five different ways to use the letter *s,* three of them morpheme suffixes, and two contractions. They are spelled similarly, with just enough differences to be confusing. The reading teacher must be prepared to make patient explanations, if necessary.

4, 5. Past Tense and Past Participle Verbs

The past tense and past participle verbs are not brought into the reading program as separate lessons, but while we are discussing inflections, we would do well to complete our list. The past and past participle are probably the most confusing aspects of English grammar. This is because although they are different morphemes and have different uses in English sentences, their regular forms are exactly alike in both spelling and pronunciation. This, in itself, causes no problem. But most common verbs are irregular. Many

English speakers are not aware that past and past participle are not inter-changeable and they confuse them in speech and writing.

The past tense is used to change a verb from present (stem form) to past; the past participle is used with the auxiliaries *have, has,* or *had*:

Present: *I walk to school* (today).

Past: *I walked to school* (yesterday).

Past participle: *I have walked to school* (many times).

Past and past participle are usually spelled by adding *d* or *ed* to the present tense form (regular verbs), and pronounced one of three ways:

/d/ after voiced phonemes /b g m n ŋ v z <u>th</u> zh y w l r j/ and vowels: open→opened, play→played, store→stored

/t/ after unvoiced phonemes / p k f s th sh ch/: drop→dropped, wish→wished, walk→walked, lock→locked

/id/ after /t d/: seat→seated, plead→pleaded

The difficulty lies with the many irregular verbs used in the bulk of our speech. Some verbs do not make any changes from the stem form: *I cut the bread* (now). *I cut the bread* (yesterday). *I have cut the bread* (many times). Others have irregular but identical forms for the past and past participle: *I win the game* (now). *I won the game* (this morning). *I have won the game* (many times). Still others have three separate forms for present, past, and past participle: *I go* (now) *I went* (yesterday). *I have gone* (many times), or may have identical stem and past participle: *I run* (now). *I ran* (yesterday). *I have run* (many times).

Teaching students to read these very troublesome verb forms can be done in two ways. They may be taught by sounds alone, with no reference to their grammatical implications. Or the student may be given a brief introduction to verb forms and each form taught by whole word method, applying the Bloomfield-Barnhart theory that phonic connections will be made by the student through sheer repetition. Both methods have their advantages and limitations. The sound-letter correspondence method is simpler and runs less risk of confusing the student with excessive grammatical terminology and the introduction of concepts not necessary for reading. However, the student's overall language development can frequently be accelerated by supplying some understanding of the basic structure of the language that is being used (See page 11.) I tend to use a combination of both methods, using mainly sound-letter matching for the slower readers, for this focuses directly on reading. Because writing is a very important phase of language development, however, I find that ultimately I have to point out that *"these* words are used for past tense, but these are used with *have, has,* or *had."*

6, 7, 8. Gerund, Present Participle, and Progressive Verb Forms

The gerund, present participle, and progressive forms of the verb are spelled *-ing* and have two possible pronunciations. In isolation these morphemes are usually pronounced /iŋ/ (*walking:* /wȯkiŋ/, but in fast conversation are more likely to be /in/ (I'm *walking:* /īm wȯkin/). Because all three forms are spelled and pronounced exactly alike, they are sometimes considered a single morpheme, although their use for different purposes would indicate otherwise. What you call them is immaterial. It is only important to teach readers to recognize the form *ing* added to verbs and to associate it with any of its uses. These uses are:

Gerund: a verb form used as a noun, that is, used in a sentence position generally reserved for nouns:

I like *pizza.*	I like *hiking.*
I like *Margie.*	I like *sewing.*
I like *San Francisco.*	I like *going* down town.

Present participle: a verb form used as an adjective, in a sentence position generally reserved for adjectives:

The *tall* man	The *grinning* man
The *fat* man	The man *walking* away
The *funny* man	The *crying* man

Progressive tenses: a verb form used in conjunction with some form of *be*:

I *am going* home.	They *were helping* us with the homework.
I *was leaving.*	You *will be coming* to visit me tomorrow.
He *is running* away.	The waiter *should be bringing* some food soon.
The students *are finishing* the assignment.	

This completes the list of verb suffixes. In summary, verbs can be said to have five forms:

stem	*go*
3rd person singular	*goes*
past tense	*went*

past participle	*gone*
gerund	
present participle ⎫	*going*
progressive form ⎭	

One more pair of inflectional morphemes, and our list will be complete.

9, 10. Comparative and Superlative Adjectives

The comparative and superlative adjectives. The comparative adjective morpheme is usually spelled *er,* and pronounced /ər/; the superlative form is usually spelled *est* and pronounced /ist/. Some adjectives are regular:

large larger largest
brave braver bravest

Some involve minor spelling changes:

happy happier happiest

Others are irregular:

good better best
bad worse worst

And adjectives of three or more syllables do not take the inflectional form, but use the words *more* and *most:*

beautiful → more beautiful → most beautiful
generous → more generous → most generous

This completes one of the three morphological systems of English—the inflectional system. Before looking at the other systems, let us return to *Let's Read* for a comprehensive look at the suggested teaching order of phonic elements.[1] So far, we have discussed the first 52 lessons (Books 1, 2, and 3 in the new series), which have included:

a as in *can*	*These are the five common short*
i as in *big*	*vowels, introduced one at a time*
u as in *bun*	*and spread over 36 lessons. With*
e as in *bet*	*these are included the 19 common,*
o as in *cot*	*regular consonant letters: b, c, d, f,*
	g, h, j, k, l, m, n, p, r, s, t, v, w, y, and
	z. The rule is always introduce the
	short vowels first. The schwa sound

[1]Pronunciation in *Let's Read* is based on that of the Thorndike-Barnhart Dictionary.

/ə/ up to this point is spelled with the letter *u*. The single-letter word *a* is introduced as a sight word. Note that a single vowel beginning or in the middle of a one syllable word is usually short.

an   get   in   pot   sun

The word *the* (*The man—the apple:* /thə man thē apəl/)

Irregular pronunciation. *Th* is voiced /th/, e is sometimes schwa /ə/, sometimes long e /ē/, conditioned by whether the succeeding phomene is consonant or vowel. Teach as a sight word, and point out that its pronunciation is irregular.

The plural suffix of nouns: *caps*. The third person singular present tense suffix of verbs: (Dan) *bats*. The possessive suffix: *cat's*. The unstressed form of is: *Nat's*. The unstressed form of us: *let's*.

The first three are the first morphemes introduced. They may be taught by sound-letter only or by discussion of suffixes. The last two are contractions. Putting these five uses of *s* together can be confusing. Be prepared to explain. This lesson also introduces consonant blends.

I believe that the inclusion of such similar elements so close together is unfortunate. It is a good rule to group *dissimilar* elements so that they will not be confused. For example, I used to teach students to differentiate between *there, their,* and *they're*. But I found that just putting these already-confused words into the same lesson often increased the confusion. I found it more effective to teach *there* in relation to *here* and *where* because students did not confuse them. A difficulty may arise in lesson 52 (Book 5, page 12 in the new series) with the words *its* and *it's*. You may have to explain that the apostrophe + *s* possessive ending is for *nouns only* and does not apply to any of the personal pronouns:

my	our
your (singular)	your (plural)
his	their
her	
its	

It's is a contraction and means *it is*. *It's* as used on p. 125 of *Let's Read* is a misprint. In the lesson (p. 143) *it's* and *its* are used properly.

ng as in *sing*	First consonant digraph. Explain that two letters sometimes make a single sound.
nk as in *sink*	This is the first blend. Some students blend intuitively, but many remedial readers require a lot of help learning to make blends. Note inconsistency: *sing* contains a digraph (/ŋ/), but *sink* a blend (/ŋk/). No logic—that's the way it is.
sh as in *shed, fish*	Another digraph.
ch as in *chin, much*	First affricate. Simpler if taught as a single phoneme (digraph).
th as in *thin, tenth*	Digraph.
wh as in *when*	Some pronounce this as a digraph /wen/, others as a reverse blend (hwen/). Spelling is *wh*, but pronunciation is /hw—/.
ck as in *back*	You may teach as digraph or introduce concept of silent letter. At this early stage, I prefer not to introduce silent consonants. I treat this as a digraph.
tch as in *catch*	May be taught as *trigraph* or as silent *t*. We now have two spellings for /ch/—*ch* and *tch*. May also be an extension of the *ch* pattern, as in *cat+ch*.
double letters: *sniff, less, bill, mitt, add*	Call attention to the use of double letters.
qu as in *quit* *x* as in *box*	Mention that *q* is always followed by *u*, and together they have the sound of /kw/. *X* is a single letter representing two phonemes /ks/. At this point, all the letters of the alphabet have been introduced.

led	sled	lab	slab	lob	slob	nag	snag
lid	slid	lag	slag	lop	slop	nap	snap
	slim		slam	lot	slot	nip	snip
lip	slip	lap	slap	lug	slug	nub	snub
lit	slit		slat		slum		snug

cab	scab	kid	skid	mug	smug	wag	swag
can	scan		skim		smut		swam
						wig	swig
cat	scat	kin	skin		smit		swim
cot	Scot		skip				swum
	scum	kit	skit				

Sam slid on a big red sled.
Cal at bat! Slam it, Cal! Run, Cal, run!
Did Sal slap Tip? Yes, Sal hit Tip. Bad Sal!
Let us hop, let us skip, let us run!
Pam did a skit in a red wig.

   Did Pal snap at Kit? Did Kit slap at Pal?
Scat, Kit, scat! Kit ran. Pal hid.

FIGURE 8-A   *Let's Read*, Lesson 37. (Wayne State University Press, 1961.)

ee as in *see*
eer as in *deer*
ea as in *eat*
ear as in *dear*

This is the first long vowel sound (/ē/), and the first double vowel letter. Sound repeated with *ea* spelling, and given special attention when followed by *r*. In some dialects, the sound changes for *r* ending vowels.

In many vowel digraphs the first vowel is long and the second silent:

   eat, boat, chair, people, ceiling

There are, however, many exceptions:

   oar, loud, haul, boil, steak

oo as in *moon*
oor as in *poor*

"R ending" vowels prepare students for diphthongs. *Ear* and *poor* contain

the	this	then	them	with
	that	than		without
	that's			smooth
				breathe

Bess will not drink tea without milk in it.
Did Ann and Joan have a smooth trip on the boat?
Let's eat lunch and then let's play tag.
Breathe in this fresh air.

Jack may play with this train, and Dick may play with that train. Jack must not snatch Dick's train and Dick must not grab Jack's train.

Nick and Frank cannot lift the big bench. Gus and Dan will help them. Gus and Dan will help them bring it out on the lawn. Gus will help Nick, and Dan will help Frank. Gus will help lift Nick's end, and Dan will help lift Frank's end. Gus will help at this end, and Dan will help at that end. Then Nick and Frank and Gus and Dan will get the big bench out on the lawn. That's it! Thanks! Thanks a lot, Gus and Dan!

FIGURE 8-B   *Let's Read,* Lesson 98. (Wayne State University Press, 1961.)

semidiphthongs, with /r/ often considered a semivowel.

ai as in *sail*
air as in *chair*
ay as in *day*
oa as in *boat*
oar as in *board*

Long vowel sounds (/ā/ and /ō/) introduced as digraphs first. Later single-letter long vowels will be used.

ou as in *loud*
our as in *sour*
ow as in *cow*

/aů/ is the first true diphthong. Teach both spellings (*ou* and *ow*) and continue to stress the *r* ending.

aw as in *saw*
au as in *haul*
oy as in *boy*
oi as in *boil*

Two more diphthongs, each with two spellings.

silent e at end of words

Teach this common English pattern, as students are used to pronouncing the *e* (/e/).

At this point, we have introduced all "regular" sound-letter relation-ships. These are the commonest patterns of the language, in which each letter or blend, with very few exceptions, always represents the same sound. From here on, we will be looking at less common spellings and reading will become increasingly complex. Unless the student is doing exceptionally well, it might be worthwhile to review all forms studied thus far. Have the student reread some of the more recent exercises. Make lists of troublesome words, phrases, and sentences on flash cards and drill on these. Try some nonsense syllables to test phonic recognition. Make up new sentences, being careful to use only words that have already appeared in the text, and have the student read these silently. Then ask comprehension questions. If the student is not getting meaning from what he is reading, do more com-prehension drill. Be reluctant to go on, until the student has mastered this section.

If the student appears hopelessly confused about some points and does not seem to be making progress, even after extended drill, I recommend going on without mastering the regular spellings. Important as it is to learn the fundamentals, it is even more important not to feel hopeless or stupid. Drop the troublesome points, go on, and return to them at a later date. The following exercises involve less common spellings:

th as in *then* *s* for /z/, as in *his* suffix —*es* or '*s* for /iz/, as in *dishes*, *Gus's*	Introduces the voiced forms of the *th* digraph, and of the plural, posses-sive, third person singular, and past tense suffixes, including /id/ and /iz/.
suffix —*d* or —*ed* for /d/, as in *rub-bed* suffix —*ed* with e pronounced (/i/), as in *landed*	
suffix —*ed* for /t/, as in *slipped*	Unvoiced phoneme /t/ for normally voiced letter *d*.
the words *to, of,* and *was*	These short, common words may be taught as sight words with irregular pronunciation.
one syllable words with final e for /ē/, as in *be*	First use of long vowel spelled with single letter. A single vowel in a one

syllable word ending in silent e is usually long.

the words *one, says, said, are, were, been*

These irregular spellings may be taught as sight words.

the common pronouns *I, you,* and so forth.

The personal pronouns are inflected so irregularly that there is no simple way to classify pronoun inflections, as can be done with those of nouns, verbs, and adjectives. Each form has to be taught individually. Below is a complete table of common English personal pronouns.

TABLE 8-1

NOMINATIVE	OBJECTIVE	POSSESSIVE ADJECTIVE	POSSESSIVE PRONOUN	REFLEXIVE
I	me	my	mine	myself
we	us	our	ours	ourselves
you	you	your	yours	yourself/yourselves
he	him	his	his	himself
she	her	her	hers	herself
it	it	its	its	itself
they	them	their	theirs	themselves
who	who or whom	whose	whose	

two-syllable words

Although some two-syllable words are introduced as early as Lesson 25 (*sunset*), their use is only occasional. Lesson 117 uses many two-syllable compounds whose parts can be read separately (*sun + set, black + board*). Lesson 118 introduces two-syllable single morpheme words (*picnic, chipmunk*).

the suffix *-ing*	It is not necessary to teach usage here, as English speakers know how to use *-ing* inflections properly. Only with native speakers of a foreign language, will explanations be needed.
Three and four-syllable words	These may be much more difficult than any enountered so far.
The *r* suffix	Lesson 129 introduces a new morphological system. Before we go on, let us examine that system.

THE DISTRIBUTIONAL SYSTEM

In our study of inflections, we noted that er (/ər/) is the comparative adjective morpheme (*nicer, bigger, yellower, meaner*). In Lesson 129 we encounter the comparative adjective inflection in such words as *cooler, steeper,* and *deeper.* But we also find *temper, power,* and *silver,* which are not comparative adjectives and are not adjectives at all. They are one-morpheme words, and the *er* is not a separate morpheme because it carries no meaning of its own. Thus we cannot assume that any letter or sound or combination of letters or sounds is always a morpheme, just because it happens to be one in some words.

A third group of words in this lesson consists of *hunter, helper, painter, pointer,* and others. In each of these words if you remove the final *er,* you still have a morpheme—*hunt, help, paint,* and *point.* Each of these words could be a noun or a verb without the *er* ending. But once the *er* is added, it can be only one thing—a noun. It can thus be said that the *er* establishes the word as a noun and is frequently called a *nominalizing* (noun building) morpheme. It fulfills the criteria for a morpheme: it *recurs* in different situations and always carries the same meaning and the same phonemic shape. Such morphemes are part of the *distributional system.* This means that they establish the word as a noun, verb, adjective, or adverb and determine how the word is to be distributed in a sentence, or how it is to be used.

Distributional morphemes, like inflections, are usually suffixed to the stem word. But a few are prefixed, such as *en*—prefixed to *act, tangle,* or *joy;* establishing them as verbs—*enact, entangle, enjoy.* A list of distributional suffixes of English would run into hundreds, but the most common are:

TABLE 8-2

DISTRIBUTIONAL MORPHEMES

NOUN SUFFIXES	MEANING	EXAMPLES
-age	process or state	leverage, passage
-ance	act or condition	acceptance, variance
-ard	one who does or is	drunkard, wizard
-ate	rank or position	delegate, primate
-ation	state of	insinuation, confrontation
-cy	state of	literacy, complacency
-dom	state of	wisdom, martyrdom
-er	one who	teacher, singer
-ess	feminine	tigress, waitress
-form	having the form of	uniform, multiform
-hood	state of	childhood, statehood
-ion	action of	union, differentiation
-ism	doctrine	communism, catholicism
-ist	believer or doer	socialist, moralist
-ity	state of	civility, brutality
-ment	state of	entrenchment, bewilderment
-ness	state of	troublesomeness, smallness
-or	doer	calculator, incinerator
-th	quality	length, warmth
-tion	state of	expedition, edition
-tude	quality	pulchritude, latitude
-ty	state of	joviality, activity

VERB SUFFIXES	MEANING	EXAMPLES
-ate	make	animate, educate
-en	become, make	lengthen, sharpen
-esce	become, grow	convalesce, acquiesce
-fy	make, cause to	justify, glorify
-ish	do, make	punish, finish
-ize	make, cause to be	mechanize, satirize

Source: Burt Liebert, *Linguistics and the New English Teacher.* New York: The Macmillan Publishing Co., Inc., 1971. pp. 111–112.

TABLE 8-2

DISTRIBUTIONAL MORPHEMES (cont'd)

ADJECTIVE SUFFIXES	MEANING	EXAMPLES
-able	able, like	favorable, unspeakable
-ate	having	fortunate, compassionate
-ed	having quality of	fluted, windowed
-en	made of, like	wooden, fallen
-esque	in the style of	Romanesque, picturesque
-fic	making, causing	terrific, soporific
-ful	full of	zestful, grateful
-ible	able	possible, edible
-ish	like	boyish, greenish
-less	without	helpless, childless
-like	similar	childlike, dreamlike
-ly	like	womanly, kingly
-ous	characterized by	religious, marvelous
-some	likely to, showing	wearisome, lonesome
-ward	in the direction of	upward, forward

A special case is that of the distributional adverb suffix *ly*, which is added to adjectives to make them adverbs:

> *This is a slow train.*   *This train moves slowly.*

Sometimes the addition of a morpheme will change the pronunciation of the stem, as in *mechanical → mechanize, joy → jovial, influence → influential*, or *sign → signal*.

Further steps in teaching phonics are listed in *Let's Read:*

the *l* suffix	This is not a morpheme, but the *le* ending is confusing
the *n* suffix	This is not a morpheme in such words as *kitten, mitten,* and *children,* but in *bitten, eaten,* and *hidden* it is an irregular form of the past participle. In *weaken, sadden,* and *gladden,* it is a distributional verb morpheme.
the *n't* contraction	This is not a morpheme, but a shortened form of *not.*
the *m* ending	This is a phoneme, not a morpheme. Note three ways to spell: *om, me,* and *em.*
the *y* suffix	Is not a morpheme in *body, daisy,* and *country;* but is an adjective distributional morpheme in *sandy, dusty,* and *rocky.* Teach that most nouns ending in *y* change the *y* to *ies* to form the plural (*pennies, daisies, puppies*).

Also point out that a final *y* in one-syllable words is usually sounded /ĭ/:

buy, my, fly

but in multisyllable words, it is usually pronounced /ē/: *badly, probably, twenty.*

a as in *game* ea as in *steak*	Introducing long *a* /ā/, with two spellings.
are, ear, ere as in *care, bear, there*	Variant spellings for /ār/.
a as in *father, car* a as in *ask* a as in *salt* a as in *wash*	Variant pronunciations for the letter *a.* Give particular attention to the "r ending" diphthongs.
o as in *dog*	Short sound /ȯ/.
o as in *go* ow as in *snow*	Long sound of *o* /ō/, with variant spelling.

or, ore, oor, our as in for, *core, door, pour*	Four spellings for this "r ending" diphthong.
i as in *bite* *y* as in *by*	Long *i* /ī/ spelled with vowel and semivowel.
o, ou as in *son, young*	Two ways to spell the schwa /ə/.
u as in *put*	Short vowel.
oo as in *book, room*	One spelling for two different sounds. The /ù/ (*book*) words are separated from the /ü/ (*room*) words in this lesson.
the *r*-vowel, as in *bird*	*Bird* is spelled phonetically /bərd/ or /brd/. The letter *r* is used here as a vowel.

Point out that many vowels followed by *r* are changed, called *r-ending* vowels:

   bird, hard, shirt, warm

These changes depend upon the speaker's dialect and speech habits.

u as in *cute, true; ew* as in *few, chew*	Three spellings for long *u*/yü/ in *cute, useful, few, news;* /ü/ in *rule, blue, prune, stew*
ea as in *head*	Combinations such as these are diphthongs in the written system (*ea*), but not in the sound system (/e/).
e as in *Eve*	This is the last of the five major long vowels /ē/.
c as in *cent, face*	Teach that this is another pronunciation for *c* (soft *c*), the same sound frequently spelled with *s*.
g as in *gem, page, bandage*	Teach that this is a different sound (soft *g*) from the *g* in *gone* (hard *g*).
dg as in *badge*	May be taught as "silent *d*," or as *dg* digraph. I prefer the digraph.
k (silent) as in *knee* *g* (silent) as in *gnaw* *w* (silent) as in *write, whole* *b* (silent) as in *lamb, doubt*	I prefer to introduce the concept of the silent consonant here, where *Let's Read* lists a number of examples.

l (silent) as in *talk, calm*
h (silent) as in *hour, school, John*
t (silent) as in *often, whistle*
silent *n* (*autumn*), *c* (*scene*),
gh (silent) as in *caught, high*
th (silent) in *clothes*
> In my dialect this is not silent /klōᴛʜz/ except in very fast, very casual speech /klōz/.

gh as in *rough*
ph as in *phone, orphan*
> Introduce these digraphs as variant spellings for /f/.

o, ou as in *woman, could*
> Variant of /u̇/.

o, oe, as in *do, shoe*
ou as in *soup, ui* as in *fruit,*
eau as in *beautiful, iew* as in *view*
> Here you have single vowels, diphthongs, and triphthongs spelling /ü/.
> *Beautiful* and *view* form long u /yü/.

ui as in *build, u* as in *busy,*
e as in *pretty, y* as in *hymn, ie* as in *sieve*
> Five variants for /i/, including a semivowel (y).

biscuit, mischief, minute, spinach
> Teach these difficult words by sight. Each contains /i/ twice, spelled differently.

ie as in *field, ei* as in *ceiling,*
eo as in *people, ey* as in *key, i* as in *gasoline*
> Variants for /ē/.

a as in *any, ai* as in *again, ue* as in *guess, u* as in *bury, ie* as in *friend, eo* as in *leopard*
> Variants for /e/.

ei as in *vein, ey* as in *obey*
> Variants for long a /ā/.

ou as in *soul, ew* as in *sew*
> Variants for long o /ō/.

oa as in *broad*
> Variant for /ȯ/.

eye
> Teach this difficult word as a sight word, along with *eyebrow, eyelash.*

uy as in *buy, ui* as in *guide*
> Variants of long i /ī/, spelled with vowel and semivowel.

island, isle, aisle
> Teach as sight words, noting silent *s.*

ea as in *heart, ua* as in *guard*
> Variants for /ȧ/.

ng as in *finger, angle*	Teach as digraph. Point out that this is the same phoneme /ŋ/ as *n* in *sink*.
i as in *onion, Daniel, Julia*	Can be considered semivowel /y/ or diphthong /yē/.
i as in *Columbia, champion*	Long *e* /ē/.
u as in *language*	Semivowel /w/ or vowel /ü/.
s as in *sure*, ss as in *Russia*, ce as in *ocean*, ci as in *special*, xi as in *anxious*, ch as in *machine*, ti as in *nation*	Variants of /sh/. Note *n* in *anxious* has sound of /ŋ/. This is a difficult word.
g as in *rouge*, s as in *measure*, si as in *occasion*	Variants of /zh/.
t as in *picture, question*	*T* for /ch/ affricate.
d as in *soldier, education*	*D* for /j/ voiced affricate.
x as in *exact*	Vowel added to voiced pronunciation /igz/ or /egz/.
Miscellaneous irregular words and variant pronunciations, such as *February, handkerchief, syrup*	These very difficult words are the last to be undertaken.

Students who have mastered the phonics concepts of this program should be able to read most material to about third grade reading level. From here, it is mainly a matter of skill building through practice. A reading specialist or children's librarian should be able to help you find a wealth of material. The difficulty lies in selecting reading matter that is appropriate for the age, maturity level, and interests of the student. Most reading matter with a low enough readability index will insult the secondary student by appearing juvenile. Most of the really interesting matter will be too difficult, and consequently discouraging. The quest for high interest, low readability material is endless, but if pursued diligently, it pays off. Where to go from *Let's Read* has been discussed in this text in Chapter 6, particularly pages 136 to 140. See also Appendixes 3 and 4.

THE LEXICAL SYSTEM

The third and final subsystem of English morphology is the lexical system. Although not discussed in most phonics texts, teaching students to understand and recognize lexical morphemes is an effective way to build language competence. Lexical morphemes add *meaning*. When a student has learned to read and write *precede*, *predetermine* and *prefer*, a familiar bell

TABLE 8-3

LEXICAL MORPHEMES—PREFIXES

PREFIX	MEANING	EXAMPLES
a-	against, without	atypical, atheist
a-	of, to	aware, awake
ab-	from, away	abstract, abdicate
ante-	before	antedate, anteroom
anti-	against	antiaircraft, antibody
apo-	from, away	apogee, apology
bi-	two	bicycle, bisect
cata-	down, away	catastrophe, cataract
circum-	around	circumference, circumstance
com-, con	together	comrade, contact
contra-	against	contraband, contradict
di-	many	dialogue, dichotomy
dia-	through, across	diameter, dialect
dis-	apart, away, not	distort, discourage
ex-	out	extrovert, extend
for-	away, from	forever, forget
fore-	before	forewarn, forefathers
hyper-	excessive	hypersensitive, hypertension
hypo-	under	hypochondria, hypodermic
in-	not	inflexible, incapable
inter-	among, between	interrupt, interdict
mis-	poorly, not	mistake, misinform
mono-	one	monotone, monologue
post-	after, following	postmortem, postscript
pre-	before	predict, previous
pro-	forward	problem, procure
re-	backward, again	return, reassert, regress
retro-	backward	retrogress, retrorocket
sub-	under, beneath	submarine, subdivision
sym-	with, together	symptom, sympathy
trans-	across	transport, transcontinental
un-	not	unable, uninformed
uni-	one	unit, unicorn

Source: Burt Liebert, *Linguistics and the New English Teacher.* New York: Macmillan Publishing Co., Inc., 1971, pp. 112–114.

TABLE 8-4

LEXICAL MORPHEMES—ROOTS

ROOT	MEANING	EXAMPLES
-ag-, -act-	do	agenda, actor
-am-, -amic-	love	amateur, amicable
-anthrop-	man	anthropology, anthropoid
-aqu-	water	aquatic, aqueous
-arch-	ancient, chief	archaic, archeology
-astr-, -aster-	star	asteroid, astronomy
-aud-, -audit-	hear	auditory, audible
-auto-	self	automatic, automobile
-ben-, -bene-	good	benefit, benefactor
-biblio-	book	bibliophile, bibliography
-bio-	life	biography, biology
-capit-	head	caption, capital
-carn-	flesh	carnal, carnivore
-cent-	hundred	per cent, centimeter
-chrom-	color	panchromatic, chromium
-chron-	time	chronicle, chronological
-clud, -clus-	close	include, seclude
-cogn-	know	cognition, recognize
-cred-	trust	credit, credible
-crypt-	secret	cryptic, cryptogram
-dem-, -demo-	people	democratic, epidemic
-dict-	speak	predict, dictate
-duc-, -duct-	lead	conduct, education
-fer-	yield	transfer, fertile
-fid-	faith	perfidy, fiduciary
-fin-	end, limit	infinite, final
-frag-, -fract-	break	fracture, fragment
-gen-	birth	engender, generation
-gen-	kind, race	genetic, genesis
-geo-	earth	geography, geometry
-gram-	write, writing	telegram, grammar
-graph-	write, writing	graphite, geography
-hydr-	water	hydraulic, dehydrate
-junct-	join	junction, conjunctive
-jud-	judge	judicial, prejudice
-jug-	join	conjugal, conjugate
-loc-	place	location, local
-log-	word, study	dialogue, logic
-magn-	large	magnificent, magnify
-man-	hand	manual, manipulate
-micr-	small	microcosm, microscope
-mort-	die, death	mortal, mortician
-neo-	new	neoclassic, neophyte

ROOT	MEANING	EXAMPLES
-omni-	all	omnicient, omnibus
-pan-	all, entire	pancake, pan-American
-pater-, -patr-	father	paternal, patron
-phil-	like, love	philanthropist, bibliophile
-poly-	many	polygamy, polyglot
-port-	carry, bear	transport, portable
-prim-	first, early	primitive, primary
-punct-	point	punctuation, puncture
-sci-	know, knowledge	science, omniscient
-scrib-, -script-	write	scribble, manuscript
-spec-, -spic-, -spect-	look, see	introspective, suspicion
-spir-	breath, breathe	respiration, expire
-tract-	draw, pull	tractor, traction
-vert-	turn	extrovert, invert
-vid-, -vis-	see	vision, evidence
-vit-	life	vital, vitamin
-zo-	animal	zoology, protozoa

should ring when he sees or hears *predict*. In all four words—and in dozens more—the *prefix, pre,* means *before.* Once a student learns to think in terms of *pre* and *post; pro* and *con; mono, bi,* and *poly,* he is on his way.

Lexical morphemes consist of *roots,* which form the nuclei of words, and *prefixes,* which come before the root and add meaning. A list of English prefixes and roots that recur in many words, always with the same meaning, could run into hundreds. But a working knowledge of only a few of the commonest can make a huge difference. On pages 205–207 is a list of some of the most frequently used English lexical roots and prefixes.

SUMMARY OF ENGLISH MORPHOLOGY

The English morphological system consists of three major subsystems:

1. The inflectional system, consisting of ten inflections suffixed to verbs, nouns, and adjectives. These inflections are:
   a. The plural noun, b. the possessive noun (a and b may be combined into plural-possessive.), c. the third person singular present tense verb, d. the past tense verb, e. the past participle verb, f. the gerund verb, g. the present participle verb, h. the progressive verb (6, 7, and 8 are spelled *ing*), i. the comparative adjective (*er*), and j. the

superlative adjective (*est*). Personal pronoun inflections are so irregular that they cannot be classified easily. Each personal pronoun must be learned as a unit.

2.   The distributional system consists of a number of suffixes (and a few prefixes) that determine whether words are nouns, verbs, adjectives, or adverbs. Once a distributional morpheme has been added to a word, it can only appear in a sentence position reserved for that part of speech.

Then one day the doorbell rang, and there was the old man with his boxes and bundles and his tray.

"Oh, how do you do, sir! Do come in and have a cup of tea," said Florence. "I want to tell you what wonderful times I've had walking into the picture and playing there."

The old man smiled at Florence with his blue eyes and said, "I am glad, child, that you liked the picture. But I know you haven't been going into it so much lately. All the picture was good for was to entertain you till you learned to read. Now you can read about much more wonderful things than just the few things that are in this picture. In the future you will want books to keep you company when you are alone. You will not need the picture any more. So now I am going to take it and lend it to some other child who has not yet learned how to read books."

Florence's mother helped the old man take the picture down from the wall. The old man opened one of the boxes that he carried and put the picture into it. Then Florence's mother made some tea. While they drank tea, Florence listened to what the old man and her mother were saying. She did not understand all of what they said, but she knew that they were talking about books and reading.

When the old man got up to go, Florence went with him to the door. He looked down at her with his bright blue eyes and said, "If you should need me, I'll come to see you again. But I don't think it will be necessary, because you need never again feel bored and unhappy when you are alone.

"Now you know how to read."

FIGURE 8-D   *Let's Read,* final lesson. (Wayne State University Press, 1961.)

3.   The lexical system consists of roots, which form the nuclei of words; and prefixes, which give additional meaning. For vocabulary building, this is the most useful of the three English morphological systems.

THE SYLLABLE

It is important that morpheme not be confused with *syllable*. The morpheme is a unit of meaning, and may consist of any number of syllables, even a fractional part of one syllable. The syllable is a unit of articulation, consisting of a vowel phoneme, with or without one or more consonants clustered around it. It may contain one morpheme or less, or several. *Connecticut* is a four syllable word with a single morpheme. *Boys'* contains three morphemes (boy + plural + possessive) in a single syllable. Breaking words into syllables is another method of simplifying long words. The value of teaching syllabication, although common practice in many English classrooms, is not firmly established. Probably its major virtue is not for teaching reading but for hyphenating words at the ends of lines. An attack on the practice of teaching syllabication is found in *The Reading Teacher*.[1] There are many rules for syllable division, some of them contradictory, and even the dictionaries do not always agree. But a few simple rules can be learned.

Some Rules for Syllabication[2]

1.   A single consonant usually goes with the vowel that follows when that consonant appears between two vowels.

silent	si/lent
minus	mi/nus
nomad	no/mad

2.   A single consonant appearing between two vowels usually goes with the preceding vowel, if that vowel is short and within an accented syllable.

acid	'ac/id
bigot	'big/ot

[1] Dorothy Z. Seymour, "Word Division for Decoding." *The Reading Teacher*, December 1973, 27, 275–283.
[2] Robert L. Curry, "Teaching the Decoding Skills." in Lawrence E. Hafner, *Improving Reading in Secondary Schools*. New York: Macmillan Publishing Co., Inc., 1967.

3. No syllabic division should be made between consonants that constitute a consonant blend or consonant digraph. . . . [These should be treated as single consonants, applying rules 1 and 2.]

    locket   'lock/et
    migrate   'mi/grate (*mi* is not a short vowel)
    bishop   'bish/op

4. The syllabic division of two consonants, which are neither blend nor digraph, and which appear between two vowels, usually comes between the two consonants.

    mildew   mil/dew
    millet   mil/let
    crescent   cres/cent

5. Prefixes usually form separate syllables.

    react   re/act
    defrost   de/frost
    invent   in/vent

6. Suffixes usually form separate syllables.

    peaceful   peace/ful
    worker   work/er

7. The suffix *ed*, if immediately preceded by the letter *d* or *t*, forms a separate syllable. The suffix *ed* combines with other letters to form one syllable if *not* preceded by *d* or *t*. [However, when final *d* or *t* is doubled before *ed*, divide the syllables between the double letters.]

    shrouded   shroud/ed
    posted   post/ed
    forced   forced
    sinned   sinned
    budded   bud/ded
    omitted   o/mit/ted

8. A word ending in *le*, when the *le* is preceded by a consonant forms a final syllable with that consonant and the *le*. However, *le* stands alone as the final syllable when preceded by the consonants *ck*.

    uncle   un/cle
    pebble   peb/ble
    buckle   buck/le
    freckle   freck/le

9.   A syllabic division is made between words that form a compound.

pathway   path/way
flashlight   flash/light

ELEMENTS OF PHONIC INSTRUCTION

Teaching phonics involves five major components, although not every student will have a problem with all five. The exercise on p. 173 is for teaching
component 1, auditory discrimination. This is primary, for the student who
cannot hear the sound cannot reproduce it. Inadequate auditory discrimination may be the result of an accent or dialect in which particular phonemes
are omitted or different, or it may result from a physical disability, such as
hearing loss or speech impairment. If a consistent pattern of errors is noted,
whether with a single phoneme, confusion of two or more phonemes, letter
confusion, or difficulty in blending, the teacher or aide can devise exercises
of the type illustrated. Or exercises may be taken from any good phonics
text. Persistent lack of progress indicates a serious involvement, and referral
to the speech pathologist is appropriate.

If the student can reproduce the sounds but is having difficulty distinguishing the letters, the problem involves component 2, *visual discrimination*. On p. 174 is an exercise in visual discrimination. To test whether a
student's problem is difficulty in hearing sounds or seeing letters, read aloud
a list of words and ask him to tell you which words contain the sound. For
example,

Which words contain the *bl* blend?
black   boy   break   blend   blond   lack   broil   baloney

Then give a similar list of words to read. Compare performances on the two
tests. In phonic discrimination drills, use words with which the student is
familiar, or use nonsense syllables and say that you are doing so. Prolonged
inability to make visual discriminations may indicate a vision loss and the
student should be referred to the school health officer.

Phonic instruction usually begins with the third component, learning
sound-letter relationships. That is what *Let's Read* is about. The student
usually begins learning to read by reading orally, so the teacher may notice
special problems in auditory or visual discrimination or lack of knowledge of
phonics; and if necessary, can digress from the text for special drill. As the
student progresses, however, oral instruction should give way to silent reading with written comprehension checks.

The fourth component is *word building*. It does no good to discriminate individual sounds if they cannot be put together into words. That is why most phonic drills are composed of complete words rather than isolated sounds, or else are followed immediately by words or sentences. Although some students have little difficulty with word building, others have problems making consonant or vowel blends or otherwise putting words together, and this requires extra help.

Finally, although it is not strictly a phonic problem, phonic drill should include component 5, *reading for meaning*. Use such drills as:

free.

In the middle of the meadow was a huge oak tree.

tire.

Or have students make up sentences using the problem words or sounds under study.

WHY MORPHOLOGY ?

Throughout this unit we have concentrated on learning to decode words, with as little theoretical explanation as possible. It is not necessary to teach students the phonetic alphabet or the ten English inflections to teach them to read. The system presented here is based on allowing the student to discover phonic principles for himself.

Why, then, is it necessary to go through this explanation? First, the teacher who understands the structure of language is in a better position to understand the problems the student is having. Whether that problem consists of the students' inability to recognize the phoneme /z/ because it is not part of their native language, their difficulty in making common English blends, or their failure to write plural and possessive nouns properly, the teacher should be able to diagnose the problem.

Once the problem is analyzed, the teacher may have to explain it to the student. Most of us learn language intuitively and have little need for formal teaching of structure. But others either do not see principles readily or need some framework upon which to hang their learning. Thus the good teacher is prepared to make explanations when necessary.

Finally, while structural theory does not need to be built into the teaching of reading, it does play a vital part in the student's overall language development. Earlier in the text, we stated that the student's capacity to read cannot exceed his linguistic growth, and it is with this that every teacher should be concerned. The science teacher who does his thing on *photosynthesis* without making sure his students understand that *photo* means light, and *synthesis* means putting things together, is not doing the whole job. The student will have to learn to read all over again upon encountering *photoengraving* in the industrial arts class or *synthetic* fiber in homemaking. But if the student has learned the principle of the recurring morpheme and has become acquainted with *synthesis* as a lexical stem and the distributional adjective suffix *ic,* things come into place much more easily.

If each teacher also pays a little attention to teaching the principles of language as they apply to classroom vocabulary, these principles can then be used in other classes and in learning to read. If students can learn to analyze words into components, big words become little ones.

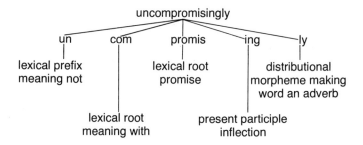

This is not to imply that every student who comes across a long word will go through this extensive analysis. But it does mean that students can learn that the longest words are composed of little bits of meaning, which English speakers can recognize because they are repeated frequently in conversation. It means that once your students learn to think in terms of word parts (morphemes), big words can no longer bully them.

CHAPTER 9
Looting the Lexicon

VOCABULARY BUILDING

In 1940 Charles Fries published *American English Grammar,*[1] in which he analyzed samples of written American English. He compared the language of highly educated men and women who work in language-oriented professions (newspaper editors, clergymen, lawyers) with uneducated (not over eighth grade) unskilled workers. He found that much of our classical textbook grammar fails to describe the differences between the two groups. What he did find was an enormous *quantitative,* not qualitative difference. Educated people, both in speaking and writing,[2] use a much larger vocabulary. They can select just the right word, while the uneducated overwork *good, bad,* and *pretty.* The educated also have at their command a greater variety of sentence structure, using more compound and complex sentences and a greater supply of modifiers and phrases.

Fries pinpointed not only the difference between educated and uneducated language, but the major obstacle your students have in bridging the gap. Many young people are unable to cope with the requirements of the classroom because their vocabularies are so meagre they lack the words needed to read, to write, and to think. Fries recommended that English instruction emphasize *expansion* of language rather than correctness—that is, learning new words and learning to handle more complex linguistic forms.

The same recommendation was made 30 years later:[3]

Expansion is the key word in the language program: expansion of communicative need, expansion of experience, expansion of confidence in the use of

[1]New York: Appleton-Century-Crofts.
[2]Another study by the same author, *The Structure of English,* New York: Harcourt, Brace & World, 1952 dealt with oral English.
[3]E. Brooks Smith, Kenneth S. Goodman, and Robert Meredith, *Language and Thinking in the Elementary School.* New York: Holt, Rinehart and Winston, 1970, p. 165.

*language, expansion of conceptual ability, expansion of control over the struc-
ture of language, expansion of vocabulary, expansion of the range of language
that is understood, expansion of the range of language used in expression and
the ability to communicate with many different people.*

They went on to recommend what amounts to a language experience
approach, making use of every opportunity to involve students in oral and
written English. This approach was called *language bombardment* by Bereiter and Engelman.[4] If every secondary student learns a few new words each
week from each teacher, the cumulative effect will be better reading, better
writing, and finer scholarship.

However, telling students to "look up all unfamiliar words in the dictionary," as many teachers do, is futile. Interrupting good reading to trot off
to the dictionary is a drag, and few students (or adults) will do this. A good
language development program is more difficult and subtle than that. It
involves understanding how language develops and clearing away some of
the common linguistic myths.

One of these myths is that one's own vernacular is, for some mysterious
reason, inferior to another language or dialect of long-ago or far-away. Just
as medieval scholars worshiped Latin and disparaged English, so have many
traditional grammarians tried to tell us just what constitutes "standard" English.

There are no "superior" or "inferior" languages or dialects, however,
as was once assumed. Linguists have combed the earth, from jungles to city
streets, looking for "primitive" languages and have found none. All adult
language is complex and uniquely suited to the communication needs of the
culture. Our students are as well equipped to communicate with their peers
as you and I are with ours. Each individual's language is quite the best for his
or her needs, hand tailored to suit the culture, the personality, and the things
we communicate about. (So what's wrong with dangling a preposition?)

Language becomes inadequate only when one moves to another language community, whether from German-speaking to French, or from the
streets to the classroom. When our students are with their friends, discussing
familiar topics, the language they learned intuitively is adequate. But we are
asking these young people to step into a new world—a world of books and
study, a world which increases in complexity as they progress through the
grades.

The real reason for language instruction, of which reading improvement is a vital phase, is not that students' intuitively acquired language is

[4]Carl Bereiter and Siegfried Engelmann, *Teaching Disadvantaged Children In the Preschool.*
Englewood Cliffs, N.J.: Prentice-Hall, Inc., 1966.

"incorrect" or inferior, but because we would like to free them from the limitations of the streets. We want students who can do more than rap with their peers. We want to produce adults who can read a newspaper intelligently; who can follow instructions in a cook book, shop manual, or clothing pattern; who can transcribe shorthand notes without looking up the spelling of every third word; who can make sense of a history or physics text; who can communicate with an author who writes for mature minds. And *that* doesn't come intuitively. That takes a lot of effort, by the student and by a bevy of teachers who are willing to teach not only subject matter, but language skills.

Another linguistic myth is that language is constant and unchanging, that newer forms are a barbaric distortion of "pure" language. Languages are continually changing, and the various processes of change can be identified.

Accretion is the addition of new forms to a language. It includes words for new things, such as *laser*; new compounds, including *rock 'n'roll*; new phrases, such as *all systems are go*; new blends and combinations of morphemes, including *motel* for *motor hotel*, *mo-ped* for *motorized peddle bike*, and *digital* computer.

Accretion comes from a number of sources. Languages are continually evolving from older languages. English grew mainly from Old German, which contributed most of our short, common words, such as *in* and *out*, *warm* and *cold*. But many of our longer words, particularly scientific and legal terms, came from Latin, including *flora* and *fauna* and *habeas corpus*. Many other words came from latin-based languages, especially Spanish by way of Mexico (*ranch* and *pinto*) and French *theatre* and *picayune*). American Indians gave us the inspiration for *bury the hatchet* and *firewater* and the words *moose* and *avocado*. (It is not accurate to speak of THE American Indian language, as over a thousand different languages have been identified with the original North and South Americans. *Moose*, for example, comes from Algonquian, of eastern United States, but *avocado* from Nahuatl, spoken by the Aztecs of Mexico.)

But many other languages have influenced English. The Dutch gave us *dollar*, Hebrew *cherub*, the Italians *piano*, and the West Africans *juke*, meaning disorderly, which Americans in the South used for *dance*, and hence *jukebox* and *jukejoint*. Truly our language is our most exotic possession, gathered from every spot on the globe.

Slang is a rich source of new forms. Henry Gleason sees slang as an attempt by some "in-group" to achieve a language of its own.[5] The group may be founded along racial lines, or by occupation, age, sex, social level,

[5]Henry Allen Gleason, Jr., *Linguistics and English Grammar*. New York: Holt, Rinehart and Winston, 1965, p. 359.

clique, or gang. It forms a private way of communicating until it either dies a natural death, as most slang does, or is overheard and adopted by out-groups. If the slang form fills a need, if it says something with greater efficiency or color, it may well begin its journey into common acceptance. But if it merely repeats what can be equally well said with a standard form, it will probably pass into oblivion. As Webster informs us, "There is no satisfactory objective test for slang."[6] There is simply a gradual transition of words and phrases from slang to popular usage.

New forms also come from occupations and subcultures. Without space science, we had neither *astronauts* nor *countdowns*. From the gold rush we acquired *roughneck* and *pull up stakes,* and the pioneers gave us *cantankerous* and *kick the bucket.*[7]

Frequently, words change their definition. *Smorgasbord* is a good example. From the Swedish meaning *open sandwich,* the word once applied to a particular style of food, including a variety of spiced fish and meats, along with cheeses and bread. Today, however, it has been applied to any variety of foods, regardless of cooking style. And with typical love for shortcuts, Americans have changed the word to *smorgy.* We have also adopted old names for new things, such as *butter* for *oleomargarine,* or transferred brand names to the product, including *Kleenex* for *cleansing tissues* and *Vaseline* for *petroleum jelly.*

Many new words come from people's names, from *Diesel,* who invented a more efficient engine, to *Maverick,* a rancher who refused to brand his cattle,[8] and *Bloomer,* an early fighter for the liberation of women.

And speaking of liberation, new social movements can profoundly affect our language. We have already added *Ms.* and *chairperson,* plus a host of other *persons* who used to be *men.* And some time soon, we will have to find some kind of neuter personal pronoun singular. It's getting difficult to write English, now that college-educated ladies object to such sentences as:

Each teacher helps *his* students use the dictionary.

But what does one say? *Her* students? Just as bad. *Their* students? Too many grammatical purists. Obviously, new social conditions require a new English third person singular neuter personal pronoun. Perhaps *its* will come

[6]*Webster's New Collegiate Dictionary.* Springfield, Mass.: G. & C. Merriam Company, 1975, p. 16a, Col. 1.

[7]Some of the information in the preceding paragraphs is from *Our Language Today, Seventh and Eighth grades.* David R. Conlin, George R. Herman, and Jerome Martin. New York: American Book Company, 1966.

[8]Richard Boning, *They Gave Their Names.* Barnell Loft, Ltd., 1971.

to be applied to people, like the Spanish *su*. Warren Farrell[9] suggests a new approach, using *te/tē/* for *he or she*, *tes* /tes/ for *his or hers*, and *tir* /tr/ for *him or her*. General acceptance of a new personal pronoun will be much more difficult than for a new noun. Yet considering the speed with which we adopted Ms., who knows?

Linguistic forms may also become victims of changing customs and changing speech patterns:

> *Obsolescence can cause a language to lose as well as gain new words, as any school student struggling with Shakespeare can testify. Before* Macbeth *is over ten lines old the student has encountered* hurly-burly, Graymalkin, Paddock, *and* anon. *This is not unique, for the same amount of reading in* Romeo and Juliet *produces* carry coals, colliers, choler, *and* take the wall. *These forms have certainly not died out of the language completely but have become uncommon or archaic expressions. Only* collier *and* anon *are listed in the Thorndike-Lorge Word list[10] as occurring once or more in a million words, whereas* hurly-burly *and* choler *are in the once in a million to once in four million group.[11]*

Words not only come into the language and go out, they change, they evolve, they grow. In a Scottish museum I encountered a *spunk box*. Do you know what one puts in a spunk box? Neither did I, but the curator informed me that "We old timers still use *spunk* for *match*." Before matches, it meant *tinder*, and before that, it was the fire itself. Then in 1773 Oliver Goldsmith, in the play *She Stoops to Conquer*, wrote:

The Squire has got spunk in him.

So now a person with spunk has "fire." What will spunk mean tomorrow? Tune in in another generation or two for the next exciting episode.

Words not only change their meaning, they change their pronunciation. Sometimes whole languages undergo drastic change, as when English experienced the "great vowel shift" a few centuries ago. What caused speakers of English to shift their pronunciation of vowels forward and upward on the vowel scale (See chart, p. 182) in a comparatively short time, we do not know. We only know it happened. Sometimes these changes involve only single words. *Rodeo* is losing its original Spanish pronunciation /rō'dāō/ and is popularly /'rōdēō/.

Sometimes words become more generalized in meaning, as in the previous example of *smorgasbord*. There is also a tendency to shorten many

[9]Warren Farrell, *The Liberated Man*. New York: Random House, 1974, p. xxxii.
[10]See: Edward L. Thorndike and Irving Lorge, *The Teacher's Word Book of 30,000 Words*. New York: Bureau of Publications, Teachers College, Columbia University, 1944.
[11]Burt Liebert, op. cit., p. 209.

words, as *gasoline* becomes *gas* and *telephone* is *phone*. Even basic grammatical structures are subject to alteration. English, for example, has lost many of its original inflections. This process is probably still going on. In the previous chapter we discussed the confusion between the plural and possessive inflections. Many speakers of English do not know where to use the apostrophe, because the two inflections are becoming blurred. Perhaps in time we will drop one or the other, or blend them into one. Something interesting is also happening to the third person singular inflection: *go— goes*. This inflection is frequently dropped in many black dialects: *He go down town now*. Interestingly, I also noticed a similar tendency in England, particularly in formal announcements:

Barclay's Bank *announce* their new summer hours.

As language changes, new dialects develop from old, and these eventually grow into new languages. Modern English, from about the time of Shakespeare, developed out of Middle English, which can be seen in the original works of Chaucer. Middle English came from Old English, the language of *Beowulf*, which has to be translated before you and I can read it. Old English is a product of Old Germanic, which itself grew from Indo-European, the language now thought to be the common ancestor of most European languages and of East Indian Hindi.

And what will be the fate of English? Will philologists some day study our native tongue as an interesting relic of a primitive time? Will the various dialects of English split into different languages, so that New Yorkers may be unable to communicate with Londoners or even Alabamans? Or will the language as a whole develop into something else?

There are some reasons to suspect that in the future, English may change at a different rate from that in the past. One of these is the universality of writing which does not change as rapidly as speech. Another is the amount of travel that brings us in contact with other English speakers. Third, we have the mass media, which permits a single broadcaster's voice to be heard throughout the nation—and international broadcasting is becoming increasingly common. But all these stabilizing influences may be counterbalanced or even overbalanced by the increasing acceleration of change in our daily lives, by the proliferation of new inventions and discoveries, and by new social movements, all of which will require new language to discuss them.

Unlike clothing styles or automobiles, language changes slowly. So little may happen to a language in one lifetime, we tend to think of it as having a fixed, unchanging vocabulary and grammar. That is why, for many of us, this is a new way of looking at language instruction. Rather than trying to shovel back the tide of linguistic change, we would do better to understand it. Instead of "correcting" our students' native tongue, we may take our cue from Fries' study, which tells us that the difference between educated and uneducated usage is less a matter of quality than of *quantity*. Thus the challenge becomes *expansion* of our students' linguistic abilities to meet the needs of the scholastic culture. And in that expansion, the building of new vocabulary is the keystone.

Extensive vocabularies are built through extensive language experience. Also, broader and deeper understanding of the meaning of many words comes with repeated use. After the word is used by a variety of writers, in many contexts, with many shades of meaning, and with different implications, it becomes part of the organic vocabulary of the reader. One of the most important functions of a teacher, regardless of subject, is to stimulate students to become readaholics, for it is wide and enthusiastic reading, more than any other activity, that promotes precision and depth with words.

But many students get caught in the "remedial reader syndrome:" They do not read because it is too difficult. And it is difficult because they do not read. To break this Catch-22 situation usually requires intervention.

The balance of this chapter will be devoted to methods by which classroom teachers can build their students' vocabularies. Some of these have already been discussed in connection with elementary methods of teaching decoding. But while each method has a value, it also has limitations. Configuration clues are limited to the most elementary reading situations, and can even hamper reading development, if not supplemented soon. Learning sight words is an important tool for beginning readers and it ultimately should become the basis for good reading. Teaching students to make educated guesses at new words on the basis of context clues is a useful skill and should be encouraged as a method of getting meaning from the page without having to stop and run to a dictionary. Letter-sound relationships must be understood, if the student is to attack new and unfamiliar words. Morphological structure can be an important method of attacking new words, but it is often neglected by classroom teachers. The study guide, which introduces students to the vocabulary of each new lesson, is probably the most important single tool for vocabulary growth. And if each teacher would point out the meaning of—*ist, poly*—, and *auto*—as they appear in the study guide, each teacher's efforts would reinforce those of his colleagues.

Vocabulary Builders

A great number of textbooks are available to increase vocabulary. Many of these are little more than lists of words either with definitions attached or for students to look up in dictionaries. Some, such as the *Harbrace Vocabulary Workshop*,[12] are based somewhat on morphological principles. Others, including Richard Boning's *They Gave Their Names*,[13] and Wilfred Funk's *Word Origins and Their Romantic Stories*,[14] give interesting etymologies.

Subject Vocabulary

While vocabulary texts are of value for English instruction, most teachers are interested in teaching the vocabulary of their own disciplines and can find ample material in their textbooks. Word lists for language growth can be taken daily from required reading.

The ultimate aim of education, however, is to free the student from dependence upon the teacher. This means that study guides are valuable only until the student has grown sufficiently to read without them. No education is complete until the student can use the tools that make him an independent learner. And a good place to start is with the most basic of all language reference, the dictionary.

But first, having dispelled some of the myths about languages, let us deal with one myth about dictionaries. There is a tendency to think of dictionaries as if they were not written by human beings at all, but handed down from the peak of Mount Sinai. Some people believe that the function of a dictionary is to police the language, to act as a final court of appeals to decide whether it's OK to *finalize* a report or use *like* as a preposition.

This is not how or why dictionaries are written. Lexicographers are observers of language, not linguistic policemen. They do not decide which usage is correct, they simply observe what people do with words and report their findings in dictionaries. Whether a particular word or usage does or does not appear in a dictionary is not a matter of correctness but of how common the usage and how complete the dictionary.

This should in no way detract from the respect we have for dictionaries and the people who write them nor from their usefulness as a reference tool. Quite the contrary, the more we learn about the complexity of language, the more respect we acquire for the enormous amount of painstaking, scholarly research that goes into making a good dictionary. And as we realize that correctness in language is nothing more than common, universal usage, the dictionary becomes an even more useful guide.

It is worth repeating that it is more important to understand the meaning of a word in context than to arrive at a general definition. A *solution* may

---

[12]New York: Harcourt, Brace, Jovanovich, Inc., 1957.
[13]Baldwin, N.Y.: Barnell Loft, Ltd., 1971.
[14]New York: Funk and Wagnalls, Inc., 1950.

be the answer to a problem in math or social studies, but a mixture of liquids and solids in chemistry. *Civil rights* may imply the beginning of a golden age to one writer, the end of it to another.

TEACHING DICTIONARY SKILLS

The "dictionary drill" offered in many English classes—long lists of evil-sounding words to be looked up and memorized—is usually disliked by students and done, if at all, in a mechanical, unproductive fashion. The two extremes of leaving students adrift with no instruction in how to use a dictionary or inundating them with rote drills concerning etymology, pronunciation, and other factors are both less than profitable. Yet a few helpful hints, a few minutes at a time as opportunities and needs arise, can pay rich dividends.

First, it is necessary for the teacher to know quite a bit about not only dictionaries but about the particular dictionary used in the classroom. Not all dictionaries are alike. Observations about one do not necessarily apply to others. It is, therefore, impossible to state any one set of rules applicable to all. But if we take two popular dictionaries and look at them methodically, we can discover certain general principles.

A good study in contrast can be made using *Webster's New Collegiate Dictionary* (G. & C. Merriam Co., 1975) and *Thorndike-Barnhart Advanced Dictionary* (Doubleday—Scott, Foresman and Company, 1974). Open the two at random, and you can observe a *difference in emphasis.* Following are reproductions of pages from each of these volumes. Note that Thorndike-Barnhart places stress on *readability.* The print is larger and the spacing more generous. Although this reproduction cannot reveal it, the paper is whiter, thus increasing readability. The emphasis in Webster is upon scholarship. It is more comprehensive, claiming over 150,000 entries to 95,000 for Thorndike-Barnhart.

THE BORN LOSER   **by Art Sansom**

Between the words *airmail* and *aisle* (See Figures 9-B and 9-C), Thorndike-Barnhart contains three words not listed in Webster, which contains fourteen not listed in Thorndike-Barnhart. Obviously, not all words in the language are found in even good dictionaries. Both publishers of these dictionaries have issued a study guide for teaching dictionary skills. Write for latest prices.

There is another major difference between the two publications. To see its significance, try listing the following words in the order in which they appear in the dictionary:

St. Patrick's Day	salmagundi	3-D
three	airflow	air gun
UNESCO	Borodin	Adams, Samuel
Sacramento	men	unknowing
safety	memorable	University of California at Davis
three-dimensional	*ami de cour*	

A naive assumption would be that these words appear in alphabetical order. This is true of Thorndike-Barnhart, except for *ami de cour,* and *University of California at Davis,* which are not listed. But in Webster five words appear in special sections at the back: *Ami de cour* is in the list of Foreign Words and Phrases, *Borodin* and *Samuel Adams* are found under Biographical Names, *Sacramento* is in the Geographical Names, and *University of California at Davis* appears under Colleges and Universities.

How do you find out all of this? Every good dictionary has an explanatory section at the beginning. This tells how the dictionary is put together and gives valuable assistance in using it. Yet seldom is this important section given proper attention. Each teacher, however, can spend some time familiarizing herself with the dictionary in her own room. Then she can pass on helpful hints to her students, as need arises. If each teacher does this, students will eventually acquire considerable skill in using the dictionary.

The information concerning the list of words given above, for example, can be found in the explanatory notes of *Webster's Dictionary,* pp. 10a–19a. *The Thorndike-Barnhart Dictionary,* on the contrary, contains one simple statement on p. 8:

One Alphabetical List

To find a word in this dictionary, you need only to know the order of the letters of the alphabet. All main entries—words in the common vocabulary, technical terms, proper names, abbreviations—are in one alphabetical list.

Look at page 1. You will find a and aardvark, abandon, and abase. You will also find Aachen, a geographical name; Aaron, the name of a person in the

Bible; the symbol A; *and the abbreviations* A.A. *and* A.B. *In this dictionary, you have only one place to look for a word.*

A page from the *Thorndike-Barnhart Advanced Dictionary* is shown in Figure 9B.

to a jet stream. Airplanes, airships, gliders, helicopters, and balloons are aircraft.

aircraft carrier, warship designed as a base for aircraft, with a large, flat deck on which to land or take off.

air crew (er′krü′, ar′krü′), *n.* the crew that flies an aircraft but does not service it.

air cushion vehicle, Hovercraft.

air drome (er′drōm′, ar′drōm′), *n.* airport. Also, BRITISH **aerodrome.** |< *air* + Greek *dromos* racecourse|

air drop (er′drop′, ar′drop′), *n., v.,* **-dropped, -drop ping.** —*n.* a delivering of food, supplies, cargo, or persons by parachute from aircraft in flight. —*v.t.* deliver (food, supplies, cargo, or persons) by parachute from aircraft in flight.

Aire dale (er′dāl, ar′dāl), *n.* any of a breed of large terriers having a wiry brown or tan coat with dark markings. |< *Airedale,* valley in Yorkshire, England|

air express, the shipment of packages by aircraft.

air field (er′fēld′, ar′fēld′), *n.* the landing area of an airport or air base.

air filter, a mechanical or electronic device that filters dust, pollen, etc., from the air, as in air conditioning.

air flow (er′flō′, ar′flō′), *n.* 1 a natural movement of air. 2 the flow of air around and relative to an object moving in air. —*adj.* 1 streamlined. 2 that is produced by air currents.

air foil (er′foil′, ar′foil′), *n.* a wing, rudder, or other surface designed to help lift or control an aircraft.

air force, 1 branch of the military forces that uses aircraft. 2 **Air Force,** a separate branch of the armed forces of the United States that includes aviation personnel, equipment, etc.

Air Force Academy, the officer-training service school of the United States Air Force at Colorado Springs, Colorado.

air frame (er′frām′, ar′frām′), *n.* framework, excluding engines, of an airplane, a ballistic missile, or a dirigible.

air glow (er′glō′, ar′glō′), *n.* a faint glow in the sky, not visible to the naked eye, believed due to chemical reactions in the upper atmosphere.

air gun, 1 air rifle. 2 device utilizing compressed air to force grease, putty, etc., into or onto something.

air hole, 1 a hole that air can pass through. 2 U.S. an open space in the ice on a river, pond, etc. 3 air pocket.

air i ly (er′ə le, ar′ə le), *adv.* in an airy manner.

air i ness (er′e nis, ar′e nis), *n.* airy quality.

air ing (er′ing, ar′ing), *n.* 1 exposure to air for drying, warming, etc. 2 a walk, ride, or drive in the open air. 3 exposure to public notice, discussion, criticism, etc.

air lane, a regular route used by aircraft; airway; skyway.

air less (er′lis, ar′lis), *adj.* 1 without fresh air; stuffy. 2 without a breeze; still.

air letter, 1 a lightweight sheet of paper designed to fold and seal as an envelope, with a message on its inner surfaces. 2 letter sent by air mail.

air lift (er′lift′, ar′lift′), *n.* 1 transportation by air of personnel, passengers, and freight in an emergency. 2 the aircraft used. 3 the cargo transported. —*v.t.* transport by airlift.

air line (er′lin′, ar′lin′), *n.* 1 an established system of transportation of people and freight by aircraft. 2 company owning or

operating such a system. 3 route for aircraft; airway. 4 a straight line through the air.

air lin er (er′li′nər, ar′li′nər), *n.* a large passenger airplane.

air lock (er′lok′, ar′lok′), *n.* an airtight compartment between places where there is a difference in air pressure. The pressure in an airlock can be raised or lowered.

air mail (er′māl′, ar′māl′), *v.t.* send by air mail: *Please airmail this letter.* —*adj.* sent or to be sent by aircraft.

air mail, 1 mail sent by aircraft. 2 system of sending mail by aircraft.

air man (er′mən, ar′mən), *n., pl.* **-men.** 1 pilot of an aircraft; aviator. 2 one of the crew of an aircraft. 3 an enlisted man or woman in the Air Force, comparable in grade to a private.

airman first class, (in the U.S. Air Force) an airman of the highest rank, ranking next below a staff sergeant.

air mass, a large body of air within the atmosphere that has nearly uniform temperature and humidity at any given level and moves horizontally over great distances without changing.

air mattress, pad that can be inflated to serve as a mattress.

air mile, a nautical mile, 6076.11549 feet, used as a measure of distance in the flight of aircraft.

air-mind ed (er′min′did, ar′min′did), *adj.* 1 interested in aviation. 2 fond of air travel. —**air′-mind′ed ness,** *n.*

airplane with jet engines

air plane (er′plān′, ar′plān′), *n.* any of various aircraft heavier than air, supported in flight by its fixed wings and driven by propeller, jet propulsion, etc. Also, BRITISH **aeroplane.**

air plant, epiphyte.

air pocket, a downward current of air formed by the sudden sinking of cooled air, that causes an aircraft to lose altitude suddenly.

air pollution, the contamination of the air by industrial waste gases, fuel exhaust, and atomic fallout.

air port (er′pôrt′, er′pōrt′; ar′pôrt′, ar′pōrt′), *n.* area, especially on land, used regularly by aircraft to land or take off, usually having several runways, buildings for passenger facilities, and hangars for

aisle (def. 2) of a church

23   **aisle**

hat, āge, fär; let, ēqual, tèrm;
it, īce; hot, ōpen, ôrder;
oil, out; cup, pùt, rüle;
ch, child; ng, long; sh, she;
th, thin; ŦH, then; zh, measure;

ə represents *a* in about, *e* in taken,
i in pencil, *o* in lemon, *u* in circus.

< = from, derived from, taken from.

storing, repairing, and servicing aircraft.

air post, BRITISH. air mail.

air pressure, atmospheric pressure.

air pump, apparatus for forcing, compressing, or removing air.

air raid, attack by enemy aircraft, especially by bombers.

air rifle, gun that uses compressed air to shoot a single pellet or dart; air gun.

air sac, any of various air-filled spaces in different parts of the body of a bird, connected with the lungs. It aids in breathing and in regulating body temperature.

air ship (er′ship′, ar′ship′), *n.* a lighter-than-air propeller-driven aircraft that can be steered; dirigible.

air sick (er′sik′, ar′sik′), *adj.* sick as a result of the motion of aircraft. —**air′sick′ness,** *n.*

air space (er′spas′, ar′spas′), *n.* space in the air, especially that belonging to a particular country.

air speed (er′sped′, ar′sped′), *n.* speed of an aircraft in relation to the speed of the air through which it moves, as distinguished from ground speed.

air stream (er′strem′, ar′strem′), *n.* the relative flow of air around or against an object in flight, usually in a direction opposite to that of the object's flight.

air strip (er′strip′, ar′strip′), *n.* a paved or cleared runway on which aircraft land and take off, especially one made hastily for temporary use; landing strip.

air tight (er′tit′, ar′tit′), *adj.* 1 so tight that no air or gas can get in or out. 2 having no weak points open to an opponent's attack: *an airtight alibi.*

air-to-air (er′tə er′, ar′tə ar′), *adj.* passing between two flying aircraft, as a rocket launched by one to destroy another: *air-to-air missiles.*

air waves (er′wavz′, ar′wavz′), *n. pl.* radio or television broadcasting.

air way (er′wa′, ar′wa′), *n.* 1 route for aircraft; air lane; airline. 2 a passage for air. 3 a specified radio frequency for broadcasting. 4 **airways,** *pl.* channels for radio or television broadcasting.

air wor thy (er′wer′ŦHe, ar′wer′ŦHe), *adj.* fit or safe for service in the air. —**air′wor′thi ness,** *n.*

air y (er′e, ar′e), *adj.,* **air i er, air i est.** 1 light as air; graceful; delicate: *an airy step.* 2 light-hearted and gay: *airy music.* 3 breezy: *a high, airy knoll.* 4 well supplied with fresh air: *a large, airy room.* 5 of or in the air; aerial: *birds and other airy creatures.* 6 reaching high into the air; lofty: *airy pinnacles.* 7 like air; not solid or substantial: *airy plans.* 8 unnatural; affected: *an airy tone of voice.* 9 flippant: *airy criticism.*

aisle (il), *n.* 1 passage between rows of seats in a hall, theater, school, etc. 2 passage on either side of a church parallel to the nave.

FIGURE 9-B   A page from the *Thorndike-Barnhart Advanced Dictionary.* (Scott, Foresman and Company, Glenview, Ill., 1974.)

A page from *Webster's New Collegiate Dictionary* is shown in Figure 9-C.

To get an idea how much information a good dictionary contains and how easily a student can become confused, a few questions based on *Webster's New Collegiate Dictionary* are listed on pages 228–229. The answers are in the dictionary's "Explanatory Notes," pp. 10a–19a. Try to answer the questions, then check your results in Webster.

If one is accustomed to using Webster, a change to another dictionary will require some adjustments. These are perfunctory and simple, and an understanding of one dictionary will indicate what to look for in another. We have already mentioned, for example, that Thorndike-Barnhart uses a single alphabetical listing, while Webster has supplements at the back. There are a number of other differences, including:

Webster encloses pronunciation in reverse slashes / / ; Thorndike-Barnhart in parentheses (   ). A few phonetic symbols are different:

Thorndike-Barnhart	*Webster*
ng	ŋ
ᴛ̵H	t̲h̲
oi	ȯi
ô	ȯ
ou	au̇

Also, some of the finer distinctions in pronunciation are more carefully defined in Webster, making that system more accurate, but also more complex.

The *order* in which information is given within each entry varies from one dictionary to the other. Webster places the etymology near the beginning of the entry, before the definitions of the word; Thorndike-Barnhart places it at the end. Even succeeding editions of the same dictionary will vary. When the *Thorndike-Barnhart advanced Dictionary* replaced the older *High School Dictionary*, it became more comprehensive. The older *Webster's Seventh Collegiate* included, in addition to a decimal system for Explanatory Notes, a "Vocabulary of Abbreviations," proofreader's marks, and a number of other Back Matter items. The New Collegiate offers an informative article on "The English Language and Its History." There are a number of other differences between dictionaries, some more important than others. But the important point is that differences in forms and organization from one dictionary to another do exist, and any dictionary can be used more effectively if some time is taken to become acquainted with it.

Some dictionary publishers issue a series of lexicons for use at various reading levels, such as the *Thorndike-Barnhart Beginning, Intermediate,* and *Advanced Dictionaries.* This makes it possible to begin teaching dictionary

intermediate chamber **2** : a stoppage of flow caused by air being in a part where liquid ought to circulate
air·mail \'a(ə)r-ˌmā(ə)l, 'e(ə)r-, -ˌmāl\ *n* : the system of transporting mail by aircraft; *also* : the mail thus transported — **airmail** *vt*
air·man \-mən\ *n* **1** : an enlisted man in the air force: as **a** : an enlisted man of one of the three ranks below sergeant **b** : an enlisted man ranking above an airman basic and below an airman first class **2** : a civilian or military pilot, aviator, or aviation technician
airman basic *n* : an enlisted man of the lowest rank in the air force
airman first class *n* : an enlisted man in the air force ranking above an airman and below a sergeant
air·man·ship \'a(ə)r-mən-ˌship, 'e(ə)r-\ *n* : skill in piloting or navigating airplanes
air marshal *n* : a commissioned officer in the British air force who ranks with a lieutenant general in the army
air mass *n* : a body of air extending hundreds or thousands of miles horizontally and sometimes as high as the stratosphere and maintaining as it travels nearly uniform conditions of temperature and humidity at any given level
air mattress *n* : MATTRESS 1b
Air Medal *n* : a U.S. military decoration awarded for meritorious achievement while participating in an aerial flight
air mile *n* : a mile in air navigation; *specif* : a unit equal to 6076.1154 feet
air-mind·ed \'a(ə)r-'mīn-dəd, 'e(ə)r-\ *adj* : interested in aviation or in air travel — **air-mind·ed·ness** *n*
air·mo·bile \-ˌmō-bəl, -ˌbēl, -ˌbil\ *adj* [*air* + ¹*mobile*] : of, relating to, or being a military unit whose members are transported to combat areas usu. by helicopter
air·park \-ˌpärk\ *n* : a small airport usu. near an industrial area
air piracy *n* : the hijacking of a flying airplane : SKYJACKING
air·plane \'a(ə)r-ˌplān, 'e(ə)r-\ *n* [alter. of *aeroplane*, prob. fr. LGk *aeroplanos* wandering in air, fr. Gk *aer-* + *planos* wandering, fr. *planasthai* to wander — more at PLANET] : a fixed-wing aircraft heavier than air that is driven by a screw propeller or by a high-velocity jet and supported by the dynamic reaction of the air against its wings

airplane: *1* weather radar, *2* cockpit, *3* jet engine, *4* engine pod, *5* pylon, *6* swept-back wing, *7* vertical stabilizer, *8* rudder, *9, 10* tabs, *11* elevator, *12* horizontal stabilizer, *13* inboard flap, *14* inboard spoiler, *15, 16* tabs, *17* aileron, *18* outboard flap, *19* outboard spoiler, *20* sound suppressor, *21* thrust reverser, *22* cabin air intake, *23* nose landing gear

air plant *n* **1** : EPIPHYTE **2** : a plant (genus *Kalanchoe*) that propagates new plants from the leaves
air pocket *n* : a condition of the atmosphere (as a local down current) that causes an airplane to drop suddenly
air police *n* : the military police of an air force
air·port \'a(ə)r-ˌpō(ə)rt, 'e(ə)r-, -ˌpȯ(ə)rt\ *n* : a tract of land or water that is maintained for the landing and takeoff of aircraft and for receiving and discharging passengers and cargo and that usu. has facilities for the shelter, supply, and repair of planes
air·post \-ˈpōst\ *n* : AIRMAIL
air power *n* : the military strength of a nation's air force
air pump *n* : a pump for exhausting air from a closed space or for compressing air or forcing it through other apparatus
air raid *n* : an attack by armed airplanes on a surface target
air right *n* : a property right to the space above a surface area or object
air sac *n* **1** : one of the air-filled spaces in the body of a bird connected with the air passages of the lungs **2** : ALVEOLUS 1b **3** : a thin-walled dilation of a trachea occurring in many insects
air·screw \'a(ə)r-ˌskrü, 'e(ə)r-\ *n* **1** : a screw propeller designed to operate in air **2** *Brit* : an airplane propeller
air·ship \-ˌship\ *n* : a lighter-than-air aircraft having propulsion and steering systems
air·sick \-ˌsik\ *adj* : affected with motion sickness associated with flying — **air·sick·ness** *n*
air·space \-ˌspās\ *n* : the space lying above the earth or above a certain area of land or water; *esp* : the space lying above a nation and coming under its jurisdiction
air·speed \-ˌspēd\ *n* : the speed (as of an airplane) with relation to the air — compare GROUND SPEED
air·stream \-ˌstrēm\ *n* : a current of air; *specif* : AIRFLOW
air strike *n* : an air attack
air·strip \-ˌstrip\ *n* : a runway without normal air base or airport facilities
¹airt \'ärt, 'ert\ *n* [ME *art*, fr. ScGael *àird*] *chiefly Scot* : compass point : DIRECTION
²airt *vt, chiefly Scot* : DIRECT, GUIDE
air·tight \'a(ə)r-ˈtīt, 'e(ə)r-\ *adj* **1** : impermeable to air or nearly so **2 a** : having no noticeable weakness, flaw, or loophole <an ~ argument> **b** : permitting no opportunity for an opponent to score <an ~ defense> — **air·tight·ness** *n*

air–to–air \ˌa(ə)rt-ə-ˈ(w)a(ə)r, ˌe(ə)rt-ə-ˈ(w)e(ə)r\ *adj* : launched from one airplane in flight at another : involving aircraft in flight <~ rockets> <~ combat>
air vice–marshal *n* : a commissioned officer in the British air force who ranks with a major general in the army
air·wave \'a(ə)r-ˌwāv, 'e(ə)r-\ *n* **1** : the medium of radio and television transmission — usu. used in pl. **2** : AIRWAY 4
air·way \-ˌwā\ *n* **1** : a passage for a current of air (as in a mine or to the lungs) **2** : a designated route along which airplanes fly from airport to airport; *esp* : such a route equipped with navigational aids **3** : AIR LINE 2 **4** : a channel of a designated radio frequency for broadcasting or other radio communication
air·wor·thy \-ˌwər-thē\ *adj* : fit for operation in the air <an ~ airplane> — **air·wor·thi·ness** *n*
airy \'a(ə)r-ē, 'e(ə)r-\ *adj* **air·i·er; -est** **1 a** : of or relating to air : ATMOSPHERIC **b** : high in the air : LOFTY <~ perches> **c** : performed in air : AERIAL <~ leaps> **2** : UNREAL, ILLUSORY <~ romances> **3 a** : being light and graceful in movement or manner : SPRIGHTLY, VIVACIOUS **b** : ETHEREAL **4** : open to the free circulation of air : BREEZY **5** : AFFECTED, PROUD <~ condescension>
aisle \'ī(ə)l\ *n* [ME *ile*, fr. MF *aile* wing, fr. L *ala*; akin to OE *eaxl* shoulder, L *axilla* armpit — more at AXIS] **1** : the side of a church nave separated by piers from the nave proper — see BASILICA illustration **2 a** : a passage (as in a theater) separating sections of seats **b** : a passage (as in a store or warehouse) for inside traffic
ait \'āt\ *n* [ME, alter. of OE *īgeoth*, fr. *īg* island — more at ISLAND] *Brit* : a little island
aitch \'āch\ *n* [F *hache*, fr. (assumed) VL *hacca*] : the letter *h*
aitch·bone \'āch-ˌbōn\ *n* [ME *hachbon*, alter. (resulting from incorrect division of *a nachebon*) of (assumed) ME *nachebon*, fr. ME *nache* buttock (fr. MF, fr. LL *natica*, fr. L *natis*) + *bon* bone — more at NATES] **1** : the hipbone esp. of cattle **2** : the cut of beef containing the aitchbone
ajar \ə-ˈjär\ *adj or adv* [earlier *on char*, fr. *on* + *char* turn — more at CHARE] : being slightly open <a door ~>
Ajax \'ā-ˌjaks\ *n* [L, fr. Gk *Aias*] **1** : a Greek hero in the Trojan War who kills himself because the armor of Achilles is awarded to Odysseus **2** : a fleet-footed Greek hero in the Trojan war — called also *Ajax the Less*
AK *abbr* Alaska
AKA *abbr* also known as
Akan \'äk-ˌän\ *n, pl* **Akan** *or* **Akans** **1** : a language spoken over a wide area in Ghana and extending into the Ivory Coast **2** : the Akan-speaking peoples
AKC *abbr* American Kennel Club
akim·bo \ə-ˈkim-(ˌ)bō\ *adj or adv* [ME *in kenebowe*] **1** : having the hand on the hip and the elbow turned outward **2** : set in a bent position <a tailor sitting with legs ~>
akin \ə-ˈkin\ *adj* **1** : related by blood : descended from a common ancestor or prototype **2** : essentially similar, related, or compatible *syn* see SIMILAR *ant* alien
Ak·ka·di·an \ə-ˈkäd-ē-ən\ *n* **1** : a Semitic inhabitant of central Mesopotamia before 2000 B.C. **2** : an ancient Semitic language of Mesopotamia used from about the 28th to the 1st century B.C. — **Akkadian** *adj*
ak·va·vit \'äk-wə-ˌvēt, 'äk-vä-\ *var of* AQUAVIT
Al *symbol* aluminum
AL *abbr* **1** Alabama **2** American League **3** American Legion
al- — see AD-
¹-al \əl, ᵊl\ *adj suffix* [ME, fr. OF & L; OF, fr. L *-alis*] : of, relating to, or characterized by <directional> <fictional>
²-al *n suffix* [ME *-aille*, fr. OF, fr. L *-alia*, neut. pl. of *-alis*] : action : process <rehearsal>
³-al \ˌal, ˌȯl, əl, ᵊl\ *n suffix* [F, fr. *alcool* alcohol, fr. ML *alcohol*] **1** : aldehyde <butanal> **2** : acetal <butyral>
ala \'ā-lə\ *n, pl* **alae** \-ˌdē\ [L — more at AISLE] : a wing or a winglike anatomic process or part — **alar** \ˈā-lər\ *adj* — **ala·ry** \-lə-rē\ *adj*
à la *or* **a la** \ä-lə, al-ə, äl-(ˌ)ä\ *prep* [F *à la*] : in the manner of
Ala *abbr* Alabama
ALA *abbr* **1** American Library Association **2** Automobile Legal Association
al·a·bas·ter \'al-ə-ˌbas-tər\ *n* [ME *alabastre*, fr. MF, fr. L *alabaster* vase of alabaster, fr. Gk *alabastros*] **1** : a compact fine-textured usu. white and translucent gypsum often carved into vases and ornaments **2** : a hard compact calcite or aragonite that is translucent and sometimes banded — **alabaster** *or* **al·a·bas·trine** \ˌal-ə-ˈbas-trən\ *adj*
à la carte \ˌal-ə-ˈkärt, ˌäl-ə\ *adv or adj* [F *à la carte* by the bill of fare] : according to a menu that prices each item separately
alack \ə-ˈlak\ *interj* [ME] *archaic* — used to express sorrow or regret
alac·ri·ty \ə-ˈlak-rət-ē\ *n* [L *alacritas*, fr. *alacr-, alacer* lively, eager; akin to OE & OHG *ellen* zeal] : promptness in response : cheerful readiness <accepted the invitation with ~> *syn* see CELERITY *ant* languor — **alac·ri·tous** \-rət-əs\ *adj*
Alad·din \ə-ˈlad-ᵊn\ *n* : a youth in the *Arabian Nights' Entertainments* who comes into possession of a magic lamp
al·a·me·da \ˌal-ə-ˈmēd-ə, -ˈmäd-\ *n* [Sp, fr. *álamo* poplar] : a public promenade bordered with trees
à la mode \ˌal-ə-ˈmōd, ˌäl-\ *adj* [F *à la mode* according to the fashion] **1** : FASHIONABLE, STYLISH **2** : topped with ice cream
al·a·nine \'al-ə-ˌnēn\ *n* [G *alanin*, irreg. fr. *aldehyd* aldehyde] : a white crystalline amino acid $C_3H_7NO_2$ formed esp. by the hydrolysis of proteins
al·a·nyl \'al-ə-ˌnil\ *n* [ISV *alanine* + *-yl*] : an acyl radical of alanine
¹alarm \ə-ˈlärm\ *also* **ala·rum** \ə-ˈlär-əm, -ˈlar-\ *n* [ME *alarme, alarom*, fr. MF *alarme*, fr. OIt *all'arme*, lit., to the weapon] **1** *usu* **alarum**, *obs* : a call to arms <the angry trumpet sounds ~ —Shak.> **2** : a signal (as a loud noise or flashing light) that warns or alerts; *also* : a device that signals <set the ~ to wake me at seven> **3** : sudden sharp apprehension and fear resulting from the

FIGURE 9-C   A page from *Webster's New Collegiate Dictionary*.

227

TABLE 9-1

QUESTIONS ABOUT WEBSTER'S NEW COLLEGIATE DICTIONARY

		Page	Column	Webster's Seventh

1.	Explain why
	    Alabaster or *alabastrine*
	    woolly also *wooly*
	What is the difference between *or* and *also*?
		11a	1	1.7.1
				1.7.2

2.	Explain the symbols \\ ' ͵	11a	2	2.1 2.2
3.	Why does the dictionary list the plural of *woman* but not *girl*?	12a	2	4.1 4.4
4.	Why does this dictionary list only the present tense form of *pump,* but also the past tense form of *find* and three forms of *go*?	13a	1 & 2	4.7
5.	Why are the forms *longer* and *longest* listed but not *shorter* and *shortest*?	13a	2	Not specified
6.	By which designations does the dictionary list frequency of capitalization?	14a	1	5.3
7.	The designation *often attrib* after the entry *vacation* means what?	14a	1	6.1 6.2
8.	What are the origins of the words *airplane* and *alarm*?	14a 26	1 & 2	7.1 20
9.	Why is one definition of *emboss* listed as *obs,* and *belike* as *archaic*? Is there a difference?	15a	2	8.1.1 8.1.2
10.	What does the dictionary say about testing for slang?	16a	1	8.2.1
11.	Is there a difference between the designations *dial, nonstand,* and *substand*? Explain.	16a	1 & 2	8.2.2 8.2.3 8.3.1
12.	Explain the use of angle brackets and boldface swung dash.	16a	2	12.1 12.2.1
13.	Why do some words have definitions, others have usage notes, still others both? What is the difference?	16a 17a	2 1	14.1 14.2

228

TABLE 9-1 *(continued)*

QUESTIONS ABOUT WEBSTER'S NEW COLLEGIATE DICTIONARY

		Page	Column	Webster's [a] Seventh
14.	A boldface colon **:** introduces what?	17a	1	10.1 10.2
15.	What do the words *see* or *compare* mean when appended to a definition?	18a	2	15.0 15.1
16.	Which of the following are one word, two words, more than two, and hyphenated? airscrew airworthiness airminded airpolice airtoair airmail	26		1.6 p. 20
17.	Explain the following abbreviations: OF n interj AF U perh	31a		p. 22
18.	A student tells you that the definition of *predate* is ANTEDATE, but he doesn't know what that means either. What good is a dictionary?	18a	2	15.2
19.	If words have more than one definition, how do you know which one to use?			
20.	A student cannot find out what *prerevolutionary history* means because it is not listed. Can you help?	19a	1 & 2	18.1 18.2

[a] In an earlier *Webster, the Seventh New Collegiate,* explanatory notes (pp. 7a–14a) are listed by decimal numbers, simplifying reference. This is an example of minor differences in successive editions of the same dictionary.

skills in the early primary grades, which I believe is very important, and continue instruction throughout the school years. If a district adopts one set of dictionaries, the transition from one level to another, as students develop reading competence, can be accomplished smoothly. I used to find the *Thorndike-Barnhart Beginning Dictionary* an excellent instructional medium for high school reluctant readers because of its readability. Interestingly, most of these students eventually decided that "this is a baby book," and demanded something more mature. So I gave them the *High School Dictionary,* but by that time they had the skills to use it.

A good language development program should include in-service work to train teachers in instructional methods for the particular dictionary adopted. For a comprehensive education, high school students should be introduced to other dictionaries in their junior and senior years, so they will learn to use them. A good program might include *Thorndike-Barnhart* series through tenth or eleventh grade (twelfth grade for less able readers) and introduction to Webster in the eleventh or twelfth.

Supplementary References

In addition to standard dictionaries, students can learn to use other reference aids. One of the most valuable of these is a *thesaurus*. This "treasure" of information about words offers lists of synonyms and, in some editions, antonyms. Some, such as Funk and Wagnal's *Modern Guide to Synonyms,* contain, in addition, detailed explanations of the differences between words that mean approximately, but not exactly, the same. These thesauri are of great value to a writer struggling to find exactly the right word. There are also dictionaries of rhyming words for struggling poets, translating dictionaries for students of foreign language, dictionaries of well-known foreign words and phrases, and specialized dictionaries in many fields.

GAMES TEACHERS PLAY

Several years ago one of the students in my "field experiences" class asked if I could supply him with six Scrabble sets. He was earning university credit for working as a teaching assistant in a high school in a low income neighborhood. He found that the students were turned off to learning and hostile to school. I secured the games, and he organized a Scrabble tournament. With four students playing at each set, he could have 24 students, the

CATHY   by Cathy Guisewite

Copyright ©, 1976, Universal Press Syndicate.

entire class, playing at once. I suggested he fudge on the rules a bit to permit students to consult a dictionary during play (except when it is their turn). Using a round robin, he had each student play every classmate, or 23 games. With one day per week allowed for the games, things moved slowly. But interest in the tournament grew, and soon students were coming in before school, after school, and during lunch to play. Even spectators appeared, and scores were posted on the bulletin board. That semester, the teacher reported more student improvement in spelling than at any time in her teaching career. She also reported more enthusiasm for school and fewer discipline problems.

This was not my first or last experience with games as teaching devices. Language games can be used in a variety of ways, from a major instructional technique to a contingency plan for one of *those* days. Some make good fillers when today's lesson plan runs out of gas ten minutes before the end of the period, or for the faster students who finish early. Carefully selected and judiciously used, games can be an excellent motivator and a real teacher.

Games come essentially from three sources. There are many commercially prepared games available from toy stores or directly from the manufacturers. A number of games and books of games can be purchased from educational publishers. But most versatile and least expensive are those which teachers themselves devise to suit the needs of their own subjects and their own students.

Commercial Games

These are of several types. First is the *spell-the-word* type, including:

SCRABBLE (Selchow & Righter)
    Players take turns filling in a word board with letter tiles, forming crossword patterns.

AD-LIB (E.S. Lowe)
    Players throw thirteen dice to form crosswords.

SCRABBLE CROSSWORD CUBES (Selchow & Righter)

SPILL AND SPELL (Parker Brothers)
    These two games are similar to Ad-Lib.

PERQUACKEY (Lakeside Industries)
    Also similar to Ad-Lib, but players are required to form more complex sets of words instead of crosswords.

SCRABBLE SCORING ANAGRAMS (Selchow & Righter)
Letter tiles are exposed one at a time and players spell words.

CROSS UP (Milton Bradley)
Letter cards are exposed one at a time. Playes try to form words from exposed letters by writing them on grids.

FOUR LETTER WORDS (Lakeside)
Players form four-letter words in any of eight different directions. A combination of Scrabble, Bingo, and three dimensional tick-tack-toe.

SCRABBLE BALI (Selchow & Righter)
Letter cards are built into columns to form words.

The second type of game involves forming sentences from words:

SCRABBLE SENTENCE CUBE GAME (Selchow & Righter)
Twenty-one word dice are thrown and the words used to form sentences.

A third type of game involves guessing words, based on "clues:"

PASSWORD (Milton Bradley)
Players give clues to their partners, who try to guess the word. Words are given to players on word cards.

LETTER PILE (Schaper)
Players construct words from transparent letter cards and other players try to guess the words from clues.

INWORD (Milton Bradley)
Players give each other short words from which they are to construct longer words.

PROBE (Parker Brothers)
Letter cards are arranged to spell words. Players try to make opponent expose the word by guessing the letters.

Finally, there is a new version of *ghost*:

GALLOPING GHOST (Lakeside)
An old game given a new twist, as four words are built simultaneously.

If these games are not available at local toy or department stores, you can send directly to the manufacturer on a school purchase order. But this list is only a sampling. New games are coming out all the time.

Some are merely the same game in new dress or with minor variations, but occasionally a really new and interesting idea appears.

Don't forget trade books, particularly paperbacks. Some students can be hooked on crossword puzzles, while others find them threatening. Interesting books of word games are occasionally found in children's book departments.

Professional Sources

Many publishers of educational material also carry flash cards and word games of many types. Maurie Taylor's *Mysticryptics* (Glenville, Ill.: Scott, Foresman and Company, 1971) uses codes to build word games.

A series of books of word games is published by:

> Word Games
> P.O. Box 305
> Healdsburg, Calif. 95448

Also send for catalogs from:

> Educational Aids
> Fremont, Calif.

> Garrard Publishing Company
> 2 Overhill Road
> Scarsdale, N.Y. 10583

Scholastic Magazines also includes word games in their publications.

Teacher-Made Games

Teachers need not depend upon commercial sources. The least expensive games and those best suited to your needs are invented by you. Commercial products are a source of ideas from which you can fabricate your own games.

For example, you can make lists of vocabulary words from your textbook—words you would like your students to learn. Most of the word games discussed so far can be played with your vocabulary list. Either limit selection to words on the list or offer bonus points for using them. You may also give bonus points for defining the word or for using it in the appropriate context.

TELEVISION GAME SHOWS   Television game shows are also a good source of ideas with which your students can identify. For example, try *Customized Concentration:* Make a list of pairs of matching terms. In a foreign language it may be words or phrases and their English translations. In geography you can use countries and capital cities or regions and products for which they are noted. In math it could be problems and answers. Or use any list of terms and definitions. Write these on cards and mount the cards on a grid of numbered rows going up and down and lettered rows going across. Cover each word card with a blank card so that it cannot be seen. As in the television game, players call out pairs of matched squares: D3, C2; A6, B3; and so forth. As each square is called, uncover it momentarily. The object is to know which items match and to remember which words and phrases are on which squares. Players try to call out a *matching pair*. Allow textbooks or dictionaries for reference, except for the player whose turn it is to call out. This will allow students to look up unfamiliar words or phrases as they are uncovered. To place greater emphasis on knowing the material and less on memorizing where each item is placed, try varying the game by leaving each item exposed permanently rather than temporarily. This speeds up the game considerably, and allows more material to be covered in a single session.

CROSSWORD PUZZLES   Not difficult to make, crossword puzzles offer an ideal medium for teaching new words, inasmuch as students are faced with the definition or other clue, and have to find the correct word and correct spelling. With a bit of practice, you can become quite adept at composing them; once drawn up, they can be kept on file and used for years. A teacher-made crossword puzzle in Spanish by Candy Jones is shown in Figure 9-E.

Inword puzzles are also popular. Subject vocabulary can be hidden in a letter grid, as in the samples done by my daughter Judy in junior high school. Having students make up puzzles and games gives an added dimension. For extra fun, the "unused" letters spell a secret message. Can you find the messages in these puzzles?

Bingo cards can be adapted to any subject. In math, Bingo squares can have numbers written on them. The leader calls out a series of problems, and the students mark the correct answer, if they have it on their card. The leader keeps track of all answers called, to check players' responses when they claim to have a "Bingo."

In other subjects, the cards can have words filled in. The leader reads definitions or otherwise identifies particular items. Students mark whenever

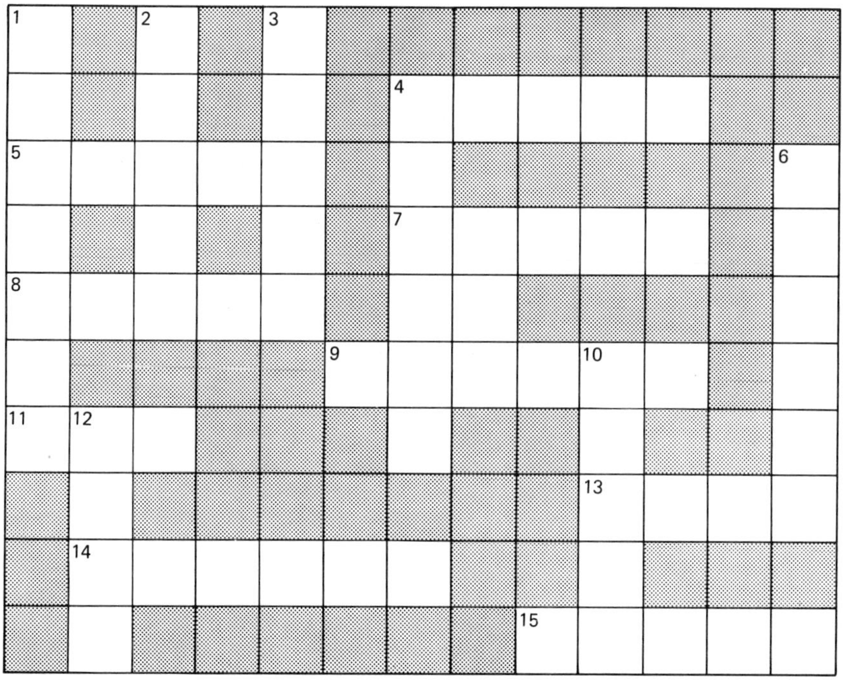

DOWN

1 horse
2 bulls
3 lion (feminine)
4 bird
6 pretty
10 tiger
12 toad

ACROSS

4 poor
5 donkey
7 young
8 smart (feminine)
9 sad
11 bear
13 cat
14 dove
15 dog

FIGURE 9-E   Animales y Adjetivos.

they think they have an answer on their card and try for a complete top-to-bottom, across, or diagonal set.

Game Boards, such as the one illustrated on the following page, are basic equipment. They can be drawn on posterboard and, for permanence,

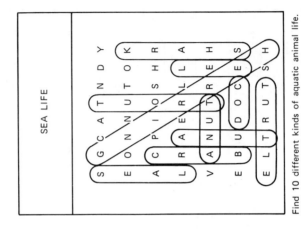

Find 10 different kinds of aquatic animal life.

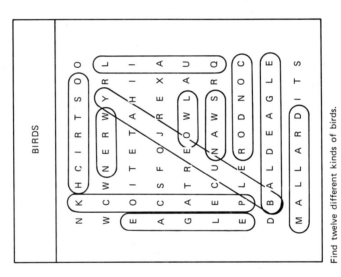

Find twelve different kinds of birds.
There are two of one kind of bird.

236

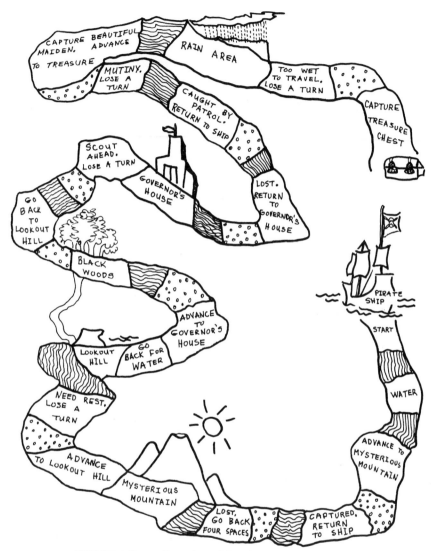

FIGURE 9-F   Game board for playing *Treasure Hunt*.

The following labels appear on the game board:

CAPTURE BEAUTIFUL MAIDEN. ADVANCE TO TREASURE

RAIN AREA

TOO WET TO TRAVEL. LOSE A TURN

CAPTURE TREASURE CHEST

MUTINY. LOSE A TURN

CAUGHT BY PATROL. RETURN TO SHIP

SCOUT AHEAD. LOSE A TURN

GOVERNOR'S HOUSE

LOST. RETURN TO GOVERNOR'S HOUSE

GO BACK TO LOOKOUT HILL

BLACK WOODS

PIRATE SHIP

ADVANCE TO GOVERNOR'S HOUSE

START

LOOKOUT HILL

GO BACK FOR WATER

WATER

NEED REST. LOSE A TURN

ADVANCE TO MYSTERIOUS MOUNTAIN

ADVANCE TO LOOKOUT HILL

MYSTERIOUS MOUNTAIN

LOST, GO BACK FOUR SPACES

CAPTURED, RETURN TO SHIP

covered with clear Contact. Longer lasting boards can be drawn on painted plywood or Masonite. They can have a great variety of themes, but the objective is always the same: to advance from starting position to the goal. Players roll a die or spin a dial to determine how many spaces they may advance a token. (Golf tees in assorted colors make inexpensive tokens, or save the caps from worn-out felt pens.) After advancing, they draw a question from a stack of question cards. Questions can be taken from your own text. For variety, have students write the question cards. If players cannot answer the question, they must return to their original place. If they land on special spaces, they follow the directions indicated. Special stacks of more difficult question cards must be answered if the player lands on certain spaces. For the board shown, you could have special sets of questions for *Mysterious Mountain, Governor's House,* and *Lookout Hill* (Players answering Lookout Hill questions may take a shortcut to Black Woods.) Up to six may play on one game board, but I like to limit the number to four.

Variations of the game board may be built by substituting playing fields of popular sports, such as a football gridiron or baseball diamond. In football, students first answer a question, then spin a dial to see how many yards their team may advance. "Forward pass" questions may be requested. These are more difficult, but they pay off in longer yardage. Each team has four players, each takes a turn at "carrying the ball" (answering a question). If the team makes ten yards in four tries, they have a first down and they may keep going until they lose the ball on downs.

In baseball, each question answered advances the "runner" one base and allows each runner on base ahead of him to advance. If a player "strikes out", all the runners on base remain in place. Any runner who is batted "home" scores a point. Each team bats until three strikeouts retire the side.

Try inventing similar games for other sports, such as basketball or soccer. Or build a tennis game, with each player "returning the ball over the net" by answering a question served at him by his opponent, then asking a question of his own. Use regular tennis scoring.[15]

Traditional card games may be adapted for classroom use. Scrabble Bali is an example of a commercial game that is patterned after solitaire. Go Fish is another game that is easily adapted. The teacher makes a list of pairs of matching items. These may be foreign words and translations, math problems and answers, authors and works, dates and events, chemical formulas and popular names, questions and answers—anything the class is concerned

---

[15]Larry Chance explains how to build a golf game, with students earning a birdie, a par, or a bogey. See "Tee Off On Reading Skills." *Journal of Reading,* March 1976, 19, 501–503.

with. These are written, each item on a separate card, and the cards dealt to the players. Players examine their hands to determine if they have any pairs. If they do, they may put the pairs in their "stack" and draw additional cards to replace them. Then each player, in turn, calls out what is written on one of his cards. If another player thinks he has the match to it, he immediately calls out his card. If he is correct, he gets to put the pair in his stack, and both players draw one additional card. If he is wrong, he gives his card to the player who called out the original, and that player adds to his stack. The object is to get the greatest number of cards in one's stack.

There are countless variations of the *Go Fish* game. Jerry Mallett[16] suggested *Have a Heart,* in which matching cards are drawn on red half-hearts. Students who successfully match a question with the correct answer receive the complete "heart." The object is to collect as many hearts as possible. An excellent idea for Valentine season.

When our bilingual program needed a game to teach Spanish—one that could be played without teacher supervision—we devised *Parejas* (couples), in which Spanish sentences and English translations appeared on opposite halves of a card. Then we cut the card apart with an irregularly shaped cut. Each time a student answered a question, his answer could be checked by putting the two halves of the card together to see if they fit. If they fit, he got a *pareja.* If not, he lost his card to the caller (see Figure 9-G).

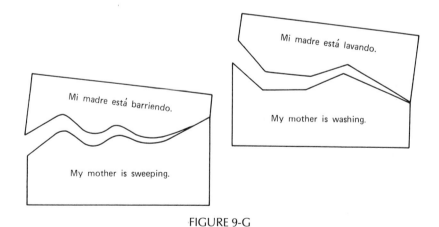

FIGURE 9-G

[16]*The Reading Clinic,* The Center For Applied Research in Education, Inc., February 1977, p. 15.

Big Muscle Games

Young bodies were not designed to be scrunched into desks for six hours a day. One of the major causes of discipline problems, I find, is that youngsters get restless and fidgety, and need an outlet for their physical energy. Properly used, games can provide that outlet. Many of the games described in this chapter can be converted to big muscle activities. Here are a few ideas:

GAME BOARDS   Butcher paper spread from one end of the room to another can be used to make game boards. Or, giant game boards can be drawn in chalk on the floor or concrete play area. Players can walk the board instead of pushing a token.

RELAY RACES   Add excitement. Divide into teams and have each team get in line. One player from each team races to a table at the other end of the room, picks up a question, writes the answer on the chalk board, then picks up another question and races back to hand it to the next player. If the first player misses the answer (The teacher can serve as judge.), he has to hand the first question to the second player, who tries to answer. The game continues until one team has answered all its questions.

In games such as Customized Concentration, have students, instead of the teacher, walk to the front of the room to uncover the cards they have called out.

And a Word of Caution

Like any other educational tool, games have both value and limitations. Big muscle games can easily get out of hand and bring unhappy looks from teachers down the hall. Some classes can play them and some cannot. Some teachers can use them effectively and some cannot. While games can be a great diversion for students, and a profitable one, they can also be overdone. Students can get tired of games just as they can any other activity.

Games can also become a substitute for real teaching. Students may become lost in a game, but the teacher must have a legitimate objective and must be continually evaluating whether the game is moving towards that objective. Playing Scrabble or doing crossword puzzles *may* lead to better spelling, or it may not. Much depends on the teacher's sensitivity to what is happening. Throughout this volume, much stress has been placed on motivation, for that is the key to learning in secondary classrooms. But there is a difference between keeping kids happy and turning them on to learning.

Another difficulty that can arise is a tendency towards overcompetitiveness. Students can get so involved in keeping score, in winning the game, that the real purpose becomes neglected and players of lesser stature feel the scorn of their teammates. This can best be avoided by a teacher who plays down the scoring and plays up the learning experience. Change the game quickly if a battle seems to be brewing. Keep games short and say little about the score. The round robin Scrabble tournament discussed earlier accomplished its purpose. It got a roomful of youngsters to use their dictionaries to check spelling and to search for new words. But the scoring mechanism for this process was, I felt, too complex.

This has been the merest sampling of ideas. New games, both commercial and teacher-made, appear all the time. Rayanne Cupps buys picture story books, blacks out the writing, and has students make up their own stories to go with the pictures. A group of my students devised a poker game for English, using noun cards, verb cards, adjective cards, and adverb cards. Students must form sentences with their cards, and certain combinations of noun—verb—adjective—noun, for example, are given rankings, just as full house, flush, and so forth, rank in poker. This idea, along with dozens of others, could be adapted for many subjects.

The past few chapters have been concerned largely with teaching *decoding*, the basic word-attack skills associated with the most elementary phases of reading. These decoding skills are essential for anyone learning to read. But there is also a danger in overemphasizing decoding. If too much stress in the reading program is placed upon learning *words*, it is quite possible to lose sight of the real purpose of language—communication.

Lack of attention to higher level comprehension skills can result in the word caller discussed previously. This person looks at reading matter as a series of words, with little meaning attached to the complete sentence or the work as a whole. He reads one word at a time, sometimes reading aloud to the complete satisfaction of the teacher, who does not realize that the words mean little or nothing to the reader. Therefore, the teaching of reading is not complete if it does not go beyond simple decoding, and it is to the higher level reading skills that we shall devote the remaining chapters.

CHAPTER 10
An Action Plan for Independent Readers

THE OATS HAVE EATEN THE HORSES

"In 1980 American inventor Omas Teddison perfected the wishet. Realizing the importance of his work, he took out a patent and brought his invention to the great industrialist, Howard Falsify. Falsify's engineers ran tests on the wishet and reported that it was practical and could be mass produced cheaply. Market Research forecast annual sales volume of 900,000 units.

"That's how Falsify Wishets, Inc. got started. Inside of a year the plant was employing 150 men and women, with an annual gross sales about 10 percent above the estimate and a volume of close to $2 million. Just as sales were stabilizing at those figures, the superintendent of Number Two production line, Louie Arriba, noticed, to his distress, that the superintendent of Number One had more men on his crew, a larger desk in his office, and his own key to the management rest room. So Arriba put on a campaign to convince the production manager that his job was just as responsible and just as productive as Number One's. Number One countered that Old Man Falsify himself had set the policy of seniority.

"The production manager had also received complaints from a number of other department heads about being understaffed. Inasmuch as he had recently had several stormy sessions with the union Reps. about overworked crews, he finally decided upon a bold course of action: he boosted the personnel of all departments, making everyone happy, particularly himself, as he had always wanted to command a work force of 200 men and women.

"But now the sales volume, which had been producing a satisfactory profit, was insufficient to meet the expanded payroll. So an advertising agency, Pacifier Promotions, was called in. Pacifier took out some full page, full color spreads in leading magazines to let America know, not that wishets are useful, but that they are used by mothers who really love their children and by young executives on the way up. Prices rose and sales increased, but the staff at Pacifier pointed out that to make a real break-through in sales, wishets needs a gimmick.

"This gimmick was provided in 1982 when Engineering and Design produced a model that came equipped with a built-in noodnick. No need to ever look for a noodnick again, as long as you had your trusty wishet handy. The new wishets were more awkward to use, but made up for it by being more expensive. Sales increased and things began to look rosy again.

"Then in 1985 Octopus Conglomerates broke the wishet patent and went into production on their own model. Their product, however, not only had the noodnick at one end, but a gahutengaheimer at the other, and was marketed as a '3-in-1.' It was an instant success because of the increased complexity of the 3-in-1, which resulted in frequent repairs and short life span.

"By 1988 there were eight companies manufacturing wishets in various styles and with many options. The industry now employed over three thousand people and grossed sixty million annually. Their advertising bill alone exceeded their first year's gross income.

"Then came the big breakthrough. Engineers at Chicanery Industries came up with a new concept—the wogget. The wogget was the twentieth century's answer to the old-fashioned wishet, which, Chicanery announced, is now hopelessly obsolete. The new television series *Typical American Family* was selected to spread the word throughout the land that no one need ever again put up with the old-fashioned wishet, now that the wogget had arrived. Woggets cost more, but are streamlined, loaded with sex symbols, and come in a full range of decorator colors. After a few episodes of *Typical American Family,* America was convinced that the most virile men and most desirable women use woggets. Garbage cans were filled with wishets and the industry thrived.

"When the market for woggets was glutted, the industry came out with the dainty, feminine 'Lady Wogget.' It was almost nonfunctional but available in mauve, chartreuse, or for just a little extra, red plush. For HIM the 'Mr. Wogget' was available with a built-in cologne dispenser and a sample bottle of that new masculine fragrance, eau de gymnasium. Another model came in imitation tiger skin. For Christmas you could buy the kiddies their own 'Wogget Junior,' for, even though children do not really *use* woggets, once presented to parents as 'training woggets' and to children as 'just like Mommy's and Daddy's,' sales rose to a new all-time high.

"And that, ladies and gentlemen, is the inspiring story of an industry that began as a simple supplier of a human need. But with truly creative marketing, it has, in less than a decade, generated an annual sales volume of ten million units and over a hundred million dollars. This, in addition to last year's exciting export deal with the Russians, as negotiated by their Ambassador Ripoff. I feel honored to have been asked to speak before this distinguished body on this important occasion. In conclusion, I can leave you with no nobler thought than this: If the woggets can do it, so can we all!"

I gave copies of *The Oats Have Eaten the Horses* to a friend who teaches at a nearby high school to use as a reading exercise. All the students were able to decode the article. They could read the words. They could even put the words together and come up with facts. None of them needed the techniques for frustration readers suggested in the preceding chapters. To many teachers, there would be no reading problem.

After reading the article, the students answered questions, including *queries about the meaning of the work. Some gave rather perceptive answers, showing clear understanding of the satire on our industrial-commercial system. One student likened the whole process to a germ that starts to grow and cannot be stopped until ultimately "the produce will eat the eater." But most were at a loss, including one who commented:*

This has no future possibilities of reality, because a wishet has not been invented yet (and probably never will).

From these answers, it was obvious that only a few could read the passage. Only a few could understand the satire, could see any connection between the written word and the real world. It thus becomes apparent that, although decoding is a prerequisite to progress in reading, it is only the first step.

READING LEVELS

As discussed in the previous chapter, there is danger in concentrating too heavily on decoding, to the exclusion or near exclusion of other reading skills. The product of such instruction is often a word caller, who expends his reading energy on deciphering words and gives little attention to putting the words together into meaning. To teach reading only by having students read out loud to the teacher is flirting with word calling. That is why, throughout this volume, emphasis has been on asking questions about the meaning of what is read. Word callers may develop considerable skill in reading aloud and sounding as if they understand.

After decoding, the next level of reading skill, *data processing,* tells the reader that the name of the gadget is a *wishet,* that it was invented by *Omas Teddison,* and that it all began in the year 1980.

Perhaps a better term would be *data gathering,* but I prefer to imply that as soon as the facts are gathered, they are *processed.* This means that as data are secured from the page, the reader begins to think, begins to question, begins to place that information into perspective. Just as the reader goes immediately from the first level of reading (decoding) to the second (data processing), so should he go immediately from the second to the third level, *interpretation.* Interpretation involves reading "between the lines," seeing the significance of what is read, making connections with other reading and with life. On the interpretive level one can view a television commercial for anything from deodorant to automobiles and exclaim: "The oats are eating the horses."

It is not only in the humanities that interpretive reading is important. Math teachers would do well to have their charges read Darrell Huff's *How To Lie With Statistics.*[1] Some science programs still see the mastery of data as the goal. Too little attention is paid to helping students see how knowledge of mathematics and the sciences can be utilized to improve their health and the health of the community, to increase available fuel and energy, to feed the hungry, and to provide better medical care. Education needs purpose beyond cramming heads with facts. If any teacher can honestly say that there is no way his subject can stimulate interpretive reading, I would question whether that subject—the way he is teaching it—belongs in the secondary school curriculum.

One may interpret *Romeo And Juliet* as a reminder that prolonged hatred can lead to destruction, but the reader who weeps for the tragic death of the star-crossed lovers has attained the highest reading level—*involvement*. Even an unemotional, purely intellectual response can include involvement. Once reading influences the individual—has some effect upon the products he buys, the votes he casts, the friends he seeks out—then he is truly participating in what he has read.

But involvement reading may not always involve the most beneficial reactions. Clever advertisers, charismatic politicians, and a wide variety of hucksters and charlatans are skilled at influencing the thoughts, the feelings, and the actions of the unwary. The task of the teacher is to train the students not only to read words, but to evaluate those words to form opinions, and to understand the implications of their opinions.

TEACHING HIGHER-LEVEL READING SKILLS

Questioning Strategies

The teacher can focus the attention of the students by the level of questions asked. In *The Oats Have Eaten the Horses,* decoding can be taught with a study guide calling attention to new words, such as *industrialist, estimate,* and *stabilizing.*

Or the teacher can focus attention on simple data processing by asking:

In what year was the wishet perfected?

What is the name of the first company to manufacture wishets?

Who was superintendent of Number Two production line?

[1]New York: Norton & Company, Inc., 1954.

These questions are so simple, so unrelated to the purpose of the article, that the reader who does not go beyond this level is not really reading. Yet I have observed that in most remedial reading situations this is as far as the teacher tries to go. The theory is obvious: these students are remedial readers. They are barely able to decode the simplest material, so we give them lots of practice decoding. And to be sure that they have *some* knowledge of what they are reading, we ask a few simple data questions.

The difficulty with this approach is that simple data questions, day after day, can be a drag. After all, who cares when the wishet was invented? Not only are such questions boring, they insult the intelligence of students and confirm their feelings about the uselessness of school.

This problem cuts across all segments of the student population. A teacher may become so sensitized to the struggles of the reluctant reader that the needs of the bright student are forgotten. The result can be that our potential leaders receive only a mediocre education in terms of developing their power to explore, to think, and to care.

I have found that as more stimulating questions are asked, the brighter students are challenged, and those of less ability benefit from the insights that are revealed. This is particularly true if the teacher asks penetrating follow-up questions: *Where did you find that information? How did you figure that out? But how do you account for the statement that . . .?*

Even data questions can be made a little more challenging by requiring some thinking:

Approximately how much did wishets cost the first year of manufacture? How did you figure this out?
> The answer, about $2.00, must be derived by putting together data from several sources: original sale estimate 900,000 units + "about 10 percent" = nearly a million units. The sales total was $2 million.

Approximately how much did they cost the evening of the speech?
> Again, the answer requires putting together ten million units with $100 million. Of course we do not know whether these figures represent wholesale or retail prices.

List the "creative marketing" ideas that boosted wishet sales from one million to ten million annually.
> The student must scan the article. Beginning with full page, full color magazine spreads, with their appeals to motherhood and status, the list concludes with the manufacture of the useless "Wogget Junior." The student has to search the article to determine which data belong in the category of "creative marketing."

If nobody in class is able to attack these problems, the teacher can help with a few well-placed questions: "What was the estimate of sales for the first year? Did sales actually go over or under that number? By how much? If the estimate was 900,000 units, and sales came to 10 percent more than that . . .? For easy computing, 990,000 is very close to what round number? If there were close to a million units sold, and two million dollars taken in, the cost for one is close to . . ." By asking such questions, the teacher is not just helping elicit an answer, but is demonstrating problem solving techniques. Continual exposure to such practices can lead students to independence.

We still have not come to grips, however, with the important question of the *meaning* of the article. Moving to interpretation, we might ask such questions as:

The title of this essay is a quotation from Shakespeare.[2] But nowhere is there any mention of either oats or horses. Explain the title.

Is the author talking about wishets? If so, why doesn't he tell us what a wishet is? If not, what is he talking about?

Make a list of all the names in the article and explain why those particular names were selected.

This article contains three attempts at "ethnic humor," which you can understand only if you belong to a particular group, or at least know the language or the culture. Can you find and explain the ethnic humor?

Note: Arriba in Spanish means upward, or higher. A noodnick in Yiddish is a pest, a nuisance. Another reference is to the sale of American wheat to Russia several years ago, and the phrase rip off.

In the final paragraph, what do we find out is happening? What is the implication of the last sentence?

These questions are beginning to dig for meaning. But we are only on level three, interpretation. To deepen the involvement we might try:

Which of the following statements do you think the author would support? Explain why. Which do you believe? Explain why.
  American industry is the finest in the world.
  Man builds institutions to serve his needs, then toils endlessly to serve the institutions.
  The last sentence of the article promises you and me a brighter future.

[2]Taming of the Shrew, Act III, Scene 2.

Write a newspaper headline for the article:
    On a data level. Example:
        Speaker Lauds Wishet Industry
    On an interpretive level. Example:
        Industry Uses "Creative Marketing" to Increase Sales, Raise Prices
    On an involvement level. Example:
        If You Can't Sell Them Goods, Sell Them Images

Does reading the article change any of your beliefs, attitudes, or feelings? Does it make you want to change any of your behavior patterns? If so, explain.

DEALING WITH DATA —EXERCISES

Except for the most extreme word callers, readers who can decode words also have some skills in data processing. The degree of skill varies tremendously from one reader to another, however. The untrained reader sprays the page with her eyes and comes up with an impression of what the author says. This impression is imprecise and fuzzy, though, and the gap between what the author intended and what the reader comes out with can be abysmal. Of course, there will always be some author-reader gap, for communication is inaccurate. But as readers' skills increase, they learn to narrow that gap. There are a number of techniques that the teacher can use to help the reader outgrow sloppy, fuzzy approximate reading. All are based on focusing the students' attention on the reading by having them reproduce the meaning in some form. The choice of form depends upon the abilities of the class and the length and structure of the reading material.

Paraphrasing

Paraphrasing involves rewriting an entire passage in one's own words. The reader tries to reproduce exactly what the author has stated, thought by thought, leaving nothing out and adding nothing. Emphasis is on careful, accurate rewriting. Except for names and a few key words that do not lend themselves to paraphrasing, the writer avoids using the same words as those found in the original.

    When having a class do this exercise, allow plenty of time. Stress careful reading and faithful reproduction, not speed. Assure the students that they are not expected to imitate the author's style or to write as well, but to write in clear, understandable sentences. Paraphrasing is a good exercise to use with material that is meaty and heavily concentrated. It demands precision reading and precision thinking. For an example of paraphrasing, see pages 132–133.

Précis Writing

Précis writing is similar to paraphrasing, except that the wordage is reduced. But the writer still does not leave out anything. He must do the same careful reading as in paraphrasing and the same careful thinking out of each idea as he puts it down on paper.

Some writing lends itself better to précis than to paraphrasing. Such writing is looser, using more words, perhaps in pursuit of style, or to give breadth and depth to each point. The teacher can decide which technique is more appropriate in each case. It may help to set a word limit: "Précis this article in not over five hundred words."

Summarizing

Summarizing differs from précis writing in that the length is reduced even further by picking out the essential points and leaving out supporting details, such as descriptions or examples. The writer of a summary must decide which points are essential and which can be left out. Summaries can be of any length, depending largely upon the original. A dissertation of 10,000 words may make three essential points and be summarized in a hundred. An article of a thousand words may be so concentrated that a good summary requires over 500. The teacher may allow the students the freedom to decide the proper length for a summary, or may assign a summary of 500 words, 200 words, or 50 words. Sometimes it is interesting to say to a class, "Summarize this selection in a single sentence." This causes students to look for the one main idea.

Summaries may be written in sentences and paragraphs or may be abbreviated. For example, parts of *The Oats Have Eaten The Horses* would be difficult to summarize because the writing style is concentrated. But the essentials could be summarized:

> 1980: Wishet perfected by Omas Teddison, brought to industrialist Howard Falsify. Production begun; within year employed 150 people, grossed $2 million. Louie Arriba protested his inferior position. And so forth.

Headlining

Headlining is the ultimate in summarizing. The writer produces a newspaper-type headline, expressing the essence of the entire work. A good headline does more than catch the essentials of the work in a single phrase. It is also dramatic and eye-catching, possibly humorous. Writing headlines can be fun as well as worthwhile, if students are challenged to combine precision reading with creative expression. See page 249.

Outlining

Outlining is a highly disciplined method of expressing the organizational structure of a work. Many so-called outlines are not outlines at all, merely a random selection of numbers and letters placed at respectable intervals in front of an equally random selection of headings. Proper outlining, like all the data exercises suggested so far, begins with a careful, point-by-point reading, followed by an equally careful expression of what has been read. Because the rules of outlining are precise and exacting, the teacher should know them well before making such an assignment. Following is a summary of outlining methods.

The writer of an outline must distinguish between the external organization of the work and its internal structure. The former consists of the title, table of contents, headings, subheads, and other clues put there by the author. The internal structure is the content of the work itself. External organization often contains clues to the internal structure, but must be verified by careful reading. The outline may or may not eventually resemble the author's structural clues.

Outlining is a method of dividing a written work into its parts, just as you and I might quarter an orange or tear a piece of paper. It thus becomes obvious that YOU CANNOT DIVIDE A THING INTO LESS THAN TWO PARTS. In a proper outline you cannot have *I* without at least *II*, *A* without at least *B*, *1* without at least *2*, or *a* without at least *b*. Suppose you are outlining *The Oats Have Eaten The Horses*, and you decide that your first topic heading should be:

I.   Ivention of the wishet

    A.   Originally by Omas Teddison

    B.   Later verified by Falsify's engineers

On second thought, you decide that Part B, *verification,* is not part of the *invention,* and really belongs in the next Roman numeral. You cannot, in this case, leave your outline reading *I A* without *I B.* The *A* part, being the *only* point under *I* is not a division at all, but part of the main topic. It could thus be changed to:

I.   Invention of the wishet by Omas Teddison

II.   Later verification by Falsify's staff

      A.   Practical nature confirmed by engineers

      B.   Sales potential confirmed by Promotion and Sales

If you cut up an apple pie you can only come up with pieces of apple pie, not chocolate cake. Every main heading must be *part of* the title, and each subdivision part of the superior heading. For example, if *II,* above, remains *Later verification by Falsify's staff,* the *A* and *B* can be two types of verification, *A,* by engineers, and *B,* by Promotion and Sales. But you cannot add *C, Employment of 150 people the first year.* That has nothing to do with verification.

An outline contains everything of consequence in the original, nothing more. There is no set number of topic headings. If the author makes only two points, your outline will have *I* and *II.* If he makes a hunded points, the outline goes to Roman numeral *C* (100). Some main headings may have over a dozen subheads, others none. The only number you cannot have is one. But an outline should not contain extraneous material to make it look "balanced," or pretty.

The title of the outline must be carefully worded. Titles are chosen for a variety of purposes. The title of this volume, for example, was selected for two purposes. First, I tried to give the potential reader some inkling of the contents. But I also tried to create an *impression* and to make teachers *want* to read it.

It is, in short, a blend of information and salesmanship. But such a *literary* title would never do for an outline. It is too vague, too unspecific, lacking in real definition of contents. In outlining this text you may decide that it is mainly a methods book. Therefore, the word *methods,* or a synonym, would be fairly certain to appear in the title, probably something like *Methods of Helping Secondary School Students Improve Their Reading.* This is a common form for good outline titles, which are often introduced by plural nouns: *Steps in . . . Places where . . . People who . . . Types of. . . .* This is much more specific than *How to . . .* or *Making a. . . .*

Because each of the main headings must be a subdivision of the title, every main heading of the outline of this book must be a method or group of methods. A clear expression of the work could be made by grouping the methods, for example,

I.   *Diagnostic methods*

    A.   *Standardized tests*

    B.   *Informal and specific reading inventories*

But before the book goes into methods, it discusses an "Incident In A Public School." Such material can hardly be labeled *I* because it is not a method and does not belong as a main heading under the title.

Yet this is a common literary device—to introduce the topic with something designed to make the reader more receptive to what is coming. To provide for it in the outline, we can label it *Introduction*. Some written works have introductions, some do not.

Some written works also have material at the end to tie it all together, and in outlining this is the *Conclusion*. An introduction and conclusion are included in the outline only if they exist in the original.

If we accept *methods* as the key to main topic headings, we run into difficulty in Chapter 3. *Causes of reading difficulties* may be important, but hardly methods. I know of no generally accepted way of incorporating such perambulations in an outline, and it is usually at such places that writers of outlines go astray, attempting somehow to twist the material into outline form or violating outline form to accommodate the material. If such problems come at the beginning or the end, we can simply label them *Introduction* or *Conclusion*. But in the middle of the text we have no standard way of accounting for them. I usually label such items *Digressions,* a device that is my own, not acceptable in any outlining text I have ever seen, but honest.

This indicates that not every work lends itself to outlining. In order to be outlined, a work has to be so organized that an outline exists. If a work is written with many digressions, or in a rambling style with no central idea that can be subdivided, it is better not to assign such material for outlining. You will only end up with the aforementioned collection of random numbers and letters.

A good outline must be consistent. All main headings and the introduction and conclusion, if there are such, are lined up directly underneath each other. Primary subheadings are evenly indented, as are secondary, tertiary, and so forth. If one topic heading marker carries a period or a capital letter, all should. Otherwise, none.

The form of the headings themselves should be parallel. Either make *all* items on the outline sentences, or make them all nonsentences. Do not, for example, say:

I.   Some countries had a representative form of government.

II.   Royalty

III. Where the church made the laws

Change *all* topic headings to sentences:

I.   Some countries had a representative form of government.

II.   Some countries had a king who served as a symbol of state.

III. Some countries had a system by which the church made the laws.

or make all headings nouns:

I.   Republics

II.   Monarchies

III. Theocracies

or make all headings phrases:

I.   Where the people elected representatives to govern

II.   Where a king made the laws

III. Where the church was the government

The most common outline form consists of a centered title, with Roman numerals for main topic headings. The introduction and conclusion are margined with the Roman numerals. Primary subheadings are indented and are headed by capital letters, secondary subheads indented again with arabic numerals. Tertiary subheads are indented again with lower-case letters. Further subdivisions are achieved by alternating arabic numerals with lower case letters. Following is a sample outline form:

Title

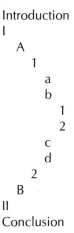

Introduction
I
    A
       1
           a
           b
              1
              2
           c
           d
       2
    B
II
Conclusion

Flow Charting

For variety, the class may be asked to make a flow chart of events presented in the reading. Suppose, for example, students read the following dramatization:

> Did you ever wonder what it would be like if there were no such game as baseball, and some enterprising promotor tried to sell the idea to a friend? The conversation might go something like this:
>
> Abner: Hey, Charlie, guess what! I just got this great idea for a new game. It's called baseball.
>
> Charlie: Basewhat?
>
> Abner: Baseball. Let me tell you about it. There are two teams, see. And one of them is out in the field. And the other team is up.
>
> Charlie: Up where?
>
> Abner: No, I mean up at bat. It's their time to go to bat. The pitcher of one team stands on a little mound at the center of the diamond. . . .

Charlie: Sounds expensive—diamonds.

Abner: The pitcher throws this little—thing—covered with horse-hide over the plate where the batter is standing.

Charlie: He tries to hit the batter?

Abner: No, he just throws it near the batter, so the batter can hit it with his bat, only he's not supposed to be able to.

Charlie: Wait a minute. First you say the batter is supposed to hit it, then he's not. Make up your mind.

Abner: Actually, the batter may decide not to swing at it at all. He may just let the thing go by.

Charlie: Sounds terribly exciting.

Abner: In that case, the umpire may call a strike.

Charlie: Some game. One pitch and already we have labor problems.

Abner: Or he may call a ball.

Charlie: I don't like to dance.

Abner: Or the batter may swing and miss. That's a strike. Or he may hit a foul.

Charlie: Is there a penalty for fouls?

Abner: Yeah. One strike.

Charlie: Who strikes who?

Abner: Or the batter may hit a fair ball.

Charlie: That sounds fair.

Abner: If he hits a fair ball, he runs to first while the team that's on field tries to throw him out. But if he doesn't hit the ball at all, and he gets three strikes, he's out. But if he gets four balls, he gets a free ride to first. Well, what do you think?

Charlie: You really want to know?

Abner: Yeah.

Charlie: Frankly, Abner, if anybody goes for a nutty idea like that, I'll eat my shirt.

(Scene 11—years later)

Abner: Well, Charlie—

Charlie: Munch, chomp, burp!

Such an article could be flow-charted as shown in Figure 10−A.

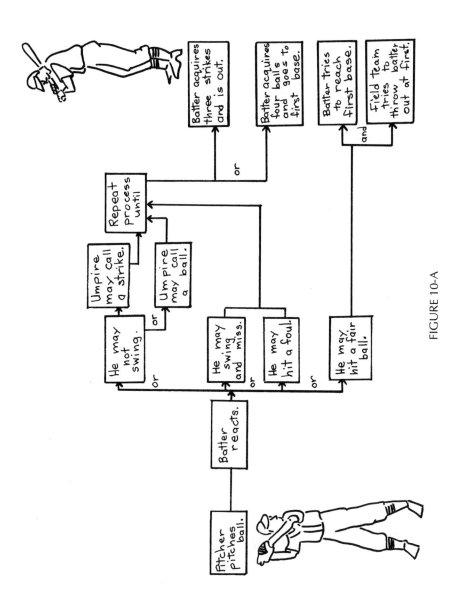

FIGURE 10-A

257

Flow charts can be made for anything from the life cycle of a butterfly to historical events, or to show cause and effect. They require careful reading for comprehension, summarizing, and sometimes a generous amount of creative thinking and design. The teacher may demonstate flow charting methods first, then give the students an exercise.

Composing Questions

Composing questions can focus attention on reading matter. Instead of continually answering, students enjoy doing the asking. Try games, with teams attempting to stump each other. Or use student questions in your test, giving bonus points to the authors of items used. Students may be encouraged to involve thought-provoking problems of inference, conclusion, or opinion, except in games, where data questions are usually more appropriate.

Creative Drama

The field of creative drama is a rich and enjoyable source of learning. After reading about Alexander Hamilton's and Thomas Jefferson's concepts of democracy, two students can assume these roles and argue about what kind of government the new nation should have. After the performance, the class can discuss whether the dialogue represented the thinking of these two men, as described in the reading. To do this properly requires careful study.

Creative drama zeroes in on human relationships, and is especially useful in social studies, home economics (family relations), and psychology. It can add zest to an English class, as Sir Launfal awakens and tells his fellow knights what happened to him during his dream about his quest for the Holy Grail and what he learned from the experience; or the spirits of the dead Romeo and Juliet (or Macbeth and Lady Macbeth, or Hamlet and Ophelia) meet in the after-world and try to explain why they acted as they did.

With imagination, any school subject can provide a dramatic situation. Have a student become Pasteur or Galileo, attempting to persuade a skeptical audience that diseases are caused by germs we cannot see, or that falling bodies fall at equal velocities regardless of weight. Or depict a parent trying to help a son or daughter with algebra.

Less spontaneous but just as creative is the *written dramatization*. Let the students write a play or a radio or TV show about what they have read. Encourage a creative mix of fact and fantasy:[3]

[3]Many other interesting ideas for oral presentation are found in James Moffett's *A Student-Centered Language Arts Curriculum Grades k-13: A Handbook for Teachers.* Boston: Houghton Mifflin Company, 1973.

Announcer:

Good evening, Thanes and Dames, this is John X_____ of the Anglo-Saxon Broadcasting Company, speaking from the great hall of Heorot. We're about to bring you a live blow-by-blow broadcast of the Beowulf-Grendel fight. As many of you know, Grendel, the direct descendent of Cain, has been terrorizing the gallant warriors of Hrothgar the scylding, having carried off as many as thirty at a time. Beowulf the Geat has just created a sensation here in the Hall by removing his armor and sword and vowing to fight Grendel in unarmed, hand-to-hand, single combat. Before the monster makes his appearance, let me see if I can get this gallant son of Ecgtheow to say a few words to our audience. Oh, Mr. Beowulf—Mr.—Beowulf . . .

One of the liveliest dramatizations I have witnessed was by students who had just read an article on the effects of liquor on various parts of the anatomy. While a narrator, in his own words, explained the main points of the article, another student wore a costume labeled "booze." Still others represented the brain, lungs, heart, liver, and other organs. As the narrator recited, Booze "attacked" each of the organs of the body, which demonstrated euphoria, drowsiness, lack of inhibition, and finally destruction. Despite a great deal of buffonery, the cast got their facts straight, demonstrating that they had read the article carefully. The point they made will be hard to forget.

Another possibility would be to have the class read a news story, a historical event, or even an incident from fiction. Then have different members of the class write an account from the point of view of one character. For example, suppose the class reads a newspaper account of the rescue of a drowning man by a teenager. Have some class members "become" the drowning man and write the story:

When I went out on the lake this morning, I didn't realize how dangerous the high wind could be for a person in a small sailboat. I was returning to the dock when. . . .

Others can be the rescuer:

I was heading back toward shore in my motorboat. The wind was getting strong, and I was afraid we were in for a storm. There was only one other boat on the lake, a small sailboat. Suddenly . . . .

Still other classmates can be boating companions of one or the other, observers on the shore, the officer who takes the accident report, or whatever characters are involved—or can be invented. Allow students to use their imaginations to embellish their stories, but do not allow them to disregard or change the facts as stated in the article. This insures a careful reading as well as imaginative writing. This technique can be particularly interesting when it involves a controversial subject.

Don't get upset if first attempts at dramatization or creative drama hardly make educational or theatrical history. I found that most secondary students are too inhibited to get up and act out a scene the first time around. It takes a while to train a class (and yourself). I like to start the class off by acting in the first scene myself, perhaps with one uninhibited student or aide, then slowly working more students into participating.

The key to learning is the discussion afterwards: did the actors follow the script, as laid out in the reading? On occasion I have let only the actors, not the entire class, read the material. Afterwards, the other students wrote or described orally what they thought the performers had read. This is an excellent test of the actors' careful reading and accurate portrayal.

The students' tendency to have fun with a scene can add zest to an otherwise dull day. But it takes skill to permit this healthy humor and at the same time keep the "horsing around" from becoming destructive. Yet once you have developed creative drama as a teaching tool—with a bit of persuasion, tact, and leadership—you'll never let it go.

Other Oral Presentations

Included in other oral presentations are the impromptu talk, formal and informal discussion, and debate. These are usually less precise than the written methods described earlier, but lend themselves well to exercises such as synthesizing a single idea from a number of sources.

THE IMPROMPTU TALK   The impromptu talk is usually given without a prepared script, but from notes. Students read a number of articles and select the information that is relevant to their subject. They should learn to put notes on index cards that can be held in the hand or placed on a podium. After each talk, discuss whether the student has understood the reading and has accurately reported its contents.

THE FORMAL, OR PANEL, DISCUSSION   Four to eight students usually present the formal, or panel, discussion. Each student gives an introductory talk, perhaps from three to ten minutes. After the presentations, the topic is thrown open for general discussion, first among members of the panel, then to the class.

THE INFORMAL, OR ROUND TABLE, DISCUSSION   The informal discussion proceeds somewhat as the panel group, but without the formal introductory talks by each member. The discussion simply begins with members of the group volunteering to present a point of view or asking or answering questions. Both panel and round table discussions require a moderator to introduce the topic, to call upon participants, to close the discussion, and possibly to provide a summation at the end.

The purpose of a discussion is to learn. Everyone contributes something, and the most successful participant is the one who comes out with the greatest amount of new knowledge or who changes his point of view. One of the most delicate tasks of the teacher is to encourage each participant to enter the discussion with an attitude of inquiry, rather than to feel the need to convince the others.

THE DEBATE   In the debate, which is a contest, the object is to win. This is done by making "points" for the team by showing that your point of view is the correct one. A topic is stated: Resolved: *The United States should legalize marijuana and all penalties for its cultivation, possession, sale, and use should be abolished.* One team represents the affirmative, the other the negative. The debate proceeds according to rules: A moderator is appointed to call on the various participants. The judges, usually three, listen carefully and record one point for each logical and valid reason given by each team. First, an affirmative speaker presents the plan and gives reasons why it is desirable. Then the negative speaker tries to refute each of the first speaker's points and to add some reasons why the plan would not be good. Then the second affirmative, then second negative speakers attempt to make points and refute each other's points. Finally, each speaker is allowed one rebuttal. After that, the judges are given time to tally points and announce the winning team.

Oral methods, such as creative drama, discussion, and debate can be used for a number of purposes. Creative drama is a great tool for developing the imagination. Debate is excellent for building listening skills, learning to think quickly and logically, and to organize one's thoughts. Discussion methods can encourage an attitude of inquiry and willingness to learn from others. In this chapter, however, we have portrayed these techniques as methods by which the student demonstrates that he has read the material carefully. The different values of these techniques are not incompatible. One can be very creative within a data framework. For example, if a student is portraying Queen Elizabeth in creative drama, as she learns more about that famous queen, this knowledge will open up new avenues of thought and action, as the student learns more about the kinds of thoughts, feelings, and behavior that would be characteristic.

It is important for the teacher to be aware, at all times, of the objective of the lesson, and to insist that these objectives be carried out. "Where did you get that information? . . . "Is that the way Madame Curie would have acted? . . . Did you listen to what she said? . . . How did you come to that conclusion?" Much depends upon the teacher's skill in asking appropriate and penetrating questions.

Other Methods

Some writing lends itself to having students make charts or graphs, dioramas, statistical tables, models, blueprints, illustrations, or freehand or scale maps. Whatever the medium, the benefit of the exercise will be lost if the teacher does not very carefully see that whatever the student produces conforms closely in subject matter to the material read. Students may become skilled at letting neat-looking diagrams or flow charts, dramatic speeches or creative illustrations substitute for the kind of careful reading and accurate expression these exercises are intended to promote.

The intent of the exercises described thus far in this chapter is to focus the reader's attention on the content. Before one can apply any of these techniques, from paraphrasing to debating, it is necessary to read with precision, then find the best words to express what has been read. Not all methods are equally valid for all written works. Some writing is more easily summarized, some is impossible to outline. Much depends, also, on the skills of the students. Paraphrasing is usually a good place to start, since it involves the least amount of manipulation of the material. Outlining requires highly disciplined reading and writing. A good teacher is familiar with all these methods, and chooses the most appropriate for each situation.

Not all material, however, merits this time-consuming reading, nor do we have the interest in everything we read to give it that much energy. In this time-is-valuable society, it is frequently necessary to read quickly as well as accurately. But few secondary school readers know how to vary the pace of their reading to suit the material and the occasion. They read a chemistry book and a comic book at the same rate, missing the concentrated data of one and trudging painfully through the other.

Who we are and the circumstances of reading also play an important part in determining reading speed. We might have fifteen minutes to read before eating dinner or dashing to our next class. Sally reads the newspaper in ten minutes. Joe, a student of current events, takes two hours. Tom does not read it at all. *What* to read and *how fast to read* it play a vital role in determining reading effectiveness. Following are some exercises that will help students achieve greater benefit from a limited amount of time and, hopefully, to understand the many reading styles available.

Skimming

Skimming involves reading very quickly to get the main ideas. Give your students material that can be read quickly. Point out the value of looking at the author's clues—the title, topic headings and subheads, charts and graphs, boldface type and italics, and the table of contents. One technique is to read the first sentence of each paragraph, then to decide whether to read more of that paragraph. Give the students a limited amount of time to read the work, then ask questions.

Scanning

A term sometimes used interchangeably with *skimming*, scanning here means to look for specific information. Give the students the questions first, then a limited amount of time to look for answers. Teach the class to hunt for dates, statistics, names, numbers, charts and graphs, key words and phrases, and possibly summaries, often at the end. Students may be asked to answer as many questions as possible in a very limited time, or may be asked to answer all the questions in the least time possible.

Some teachers teach scanning without knowing it and without wishing to. I have found that whenever I gave my class a reading assignment with questions to answer, they scan for the answers, rather than read the material carefully. This is a legitimate teaching device and a valuable skill for students to acquire, provided that is how the teacher wants the material to be covered. But it is not a substitute for either skimming or careful reading. It is, therefore, important for the teacher to know what is wanted and how to achieve it.

Selective Reading

Selective reading can be used to synthesize many of the data skills discussed so far. The following exercise is built around reading a newspaper, but the method can be adapted to a wide range of material—magazines, textbooks or supplementary texts, the room library, or the school library.

> Give every student a newspaper and ask everyone to make a list of its various sections. Allow time for each student to hunt carefully through the paper, probably a full class period. Next day, discuss the findings and make a master list. This list should be fairly comprehensive, including front page news, local and regional news, sports, comics, advertising, amusements, radio and television programming, feature articles, classified advertising, business and finance, and dozens of other special items and syndicated material.

Once the master list has been worked out and made available to each student, ask the class: which of the many features of a newspaper are interesting to you? Given a limited amount of time to read the paper, approximately how much time would you like to spend reading each section?

On the third day supply each student with another newspaper and allow an opportunity to read at will. The class may search for those parts of the paper that they wish to read and to see if they can divide their time in proportion to the stated preference of each.

For follow-up, you may wish to discuss the budgeting of reading time by carefully selecting what is to be read and by varying reading speed. Or you may wish to discuss the content to see if this type of reading is effective. One interesting possibility would be to allow students an unlimited amount of time to read one selection but a short time to read another. Then by means of objective questions, compare the two reading styles for understanding and retention. Or you may wish no follow-up at all, but to terminate the exercise with the selective reading. Most large newspaper publishers will give schools free classroom sets.[4]

BACK TO THE STUDY GUIDE

Assigning students to write a paraphrase, a summary, or an outline is a good method of focusing attention on the reading, but if they lack certain reading skills, this is insufficient. It may be necessary to teach how to do it. The use of a study guide for this purpose has been described in Chapter 5. But a study guide can be more than a list of scattered data. Let us look at ways it can be used to increase the reader's depth of comprehension.

Vocabulary

Most of us are aware that many words have multiple meanings. *Webster's Third New International Dictionary* lists 52 separate definitions for the word *tap,* plus four more for the idiom *on tap. Tap* can be a plug in the hole in a wine barrel or the wine that flows out, a faucet in the kitchen, or a tool for cutting inside threads. It can mean to secure a loan or to steal, to hit lightly or to listen in on someone's telephone conversation. It is a style of dancing or a kind of tree root. Just what the word *tap* means in any particular passage can only be determined from context.

---

[4]For an extensive set of lessons involving the newspaper as a teaching tool, see Eileen E. Sargent, *The Newspaper As A Teaching Tool.* The Reading Laboratory, Inc., Norwalk, CT., 1975.

Some words stand for classifications. A fish can be anything from the tiniest fingerling to a 45 foot whale shark. All this may appear self-evident until you read that Mr. Jones is a *radical,* or a *reactionary,* or a *communist.* A good reader knows that one radical may be as different from another as acid rock from a symphony, although they are both *music.* In a study guide, the teacher can call attention to the need for precision in defining a word or concept:

> *What did the author mean when he stated that Franklin D. Roosevelt was considered a radical by some people, a conservative by others? As you read, look for policies of his which fit the definitions we discussed yesterday for radical and conservative. Name at least five people mentioned in the chapter that you would consider more radical than Roosevelt, and five you think were more conservative. Tell why.*

Relative Words

Is San Francisco *nearby* or far *away?* Is it a *big* city or *small?* Obviously, some words have meaning only by comparison. To your kitten you're a giant, but to a horse . . . I have some students in my classes who are considered political *liberals.* But students with the same political views in the 1960s were rather conservative.

One difficulty is that we tend to make comparisons on the basis of our own limited experience. I still remember journeying from my home town in Arizona to Chicago, and my shock at hearing people there speak of "here in *The West.* . . ." A study guide can explain how the subject matter shifts not only the meaning, but the usability of a word.

You and I may speak of a heavy bundle, while the poet has a heavy heart, the dietitian avoids heavy foods, and the military man asks for heavy artillery. But the scientist must be precise and universal. He must define weight before he can use the word. Sometimes he finds other words more accurate and less ambiguous:

> [5]The amount of mass which occupies 1 unit volume is called the *DENSITY.* You can recognize a density value by the units *grams/milliliter (g/ml); grams per liter (g/l); and grams per cubic centimeter (g/cc).* The density of any substance can be found by using the formula

[5]Bolton, et al. *Laboratory Experiments in Action Chemistry,* New York: Holt, Rinehart and Winston, 1973, pp. 1–30.

$$\text{density} = \frac{\text{mass}}{\text{volume}} \qquad \text{Example: density} = \frac{100 \text{ g mass}}{50 \text{ ml volume}}$$

$$\text{density} = 100 \text{ g} \div 50 \text{ ml}$$

$$\text{density} = 2.0 \text{ g/ml}$$

Concrete and Abstract

The more abstract a word is, the more difficulty we have communicating because of relative meanings. We are aware of the many varieties of *animals,* but are we equally aware of the many varieties of *morality* or *sin?* To many of us, if you're not using my brand, you're not using.

I remember a discussion between an American and a Russian semanticist. Both were indignant because the other claimed that his country was a *democracy.* Further discussion revealed that American democracy is a political term. We believe in equality under the law. Russian democracy is economic. The workers are supposed to share equally the fruits of their labors. Of course, both admitted that their country had failed to achieve even its own version of democracy. There are rich and poor in Russia, and in the United States a person's political clout is directly proportional to the strength of his lobby. But we all consider ourselves living in a democracy.

Words, then, have no real meaning until you and I give them meaning. And we continually find ourselves in semantic hassels because we fail to see the variety of meanings in some of the commonest words:

> *"You don't love me,"* said Suffering Sally to her husband,
> *and she was right.*
> *"But I do love you,"* replied Patient Paul, and he was
> *also right.*

In addition to the multiple definitions recognized by dictionaries, words may carry an infinite variety of shadings and implications. A good reader knows whether a word is being used with scientific precision, as in a mathematical equation; with sarcasm, as when reading the advantages of the wogget over the wishet; for dramatic effect; or with light-hearted humor. Good readers can also recognize a *euphemism* when they see one. This is an attempt to make something unpleasant more acceptable by giving it a nicer-sounding name. When the thought of death becomes oppressive, we say Grandma has *passed on,* or *gone to her final resting place.* A company that wishes to engage in price fixing merely labels the practice *fair trade,* and everything is peachy. The military are masters of euphemism. They no longer wipe out populations, they simply *neutralize the area,* just as conquerors no longer conquer, they *liberate.* Euphemisms permeate every delicate subject from politics to sex, and while they may simply preserve good taste, a good reader knows that *plump* or *husky* often means *fat.*

Whenever we communicate, a variety of "translations" interfere. Figure 10-B illustrates a verbal transaction between two people, using a common, simple word, *tree.* The box at upper left symbolizes the *referent,* a term used by Ogden and Richards[6] to mean the real object as it exists. But a real tree is a complex organism, continually changing, growing in places, dying in other places, shuttling moisture, food, and energy up and down in a never-ending symphony of movement. The human mind cannot grasp the whole of it. We can only form an *image* (Image$_1$), which is the referent after it filters through our perception. We each form a different image, depending upon who we are. The artist sees colors and form the rest of us miss, while the lumberman assesses the tree's value in board feet. The poet has yet another view of the tree, as does the weary traveler seeking shade.

But whatever our image, we communicate by writing (or speaking) the word *tree,*—which is a symbol, not of the referent, but of Image$_1$. Upon seeing the word, the reader forms an image (Image$_2$), after filtering the symbol through his or her personality. Thus reality undergoes three distortions, first as the observer imperfectly views the real object, then as he or she searches for words to symbolize this image, and finally as the reader attempts to interpret the symbols on the page.

The teaching of reading should have as its ultimate goal the clear and accurate interpretation of the written symbol, just as the teaching of writing should be less concerned with minor points of grammar than with putting together a string of symbols that as clearly and unambiguously as possible express the image of the writer. In other words, the art of communication consists of making Image$_2$ coincide as closely as possible with Image$_1$.

You and I, for example, may agree that it is good to be virtuous. But when we use the word, do we mean the same thing? What specific, observable behavior would a person have to exhibit in order to be virtuous? The uneducated have a ready stock of simplistic clichés to account for every point of morals, but neither theologians nor lawmakers have ever been

[6]C. K. Ogden and I. A. Richards, *The Meaning of Meaning.* New York: Harcourt, Brace & World, 1923, p. 11.

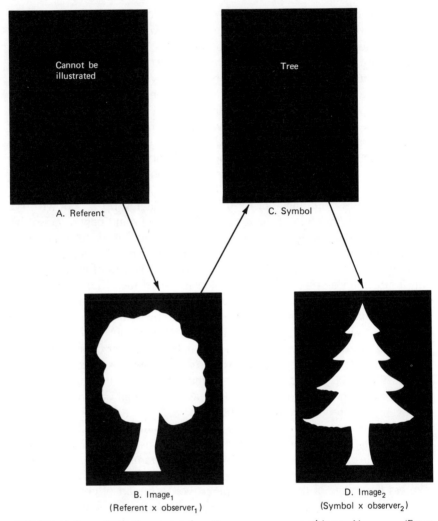

FIGURE 10-B   What happens when X ——— says something to Y ———. (From Burt Liebert, *Linguistics and the New English Teacher,* New York: Macmillan Publishing Co., Inc., 1971, p. 243.)

unanimous. Try getting any group of intelligent people to agree about the meaning of *free speech, obscenity,* or *patriotism.* Or try asking good teachers what constitutes education. We can only agree with each other on the most superficial, unexamined level. The uneducated "knows what's right." Supreme Court justices have been disagreeing for decades.

Some Language Is Loaded

Although colorful language is associated mainly with literary authors, students are frequently asked to read material that involves high level interpretive skills. In the *Delcaration of Independence* we have simple words with highly complex meaning:

> . . . *all men are created equal.* . . .
> . . . *life, liberty, and the pursuit of happiness.*

All men are created equal. How simple to say, how difficult to understand! Charlotte Chorpenning wrote a play[7] that centered around the main character's search for the meaning of the words "All men are created equal."
     In the *Gettysburg Address,* Lincoln gave us:

> . . . *conceived in liberty.* . . .
> . . . *government of the people, by the people, and for*
> *the people.* . . .

It is a disservice to young people and to the country to allow students to read such thought-provoking material, which forms some of the basic thinking behind American democracy, without some penetrating discussion of just what such phrases mean.

Figurative Language

Even textbook writers may spice up their words with figures of speech:

> Through our history runs the ever-widening stream of liberty.[8]

> *Words can be wild and elusive. Some go galloping off in unexpected directions. Others stand when they should be seated. The artist with words is the man who can tame them, who can conquer their whims and variables and make them behave as they should.*[9]

Many students are unable to put such material into perspective. Carter found this to be true of seventh grade social studies students. She had them

[7]*Paul Bunyan's First Christmas.* Children's Theatre Press.
[8]John W. Caughey et al., *Land of the Free: A History of the United States.* p. 13.
[9]Warren Weaver, "The Case of the Wayward Words." in Jack C. Gray, *Words, Words, and Words about Dictionaries.* Chandler Publishing Company, 1963, p. 3. Reprinted from *The Saturday Review,* March 5, 1960.

read a textbook passage that contained figurative language, then tested them with questions that could not be answered without understanding the figure. She found literal interpretations being attached to figurative language:[10]

> *Thomas Paine was judged to "use his pen as a weapon" by squirting ink on the Tories; as a "framer of the Constitution," James Madison was believed to have prepared it for hanging on a wall; and Warren G. Harding, a "dark horse candidate," was interpreted as being the first Black President of the U.S.*

Sometimes a question can be very effective, allowing the student to exercise his mental faculties:

> When the author called this period of history an *anemic* society, he didn't mean that everyone was suffering from a lack of hemoglobin. What do you suppose he did mean? Read his description and think about the main characteristics of the period. What did it have in common with people who are anemic?

There are a number of types of figurative language with which students should be familiar. These include:

> *Hyperbole* (exaggeration).   *On the dance floor he is a three-legged grizzly bear.*
>
> *Metaphor* (See p. 159).   *The lark is the messenger of morning.*
>
> *Simile* (See p. 159).   *She is like a daisy in a field of thistles.*
>
> *Personification* (Treating a nonhuman object as if it had human characteristics).   *The weather was doing everything it could to make the day perfect.*

Having advanced from decoding to data processing, we still have much to do, for beyond the fact there is *meaning.* Beyond data are higher level skills—*thinking* skills—skills that apply equally to reading, hearing a speech or news report, or arguing politics or philosophy. Without these thinking skills, the reader's capacity to come to terms with a writer is limited. James Moffett pointed out that the skills discussed in our final chapter are not strictly reading skills:

> *A long list of mental activities that any psychologist would consider general properties of thinking that occur in many different areas of human experience*

---

[10]Betty B. Carter, "Helping Seventh Graders to Understand Figurative Expressions." *Journal of Reading,* April 1977, 20:553–558, p. 555.

[11]Moffett, op cit., p. 16.

have somehow or other all been tucked under the skirts of reading. "Recalling," "comprehending," "relating facts," "making inferences," "drawing conclusions," "interpreting," and "predicting outcomes" are all mental operations that go on in the head of a nonliterate aborigine navigating his outrigger according to cues from weather, sea life, currents, and the positions of heavenly bodies. Not only do these kinds of thinking have no necessary connection with reading, but they have no necessary connection with language whatever.[11]

But if these skills are not the exclusive territory of the reading teacher, or even the language teacher, they are certainly a vital component of the reading process, a component I find receiving insufficient attention in most secondary classrooms. It is, therefore, important that we turn our attention next to the more abstract and the cognitive, to the ability to feel deeply, to relate, and to refuse to be fooled.

CHAPTER 11
Beyond the Word: Teaching Higher-level Reading Skills

I am not just teaching dull, barren facts–I am teaching students to think.

How often have we heard that noble objective from teachers! Yet my impression is that however high the ideal, teachers do not teach anybody to think because thinking cannot be taught. Wisdom is not transferable, wrote Hermann Hesse, and he might have added that neither is thinking.

What is usually meant by *teaching students to think* is teaching them to *think the way I think.* If I am a political liberal, I know that right-minded thinkers think as liberals. I don't *believe* I am right; I *know* I am right. That is why I am a liberal. So my students are not really thinking until they are thinking as liberals. On the other hand, if I am conservative, I know that liberals are muddle-headed bleeding hearts, and my mission in life is carrying the banner of *status quo.*

Once I start messing with anyone else's thinking, I am not teaching thinking at all—just indoctrinating. Fortunately, most young people have a pretty healthy capacity to resist indoctrination. Given half a chance, they will *teach themselves to think,* and it is the giving of that half chance that concerns us now.

That half chance to develop thinking capacity involves two things the teacher can do:

First, set up an intellectually stimulating classroom. Then keep out of the way.

Both of these are a lot more difficult than they seem. They consist not of teaching to think, but *allowing* to think. Much of the process has already been described in Chapter 4—discovery teaching, freedom from fear of reprisal for disagreeing with the teacher, an atmosphere of acceptance, individualizing instruction to meet the needs of the student, establishing open classrooms and active rather than passive learning. However, it also consists of continually questioning, continually challenging. The teacher who can do this must be a liberal who can listen to super-conservative arguments without needing to set the erring student straight, or a conservative who can hear radical ideas and be quiet despite tension in the midsection.

Difficult as it is to set up a truly stimulating classroom, allowing students to think for themselves is even more difficult. I recently had a materials requisition returned by a junior high school principal because the books "had not been approved by the board." It takes courage and wisdom to let people read what they want and to think freely.

But beyond this, there are specifics. While thinking skills cannot be taught directly, a teacher can introduce his charges to some of the thinking *tools*. These tools are questions that can be asked and concepts that can be explored. Let us look at some of these.

THE FALLACY OF FACT, OR HOW MUCH IS TWO PLUS TWO TODAY?

Once upon a time the world was flat. No, I don't mean people thought it was flat, I mean it really *was* flat. Anybody could see that just by looking out the window. Of course, there were the usual hills and valleys, lakes and rivers, even mountains, but except for comparatively minor little bumps and dips, the world was flat.

A few philosophers and assorted eggheads formed some sort of theory about the world being shaped like a ball and revolving around the sun. But these were obviously nuts, because everybody knew that if the earth were shaped like a ball, and half the people lived on the underside, they would fall off.

Strangely, however, as time went by, more and more people said they had *evidence* that the world is round. In the sixteenth century Copernicus did a lot of mumble-jumble calculations and said he had proved it, and Galileo, with his telescope, agreed. Christopher Columbus probably received too much credit in the history books, for his theory about going to the East by sailing west was not all that new. But while others were speculating, he did something about it. Of course, he missed the target by a hemisphere, so it remained for Magellan, or at least his crew, for Magellan himself was killed en route, to sail around the world and pile up still more evidence. One of Magellan's ships returned to home port without turning back, and that made the *world is round* folks a bit harder to argue with.

Today the sciences of geography, geology, physics, and astronomy seem to agree that the world is round, just as a bevy of assorted kooks

"I'm sorry, Mrs. Columbus . . . but Christopher flunked geography again!"

FIGURE 11-A   (Courtesy of United Feature Syndicate, Inc.)

throughout history have insisted. All of which seems to indicate that it doesn't pay to be too sure.

Can we now, for example, be sure that the world is round? Oh, it's round, all right, but only in the sense that it was once flat. That is, as far as we are able to look, listen, smell, calculate, and speculate—as far as anybody I know has been able to OBSERVE, the world is round. And we have some pretty sophisticated instruments—(well, we think they are, at least—) to confirm the theory.

I say *theory* because that's all it is. If today's instruments are so sophisticated that they can lay to rest the best observations of the ancients (through the window with their own eyes), how can we know what SUPERSOPHISTICATED instruments will come along tomorrow?

The point is, there is no such thing as a fact. We have only theories. And we never know when *new evidence* can disprove a theory. That *two plus two equals four* would seem reasonable to call a fact. But can we even be sure of this? How do we know what new conditions will present themselves tomorrow, conditions under which two plus two may not equal four? As a matter of fact (Note that even our language pays homage to the Great God Fact: "As a matter of fact . . ."), we do not have to wait at all. Try adding two plus two, using a base three numerical system. I get 11. What do you get? Nor do we even have to change bases. Next time you are in the kitchen try adding two cups of sugar to two cups of water. Just try to come out with four cups without cheating.

All this sounds like a batch of harmless but useless theorizing until we look at what failure to understand the fallacy of fact does to us. For example, a few years ago some members of a State Board of Education discovered that evolution constituted part of our curriculum in science. After months of furious debate, they finally reached a conclusion:

> Evolution may be taught in the public schools, but only as a theory, not as fact.

But how else could it conscientiously be taught? How can anything be taught with any validity, except as a theory? Even *the world is round* theory was modified when it was discovered that it is actually flattened at the poles. And how do we know what Copernicus, what Galileo, what Einstein is lurking in the shadows of the future with new measuring devices, new calculations, new ways of looking at the universe? Next time you decide to tell your class you are going to teach them to tell fact from theory, think of Magellan.

So if everything is only theory, then my theory is as good as yours, isn't it? Let's see:

> Every Midsummer's Eve a dozen little fairies emerge from their home underground and dance on the quad of this revered university. Of course, fairies are invisible, and they make no sound, and mortals can walk right through them and never feel a thing, for fairies live in another dimension. But they are there, nevertheless, and they can sense whether you believe in them. If you believe, they will shower great blessings upon this university, but if you disbelieve–Oh, I tremble to think . . .

Well, that's my theory. Try to prove me wrong. Go ahead—prove that I am wrong. That's a challenge.

The point, of course, is that you don't have to prove me wrong. It's my theory, so it's up to me to prove myself right. And I can't. There's no way to do that. My theory lacks *observability*. Observability, or lack of it, is what makes one theory as different from another as a mouse from an elephant. So, science teacher, when you're teaching evolution as a theory, teach students to investigate its *observability*. Charles Darwin spent years painstakingly collecting evidence and putting together research, until the picture emerged. And since Darwin, thousands of scientists have gone over his ground trying to refute or verify his conclusions. So before you pooh-pooh Darwin, you have to show *evidence* to counter his evidence. And that's what you can teach your students—to consider everything a theory, to look for evidence, and to value theories as comparatively *high or low in observability.*

Of course, I am not saying that two plus two does not equal four, or that the world is not round. Considering the evidence, that would be ridiculous. Nor can I predict that any particular theory will be upset in the future. But the *habit of thinking* as if every aspect of the universe were known and unchanging is one of the great barriers to clear thinking. Inability to change to meet new conditions, refusal to examine new theories or modes of operation, are bitter enemies of progress.

I recently read about a man who operates a privately owned garbage dump. Instead of the usual methods of sanitary fill—dumping the refuse in natural or man-made canyons to level the land—he piled it up to build a man-made "mountain," which he intends to develop eventually for recreation. Of course, the local board of supervisors, knowing that that isn't the way it is done (two plus two always equals four), is trying to close his operation.

Another man has learned to grow salmon in reclaimed sewer water. But he is now fighting the bureaucracy to convince them to develop such projects instead of wasting a valuable resource.

Have you heard the one about the lion? Captured in his native jungle and brought to "civilization," he was put into a cage at the zoo. Hating captivity, he paced the cage, back and forth, back and forth, looking for a way out, looking for a weak spot in the bars. But with no success. There was no way out. All the poor beast could do was to continue pacing back and forth, back and forth, back and forth. Then one day the keeper carelessly left the door open. What did the lion do? He continued to pace back and forth, back and forth, back and forth, staring longingly through the open door at the freedom that was, alas, just out of reach. How many lions have you seen recently?

There is the classic experiment by a catsup company. Hearing complaints about how difficult it is to get catsup out of the long-necked bottle, they marketed it in wide-mouth jars. But sales plummeted because people had a hard time thinking of catsup in anything but the traditional bottle.

But let's not succumb to the curse of the educated class—getting so tied up in theories about theories that we paralyze ourselves into inaction. You have sufficient evidence, for example, that if you flick that little *thing* over there, the lights will go on. So flick it. No need to sit in the dark, just because it is only a theory that the lights will go on. After all, civilization is built upon just such theories. And the sky hasn't fallen in yet. So it seems reasonable to help our students understand that *it is O.K. to act on the theory of highest observability, and if future events create new theories of higher observability it's no crime to switch.*

SORTING THINGS OUT

Thus far in this chapter, we have dealt with cognitive problems, questions that involve thinking skills. But this does not deny the existence of a whole other dimension, the *affective domain.* (See p. 10). Nor is it intended to diminish, in the slightest, the importance of that dimension. Our feelings are as vital as our thoughts and I suspect they have more to say about decision-making.

The trouble begins when we confuse one dimension with the other—when our emotions cloud our thinking, or when we try to rationalize our feelings. And inasmuch as the two dimensions are closely interwoven and are continually interacting, we are in continual trouble.

It thus falls upon the teacher to help his charges sort out reactions that are based on feelings—which cannot be held responsible for observability from reactions based on the intellect, which can. When I read Alvin Toffler's *Future Shock,* something human within me cries out, "It's not so! I don't believe it." I don't *want* to live in the plastic, mechanized, temporary, throw-away world he depicts. So my feelings contaminate my reason and urge me to disbelieve. Then a student enters my office to tell me that the computer rejected his registration in my class because he left his card on a chair and the baby chewed on it, and would I please fill out the appropriate form and send it through appropriate channels. To read *Future Shock,* one needs to have both dimensions working overtime. The primary question, is Toffler correct?, must be examined on the basis of evidence. But equally important is the second question, which of his statements (or misstatements) offer a better world and which indicate a lowering of the quality of life? This must not only be answered on the basis of reason, but dealt with by our feelings about the kind of world in which we want to live. Finally, we utilize the fourth level of reading, the involvement level, when we ask the ultimate question: given certain conclusions about what we have just read, what are we going to do about it?

In contrast, when I read *The Mouse That Roared,* I am faced with a situation so implausible, so ridiculous—New York captured by a band of 23 stalwarts with bows and arrows—a single scientist and his (of course, beautiful) daughter alone and unguarded with a bomb powerful enough to blow up all of Europe—that there is no way for my intellect to cope. But that doesn't matter. I don't have to cope intellectually with a story that was not written for plausibility. I need only lose myself in this utterly delightful tale—enjoy its humor, its romance, and even the surprisingly serious theme.

My experience has been, on the other hand, that many students miss the delight of *The Mouse* in the search for believability. And they are unable to read Toffler (and similar works) intelligently because their feelings hamper their reason.

It is not literature alone that can elicit a feeling response from a good reader. George Leonard depicts youngsters of the future reading history with tears in their eyes, trying to comprehend humanity's inhumanity.[1] In science, too many classes deal with data alone, failing to consider the vital questions:

In what kind of world do I want to live?

How can that world be achieved?

What contributions can the scientist make to that world?

Industrial arts students should not cut into the lumber pile without reading what has happened to the great forests of North America and the world, and consequently, to our timber supply. No cooking class is complete without some understanding of what is happening to our farm land, and how this relates to predicted world-wide famine. Nor should the young dressmaker escape without knowing the difference between natural and synthetic fibres in terms of air and water pollution and consumption of farmland and energy.

These are not, of course, purely emotional questions. Much profound thinking will be required to search for answers. But we will also need to feel something about our value system, about the position of the human race in the ecology of Spaceship Earth, and about our relationship with other people in the world.

But in the quest for cognitive skills, too many teachers ignore this whole vital affective area. The result can be a classroom full of students who are unexcited about school because school is offering little to be excited about.

But human emotions will not be put down. They crop up in whatever we do, including reading. They add to the joy of the page, whether we are carried away by the horror of Macbeth and the bloody daggers or by the discovery of how to solve for X.

Thus a teacher can further the quest for high level reading skills by asking (not by telling, but by asking): Is your conclusion based on observable data, or is it based on your personal life position—on your political and

[1]George Leonard, *Education and Ecstasy*. New York: Delacorte Press, 1968, p. 172.

religious convictions, your fears and insecurities, your vested interests, and other emotional factors? Both areas, the cognitive and the affective, are legitimate. But a good reader—a good thinker—knows which is which.

HOW MUCH IS IT WORTH?

People read for a variety of reasons, just as they write for a variety of reasons. These reasons, however, can be grouped under two main headings: reading for enjoyment and reading for information. Frequently, of course, we combine the two, but for purposes of instruction we can look at each separately.

For Enjoyment

Most students who tell me they do not enjoy reading are poor readers. It is difficult to enjoy anything we find tedious and frustrating. I have seen many students who, with a dramatic improvement in reading skills, experienced a dramatic improvement in enjoyment. It also works in reverse. When students' interests are caught by reading, their skills are almost sure to improve with use. This is why so much emphasis has been placed on study guides, alternate lessons, and other devices to make reading both easier and more enjoyable.

Another important factor is a healthy affective domain. The reader who feels deeply has a good start. To be angry at injustice; to empathize with the loves, fears, hates and joys of literary characters; to relish a clever mataphor or poetic language—these are the stuff of reading enjoyment.

But rugged emotions are not easy to develop. Many English teachers who think they are developing "appreciation" for literature are only developing a distaste. Exposure, of course, is essential, particularly when bolstered by lively and enlightening discussion, although both exposure and discussion can be deadening as well as supportive, depending upon their appropriateness for the student.

A teacher with talent for oral reading can help students see the drama and poetry of words. There are also hundreds of spoken recordings available at record stores, featuring the world's finest actors. A teacher with a well-developed sense of humor can help students see the humor in what they read, more by exhibiting appreciation than by trying to explain the "point." But exposure to reading alone is not enough. One also needs exposure to the whole process of living. One has to be *involved,* to experience the joys and frustrations of being human. A person who is raised in an intellectually unstimulating environment is not likely to be turned on to reading. We can only bring to the page the total of our life experiences. This is why reading instruction begins with the turned-on classroom.

For Information

Some textbook material is limited to simple data and does not require highest level reading skills. But suppose the reader comes across the following:

THE REAL TRUTH ABOUT UNESCO

The crackpots and fuzzy-minded liberals pushing UNESCO in the United States have not succeeded in polluting the minds of American school children yet, but not because they haven't tried. In a recent issue of *Forward Magazine* John Smite wrote a tear-jerking piece about the "sad fate" of UNESCO in school districts across the land. Wise school board members, it seems, have barred UNESCO propaganda from the schools in many communities. Smite and his fellow one-worlders have been trying to shove UNESCO down the throats of Americans for years, but Americans aren't swallowing the stuff.

How is such material to be interpreted? What should be the reader's attitude towards UNESCO? With a twist of fate he might instead have read:

The enlightened liberals who are telling the dramatic story of UNESCO's many accomplishments to the American people are being continually thwarted by the forces of fear and status quo. In a recent issue of *Forward Magazine* John Smite told a heart-breaking story of his frustration in attempting to reach the school children of America. School board bureaucrats in many areas, fearful lest their own narrow concepts be questioned, have censored UNESCO material out of the course of study. Smite and his enthusiastic group have been trying for years to explain the many benefits that could come to all of us through the activities of UNESCO, but he finds it difficult to counteract the chauvinism that is consistently promoted by the establishment.

It is obvious to all but the most naive and the most opinionated that the writers of both paragraphs are more interested in influencing the reader than enlightening. But consider the next two versions:

The liberals supporting UNESCO in the United States have not yet succeeded in influencing the minds of American school children, although they have tried. In a recent issue of *Forward Magazine* John Smite wrote an analysis of the reaction toward UNESCO in school districts across the land. Careful school board members have barred UNESCO materials from schools in many communities. Smite and his internationally-minded followers have been promoting UNESCO to Americans for years, but Americans have not been as enthusiastic as Smite would like them to be.

UNESCO enthusiasts have been meeting many obstacles in telling their story to American school children. In a recent issue of *Forward Magazine* John Smite wrote a moving account of the unfair treatment UNESCO has received in many school districts. Conservative school board members have prevented UNESCO's material from reaching the children. Smite and his fellow humanitarians have been explaining the benefits of UNESCO to Americans for years, but have been frustrated in their attempts to reach the school children.

The second pair of paragraphs are more "dangerous," because the propaganda is more subtle. Even good readers can be trapped by such writing, if their skills are confined to word-attack and data processing. Therefore, no reading program is complete if it does not involve training in the higher level skills of interpretation and involvement.

Evaluation

A teacher would be off base attempting to teach students that UNESCO is good or bad on the basis of this (or any other) essay. That's what I mean by teaching to think the way the teacher thinks. But there are some objective questions that can be asked. These questions revolve around three major subjects: the author, the reader, and the work itself.

THE AUTHOR   How qualified is the author to make these statements? How much *observation* has she done in this area? How much research or study has she undertaken? The Sunday morning philosopher will cheerfully advise the President, but the opinions of the career economist, political scientist, or student of foreign affairs are in a different league.

But there is also the question: an authority on what? Fireball Freely may be the world's greatest baseball player, and a handsome son-of-a-gun to boot, grinning at us from a newspaper or TV tube, but is he qualified to tell us about shaving cream?

Sometimes we are led to believe there is a connection when there isn't. The movie starlet who tells us that "We actresses must know how to care for our complexions," probably doesn't. And the doctor who writes about the national health care proposal may be a great brain surgeon, but may or may not be better informed than his readers about the economics of the proposal.

There is also the question of motive. This is an extremely difficult area to deal with, for human beings are loaded with hidden agendas. The baseball player's and the starlet's motives are obvious. They are getting paid for an endorsement. If another company paid them more, they would happily switch brands.

Yet such tactics sell millions of dollars worth of shaving cream and glop for the face. This is because many people have not learned to sort out their feelings (Isn't she *darling*. Wouldn't I love to look like her! Maybe if I use the same brand of glop. . . .) from their intellect (What evidence is there that the stuff will do anything for me?).

The doctor is another story. He has been through college and medical school. He is a professional, and deals with health problems every working day of his life. Let's assume he is chairman of his medical association Legislative Committee, and in this capacity spends many hours every week studying health legislation. Therefore, he is knowledgeable. He quotes statistics. He uses big words. He is an articulate speaker and a convincing writer. That is why he is chairman of his committee.

But he is something else as well. He is also human. He views issues from the human point of view—how will it affect me? And the national health plan will affect the amount of money he earns, the number of patients he has, the degree of regulation to be imposed on him. Although his opinion will be stated in terms of the public good, he cannot help being influenced to a greater or lesser degree by the old, but very human, *what's in it for me?*

This is not to imply that doctors, or other human beings, are unable at times to put their own selfish motives aside and come out for the greatest good for the greatest number. I am only cautioning that some of the most authoritative-looking writing may be, and frequently is, influenced by an obscure motive. This motive is not determined by occupation alone, but by age, sex, political orientation, religious conviction, economic status, education, and a host of other factors.

The search for authority, however, can be a double-edged sword. On the one hand, I believe there is in this country a generic distrust of "eggheads," a tendency to romanticize the school of hard knocks. It is part of the Great American Myth that the man of action can solve the most difficult problems with good old common sense. But it is just such common sense that Stuart Chase says causes us to look out the window and declare that the world is flat.

But on the other hand lies the danger of becoming overimpressed by authority. Plenty of utter drivel finds its way into print; even textbooks are not immune. Many a degree is awarded for sitting still long enough without causing too many ripples. As the Wizard of Oz remarked in the film, If I cannot give you wisdom I can give you a diploma.

WE READ WHAT WE ARE   It is not only the author, but ourselves, who are subject to the frailties of humanity. We react to what we read, we think and we act on our thoughts not alone on the basis of clear, objective reasoning, but because *we are what we are.* We have a point of view, based upon our total experiences to date, and that point of view largely determines our understanding. The current state of our intellectual development, our emotional condition, and many other factors are involved. So are we also influenced by friends and relatives, by neighbors and work associates, as well as our limited perceptions. The universe consists of one dog. Ask any flea.

We are all "culturally deprived" to the extent that we belong to a culture, and that culture shapes our reactions. Even if we became authorities on, say, William Shakespeare or Leo Tolstoy, we would still view their works as twentieth century thinkers, not as Elizabethans or Czarist Russians. And by the time we are teen-agers, we have deeply ingrained political, religious, and philosophical attitudes.

When a person says, "I am not prejudiced," he ought to be saying, "My prejudices run so deep that I cannot recognize them. If I knew my prejudices, I would not have them." To deny being biased is to deny being human.

If I tell you that Green Haired People control the money and the banks in this country, I may or may not know what I am talking about. If my research has shown that 86 percent of bank directors and 79 percent of major corporation directors are Green Hairs, this is not a prejudice, but theory based on observation. But if I believe this statement to be true without investigation, I have literally *pre-judiced,* or judged beforehand. Once I discover that my belief is unfounded, I may still have feelings to deal with, but I no longer have the prejudice.

All this should not keep us from thinking about what we read, from forming opinions, and from acting on those opinions. Like the umpire, all we can do is "call 'em like we see 'em." But while calling, we can also be aware of the many facets of the question that our point of view hides from us and we can be ready to change our opinions and actions as new evidence indicates.

THE EVIDENCE   Looking at the author's credentials and at our own is, of course, only the beginning. Ultimately good readers look at the work itself.

Literary works may quite legitimately be judged largely on the basis of personal reaction. The reader was either interested or not interested, and if the writer moved the reader, he accomplished his purpose. This is not to imply that some literature does not have more depth, is not written with finer style, and is not more skillfully constructed. But these literary values are frequently difficult—sometimes impossible—for an immature reader to comprehend. Many teachers turn students off to reading by showing their obvious contempt for the kinds of things their students want to read. Frequently, it is the teacher who is so wrapped up in his own university major that he fails to see how much knowledge and talent go into writing an article or book that appeals to a tenth grader with fifth grade reading skills.

In reading nonfiction, however, different criteria may be applied. "Facts" are nothing more than theories that are subject to varying degrees of verifiability, while opinions are more difficult to pin down. There is no sharp dividing line between the two, and what I may consider verified, you may consider opinion.

Surface Validity

It is frequently possible to estimate the care with which something is written by inspecting the writing style. A reliable writer is very careful about the statements he makes. His works are permeated with words such as *possibly, probably, may,* and *could.* The careless writer tends to use *always, never,* and *everybody* with abandon. What may be proof (fact) to the unwary, is evidence (probability) to the careful. A good writer may be just as likely to hold strong opinions, but usually tells why he believes as he does. He bases his opinion on *evidence.* The four paragraphs on UNESCO are distinguished by the carelessness with which they state that "Americans aren't swallowing the stuff," "he finds it difficult to counteract the chauvinism," "careful school board members have barred UNESCO materials" and "have been explaining the benefits of UNESCO." Nowhere is there any real evidence that school board members are either chauvinistic or careful, that there is anything good or bad about UNESCO. If any of these paragraphs contain a modicum of truth, that truth is obscured by careless writing.

Snarl Words and Purr Words

These terms were coined by S. I. Hayakawa[2] to indicate that certain words have no real meaning as used in certain contexts. They are like a snarling dog or a purring cat, representing only states of emotion. "Fuzzy-minded liberals" and "enlightened liberals" are good examples, as are "UNESCO propaganda" and "the dramatic story of UNESCO's many accomplishments."

Sometimes these emotion-packed words are obvious and easy to de-

[2]*Language in Thought And Action.* New York: Harcourt, Brace Jovanovich, Inc., 1964, pp. 44–48.

tect; sometimes they are subtle and insidious. Advertisers, politicians, anybody with a point to make may resort to emotion-packed words to soothe, inflame, or incite fear. An interesting "game," called *conjugating irregular verbs,* from an idea by Bertrand Russell is suggested by Hayakawa[3] to develop sensitivity to emotional use of words. It may be played any number of ways, but it consists of making up three ways to say the same thing:

I am clever.	You are calculating.	She is tricky.
I am an officer of the law.	You are a cop.	He is a pig.
I am slender.	You are thin.	She is skinny.
I am husky.	You are fleshy.	He is fat.
I am fond of people.	You are a nuisance.	He is lecherous.

Try this with a class some time. Give them a few examples and let them make up more. Or let three teams take turns starting, continuing, and completing the "conjugations." Or place several dozen cards around the room, each card containing a starter. Let the students walk around the room and complete the cards. Here are a few ideas for starters:

I believe in being honest.

I am diplomatic.

I am the life of the party.

I am beautiful.

I find it challenging to restore old automobiles.

I am a natural born leader.

I am a specialist.

I don't run off half-cocked. I check the facts before I act.

I am a person of quiet, serene dignity.

I have set for myself a high standard of morality.

I have faith in myself.

I am always gentle.

I am a man of action.

Here is another game that points out the subtle differences between words. The first player whispers a word into the ear of the second. It should

[3]Ibid., pp. 95–96.

be a meaning word, not a short function word such as *of, the,* or *but.* The second player thinks of a synonym for that word—the closest synonym he can. Then he whispers the synonym into the ear of the third player. He should speak clearly to be sure the other player hears the correct word. The third player whispers a synonym for what he heard into the ear of the fourth. This goes around the room. Finally, the first and last players tell the rest of the group their words. It seldom takes half a dozen players for the meaning to change completely, showing that synonyms do not mean the same thing.

A variation would be to have several "teams." The starter whispers the same word to the first player from each team. As the last player on each team tells his word, we see how completely unrelated each final word is to the other, as well as from the original word.

The Vague Generality, or the Meaningless Abstraction

Try this with your class some time. Write on the chalk board a statement such as:

Teen-agers are lousy drivers.

Ask them to "discuss" it. One comment I frequently get to this statement is something like: *Yeah, but those old biddies who drive down the road are worse.* You could point out that this comment may represent either or both of these thought processes:

A. *Defensiveness:* I am a teen-ager (We read [or hear] what we are.) I don't want to be "lousy." If I throw mud at someone else, it takes the heat off me.

Such an argument is utter futility, just so many snarl words. On the other hand, if viewed differently, the statement does have a modicum of logic.

B. *Comparison:* How do you define "lousy"? What is your standard? Let's compare teen-age drivers with older drivers. Thus this statement may be a crude groping for the first step in unraveling vague generalities:

1. *Define your terms.*
    What is a lousy driver? One who has been in an accident? Two accidents? One accident per year? One accident per ten thousand miles of driving? A serious accident? Or do you include drivers with no accidents but many traffic tickets? And how many accidents is *many*? And how serious must they be? Do you count overtime parking

tickets along with drunken driving? The deeper you think, the more difficult it becomes to define.

Also in need of definition is *teen-age*. Do we mean all teen-agers? Does the age group run from 13 to 19? Sixteen to 19? Are all age groups in this bracket equally bad drivers? Boys and girls equally? Intelligent and unintelligent? Aggressive and submissive types? Do we mean all? Or are we speaking of averages? Or was this statement based on observation of certain incidents or even a single incident (inadequate sample)? This leads to the next important step:

2.   *Present your evidence.*
"Well, I teach in this high school, and I see how kids burn out of the parking lot!"

"Now we are getting somewhere. *I have personally observed driving practices at X_____ High* is a far cry from *teen-agers are* . . . But how methodically have you observed?"

"I hear their tires screeching every time they leave the lot."

"Then by your definition, *screeching tires* means *lousy drivers?*"

"Well, not just tires, but if they burn rubber like that, think how they must drive."

"Burning out *may* be a sign of careless driving. Your only observation has been the parking lot?"

"I suppose so. But everybody knows. . . ."

"I don't know it, and I'm somebody. Have you ever counted the number of students who do not burn rubber when they leave the parking lot?"

"Sounds like they all do."

"But you can't hear the ones who leave quietly. Tell you what. Go to the parking lot when school is out and count."
(Scene 2. Next day)

"Well?"

"I counted 27 burnouts and 42 nonburnouts, and five made such little burns I didn't know whether to count them."

"Interesting. Even a grey area. People don't fit into neat little categories. But now you have an acceptable statement: *I have observed that. . . .* You've come a long way from *Teen-agers are. . . ."*

"How come kids have to pay more for insurance, if they're such wonderful drivers?"

"I didn't say they were. I only asked you to define your terms and present evidence. Actually, it's my understanding that insurance company statistics do indicate that young drivers have a higher accident rate. Whether it is poor driving or some other factor, I don't know. Maybe they drive unsafe cars. I have never studied the tables, but my insurance agent told me that my son would have to pay the higher rate until he is 25. But it's not that simple. My son pays a higher rate than my daughter. And some companies have a "good student" discount. (Interesting. Students with a B average or better have fewer accidents.) So do married students. Again, the more you investigate, the more complex it becomes."

Such dialogues are needed for students to learn that evidence can be gathered by direct observation (in the parking lot) or by study of other people's observations (insurance statistics). They can learn about *representative samples:* Count the burn-outs the day of the big pregame football rally. Then count them the day a classmate died. Or compare sunny days with rainy days. Or compare our high school with other schools. Students can learn to spot the vague generality, and to sift the verifiable from the unverifiable.

In the article about UNESCO, the most verifiable datum is that John Smite published an article in *Forward Magazine* praising UNESCO. This can be checked at any good reference library. The four articles seem to agree that UNESCO material has not been favorably received by school boards across the nation, but to verify this, one would have to research enough school districts (and there are tens of thousands) to have a representative sample. Also, what *specific action* would a school board have to take to constitute a favorable or unfavorable response? Did they refuse to purchase UNESCO material for school use, and if so, was this for philosophical or budgetary reasons? Or was the material poorly prepared or overpriced? Or did the school boards refuse to accept it as a gift? Or did they forbid the mention of UNESCO in the classrooms?

How many "school districts across the land" were contacted, and where? A campaign in Utah may have a different outcome from the same in New York. School districts in urban, suburban, and rural areas may have different characteristics, as may large, small, or medium-sized units.

Thus a good reader recognizes that the phrases, "school districts across the land" and "prevented UNESCO's materials from reaching the children", are abstract and vague. She recognizes that calling John Smite "enlightened" or "fuzzy-minded" tells you more about the political stance of the writer than about Smite.

The Don't-We-Wish Cause and Effect

The advertisement shown in Figure 11−B implies that if you send your child to their school, that child will excel in reading and arithmetic. And they quote the prestigious Stanford Achievement Test as "proof." Wow! Here you have a perfect case of implied cause and effect. But are there factors that can cause students to come out with superior ratings—factors that are not related to the merits of the school?

```
WE'RE
PROUD . . . WHY?
    We teach reading!
    We teach arithmetic!
    We teach much more!
How do we know?
    Stanford Achievement
    tests say so!
Prove it! . . . okay!
Grade 1:30 students
    63% above national
    average
    2.7 grade equivalent
Grade 2:18 students
    50% above national
    average
    3.6 grade equivalent
Grade 3:23 students
    38% above national
    average
    4.6 grade equivalent
How many below
national average?
Grades 1, 2, and 3 − Zero!
WOULD YOU LIKE TO
KNOW OUR SECRET?
Call 967−6500, 967−7748
and more proof of academic
excellence will be supplied.
```

FIGURE 11-B

We shall give the school the benefit of the doubt and not consider the possibility that the test results may not be accurate. The doubt does exist, because when my students take a test, I naturally want them to do as well as possible. Their success is my success; likewise their deficiencies. There are many ways the tester may tilt the results—consciously or otherwise. Some extras in giving directions, or a bit of "carelessness" in timing, and the results are skewed. But let's assume the test was administered fairly and objectively.

I think most teachers know that the most reliable way to be "successful" is to choose your students carefully. What kind of student body would a school such as this have? To begin with, this school seems to be heavily oriented towards academic, college-preparatory skills. It would seem reasonable to assume that the mothers and fathers who bring their youngsters here would be oriented to study hard, work hard, get into college. It thus seems probable that so would the bulk of the youngsters.

The school was charging, several years ago when they ran the advertisement, a tuition of $550.00 per year. Who can afford such tuition? It is possible to assume that most students come from upper middle class families—the socio-economic group that contributes the highest achievers to the public schools. In other words, there is a good possibility that this school owes its "success" to having a student body that would have made high scores in any school.

This brings up the question of a representative sample again. Show me that this school's student body contains the same proportion of members of every economic class that is found in the public school, and I'll try to learn how they do it.

The Judicious Deletion, or the Truest Story Never Told

"Tell me what you wish to prove, and I'll prove it." This remark was made to me by the director of research of a large statewide organization. Although he was speaking with tongue-in-cheek, his point is well taken.

Sometimes it isn't what a writer says, but what he fails to say that is most significant. In a small private school, for example, the presence of a few very bright students can unduly influence the average. As students come and go, it is conceivable that there will be good years and poor ones. All you have to do is test students during the good years and report only those results.

It is also possible, through selective teaching, to achieve high scores in certain areas at the expense of others. A school may have a strong program in reading and math, but neglect art, music, science, social studies, and physical education. There are also other factors that go into the making of a good school, such as the warmth and sensitivity of the teachers; and the diversity of the student body, which enables students to learn from classmates of other cultures and other persuasions. Yet year after year, teachers and schools are unofficially "rated" according to test results that may reveal only the most insignificant data.

Rhetoric and Reality

"If you can't pound in your points," my debate coach used to say, "pound on the table." "Promise her anything," advises an advertiser, "but. . . ." It is all a matter of images. Reality is one thing. How we view reality, however, may be quite another. Whether it is the tree discussed on page 268, a political campaign, an advertised product, or any other issue, we are continually confronted with a potpourri of carefully put together images designed to seduce us into buying, voting, thinking, feeling, and doing.

Take, for example, the women's movement. In recent years the image of woman has been changing. More and more women are achieving in business, the professions, and the trades, and are even competing with men in athletics.

The Feminist Movement is neither new nor limited to females. James Barrie and Henrik Ibsen are only a few who dramatized the plight of women with works such as *The Twelve Pound Look* and *The Doll's House* before Gloria Steinem and Germaine Greer were born. Even the classical Greek Theatre, from *Agamemnon* and *Medea* to *Lysistrata* portrayed women who were sick and tired of being taken for granted. But of course, humanity has always had sages whose works we have venerated, but whose wisdom we have ignored.

Now men are getting into the act. Led by Warren Farrell[4] and others, the male stereotype is also breaking down. And the more we look at stereotypes, the more obvious it becomes that we are all a mass of them. We have stereotypes of our government, our school system, and our community. We carry around with us stereotypes of Blacks, Whites, Asians, Indians, and Chicanos; of foreigners, teen-agers, college students, doctors, professors, and cops. These stereotypes are built into us by single incidents (imperfect sample), by inaccurate observation (Image₁ does not match referent), by television and other mass media, and by heresay from friends and family.

The art of persuasion is largely a matter of understanding people's stereotypes and using them to induce fear, anger, hope, greed, or euphoria.

[4]Warren Farrell, *The Liberated Man.* New York: Random House, Inc., 1974.

Let's look at the record was a political slogan many years ago, and it is pretty sound advice. But before voting for a person who says it, I would want to *look* at the record. Does this politician really want me to look at the record, or does he only want me to *think* he wants me to look at the record? How available does he make the record? How accurate and how complete is the record he makes available? How well does it seem to mesh with my own observation? Sifting rhetoric from reality is not easy, and too many of us have stopped trying.

TEACHING STRATEGIES

1. Have the class read a thought-provoking passage, then present a series of statements. Let them classify each statement as:

According to the reading, this is true.

According to the reading, this is not true.

This seems to be implied in the reading.

This is not stated in the reading.

Include, if possible, some "open end" questions, for which there are no specific answers. Also include statements such as:

The author says _____, but I disagree because. . . .

The author says _____, and I agree because. . . .

Stress the importance of understanding and feeling comfortable with ambiguity and differing points of view. Help students realize that many important problems have no textbook solutions.

2. Present a controversial newspaper or magazine article or selection from a book, or a television or motion picture drama. Ask the class which parts of the work present data (Are the data documented?), which contain reasoning (Is the reasoning logical?), and which appeal to the emotions. Does the work contain humor? If so, does the humor say anything (satire)?

Present the class a set of conflicting opinions related to the work:

Every human being should take responsibility for his own destiny and not expect others to support him.

In a civilized society the young, the aged, the sick, the weak, and the unfortunate should be helped by their more fortunate neighbors.

It takes real skill for the teacher to play his proper role in such discussions, permitting each student to express himself freely, resisting the temptation to inject the "correct" answer, yet continually challenging the class with questions:

Sally, where did you get that information?

Joe, you said that X_____ happened as the result of Y_____. We have seen both happen, but do we know that one caused the other?

Theresa, suppose your father and mother were farm workers (or storekeepers, or doctors, and so forth). Do you think you would feel the same way?

3. Display a picture, map, chart, graph, model, or any visual object. Then present a series of statements. Ask which statements:

Are true, according to the information displayed.

Are not true, according to the information displayed.

Would seem to be reasonable assumptions.

Are not dealt with.

Such questions can be more complex than they appear. For example, if the picture includes a cat curled up by the fireplace, eyes closed, the statement *The cat is sleeping by the fireplace* would seem true. But she may not have fallen asleep. It could even be a stuffed cat or a sculpture. Capitalize on such problems to point out that we frequently make assumptions on the basis of incomplete data, cultural conditioning, faulty observation, or logic clouded by emotionalism, prejudice, or wishful thinking. Whether it is a *reasonable assumption* that the cat is sleeping, is one of those open-ended questions.

Relate such problems to their counterparts in the real world:

Yesterday we heard the speech of A_____, who promised that if elected, he will reduce taxes. Therefore, is it true, untrue, or a reasonable assumption that if he wins the election, taxes will be cut?

The art of asking questions: I know a teacher who made a poster for the front of her room. It said:

Have You Asked an Intelligent Question Today?

Will the politician really cut taxes, or is this campaign oratory? What is his record? Is this statement consistent with other statements he has made and *things he has done?* Does the office he is seeking carry the authority to do what he says? Suppose he did cut taxes, how will he meet the expenses of government? Which taxes will be cut (on the rich or on the poor)? Which programs will be cut? Who will be thrown out of work? What will be the ultimate consequences of this act?

Although such discussions need not involve closure (definite answers), they should aim towards some type of decision. Otherwise, we get ourselves into the aforementioned bind of paralysis and inaction. Ultimately, we have to vote for somebody, we have to buy the Ford, the Chevy, or the Plymouth. Even to go without a car is a decision. Each student may come to a different conclusion, which is O.K., especially if the discussion has broadened some points of view. Making imperfect decisions is an occupational hazard equated with being human. It's that theory of highest observability, and considering the risks, things seem to come out surprisingly well.

This has been but a brief introduction to teaching high level reading skills. We could spend an entire volume and an entire lifetime on the problem of creating an intellectually stimulating environment and permitting the student to grow in it. Although teaching the less able reader has consumed the greater number of pages in this volume, that is not meant to imply that the development of clear and precise thinking habits is less important. A clear-thinking citizenry is vital to a democratic society, and for a teacher, the implications are enormous.

CHAPTER 12
Lesson Plans

As the following lesson plans indicate, any subject can be taught in an imaginative and creative fashion, and can include a language growth activity, without sacrificing subject matter. Each lesson plan incorporates a reading experience and a writing experience. These range in length and difficulty, according to the subject. The lessons may be done exactly as indicated here, or may be adapted to meet the needs of any classroom.

SOCIAL STUDIES[1]

Introduction   This lesson may be used in any class that deals with values clarification.

Objectives

Students will read and demonstrate comprehension of the handout by selecting the "survivors" to enter the fallout shelter and writing their reasons for the selection.

Students will demonstrate a critical attitude towards human values by the care with which they make their selections.

Students will demonstrate (1) listening skills and (2) an attitude of inquiry by comparing their original selections with those after participating in the discussion.

Students will demonstrate ability to write coherent English by (1) writing their reasons for their original selections and (2) writing a comparison of their original selections with their selections after participating in the discussion.

[1]Suggested by Betty Kanekó.

Materials

1.   Study guide for handout (class set).

2.   Handout: *Who Shall Survive?* (class set).

3.   Paper and pencil (class).

Procedure

Present the study guide (if needed).

Pass out the handout. Allow the class time to read it.

Assign: List the people you would invite to join you in the fallout shelter. Write your reasons for including each person. Ten minutes will be allowed.

Divide the class into groups of approximately six. Allow the groups 15 minutes to discuss the question and arrive at a group decision. Have each group report its findings to the class, orally through a spokesperson.

Assign: Each student is to list the people he or she would choose now, after hearing the discussion, and write an essay on the differences between the choices made before and after participating in the discussion and hearing the reports, and the reasons for making or not making changes. Collect the papers.

Tell the class that this was an exercise in listening skills, in learning to learn from others, and in mental flexibility. Inform them that who they chose is less important than having valid reasons for making the decision. Also, whether they changed their minds or stuck to their original choices is not important. What is important is that they heard, understood, and carefully considered what the others were saying.

If time permits, discuss with the class any of the following questions that have not already been brought up:

A.   Which is more important—the lives of the survivors or repopulating the world?
If the former, should age be a major factor?
If the latter, should the sexes be evenly divided so there will be four couples? Or should there be more women than men, so more children can be born? And if that is the case, (for example,

five women and three men) how important is our traditional monogamous marriage system?

B.   How important to the future will each of the following values be, as represented by each of the individuals:

   1.   Law and order, with weapons to enforce it. When the policeman refuses to go without his weapons, what does that tell us?

   2.   Science and scientific knowledge. How can biochemistry be put to use?

   3.   How important will a doctor be? How do you feel about political militants? If she is not taken, there will be no black people left. Will this solve the racial problem, or will it be a loss?

   4.   How important is religion in the new society? You do not know the religion of the other people. Keep in mind that a catholic priest is not supposed to father children.

   5.   What kind of contribution, if any, can the actress make? Remember that the days of the dumb chorus girl are over. Today's starlets have to be intelligent, educated, and well trained, as well as talented.

   6.   Will the clerk have more or less than the others to offer? Will this tiny cluster of survivors be able to use his ability to build boats?

   7.   Six and seven are the only husband-wife team. Should you take both or neither, or would it be better to take one? Would the presence of a married couple lend the group stability, or would their feeling that they are a "pair" make them less able to relate to the rest of the group?

   8.   A speaker of German could provide access to a lot of literature, particularly of a scientific nature. But would this be disrupting or a strength? How much of the group's energy would have to be spent teaching her to communicate with the others?

9. How important is it to have a historian to keep records? What other abilities and characteristics would a professor of history have? Is his age important?

10 and 11. What priority should be given to youth? They have the longest life expectancy, they would be strong and virile when the others are past their prime. On the other hand, they have the least amount of experience, knowledge, and skill.

12. What contributions could the inventor make? What kind of person would he have to be to invent a hydraulic, electronic, automatic, self-adjusting nemaflier?

Who Shall Survive? Study Guide

Radiation: The poisonous effect of an atomic bomb. It is deadly and long-lasting.

Biochemistry: The study of the chemical qualities of living things.

Doctorate: An advanced graduate university degree. It is not necessarily a medical degree.

Militant: Inclined to fight for what one believes in. This fight may be physical or a battle of words.

Broadway: A famous street in New York which runs through the theater district. A "Broadway" play is a top level professional play.

Hydraulic: Controlled by the use of fluids.

Electronic: Controlled by electricity.

Automatic: Self-operating, with controls that make it work by itself.

Namaflier: There really is no such thing. You may imagine what a nemaflier is. But what kind of person would the inventor of such a device be?

This is an exercise in deciding what your *values* are, or what is important to you. Each of the people you will read about represents certain values, can make a unique contribution to the new civilization, but also has certain limitations. Some of the questions you might keep in mind are:

How many men and how many women are to go into the shelter?

Which knowledge, skills, and attitudes will be most valuable?
Is age important?

What are the probable values, or ways of thinking, of each person?

Who Shall Survive?

World War III has broken out, an atomic war that threatens to destroy civilization and wipe out the human race. However, you own a fallout shelter capable of sustaining life until the radiation has "cooled." But the shelter will only hold eight people, and there are twelve, plus yourself, in your home at the time. Everyone realizes that you must make the decision concerning which seven may join you in the shelter, and they promise to abide by your decision. You have fifteen minutes before the radiation will reach your area, and you know that if you fail to make a decision in that time, everyone will rush for the shelter and fight for entrance. Many may be killed in the battle, including yourself.

Yours is one of the world's few completely equipped fallout shelters, and there is a possibility that your eight people may be the only ones left to repopulate the world. Think carefully about who will make the best future citizens, whose children you will want to begin a new civilization, and who you will want as your sole companions for the rest of your life. The choices include:

1. A policeman, fully armed with gun, club, and so forth. He refuses to go without all his equipment.

2. A student of biochemistry, working on her doctorate.

3. The first woman and the first Black to graduate from her medical school. Now 42 years old, she is famous as a militant campaigner for women's and black people's movements, as well as a fine doctor.

4. A Catholic priest, 46 years old.

5.   A promising young actress, very beautiful, who has sung and danced on Broadway as well as Hollywood.

6.   A department store clerk, 36 years old. His hobby is building and sailing boats.

7.   The clerk's wife, four months pregnant. She has worked as a bookkeeper.

8.   A famous olympic ice skater, visiting from Germany. She speaks only German.

9.   A professor of history from the local university. He is 53 years old.

10.   A teenage cheer leader from the high school.

11.   The cheer leader's boy friend.

12.   The male, 26 year old inventor of the hydraulic, electronic, automatic, self-adjusting nemaflier.

ENGLISH

Introduction   This lesson consists of two parts, creative dramatics and unscrambling. Each may be used as a separate lesson, or they may be combined, as here. Although this lesson is labeled for an English class, it has applications in any subject area. Without changing the handout (Maud Muller), the lesson can lead into a discussion appropriate for a family living or psychology class. By changing the hand-out, the unscrambling idea can be used with any textbook. However, it involves duplicating a class set of the material to be read, and this is of doubtful legality because of copyright laws. The selection used here is in public domain, and can be used freely.

Objectives

Students will read and demonstrate comprehension of the poem Maud Muller by placing the verses in proper sequence.

Students will demonstrate knowledge of the theme of the poem by criticizing the scene portrayed by their fellow students.

Students will demonstrate ability to (1) listen carefully for detail, and (2) write coherent English by writing the story of *Maud Muller* in their own words, as they reconstruct it, after watching the scene.

Materials

Handouts:

1.   *Maud Muller* poem and instructions for doing the scene (two copies).

2.   Study guide for *Maud Muller* (class set).

3.   *Maud Muller* poem, cut into sections of approximately three verses (class set).

4.   Paper and pencil (class).

Procedure   Ask the class for two volunteers, a boy and a girl. Give them each a copy of the poem and instructions, excuse them from the classroom, and tell them they have fifteen minutes to read the poem and decide how they are going to plot the drama.

While they are preparing the scene, the rest of the class can work on the study guide.

After 15 minutes, or when the study guide has been completed, call the actors back to create the drama, based on the handout.

After watching the scene, ask each student to write what he thinks happened in the story that the two actors read (not the story they enacted, but what happened before that.) Suggest that the class include the information from the handout:

What happened at the spring?

How did Maud and the Judge feel about it then?

How do they feel about it now?

What happened to Maud and the Judge after the incident?

After collecting these papers, discuss with the class what they think was the content of the poem. This can be followed by a discussion of whether the scene, as they portrayed it, is appropriate.

Then pass out copies of the poem to everyone, but with the verses cut apart so not more than three appear on each little piece of paper. Ask each student to place the verses of the poem in proper order on the basis of careful reading combined with information gleaned from watching the scene and participating in the discussion.

Note: It has been my experience in doing this exercise a number of times that students doing the creative drama tend to come up with a "Hollywood ending," saying something like: "It isn't too late—we still have an eternity to make up for lost time." After the class has read the poem, if nobody questions the ending, I point out that the reading has not been done carefully. The entire basis for the attraction between Maud and the judge is that she is in love with her *fantasy* of him, and he with his *fantasy* of her. Their marriage would have been one of shock and disillusion, as each found out that the other hates his or her life style. And the handout stated that they were supposed to have acquired wisdom. This should provide lively material for discussion after the class has put the poem into proper sequence and each student has read it.

Evaluation:

By the ability of the class to put the verses of the poem into proper sequence.

By the insight displayed in commenting about the scene.

By the quality of the compositions.

Maud Muller Study Guide

Rustic:	Rural. Having to do with the country rather than the city.
Wrought:	Old-fashioned word for *did*. Also means *made*.
Tattered:	Torn.
Draught:	A drink.
Quaffed:	Past tense of *quaff,* which means to drink.

Hazel eyes:	Her eyes were the color of hazel nuts.
Doubtful balance of rights and wrongs. . . :	He was a judge and had to decide in court who was right and who was wrong.
Low of cattle:	Sound that cattle make.
Mused:	Thought quietly and meditatively.
Richest dower:	The custom was for a bride to bring her husband a *dowry,* or sum of money and goods to begin their marriage. He married a woman with a large dowry, a rich woman.
Garnished:	Richly decorated.
Spinnet:	An early piano, associated with fine, rich drawing rooms.
Weary wheel:	Spinning wheel, over which she labored to make threads for weaving.
Astral:	An expensive oil lamp.
Chimney lug:	The side wall, or corner of the chimney.
Repiner:	One who repines, regrets.
Roll the stone from the grave away!	A reference to the resurrection of Jesus, when the stone was rolled away from his grave. It means that some day human beings may find salvation, may achieve wisdom.

MAUD MULLER

By John Greenleaf Whittier

Maud Muller on a summer's day

Raked the Meadow sweet with hay.

Beneath her torn hat glowed the wealth

Of simple beauty and rustic health.

Singing, she wrought, and her merry glee

The mock-bird echoed from his tree.

But when she glanced to the far-off town,

White from its hill-slope looking down,

The sweet song died, and a vague unrest

And a nameless longing filled her breast,

A wish, that she hardly dared to own,

For something better than she had known.

The Judge rode slowly down the lane,

Smoothing his horse's chestnut mane.

He drew his bridle in the shade

Of the apple-trees, to greet the maid,

And asked a draught from the spring that flowed

Through the meadow across the road.

She stooped where the cool spring bubbled up,

And she filled for him her small tin cup,

And she blushed as she gave it, looking down

On her feet so bare and her tattered gown.

"Thanks!" said the Judge; "a sweeter draught

From a fairer hand was never quaffed."

He spoke of the grass and flowers and trees,

Of the singing birds and humming bees;

Then talked of the haying, and wondered whether

The cloud in the west would bring foul weather.

And Maud forgot her brier-torn gown,

And graceful ankles bare and brown;

And listened, while a pleased surprise

Looked from her long-lashed hazel eyes.

At last, like the one who for delay

Seeks a vain excuse, he rode away.

Maud Muller looked and sighed: "Ah me!

That I the Judge's bride might be!

"He would dress me up in silks so fine,

And praise and toast me at his wine.

"My father should wear a broadcloth coat;

My brother should sail a painted boat.

"I'd dress my mother so grand and gay,

And the baby should have a new toy each day.

"And I'd feed the hungry and clothe the poor,

And all should bless me who left our door."

The Judge looked back as he climbed the hill,

And saw Maud Muller standing still.

"A form more fair, a face more sweet

Ne'er hath it been my lot to meet.

"And her modest answer and graceful air

Show her wise and good as she is fair.

"Would she were mine, and I today,

Like her, a harvester of hay:

"No doubtful balance of rights and wrongs,

Nor weary lawyers with endless tongues,

"But low of cattle and song of birds,

And health and quiet and loving words."

But he thought of his sisters proud and cold

And his mother vain of her rank and gold.

So, closing his heart, the Judge rode on,

And Maud was left in the field alone.

But the lawyers smiled that afternoon,

When he hummed in court an old love-tune;

And the young girl mused beside the well

Till the rain on the unraked clover fell.

He wedded a wife of richest dower,

Who lived for fashion as he for power.

Yet oft, in his marble hearth's bright glow,

He watched a picture come and go;

And sweet Maud Muller's hazel eyes

Looked out in their innocent surprise.

Oft, when the wine in his glass was red,

He longed for the wayside well instead;

And closed his eyes on his garnished rooms

To dream of meadows and clover-blooms.

And the proud man sighed, with a secret pain,

"Ah, that I were free again!

"Free as when I rode that day,

Where the barefoot maiden raked her hay."

She wedded a man unlearned and poor,

And many children played round her door.

But care and sorrow, and childbirth pain,

Left their traces on heart and brain.

And oft, when the summer sun shone hot

On the new-mown hay in the meadow lot,

And she heard the little spring brook fall

Over the roadside, through the wall,

In the shade of the apple-tree again

She saw a rider draw his rein.

And, gazing down with timid grace,

She felt his pleased eyes read her face.

Sometimes her narrow kitchen walls

Stretched away into stately halls;

The weary wheel to a spinnet turned,

The tallow candle an astral burned,

And for him who sat by the chimney lug,

Dozing and grumbling o'er pipe and mug,

A manly form at her side she saw,

And joy was duty and love was law.

Then she took up her burden of life again,

Saying only, "It might have been."

Alas for maiden, alas for Judge,

For rich repiner and household drudge.

God pity them both! and pity us all,

Who vainly the dreams of youth recall.

For of all sad words of tongue or pen,

The saddest are these: "It might have been!"

Ah, well! for us all some sweet hope lies

Deeply buried from human eyes;

And, in the hereafter, angels may

Roll the stone from its grave away!

Instructions (for the two actors only)

Maud and the Judge have lived out their lives and have gone to their final reward. Act out the following:

The scene is the Afterworld. Maud and the Judge meet and recognize each other. They remember the day at the spring and discuss it, now that they have acquired wisdom. By the end of the scene, the class should know:
> *What happened at the spring.*
> *How you felt about it then.*
> *How you feel about it now.*
> *What happened to Maud.*
> *What happened to the Judge.*
> *What the author was saying (the theme of the poem).*

Note: Although you are now eternal, you are not mind readers. You are both surprised to find out how the other feels.

PHYSICAL EDUCATION

For a break from the usual routine, try an occasional field day. Here is one suggestion.

Objectives

Students will read and demonstrate comprehension by carrying out instructions.

Students will demonstrate skills necessary to perform assigned tasks in a minimum amount of time.

Students will demonstrate ability to 1) critically evaluate a physical education experience and 2) write coherent English by writing a critical paragraph answering the questions at the end of the session.

Materials

Table tennis paddles and balls

Basketballs

Footballs

Softballs and bats

Soccer balls

Tennis rackets and balls

Golf clubs and balls

Other equipment as other activities are added

The amount of equipment needed will depend on the number of teams on the field and the number of team members active at any one time.

Procedure   Place all equipment in one big pile. Divide the class into teams. Any number of teams can be used, with any number on a team. Teams of four will keep many students exercising, with sufficient resting time between tasks. For each team there is a container (hat, can, box, anything). In each container is a cluster of papers, and on each paper is a set of instructions. Each container holds the same instructions, but not necessarily in the same order. One at a time (or two or three at a time if there is enough equipment) team members run to their container and take out one instruction, which they carry out. The first team to empty their container wins. Instructions may include:

Take a table tennis ball and paddle. Bounce the ball on the paddle as you make a complete circle around a basketball court. Return the paddle and ball to the equipment pile.

Take a basketball and dribble it around the tennis court. Return the basketball to the equipment pile.

Take a football from the equipment pile and place it on the sideline of the football field. Center it towards the opposite sideline, run and pick it up, and center it again. Repeat until you have centered the ball past the opposite sideline and back. Return the football to the equipment pile.

Go to the equipment pile and pick up a softball and bat. Run to the baseball field and stand on home plate. Throw the ball in the air and bat it as close as you can to second base. Run and pick up the ball and bat it closer to second base. Repeat until you can pick up the ball and touch second base with a single step. Repeat back to home plate. Return the bat and ball to the equipment pile. (This can also be done by throwing the ball or throwing a football, a discus, a shot put, or almost anything. Or a player can run the bases instead of going to second and back, or can take any designated course.)

Go to the equipment pile and get a soccer ball. Kick the soccer ball around the gym and back to the equipment pile.

Bounce a tennis ball on a tennis racket (or badminton) from the equipment pile to the gym (touch the gym) and back. Replace the ball and racket on the equipment pile.

Take a golf ball and golf club from the equipment pile and place the ball in the end zone of the football field. Hit the ball with the club as many times as necessary to get it into the opposite end zone and back. Replace the ball and club on the equipment pile. (Locate where nobody can get hit, or use the soft practice balls.)

Many other interesting activities can be devised, depending on the equipment available. Teams can roll tires or hula hoops, push wheelbarrows with team mates in them, ride bicycles or scooters, or use different combinations of equipment, such as hitting a table tennis ball with a golf club, or a tennis ball with a baseball bat.

At the end of the session, pass out paper and pencils and ask each student to:

Write a paragraph evaluating today's program. Include the following information:

Which of the exercises did you consider the most fun?

Were there any exercises you did not like to do?

Would you like to have another field day such as today again, or would you rather stay with the regular program? Give your reasons.

Evaluation

By the ability of students to read and understand the directions.

By the enthusiasm shown in the performance of the exercises.

By student comments on the paragraphs.

By the quality of the paragraphs.

MATH—SOCIAL STUDIES[2]
(Introduction to Computers—Social Awareness)

Objectives

Students will demonstrate knowledge of how the simple binary operations of a computer can be used to process complex data. They will do this by "becoming" computers to find the most likely "suspects" in a burglary.

In their compositions students will explain how unsuspecting individuals can be tricked into giving away personal information that may at some time be used against them.

Students will read and demonstrate comprehension of the handouts by matching the "Date-A-Mate" data with the description of the suspects. Students will demonstrate ability to write cohesive English by writing a well-organized composition.

[2]Suggested by John Charles Patterson.

Materials

"Date-A-Mate" questionnaire (class set).

Police description of the two burglars (class set).

Computer program (one for each member of group II).

Procedure   Announce to the class that there is a new computer matching service in town and that as a promotional effort, they are offering their service free to selected individuals, and that the students of this class have been offered the service. All they have to do is fill out the questionnaire. The company will run it through their computer and give them interesting insights about their personalities and what qualities they should look for (and avoid) when selecting a partner of the opposite sex.

Pass out the questionnaires and allow time for students to fill them in. Collect the questionnaires and tell the students you will send them to the company for processing.

Introduce the "next" topic—the principle of computers. Explain that the heart of a computer is an electric switch that can open or close, registering one of two responses. We call these responses 1 or 0. The computer can be programmed to respond with a 1 or a 0 to any data fed into it. By combining a series of 1—0 responses, the computer can come up with complex information in a short time.

Announce that you will now give a demonstration of how this works, that the Date-A-Mate corporation doesn't really exist, that the fact is that last night the school office was robbed, and the police have obtained a description of the burglars. They are fairly sure the burglars are students, and have asked the teachers to cooperate in the search. Now, with the help of the questionnaires the students have just filled out, you will see if there are any prime suspects in this case.

Pass out the police description of the suspects.

After the students have read this handout, divide the class into three groups. Announce that the class is going to "become" a computer to help the police isolate the suspects. Group I will function as the computer "data input." Their job will be to take each of the questionnaires and read the data to a classmate from Group II, who will "process" it by recording 1 or 0 for each bit of information, then pass it to a member of Group III, the "data storage bank." This group will compute each student's data and arrange the questionnaires in the order of their suspiciousness. Separate stacks may be kept for the boys and the girls.

Now give each member of Group II the computer "program." This will tell them how to process the information they receive from data input.

After scores have been computed for all questionnaires, announce the prime girl and boy "suspects."

Then ask the class: Why did you give me this information? Didn't it occur to you that it is none of my business what your religious or political feelings are or where your parents were born? How many times have you filled out such forms (credit and job applications, tax forms, and others)? Did it ever occur to you that such information may be used for purposes other than those stated? Let the class know that there really was no burglary, that this was simply a demonstration of how the information you give freely may be improperly used.

This should lead to a lively discussion of data banks, personal privacy, and unethical or even unlawful use of information given by citizens in innocence. Some of these misuses of information may be by law enforcement agencies (Note the ultimate irony: churchgoers and people of deep religious conviction were classified by the impersonal $1-0$ system of the computer as prime suspects. Data bank information may also be made available to companies with products to sell, politicians making up lists of "friends" and "enemies," and many others whose activities may not be in the public interest.

Point out that information so amassed is vital in such areas as credit approval, tax accounting, social security and other pension payments, insurance statistics, and many other branches of government and business. Allowing sufficient information for government and industry to function smoothly, but keeping that information out of the hands of those who would abuse it, is an increasingly complex and difficult problem.

Assign students to write an essay about their current feelings concerning use of data bank storage of personal information about American citizens.

Evaluation

By the enthusiasm with which students attempt to find the "suspects."

By the quality of the compositions.

By the understanding of the operation and function of data banks exhibited in the composition.

By the grasp of the problem of invasion of privacy versus the need for information for the normal functioning of business and industry, as expressed in the compositions.

THE DATE-A-MATE CORPORATION
Questionnaire

Name _____   telephone _____

Address _____   sex: M ☐

                                                                     F ☐

Age _____   Weight _____   Height _____   eye color _____   hair color _____

Skin color: light   medium   dark   very dark   black

Ethnic identity: White   Black   Hispanic   Asian

                                Native American

Father's birthplace _____   Date of birth _____

Mother's birthplace _____   Date of birth _____

I attend church: regularly   occasionally   rarely   never

My religious convictions are: deeply felt   moderate   slight or none

I believe the following: Agree   Oppose

The Equal Rights Amendment is good for the country.   _____   _____

A woman should have the right to an abortion if she wishes.   _____   _____

Minorities and other disadvantaged people should be given job preference.   _____   _____

A license should be needed to possess a handgun.   _____   _____

The use of marijuana should be legalized.   _____   _____

THE DATE-A-MATE CORPORATION
Questionnaire *(continued)*

Which of the following activities do you consider among your favorites:

Participating in sports	_____	Talking with friends.	_____
Reading	_____	Discussing politics, philosophy, or religion	_____
Dancing	_____	Playing cards, chess, and other games.	_____

My favorite television programs are:

Quiz shows	_____	Family comedies	_____
Sports shows	_____	Dramas	_____
Crime shows	_____	Westerns	_____

Which of the following people do you admire:

Albert Einstein, great scientist and mathematician _____

General Patton, hero of World War II _____

William Shakespeare, greatest of all dramatists _____

O. J. Simpson, professional football player _____

Stokely Carmichael, black militant _____

George Wallace, fighter for racial segregation _____

Farrah Fawcett Majors, beautiful movie star _____

Betty Friedan, leader in the women's movement _____

Which of the following books do you think has an important message:

A Study of Communism, J. Edgar Hoover's warning about the communist menace. _____

The Greening Of America, Charles Reich's discussion of how the hip youth movement of the 1960's enriched the nation. _____

Mein Kampf, the philosophy of Adolf Hitler and his struggle for power. _____

Why We Can't Wait, Martin Luther King's story of his civil rights crusade. _____

POLICE DESCRIPTION OF SUSPECTS

Two people are known to have been involved. They wore masks, but enough of them showed to get a description. One was a woman.

Description:

teenager

about 5' 4" tall

weight about 125 pounds

blue eyes

blonde hair

light skin

The Other Was a Man:

teenager

about 5' 11" tall

weight about 165 pounds

brown eyes

brown hair

medium complexion

Other clues:

The man climbed a wall and jumped from one building to another. He would have to be very athletic. He also vandalized the office, writing political slogans over the walls. This writing expressed the feeling that America was going downhill because of communist-hippie race mixing, and it is time for God-fearing patriotic Americans to take charge. He seems to be a member of a right-wing fanatic group and considers himself on some sort of religious-political crusade. The woman did not enter the building, but drove the getaway car and apparently helped load the loot into their vehicle. It seems a reasonable assumption that she shares the man's political and religious convictions.

COMPUTER PROGRAM

M = send to Male program, below: F = send to Female program, below:

Age: 14-19 = 1; all else = 0   Age: 14-19 = 1; all else = 0

(Presumably everyone in the class will receive a "1" for age.)

Weight: 150−180 = 1; all else = 0   Weight: 115−135 = 1; all else = 0

(These ranges allow considerable margin for human error in reporting.)

Height: 5' 9"-6' 1" = 1; all else = 0   Height: 5' 2"-5' 6" = 1; all else = 0
Eye color: brown = 1; all else = 0   Eye color: blue = 1; all else = 0
Hair color: brown = 1; all else = 0   Hair color: blonde = 1; all else = 0

Compute boys and girls together on the following items:

   Ethnic identity: White = 1; all else = 0

   Father and mother birthplace: Do not compute.

   Father and mother birthdate: Do not compute.

   Attend church: regularly = 1; all else = 0

   (The value of the item above may be debatable, but it is the sort of
   evidence that can be used to build a case.)

   Religious convictions: deeply felt = 1; all else = 0

   Political questions: each "oppose" = 1; "agree" = 0

   (Shows strong right-wing politics.)

   Activities: Participating in sports = 1
             Dancing = 1
             Discussing politics, philosophy, religion = 1
             all else = 0

   Television programs: sports shows = 1

             crime shows = 1
             westerns = 1
             all else = 0

   (Shows a preference for violence.)

People admired: Patton, Simpson, Wallace = 1 each; all else = 0

(Admires war hero, sports hero, racist)

Books: *Mein Kampf, A Study of Communism* = 1 each; all else = 0

(Admires authoritarian figures.)

Note: This computer can be changed (reprogrammed) to meet the needs of any classroom.)

INTERDISCIPLINARY LESSON

Introduction   This lesson, based on using a bicycle, can be adapted to a variety of subjects or combinations of subjects by emphasizing various phases of the operation. For example, for an industrial arts class, the stress can be placed on repair and maintenance of the bicycle. Physical education can emphasize the many activities that revolve around bicycle riding, science can feature the observations of the physical and biological world made during bike rides, social studies can look upon the steps in formation of a bicycle club as a study of social institutions. The English class can use the activities as a springboard for reading and writing, and home economics can accent bicycling as a family activity and the planning of balanced, nutritious, low budget meals during extended trips.

Objectives

Students will become sufficiently interested in bicycling to form a bicycle club.

Students will read one or more bicycle publications with sufficient comprehension to list four major characteristics of that publication (content, length of articles, reading level, writing style, illustrations, and other observed information).

Students will demonstrate ability to write coherent English by writing an article appropriate for submission to any publication listed under *materials*.

Materials

A bicycle for each student (ask students to bring a bicycle at the previous session).

A whistle.

A collection of bicycle literature. Some ideas for this collection are:
> *Bicycling* magazine
> American Youth Hostels Handbook
> International Youth Hostels Handbook
> Ride schedule from a local bicycle club
> Cyclists Touring Club handbook and publications (British)
> Bicycle catalogs, available free from bicycle dealers
> Books on bicycle repair and bike touring.

See Appendix 4—physical education and industrial arts for ideas for contributions to this collection.

Procedure   Pass out bicycling literature. Allow time to browse and read.

Discuss: Should we consider forming a bicycle club as part of our school extracurricular program? What are some possible activities?

Touring rides: after school, on Saturdays or Sundays, overnight camping or hosteling trips on weekends, extended vacation trips.

Competition events: races, short or long distance; skill contests, such as bike decathelon; games, such as bicycle polo.

Bicycle repair and maintenance instruction.

Social action:

1.   Form a group to promote bicycling as an alternative to automobile travel for going to work or school, for shopping or recreation.

2.   Form a group to lobby for bike paths and hostels. Promote bicycle safety by forming a speakers bureau to talk to schools, service clubs, and other organizations.

3.   Fund-raising events to buy equipment for the club.

Discuss: The values of bicycling in comparison with motor-driven transportation (It is cheaper, energy efficient, smog-free, good exercise, and the best way to see the countryside [Walking is too slow; automobiles are too fast]). Limit discussion time. This is only to stimulate thinking. Decisions can be made later, after the bicycle ride.

This may conclude the first class session. Ask students to bring bicycles to school tomorrow.

Bicycle ride: Select a route as free of traffic, as interesting, and as scenic as possible.

Establish safety procedures for the ride:

> The leader rides ahead. Nobody passes the leader.
>
> Everyone rides single file on right side of path or road.
>
> One person is selected to be the rear scout, who carries a whistle for emergencies. Everyone stops when the whistle blows.

After the ride return to the classroom. (This may require a third session.)

Complete the discussion about the bicycle club.

Redistribute the literature, allow more reading time.

Assign: Write something that would be appropriate for any of the publications available.

Evaluation

> By whether sufficient interest is aroused to form a bike club.
> By the quality of the assigned compositions.

APPENDIX 1
Sources for Reading Improvement Equipment

Because new equipment is continually coming on the market, along with new models of existing instruments, this list should be supplemented when ordering. Consult your school district purchasing agent for current information, and send to each company for their latest catalog and price list or contact their local representative.

Borg-Warner Educational Systems
600 West University Drive
Arlington Heights, Illinois 60004

System 80
    A microgroove disc record is coordinated with a miniaturized filmstrip so that pushing a button provides both the sound and the picture. Incorrect responses trigger repetition of the question; correct responses cause the machine to continue to the next frame. Each program contains 80 frames. Programs in language arts, phonics, structural (morphological) analysis, words in context, spelling, and reading comprehension. Also programs in math and French. This machine has more widespread application in elementary school, but some carefully selected programs may be used in secondary.

Communicad
The Communications Academy
Box 541
Wilton, Connecticut 06897

The Acceleread Phrase-Flasher
    The student progresses from a series of short words to long phrases, 1200 lines on a 60-card set. Individualized, used at normal reading distance. Student advances at own pace.

323

This company also carries a number of vocabulary development programs at various grade levels.

FIGURE A-1   Phrase flasher. (Courtesy of The Communications Academy.)

Craig Education
921 West Artesia Boulevard
Compton, California 90220

The Craig Reader
A reading simulator with a viewing screen for rear projection of 12-frame slides. May be used for tachistoscopic flashing or controlled reading. May be adjusted to exhibit a single line at a time, a pacing segment, or the entire frame.

The Comparative Cassette Recorder
A four-track, two-channel tape recorder that functions similar to a language master, but uses a continuous cas-

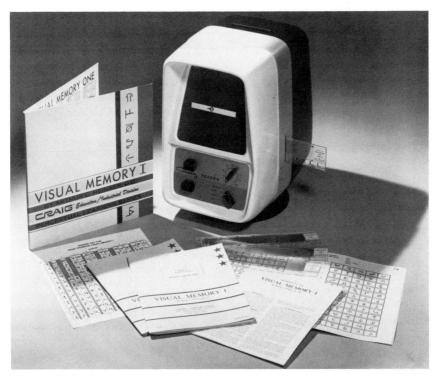

FIGURE A-2   Craig Reader. (Courtesy of Craig Education.)

sette tape. Allows the student to record responses on a cassette tape without erasing the prerecorded material. Useful for foreign language, ESL, and other situations requiring auditory training.

Programs in language arts, perceptual training, reading acceleration, comprehension/study skills, American history, and vocabulary development are available to use with these two instruments.

Creative Visuals
Box 1911
Big Springs, Texas 79720

Singer Graflex Projection and Tachistoscopic Equipment:
Reader Mate
A low-cost, portable unit for table or carrel use for individual practice or

study. 3″ × 4″ viewing area, adjustable from 20 to 120 lines per minute.

Projection Reader, Junior and Senior Models

Junior model with 50 watt lamp, primarily for individual or small group study. Senior model for class use has 500-watt lamp. Can be used as controlled reader with variable speed projection, or as a tachistoscope, if special attachment is used. Adjusts from 60 through 1000 words per minute.

Messenger VII

Couples a rear-view filmstrip projector with a built-in cassette to provide synchronized audio-visual programs.

Also available through Creative Visuals are a variety of filmstrips, cassettes, and transparencies on literature, language, journalism, research methods, study habits, reading skills, foreign language, and fine arts.

Educational Developmental
Laboratories, Inc.
1188 Adrienne Lane
Huntington, New York 11743

The Reading Eye

Records the eye movements of students during reading, providing a means of studying the student's reading habits in relation to eye fixations, regressions, return sweeps, and duration of fixation. (See pp. 20–22.) Eye movements are recorded on a sheet of graph paper for analysis by the reading specialist.

The Controlled Reader, Junior and Senior Models.

Reading material is flashed on a screen at a controlled rate from 60 to 900 words per minute. The moving slot of light is intended to coordinate and speed eye movement. The student sees the material only once, is forced to concentrate. Senior model projects ten to twenty feet for class use, junior model for individual or small group use.

Tach-X

A 500-watt tachistoscopic projector used with special 35 mm quarter-frame filmstrips. Exposes images from 1/100 of a second to 1½ seconds.

Flash-X

Individually used, hand-held tachistoscope. Exposes pictures, numbers, letters, or words presented on special discs at a preset exposure rate of 1/25 of a second.

Aud-X

A sound-filmstrip projector for use with 35mm filmstrips and tape cassettes. Used with small groups of students at a projection distance of 4' to 8'.

EDL also makes available a large variety of programs in a number of subjects for use with their equipment.

Educational-Instructional
Systems
2225 Grant Road, Suite 3
Los Altos, California 94022

Eye-trac

Similar to the Reading Eye described under Educational Developmental Laboratories.

Guided Reader

Similar to controlled reader, two models available, both can be used for groups or individuals. Left-to-right or full line presentation. Reading rates adjustable from 40 to 1050 words per minute. Available with special attachment that adds tachistoscopic dimension.

Tach-Mate

Three models available. Projects at 1/25 second.

Vu-Mate

Individual perceptual training device that can be hand-held or used on desk. Adjustable speeds of 1/25, 1/50, and 1/100 second.

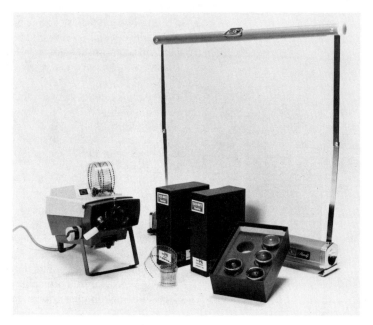

FIGURE A-3   Tach-Mate. (Courtesy of Educational-Instructional Systems.)

Ralph Gerbrands Company
8 Beck Road
Arlington, Massachusetts 02174

Psychotecnics, Inc.
1900 Pickwick Avenue
Glenview, Illinois 60025

Also available from EIS are tape recorders that shut off on a prerecorded cue and programs to fit their instruments.

A number of highly accurate individual and projection tachistoscopes. For most classrooms, however, these would be expensive.

Tachomatic ×500
Controlled reader permits reading speeds ranging from 60 to 1000 words per minute, although special setting combinations allow processing up to 5000 words per minute. Remote control available.

T-matic ×150
Smaller, manually advanced tachistoscope-controlled reader combi-

FIGURE A-4   Vu-Mate. (Courtesy of Educational-Instructional Systems.)

nation. A hold button permits the image to be retained for prolonged observation.

Shadowscope Reading Pacer
    For individual study. A book or other reading material is placed on a tray, and an inch-wide beam of light moves down the page. Can be adjusted from almost zero to over 2000 words per minute, depending on the material. Has the advantage of using ordinary reading matter rather than special filmstrips or slides, therefore requiring less transfer.
    Programs are available for these instruments.

FIGURE A-5   Shadowscope. (Courtesy of Psychotecnics, Inc.)

The Reading Laboratory, Inc.
55 Day Street
Norwalk, Connecticut 06858

Phrase Flasher
    See Acceleread Phrase Flasher, Communicad.

Prep Pacer
    Books and other reading material are placed on a desk or table, and the Prep Pacer controls reading rate from 80 to 3000 words per minute, depending on the material. Similar to the Shadowscope, except that the reading rate is controlled by an arm that extends over the reading material instead of a beam of light.
    My last report indicated that the Prep Pacer was being reengineered and

was temporarily unavailable. Check with The Reading Laboratory for information concerning the new model.

This company also carries books, reading skill kits, films, cassettes, and timing equipment.

Tutorsystems
Division of:
Sargent-Welch Scientific Company
7300 Linder Avenue
Skokie, Illinois 60076

Tutorsystems

A complex, sophisticated teaching machine featuring "branched" programming. This means that instead of simply following one linear program, the system can branch out either because the student needs special remedial instruction or because he or she can omit some of the drill. Programs are available in math, reading, communication, English, science, electronics, health and medicine, and business and industrial skills.

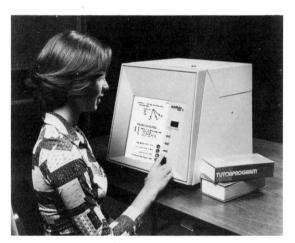

FIGURE A-6   Tutorsystem (Courtesy Sargent Welch Scientific Company.)

APPENDIX 2
Bibliography of Standardized Tests

Dozens of excellent reading tests are available from publishers, and this list is by no means complete. I have tried to place here a selection of different types of tests, rather than many tests which do essentially the same thing. For a comprehensive list of testing materials, see:

> Oscar Buros, *Mental Measurements Yearbooks*. Gryphon Press. Seventh Yearbook is in two volumes; reading tests are in Volume II.

> Oscar Buros, *Reading Tests and Reviews*. Gryphon Press, 1968. This volume lists all the reading tests from the first six *Mental Measurements Yearbooks*. Indexed.

TEST AND PUBLISHER	LEVELS	SECTIONS	NORMS
Adult Basic Learning Examination (ABLE) Harcourt, Brace Jovanovich, Inc.	Levels I, II, III for adults	Vocabulary, reading, spelling, math	Norms not listed. To be scored by local norms
California Achievement Tests (CAT) Calif. Test Bureau/McGraw-Hill	Levels I-V Grades 1.5-12 Level V: 9-12	Reading vocabulary & composition +	Norms by percentile, stanine, and grade level
California Phonics Survey (CPS) CTB/McGraw-Hill	Forms I & II Grades 7-college	5 tape recorded exercises to survey phonic recognition	Individual profile shows 8 areas of possible phonic deficiency
Comprehensive Tests of Basic Skills (CTBS) CTB/McGraw-Hill	Grades 2.5-12 Level III: 6-8 Level IV: 8-12	Reading vocabulary and comprehension	

TEST AND PUBLISHER	LEVELS	SECTIONS	NORMS
Davis-Eels Test of General Intelligence, or Problem Solving Ability (Davis-Eels Games) Harcourt, Brace, Jovanovich, Inc.	Levels I and II Grades 1-6 or for older students with culture block	Pictures designed to render a "culture fair" score	Intelligence quotient
Durrell Listening-Reading Series Harcourt, Brace, Jovanovich, Inc.	Grades 1-9 Advanced Level: 7-9	Two tests to compare listening and reading comprehension	Compare Listening and reading scores or use grade level norms
Gates-MacGinitie Reading Tests Teachers College Press Columbia University	Forms Primary A to Survey F Grades 1-12 Survey E: 7-9 Survey F: 10-12	Speed and accuracy, vocabulary and comprehension	Percentiles by grade level
Gilmore Oral Reading Test Harcourt, Brace, Jovanovich, Inc.	One form Grades 1-8	Student reads aloud to examiner, who records reading problems	Scored for accuracy, comprehension, and rate
Iowa Silent Reading Tests Harcourt, Brace, Jovanovich, Inc.	Levels I, II, III Grades 6-college	Vocabulary, reading comprehension, reading efficiency	Stanine and percentile
McGraw-Hill Basic Skills System CTB/McGraw-Hill	"centers on Grades 10 through 13"	Reading and other disciplines	Local norms recommended, also stanines and percentiles stated
Metropolitan Achievement Tests (MAT) Harcourt, Brace, Jovanovich, Inc.	Primer, Primary I, Primary II, Elementary, Intermediate, Advanced Advanced: 7.0-9.5	Vocabulary, reading and other disciplines	Grade equivalent, stanine, and percentile
Slosson Oral Reading Test (SORT) Slosson Educational Publications	One form only Grades 1-12	List of 200 words of graded difficulty	Grade level score
Stanford Achievement Test Harcourt, Brace, Jovanovich, Inc.	Grades 1-12 Advanced Battery: 7-9; H.S. Bat: 9-12	Reading and other disciplines	Stanines and percentile by grade level

TEST AND PUBLISHER	LEVELS	SECTIONS	NORMS
Stanford Diagnostic Reading Test Harcourt, Brace, Jovanovich, Inc.	Elem., Jr. Hi, H.S. 2.5-H.S.	Reading, composition, word structure, word meaning, phonics, word synthesis, skimming, scanning	Stanines and percentiles
Tests of Academic Progress (TAP) Houghton Mifflin Co.	4 grade levels, 9-12 in one test	Reading and other disciplines	Percentiles at various grades
Inter-American Series Guidance Testing Associates	This company carries a number of tests in English and Spanish, grades 1-13. Catalog available upon request.		

ADDRESSES OF TEST PUBLISHERS

California Test Bureau/McGraw-Hill
Del Monte Research Park
Monterey, California 93940

Guidance Testing Associates
6516 Shirley Avenue
Austin, Texas 78752

Harcourt, Brace, Jovanovich, Inc.
Test Department
757 Third Avenue
New York, N. Y. 10017

Houghton Mifflin Company
Educational Division
110 Tremont Street
Boston, Mass. 02107

Slosson Educational Publications
140 Pine Street
East Auroroa, N. Y. 14052

Teachers College Press
Columbia University
New York, N. Y. 10027

APPENDIX 3
Material for Teaching Reading

Anything that students will read with interest is potential material for a reading program. Not only books and magazines, but pamphlets of all kinds, catalogs, sales brochures about anything from cars to records, other students' compositions, or textbooks from other classes have a place on the shelf of the reading class. This list contains a few suggestions for sources.

BIBLIOGRAPHY

Martha H. Dillner and Joanne P. Olson, *Personalizing Reading Instruction in Middle, Junior, and Senior High Schools.* Macmillan Publishing Company, 1977. Chapter 11.

Daniel N. Fader and Elton B. McNeil, *Hooked on Books: Program and Proof.* Berkley Publishing Corporation, 1968.

Robert Karlin, *Teaching Reading in High School,* Second Edition. The Bobbs-Merrill Company, 1972, pp. 363–364.

Eddie C. Kennedy, *Classroom Approaches to Remedial Reading,* Second Edition. F. E. Peacock, Publishers, 1977, pp. 465–474.

Hilda Stauffer, "New Materials on the Market," *Journal of Reading,* 19:392–403, February, 1976.

Some publishers of paperback books put out guides for teachers to their own publications. The leader in this area is Dell Publishing Company, with such publications as:

When Children Read

Where the Readers Are

Releasing Children to Literature

A Teacher's Guide to Contemporary Teenage Fiction

A Teacher's Guide to Poetry

A Teacher's Guide to Senior High School Literature

A Teacher's Guide to Selected Literary Works

Dell also publishes a catalog of paperback books recommended for teen-agers.

See also: G. Robert Carlsen, *Books and the Teen-Age Reader*. Bantam Books. Paperback, 1967.

PHONICS

Building Your Language Power
Frank C. Laubach
Silver Burdett Company
250 James Street
Morristown, New Jersey 07960

A reading-writing program for total illiterates. Begins with writing simple consonants, builds to words. First grade skills only. Not built along linguistic principles.

Sam
Harry E. Huls, Principal Author
San Diego State University Foundation
San Diego State University
San Diego, California 92182

A basal reader using phonic-linguistic principles. Subject matter is somewhat more interesting than that of *Let's Read*. Comes with teacher editions containing many suggestions for teaching.

Let's Read
Leonard Bloomfield and Clarence L. Barnhart

For description see page 26 and Chapters 7 and 8 of the text.

Wayne State University Press
5980 Cass Avenue
Detroit, Michigan 48202

The same program is available in a series of short paperback books from:
Clarence L. Barnhart, Inc.
P.O. Box 250
Bronxville, New York 10708

HIGH-INTEREST, LOW READING LEVEL SERIES

These series of books were written particularly for secondary age students with reading difficulties. The interest levels are appropriate for the age group, but the reading levels are low enough for the students to cope with them. Write to publishers for more complete information, since new books are coming out all the time while others go out of print.

Caution should be exercised in selecting titles dealing with frontier characters. These books should be reviewed carefully for material that may be offensive to Native Americans, Chicanos, or other minority groups.

American Adventure Series
Harper & Row, Publishers
49 East 33rd Street
New York, New York 10016

Mainly stories of the frontier, with a few war tales included. Reading levels: grades 2–5.

Childhood of Famous Americans Series
The Bobbs-Merrill Company, Inc.
4300 West 62nd Street
Indianapolis, Indiana 46268

Stories from the early years of famous Americans, including athletes, statesmen, soldiers, Indians, and many others. Reading levels: grades 3–9.

The Deep-Sea Adventure Series
Field Educational Publications, Inc.
510 Merchandise Mart Pl.
Chicago, Illinois 60654

Sharks, whales, and buried treasure are some of the elements that make up these tales of adventure in and over the sea. Reading levels: grades 2–7

The Morgan Bay Mysteries
Field Educational Publications, Inc.
510 Merchandise Mart Pl.
Chicago, Illinois 60654

Mystery and adventure on land and ocean.

Reading levels: grades 2–4

Reading Motivated Series
Field Educational Publications, Inc.
510 Merchandise Mart Pl.
Chicago, Illinois 60654

Tales of the West.
Reading levels: grades 3–9

The Incredible Series
Dexter & Westbrook, Ltd.
958 Church Street
Baldwin, New York 11510

Action-packed adventure stories, written with simplicity and drama. Beautifully illustrated. Titles include *Escape,* a tale of the daring dash for freedom of a pair of slaves; *Horror Overhead,* the terrifying last flight of the "super safe" dirigible the Hindenburg; and *Alone,* the story of a courageous and resourceful seacook who saved himself from drowning by drifting 1200 miles in open ocean on a raft no larger than a table top. Reading levels: grades 3–7

Jamestown Classics
Various authors
Walter Pauk and Raymond Harris, editors

A series of classic stories rewritten in simplified form, each in a separate paperback book, with glossary, questions, discussion material, and suggested

Jamestown Publishers
P.O. Box 6743
Providence, Rhode Island 02940

activities. A teacher's Planning and Resource Guide is available with each volume.

On an accompanying tape, the student can hear the story read, with sound and musical accompaniment. The supplementary study material is also on tape.
Reading levels: grades 6−9

Pleasure Reading Series
Edward W. Dolch
Marguerite P. Dolch
Beulah F. Jackson
Garrard Publishing Company
1607 North Market Street
Champaign, Illinois 61820

". . . famous stories and legends rewritten in a simple easy style." Stories are more juvenile in appeal than most of the others in this section, and are written around the Dolch First Thousand Words for Children's Reading.
Reading levels: grades 2−6

Reading Incentive Series
Ed and Ruth Radlauer
Bowmar
622 Rodier Drive
Glendale, California 91201

Striking Illustrations and dynamic, one-paragraph pages give this series lots of appeal. Titles include *Motorcycles, Dogs, Drag Racing, Karting,* and many others. Available with each volume are cassette and skill development sheets on spirit masters.
Reading levels: grades 2−4

Troll Books
Troll Associates, Inc.
320 Route 17
Mahwah, New Jersey 07430

A series of short books on a variety of topics. Includes such titles as *Ballooning: High and Wild, Hunting the Killer Shark, The Baja Run,* and *Rock* (music). Each page contains a single paragraph, accompanied by a beautiful full-color photograph.
Reading levels: grades 5−9

The Tom Logan Series
Benefic Press
1900 N. Narragansett
Chicago, Illinois 60639

Tales of the Old West
Reading levels: grades 2−3

The Dan Frontier Series
Benefic Press
1900 N. Narragansett
Chicago, Illinois 60639

Dan Frontier, the central character, has a career that runs from frontiersman and trapper to congressman.
Reading levels: grades 2−4

World of Adventure Series
Benefic Press
1900 N. Narragansett
Chicago, Illinois 60639

Adventure in exotic places.
Reading levels: grades 3–5

Scholastic Book Services
904 Sylvan Avenue
Englewood Cliffs, New Jersey 07632

Scholastic publishes a great variety of paperback books suitable for use in a reading class. Some can be purchased individually, some come in collections. Racks for displaying can also be purchased, or sent as a bonus with large book orders. Send for complete catalog. Multiple readability levels.

Skill Building

Specific Skill Series
Richard A. Boning
Barnell, Loft, Ltd.
958 Church Street
Baldwin, New York 11510

Eight "specific skills" are isolated and drilled in each of the eight volumes, each available on six different levels. Skills include *Getting the Facts, Drawing Conclusions, Using the Context,* and five others.
Reading levels: grades 4–12

Reading and Study Techniques
for Academic Subjects
Baldridge Reading Instruction
Materials, Inc.
14 Grigg Street
Greenwich, Connecticut 06830

A book of instructions and suggestions for improving reading rate and comprehension accompanied by another book of exercises. For more advanced students.

Reading Skills Check List and Activities
Walter B. Barbe
The Center For Applied Research in Education, Inc.
West Nyack, New York, 10994

A series of eight volumes of suggested activities to develop specific reading skills. The skills are grouped into those relating to vocabulary, word-attack, comprehension, and oral and silent reading. Multiple readability levels.

Supportive Reading Skills Series
Richard A. Boning
Dexter & Westbrook, Ltd.
958 Church Street
Baldwin, New York 11510

Reading Homonyms, Reading Compound Words, and *Using a Table of Contents* are a few in this series of eleven booklets, each on six levels, which "complements and supplements" the Specific Skills Series. May be used independently, however. Exercises are single sentence, short answer variety. Multiple readability levels.

Follett Coping Skills Series
Follett Publishing Company
1010 West Washington Boulevard
Chicago, Illinois 60607

Finding Work, Budgeting, and other titles compose this series of workbooks for reading handicapped secondary students. Each lesson has a prereading study guide and comprehension questions.

Programmed Reading
Jerrold Glassman
Globe Book Company .
175 Fifth Avenue
New York, New York 10010

Such skills as "Finding the Main Thought," "Following Directions," "Learning New Words Through Clues," and others are taught in a programmed instructional framework.

Comprehension Skills Series
James A. Giroux et al.
Jamestown Publishers
P.O. Box 6743
Providence, Rhode Island 02940

Individual short paperback booklets, each devoted to a specific skill. Titles include *Drawing a Conclusion, Making an Inference, Understanding Characters,* and others. A series of very short exercises, with questions for developing skills. Emphasis is on reasoning as well as reading.

Students can listen to the material read on a cassette tape that accompanies each book.
Readability levels: 7−12

Reading Drills for Speed and Comprehension
Edward B. Fry
Jamestown Publishers
P.O. Box 6743
Providence, Rhode Island 02940

A book of 1000 word exercises with comprehension questions.
Reading level: grade 12

A Skill At A Time Series
Walter Pauk
Jamestown Publishers
P.O. Box 6743
Providence, Rhode Island 02940

A series of 10 short paperbacks, each one dealing with a particular reading skill. Titles include *Perceiving the Author's Intent, Recognizing Points of View, Reading Between the Lines,* and others.

Each booklet contains paragraphs from literature, with questions designed to delve for the specific skill under study.
Reading levels: grades 4−12

Skimming and Scanning
Edward B. Fry

Directions and exercises for practice in these two important reading skills.

Jamestown Publishers
P.O. Box 6743
Providence, Rhode Island 02940

Timed Readings Levels 1 through 8 Edward Spargo and Glenn R. Williston Jamestown Publishers P.O. Box 6743 Providence, Rhode Island 02940	A series of fifty 400-word passages in each volume (level) with questions. Multiple readability levels.
Reading For Meaning Series Grades 7 through 12 Revised by John H. Coleman and Ann Jungeblut J. B. Lippincott Company East Washington Square Philadelphia, Pennsylvania 19105	Short reading selections followed by comprehension drills. Includes such exercises as "Getting Word Meanings," "Choosing the Best Title," "Getting the Main Idea," and "Getting the Facts."
Yellow Pages of Learning Resources Richard Saul Wurman, Editor The MIS Press Cambridge, Massachusetts Educational Facilities Laboratories, Inc. 477 Madison Avenue New York, New York 10022	A treasure house of ideas for using the community as a place to learn. Dozens of learning ideas involving trips to places of interest throughout the community: "What can you learn at a bakery?" "What can you learn from an electrician?" and many more. Reading level: grade 9
The Newspaper as a Teaching Tool Eileen E. Sargent The Reading Laboratory, Inc. 55 Day Street South Norwalk, Connecticut 06854	Exercises built around reading specific parts of a daily newspaper. Some are for general reading, other exercises are designed for particular subject matter classrooms such as math, physical education, social sciences, and others. Reading level: grade 12
SRA Reading Laboratory Kits Don H. Parker Science Research Associates, Inc. 259 East Erie Street Chicago, Illinois 60611	Individual reading assignments on single sheets of heavy paper or cards. These kits come in boxed sets. The company puts out a number of kits at various grade levels, plus a variety of other instructional material. Send for complete catalog. Multiple readability levels.

Reading Essentials Series
Ullin W. Leavell et al.
Steck-Vaughan Company
P.O. Box 2028
Austin, Texas 78767

Exercises for developmental skills, with comprehension questions. Also includes such areas as studying illustrations and dictionary work. Brief study guides with each lesson.
Reading levels: 1–12

Survival Reading Task Cards
Paula Wheatley
Teachers Exchange of San Francisco
600-35th Avenue
San Francisco, California 94121

A packet of cards, each with a task to perform that involves reading: getting information from a telephone directory, finding information in a newspaper, checking a bus schedule, and many other interesting "survival" tasks. Multiple reading levels.

Developing Reading Efficiency
Karen M. Hess, Robert E. Shafer, and Lanny E. Morreau
John Wiley & Sons, Inc.
605 Third Avenue
New York, New York 10016

Longer, more advanced, more complex reading exercises. Excellent for developing higher level reading skills.

Periodicals

Real World
9 issues per year
King Features Syndicate
235 East 45th Street
New York, New York 10017

In tabloid newspaper form, this publication features a series of articles of interest to secondary students. Largely oriented towards vocational education, but includes other general interest features also.

Scope
Scholastic Book Services
904 Sylvan Avenue
Englewood Cliffs, New Jersey 07632

A high-interest, low reading level publication, very popular in English and reading classes. Good reading—plays, mystery stories, puzzles, and a wide variety of features.

The same publisher issues other periodicals on higher reading levels. Send for catalog.

The following general circulation magazines are popular with teenage readers, and a check at a local magazine counter will reveal many more. They may be ordered from your local wholesaler. Your librarian or district purchasing agent can give you the name and address of the local source.

Sports

Sports Illustrated
Bicycling
Field and Stream
Black Belt
Women in Sports
Road and Track
Hot Rod
Dirt Bike
Outdoor Life
Sporting News
Football Digest
Basketball Digest
Auto Racing Digest
Baseball Digest
Skiing
Official Karate
Cycle Guide

Miscellaneous

Dell Crosswords
Vogue
National Geographic
Ms.
People
Psychology Today

Teen Magazines

Seventeen
Sixteen
American Girl
Rolling Stone
Teen

For Black Students

Ebony
Jet

Industrial Arts

Popular Mechanics
Popular Science

News Magazines

Time
Newsweek

Humor

Mad

APPENDIX 4
Suggestions for Classroom Libraries, by Subject

Basic to any attempt to improve reading skills, or to expand student growth in any subject, is the classroom library. It is here that the student's attention can be caught by the infinite variety of interesting material, some directly related to the subject matter of the class, some leading to new directions. All, however, can be worthy of exploration. No matter how popular the school or public libraries may be, the carefully selected and seductively displayed classroom library provides an eye-catching invitation to learning.

With thousands of new publications appearing annually, a list such as this can only contain a few suggestions. In addition to the books listed here, there are hundreds of excellent magazines (see Appendix III), pamphlets, newspapers, tape recordings, films and filmstrips, and other material.

Many teachers maintain a clipping file, cut or duplicated from newspapers and magazines. Pictures, maps, posters, book jackets, charts and graphs, and duplicated material can find a place in this file. Many teachers haunt bookstores, libraries, and newsstands for ideas, as well as stores and commercial and public agencies for descriptive literature.

Many of the books on this list are available in many editions, both hardcover and paperback, some from more than one publisher. The edition listed here may, therefore, be one of the several available. If no edition is listed, the work has been brought out by numerous publishers.

BIBLIOGRAPHIES

Books For Secondary School Libraries. Compiled by a committee of librarians, 5th edition, R. R. Bowker, 1976.
Junior High School Library Catalog, 3rd edition, H. W. Wilson, 1975.
Senior High School Library Catalog, 11th edition, H. W. Wilson, 1977.
Magazines For Libraries. Edited by Bill Katz and Berry Gargal. R. R. Bowker, 2nd edition, 1972.
Books And The Teen-age Reader, Robert G. Carlsen, Harper, 1971.

AGRICULTURE

In addition to the thousands of pamphlets issued by federal, state, university, and other agencies, bookstores offer a tempting selection of volumes on growing everything from house plants to fruit trees.

The American Food Scandal; Why You Can't Eat Well on What You Earn
  William Robbins
  Morrow, 1974

An indictment of the entire American food industry, exposing the influence of the huge corporations. Explodes the myth that our food is produced by the traditional family farm.

The Basic Book of Organically Grown Foods

See Home Economics—foods

Cesar Chavez; Autobiography of La Causa
  Jacques E. Levy
  Norton, 1975

Story of the man who fought, and is still fighting, to organize the farm workers.

Farming the Sea
  Alexander McKee
  Crowell, 1969

A look at world-wide attempts at making the ocean more productive.

A Gardener Touched with Genius; The Life of Luther Burbank
  Peter Dreyer
  Coward, McCann, 1975

The life of one of the most famous plant breeders.

I Never Met a House Plant I Didn't Like
  Jerry Baker
  Simon and Schuster, 1974

Interesting guide to house plant culture.

Landscape Gardening
  James Underwood Crockett
  Time-Life, 1971

Design and execution of landscape plans.

The Organic Gardener
  Catharine Osgood Foster
  Knopf, 1972

Soil chemistry, composting, insect traps, and lots of useful information.

Silent Spring
  Rachel Carson
  Houghton, 1962

The devastating results of using agricultural pesticides. How we frequently achieve a result opposite from what we intend.

Sunset Garden Books
  Lane

A series of volumes on growing different types of ornamental and food-producing plants.

ART

There are many beautiful art prints and slides and books of prints available at bookstores and art museums.

Also available are textbooks on history of art and instruction books in many types of crafts, such as ceramics, leather, macrame and others.

Art Has Many Faces
  Katharine Kuh
  Harper, 1951

Introduction to art appreciation.

Artists in Perspective Series
  H. W. Janson
  Prentice-Hall

Evaluations of the lives and works of well-known artists.

The Art of Jewelry Making
  Takashi Wada
  Van Nostrand, 1975

A basic introduction to this fast-growing form of expression.

Art Today; An Introduction to the Visual Arts
  Ray Faulkner and Edwin Ziegfeld
  Holt

Influence of art on industry and city planning, as well as a study of many art media.

The ABC's of Batik
  Bernadette Hersk
  Chilton, 1975

Complete detailed instructions for following this Asian method of dying.

Crafts from Around the World
  B. J. Casselman
  Meredith, 1975

Projects suggested by folk arts from around the world.

Creating with Clay
  James E. Seidelman and Grace Mintonye
  Van Nostrand, 1972

Methods and materials for ceramics. Includes such related arts as papier-mâché.

Landscape Gardening

See agriculture.

Lust for Life
  Irving Stone
  Doubleday, 1937

The tortured, frenzied life of painter Vincent Van Gogh—his early religious years among the coal miners of Wales, his loves, and his passionate quest for artistic technique.

Origami
  Georgie Davidson
  Larousse, 1975

The ancient art of creative paper folding.

Practical Macrame
  Eugene and Ellen Andes
  Van Nostrand

Illustrated guide to decorative knot tying.

A New World History of Art
  Sheldon Chaney
  Holt, 1961

Beautifully illustrated introduction to painting, architecture, ceramics, sculpture, and other media.

BUSINESS SUBJECTS

See all titles under home economics—consumer education.

Enterprising Women

See Women's Studies.

The Hidden Persuaders
  Vance Packard
  McKay, 1957

See home economics—consumer education.

The Legend of Henry Ford
  Keith Sward
  Russell, 1968

The life story of one of America's great industrialists.

The Robber Barons; The Great American Capitalists, 1861 – 1901
  Matthew Josephson
  Harcourt, 1962

Social and economic history of this period, with emphasis on the lives and influence of such great industrialists as J. P. Morgan, Andrew Carnegie, John D. Rockefeller, and others.

Up the Organization
  Robert Townsend
  Fawcett, 1975

How to get ahead in today's corporations.

The Waste Makers
  Vance Packard
  Pocket

Exposé of the industrial system—how it sustains itself by turning out inferior products that will need quick replacement.

DRAMA

There are so many excellent plays and volumes of plays available, I will not try to list them. Ideas can be gleaned from bookstores or from libraries. Look under Dewey-Decimal numbers 808.82, 809.2, 812, 812.08, 822. Play scripts are available from Samuel French, Walter H. Baker, Harper-Row, and others. See list of publishers at end of this section.

An Actor Prepares
  Konstantin Stanislavski
  Theatre Arts Books, 1948

The founder and director of the famous Moscow Art Theatre discusses the method of acting that he originated.

The Amateur Magician's Handbook
  Henry Hay
  Crowell, 1972

Directions for performing magic tricks.

Costume Throughout the Ages
  Mary Evans
  Lippincott, 1950

Development of costume from Egypt to the twentieth century.

Historic Costume for the Stage
  Lucy Barton
  Baker, 1935

A comprehensive guide to authentic period costume.

Humphrey Bogart
  Nathaniel Benchley
  Little, 1975

Biography of one of Hollywood's most interesting actors.

Madame Sarah
  Cornelia Otis Skinner
  Watts

Biography of one of France's—and the world's—great actresses, told by a fellow actress.

The Movies
  Richard Griffith and Arthur Mayer
  Simon and Schuster, 1970

An enjoyable history of the American Film.

A Method of Lighting the Stage
  Stanley McCandless
  Theatre Arts Books

For years this has been a pacesettter in this important, but sometimes neglected area.

Scenery for the Theatre; The Organization, Processes, Materials, and Techniques Used to Set the Stage
  Harold Burris-Meyer and Edward C. Cole
  Little, Brown, 1971

Advanced and comprehensive text on scene design, construction, and painting.

Stagecraft for Nonprofessionals
  F. A. Buerki
  University of Wisconsin Press

A simple introduction to design and construction of stage settings. Includes a chapter on lighting.

Stage Makeup
  Herman Buchman
  Watson-Guptill

Specific instructions for a variety of character makeups.

The Theatre; Three Thousand Years of Drama, Acting, and Stagecraft
  Sheldon Cheney
  McKay, 1972

Theatres, actors, dramatists, and a great variety of theatre people give this history of the theatre a richness of feeling as well as comprehensiveness of content.

Theatre Props
  Motley
  Drama Book Specialists, 1975

One of the few books on how to make or otherwise obtain that vast array of items that the property master is called upon to produce.

Tyrone Guthrie on Acting
  Tyrone Guthrie
  Viking, 1971

Tips on acting, including a rich background of the author's experiences.

Stage Makeup
  Richard Corson
  Prentice-Hall, 1975

Basic techniques for straight and character makeup.

W. C. Fields by Himself; His Intended Autobiography
  Ronald J. Fields
  Prentice-Hall, 1973

Fields' grandson has put together a treasury of sketches from the life and humor of this great star of film comedy.

ENGLISH

Because literally anything in print is fair game for an English class library, I have not included literature on this list. See any bookstore or library or the bibliographies at the head of this appendix. The English list consists of material on language and communication.

All About Language
  Mario Pei
  Lippincott, 1954

History and diversity of languages, slang and dialect.

The Art of Readable Writing
  Rudolf Flesch
  Harper, 1974

Good, readable guide to writing in a simple, direct style.

Communication; From Stone Age to Space Age
  Harry Edward Neal

Development and function of language from prehistory to current media.

Dimensions of Change
Children of Change
Three Roads to Awareness
  Don Fabun, Glencoe Press

A series of mind-blowing articles on a great variety of subjects, most of them tied to the theme of communication.

Double Speak in America
  Mario Pei
  Hawthorn, 1973

How we use words to disguise our real meaning, or at least to soften the effect. Sometimes amusing, sometimes serious, this volume tells us much about the psychology of language.

Heavens to Betsy! and Other Curious Sayings
  Charles Earle Funk
  Harper, 1955

Did you ever wonder how some of our English idioms began? In this entertaining volume the author explains about 400 of them.

Language in Thought and Action
  S. I. Hayakawa
  Harcourt, 1972

Snarl words and purr words and levels of abstraction are just a few items in this introduction to general semantics.

Men, Messages, and Media
  Wilbur Schramm
  Harper, 1973

A summary of the major theories of communication.

The Modern Researcher
  Jacques Barzun and Henry Graff
  Harcourt, 1977

Guide to scholarly writing includes library research, judging values, and manuscript preparation. A readable volume, with illustrations of research writing from many areas.

The Story of the English Language
  Mario Pei
  Lippincott, 1967

English from its roots in Indo-European to the present.

Talking Your Way Around the World
  Mario Pei
  Harper, 1971

Introduction to the family of world languages.

The Tyranny of Words
  Stuart Chase
  Harcourt, 1938

Words have no meaning until you and I agree on what they mean. This basic book on semantics explains some of the intricacies of language.

Word Origins and Their Romantic Stories
  Wilfred Funk
  Funk and Wagnalls, 1950

Interesting tales of how over three thousand English words originated.

You and Your Language
  Charlton Laird
  Prentice-Hall, 1973

A look at how our language is organized and the use of language to increase our brain power, with special attention to such language uses as slang and bureaucratese.

FOREIGN LANGUAGE

Ask travel agents for tour books. They can give you beautifully illustrated brochures to stimulate interest in foreign travel. Some airlines will supply travel books and posters.

Check local bookstores, and college bookstores if available, for good literature in foreign language, particularly dual-language books for beginning classes.

HEALTH EDUCATION

See physical education, home economics—foods, and psychology.

HOME ECONOMICS—GENERAL

How to Live on Nothing
  Joan Ranson Shortney
  Pocket, 1973

A brief guide to cooking, clothing, home furnishing, travel, and many other facets of living, all with a view to survival on extremely limited budgets.

Living on the Earth
  Alicia Bay Laurel
  Vintage, 1971

Detailed instructions for seeking a simpler way of life.

A Manual for Baby-Sitters
  Marion Lowndes
  Little, 1975

Suggestions for menus, amusing children, and what to do in emergencies.

The Medically Based No-Nonsense Beauty Book
  Deborah Chase
  Knopf, 1974

Instructions for care of hair, skin, and eyes.

HOME ECONOMICS—CLOTHING

See sewing books by Vogue, Simplicity, and Singer Sewing Machine Company.

Cheap Chic
  Caterine Milinaire and Carol Troy
  Harmony, 1976

Suggestions for looking good on a budget.

Costume Throughout the Ages

See drama.

How to Make Something out of Practically Nothing
  Barbara Corrigan
  Doubleday, 1975

Making new clothing out of old. Assumes the reader has a basic knowledge of sewing.

HOME ECONOMICS— CONSUMER EDUCATION

The Consumer and Corporate Accountability
  Ralph Nader
  Harcourt, 1973

Exposé of some unscrupulous business practices in America.

The Hidden Persuaders
  Vance Packard
  McKay, 1957

How advertisers manipulate you and me to get us to buy their product or vote for their candidate.

The New York Times Book of Money

See math.

Sylvia Porter's Money Book
  Sylvia Porter
  Doubleday, 1975

A treasure house of information about household finance.

HOME ECONOMICS— FAMILY LIFE

See also titles under psychology, women's studies, sex education.

Earth: Our Crowded Spaceship
  Isaac Asimov
  Day, 1974

A scientist and fiction writer tells what can happen if we continue to overpopulate the earth.

The Family: Yesterday, Today, and Tomorrow
  Elaine and Walter Goodman
  Farrar, Straus, 1975

The family unit through the centuries, how it has changed, and what it means today.

Getting Ready for Marriage
  David R. Mace
  Abingdon, 1972

The author urges couples contemplating marriage to admit that problems arise and prepare to face them.

It's Not the End of the World
  Judy Blume
  Bradbury, 1972.

A girl conducts a futile struggle to save her parents' marriage, finally realizes that "it's not the end of the world."

Karen
  Marie Killilea
  Prentice-Hall, 1952

The struggles of a family with a daughter afflicted by cerebral palsy. A great story of courage and faith. See also *With Love from Karen,* 1963.

Love and Marriage; A Guide for Young People
  Curtis E. Avery
  Harcourt, 1971

The 10 most important areas of married life are discussed. No answers are given, but interesting questions exposed.

Mr. and Mrs. Bo Jo Jones
  Ann Head
  Putnam, 1967

Two high school youngsters, married by necessity, struggle against immaturity and differences in background. An appealing, poignant tale of young love.

A Tree Grows in Brooklyn
  Betty Smith
  Harper, 1947

A girl grows up in a Brooklyn slum. Despite economic poverty and a drunkard father, she experiences much warmth and tenderness.

A Walden Two Experiment; The First Five Years of Twin Oaks Community
  Kathleen Kinkade
  Morrow, 1973

The story of the establishment of a Skinnerian cooperative community, told by one of its members.

Young People and Parents
  Arthur H. Cain
  Day, 1971

The author advises young people how to work more effectively with their parents.

HOME ECONOMICS—FOODS

There are so many excellent cook books available that I won't attempt to list them here. A little time in a bookstore will yield rich results.

The Basic Book of Organically Grown Foods
  M. C. Goldman and William H. Hilton, editors

Instructions for buying, growing, and preparing more nutritious, less poisonous, more satisfying food.

Beware of the Food You Eat
  Ruth Winter
  Crown, 1971

Some unhappy information about what happens to food on the way to your table.

The Dieter's Companion; A Guide to Nutritional Self-sufficiency
  Nikki Goldbeck
  McGraw-Hill, 1976

Discusses the merits and limitations of various diets, with a guide to proper nutrition.

Hunger Fighters
  Paul de Kruif

True stories of scientists who have contributed to our knowledge of food and how to produce it.

INDUSTRIAL ARTS

All About Motorcycles
Max Alth
Hawthorn, 1975

Selection, maintenance, and repair.

Auto Engines of Tomorrow
  Harris Edward Dark
  Indiana University Press, 1975

Begins with examination of steam, electric, and internal combustion engines, then examines Wankel, diesel, turbine, and others. Considers economics, availability of fuels, and environmental factors.

The Coming Age of Solar Energy
  D. S. Halacy, Jr.
  Harper, 1973

Simple introduction to the history and use of solar energy.

The Complete Book of Boating
Ernest A. Zadig
Prentice-Hall, 1976

Designing, building, operating, and maintaining a variety of boats.

Complete Book of Woodworking
Rosario Capotoso
Harper, 1975

Basic work on woodworking tools and their uses.

The Complete Car Owner's Manual
Jerrold R. Clifford
Drake, 1976

Maintenance and repair of a variety of automobiles.

The Complete Handbook of Power Tools
George R. Drake
Reston Publishing Company, 1975

Using the lathe, drill press, jointer, shaper, power saws, and others.

Fix Your Small Appliances
Jack Darr
Sams, 1974

Diagnosis and repair of a variety of household gadgets.

How Things Work in Your Home and What to do When They Don't
Time-Life, 1975

Basic manual on home maintenance and repair.

Mini and Trail Bikes and How to Build Them Yourself
James C. Sparks
Dutton, 1976

Old lawn mowers furnish the engines. First directions for a simple mini-bike, then more complex models.

Small Gas Engines
James A. Gray and Richard W. Barrow
Prentice-Hall, 1976

Diagnosis and maintenance of single-cylinder engines.

Tape Recorders; How They Work
Charles G. Westcott and Richard F. Dubbe
Sams, 1974

Complete guide to how a tape recorder works.

Understanding Electricity and Electronics
Peter Buban and Marshall L. Schmitt
McGraw, 1975

Introduction to theory of electricity and its applications.

The Radio Amateur's Handbook
Fredrick A. Collins
Crowell. Frequent revisions to keep the material timely.

The complete guide to building and operating an amateur radio set, including FCC regulations for transmitting.
There is also another volume by the same name, reprinted annually by the American Radio Relay League.

Unsafe at Any Speed

See social studies, sociology.

JOURNALISM

The Art of Readable Writing

See English.

The Compact History of the American Newspaper
  John Tebbel
  Hawthorn, 1969

Problems and accomplishments of the American press.

Feature Writing for Newspapers
  Daniel R. Williamson

"How to" book for feature writers.

How to Talk to Practically Anybody About Practically Anything
  Barbara Walters
  Doubleday, 1970

A guide to the art of conversation, with emphasis on interviewing famous people.

The Journalistic Interview
  Hugh C. Sherwood
  Harper, 1972

Describes techniques for conducting interviews.

The New Muckrakers
  Leonard Downie
  New Republic, 1976

The inside story behind the headlines of investigative reporting.

The Writer's Market
  Writer's Digest, Annual

Comprehensive guide to where to sell written material.

MATHEMATICS

Albert Einstein, Creator and Rebel
  Banesh Hoffmann
  Viking, 1972

Life and work of one of the twentieth century's great geniuses.

The Calculating Book; Fun And Games with Your Pocket Calculator
  James T. Rogers

Tricks and games with a pocket calculator.

Flatland; A Romance of Many Dimensions
  Edwin A. Abbott
  Dover

An imaginative and fascinating conjecture about living in only two dimensions.

Galileo and the Scientific Revolution
  Laura Fermi and Gilberto Bernardini
  Basic, 1961

The agonizing life of one of the world's greatest scientists, mathematicians, and fighters for freedom of discovery.

Games Calculators Play
  Wallace P. Judd
  Warner, 1975

Tricks and riddles, names in numbers, and many other fun activities with a calculator.

How to Lie with Statistics
  Darrell Huff and Irving Geis
  Norton, 1973

A fascinating exposé of how numbers, graphs, and other mathematical devices can be used to say whatever the reporter wants to say.

I Hate Mathematics! Book
  Marilyn Burns
  Little, 1975

Gags, tricks, and experiments to turn the reader on to mathematics.

Magic House of Numbers
  Irving Adler
  Day, 1974

Math puzzles and riddles leading to a deeper understanding of our number system.

Martin Gardner's New Mathematical
Diversions from Scientific American
  Martin Gardner
  Simon and Schuster, 1966

A treasury of math problems and fun with numbers and math concepts.

Mathematics for the Million
  Lancelot Hogben
  Norton, 1968

Use of math to solve many everyday problems.

The New York Times Book of Money
  Richard E. Blodgett
  New York Times, 1967

Borrowing, banking, budgeting, and many other phases of economic survival.

Sylvia Porter's Money Book

See home economics—consumer education.

We Dare You to Solve This
(a series of four volumes)
  John P. Adams
  Berkley

Brain teasers and fun with word problems.

MUSIC

Check your local bookstore for good volumes of songs, popular and folk.

The Beatles: An Illustrated Record
  Roy Carr and Tony Tyler
  Harmony, 1975

Biographical sketches and information about the works of this famous musical group. In the form of a high school yearbook.

The Complete Plays of Gilbert and Sullivan
  W. S. Gilbert
  Norton, 1976

The words to 14 comic satires, with words by Gilbert and music by Sullivan.

The Fireside Book of Folk Songs
    Margaret Bradford Boni
    Simon and Schuster, 1966

An outstanding collection of ballads, work songs, marching songs, and hymns beautifully illustrated by Alice and Martin Provensen

From Satchmo to Miles
    Leonard Feather
    Stein and Day, 1972

Short sketches of Count Basie, Ray Charles, Duke Ellington, Ella Fitzgerald, and many other Black musical artists.

Giants of Jazz
    Studs Terkel
    Crowell, 1975

The lives and work of Benny Goodman, Dizzy Gillespie, Duke Ellington, and others.

Making Music for Money
    James Lincoln Collier
    Watts, 1976

Starting and leading a group. A complete guide for the aspiring band leader.

Man of La Mancha
    Dale Wasserman
    Lyrics by Joe Darion
    Music by Mitch Leigh
    Dell, 1965

The story of Don Quixote, with author Cervantes himself part of the cast, brought to the musical stage.

My Lord, What a Morning; An Autobiography
    Marian Anderson
    Viking, 1956

A great artist shares with the reader her thoughts on subjects from music to race prejudice.

The New Milton Cross' Complete Stories of the Great Operas
    Milton Cross
    Doubleday, 1955

History of opera, what to look for in an opera, and stories of 76 great operas.

Song and Dance Man; The Art of Bob Dylan
    Michael Gray
    Dutton, 1972

The works of Bob Dylan—poet, musician, philosopher, and idol of a youth generation.

West Side Story
    Book by Arthur Laurents
    Music by Leonard Bernstein
    Lyrics by Stephen Sondheim
    Based on a conception of Jerome Robbins

Musical drama of love and hate among Anglos and Puerto Ricans in New York's slums. Loosely based on *Romeo and Juliet.*
    Dell publishes an interesting edition with *Romeo and Juliet* in the same volume.

What to Listen for in Music
    Aaron Copeland
    McGraw, 1957

The three planes of musical listening—the sensuous, the expressive, and the purely musical.

OCCUPATIONS

(R.O.P. and other vocational awareness classes.)

Making Music for Money	See music
The Making of a Surgeon William A. Nolen Random House, 1970	The story of a doctor from internship to chief resident.
Raising Small Animals for Fun and Profit Paul Villiard Winchester, 1973	Short but adequate instructions for raising nearly anything from microscopic water life to expensive minks. Handling, feeding, and marketing.
Rescue Squad Larry Ferazani Morrow, 1974	The work of a fire department rescue squad, dealing with fires, drug victims, suicides, and other difficult situations. Also gives instructions for dealing with common emergencies.
The Teenager and the Interview John Keefe Richards Rosen, 1971	A manual for conducting oneself during an interview, with added remarks about the working world.
Working Studs Terkel Pantheon, 1974	Terkel interviewed people around the country, discussing their work and how they feel about what they do for a living.
Your Career in Unusual Occupations Walter Harter McKay, 1971	Such careers as fish farming, museum work, and tree trimming are explored.

PHYSICAL EDUCATION

Aaron Henry Aaron, with Furman Bisher Crowell, 1974	The story of a nice guy who made it big in baseball.
African Rhythm—American Dance; A Biography of Katherine Dunham Terry Harnan Knopf, 1974	A Black woman incorporates African and Caribbean rhythms into American choreography.
The All-American Dollar; The Big Business of Sports Joseph Durso Houghton, 1971	The development in recent years of professional athletics into a big business.

All About Bicycling
  Rand McNally

Selecting, maintaining, and using a bicycle. Bike sports, racing, touring, and camping.

American Youth Hostels, Inc. Hostel Guide and Handbook
  AYH, annual

Gets young people into bicycling by introducing them to the American Youth Hostel program, which sponsors low-cost American and international travel. Hiking and waterways travel is also popular with hostelers.

America's Camping Book
  Paul Cardwell
  Scribner, 1976

Campsites, equipment, and many other phases of camping make this a comprehensive guide for the novice camper.

Backpacking
  Tony Gibbs
  Watts, 1975

Equipment, food, and other important know-hows for the backpacker.

Back to Nature in Canoes; A Guide to American Waters
  Rainer Esslen
  Columbia, 1976

Listing of the major rivers and lakes in each state, along with an introduction to canoeing.

Balanchine's New Complete Stories of the Great Ballets
  George Balanchine
  Doubleday

Over 200 ballets are included, as well as discussion of enjoyment of the ballet and history of ballet.

Best Sports Stories Series
  Dutton

See publisher's catalog for complete list in this series.

Billie Jean King
  Jim Baker
  Grosset

Easy reading story of a great tennis champion.

Billie Jean King's Secrets of Winning Tennis
  Billie Jean King and Joe Hyams
  Holt, 1974

Pointers for developing a winning style.

The Complete Book of Boating

See industrial arts.

Crazy Legs Mcbain
  Joe Archibald
  Willow, 1961

Football story.

DeLong's Guide to Bicycles and Bicycling: The Art and Science
  Fred DeLong
  Chilton, 1974

Selection, maintenance and repair, racing, and touring.

The Football Quiz Book Al Goldberg Drake, 1975	Questions about players and plays, many aspects of the game.
From Cobb to "Catfish"; 128 Illustrated Stories from Baseball Digest John Kuenster (editor) Rand McNally, 1975	Stories of great events in the history of baseball.
Garrard Sports Library Garrard	Easy reading stories of great athletes, essays about popular sports, even a volume about coaches. Send for catalog.
Go Ask Alice	See psychology.
The Greatest, My Own Story Muhammed Ali Random House, 1975	The sometimes glorious, sometimes tormented story of a man who threw his olympic gold medal into the river after a racial brawl, changed his name and his religion, and banged and clowned his way to the heavyweight championship.
Guiness Sports Record Book	From the Guiness Book of World Records, includes interesting information from a variety of sports.
Guiness Book of Olympic Records Norris D. McWhirter and A. Ross McWhirter, editors Bantam	Companion to *The Guiness Book of World Records.*
Hillbilly Pitcher C. P. and O. B. Jackson Scholastic	Wilson knows that his odd Tennessee way of talking sets him apart from his schoolmates. When his own teammate jeers him in the middle of a game he knows the time has come for a showdown.
How Did Sports Begin? A Look at the Origins of Man at Play R. Brasch McKay, 1970	History and development of 43 popular sports.
I Know Why the Caged Bird Sings Maya Angelou Random House, 1970	After a depressing and painful childhood, this dancer tells the story of her rise to fame.
Incredible Olympic Feats Jim Benagh McGraw, 1976	Outstanding performances by olympic athletes. Emphasis on track and field results in emphasis on American athletes.

Jack Johnson is a Dandy
  An autobiography

The life and loves of this great fighter, who held the heavyweight title from 1908 to 1915.

Jackie Robinson of the Brooklyn Dodgers
  Milton J. Shapiro
  Washington Square

Dramatic story of the great National League slugger who broke baseball's color line.

Nice Guys Finish Last
  Leo Durocher
  Simon and Schuster, 1975

Autobiography of the most colorful member of baseball's most colorful team.

Nothing Venture, Nothing Win
  Sir Edmund Hillary
  Coward McKann, 1975

The many adventures in the life of this conquerer of Mt. Everest.

Paper Lion
  George Plimpton
  Harper, 1966

A journalist joins a professional football team as last-string quarterback, and comes out with some fascinating insights.

The Perfect Exercise; The Hop, Skip, and Jump Way to Health
  Curtis Mitchell
  Simon and Schuster, 1976

The value of exercise explained. Rope skipping is used as the basis for exercise routines.

Pivot Man
  Dick Friendlich
  Scholastic, 1966

Basketball story.

Rules of the Game; The Complete Illustrated Encyclopedia of All the Sports of the World

Official rules of over 400 sports.

A Sense of Where You Are
  John McPhee
  Bantam, 1965

Illustrated profile of William Warren Bradley, holder of numerous records and honors as Princeton's famed basketball captain.

Sports Illustrated Basketball
  Lippincott, 1971

Analysis and instructions for winning basketball. Also see others in this series.

Surfing: All the Young Wave Hunters
  William Cleary
  Signet, 1967

Stories and essays about surfing and the great surfers. Illustrated.

Tall Story
  Howard Lindsay and Russell Crouse
  Random House

Gamblers, basketball players, and college professors figure in this comedy-drama.

A Treasury of Sports Humor
  Milton J. Shapiro
  Messner, 1972

Interesting and humorous anecdotes from the world of sport.

Wilt: Just Like Any Other 7-Foot Black Millionaire Who Lives Next Door
  Wilt Chamberlain
  Macmillan, 1973

A wild and zany autobiography of a most unusual basketball player.

Women Who Win

See women's studies.

PSYCHOLOGY

The Art of Loving
  Erich Fromm
  Harper, 1956

Love is presented as something one does not "fall into" but works for. One can only become a good lover, says Fromm, by becoming a full human being.

Body Language
  Julius Fast
  M. Evans, 1970

Communication without words. Understanding what the body is saying.

Carl Rogers on Encounter Groups
  Carl R. Rogers
  Harper, 1970

A history of the encounter movement, with scenes from Rogers' own groups.

The Catcher in the Rye
  J. D. Salinger

A sensitive adolescent boy, about to be expelled from school, goes on an agonizing three-day odyssey in quest of making sense of a confusing and phony world.

Flowers for Algernon
  Daniel Keyes
  Harcourt, 1966

A mentally retarded young man is helped by a brain operation to become a genius. But more changes occur than anyone had foreseen.

Future Shock

See social studies—sociology

Games People Play
  Eric Berne
  Dell, 1964

The original presentation of transactional analysis by the father of the subject. Parent-Adult-Child, time structuring, the psychology of games.

Go Ask Alice
  Anonymous
  Prentice-Hall, 1971

Diary of a fifteen-year-old girl who gets hooked on LSD. An intimate picture of the teenage drug scene, with tragic conclusion.

Healing the Mind; Eight Views of Human Nature
  Robert A. Liston
  Praeger, 1974

Contributions of Freud, Rogers, Skinner, Maslow, and others to our knowledge of the mind.

I'm OK—You're OK
Thomas A. Harris
Avon, 1967

This classic explains in simple language the Parent-Adult-Child theory of transactional analysis. It also presents and discusses the four life positions, based on the OK-not OK feelings. A good introduction to TA.

Is There Life After High School?
Ralph Keyes
Little, 1976

In this sometimes humorous collection of interviews the author discovered that high school caterpillars can turn into butterflies, an encouraging report for many.

Jonathan Livingston Seagull
Richard Bach
Avon

Beautifully written, beautifully illustrated symbolic story of the eternal struggle of the nonconformist to feel OK about himself.

Lord of the Flies
William Golding
Coward-McCann

A group of British children are shipwrecked on an uninhabited island, forced to build their own civilization. The ensuing battle between order and reason on one hand, and brutal lust on the other, is a chilling statement about adult life.

The Occult Explosion
Nat Freedland
Putnam, 1972

Discussion of astrology, magic, transcendental meditation and other parapsychological experiences by one who seems to be more believer than skeptic.

On Being Human

See social science—sociology.

One Flew Over the Cuckoo's Nest
Ken Kesey
Viking, 1962

A moving novel about life in a mental hospital.

Pairing; How to Achieve Genuine Intimacy
George R. Bach and Ronald
M. Deutsch
Avon, 1970

The authors discuss reality versus image-building in human relationships, with emphasis on male-female romantic involvements. They offer suggestions for building strong, intimate relationships with the opposite sex.

T. A. for Teens (and other important people)
Alvyn M. Freed
Jalmar

Principles of transactional analysis, with emphasis on helping teenagers feel OK about themselves and understand others.

A Whale for the Killing
Farley Mowat
Little, 1972

The reader is first intrigued as a whale became trapped in a small Newfoundland bay, then enraged at the senseless cruelty of people.

PUBLIC SPEAKING

"Come to Order," Essentials of Parliamentary Practice and Group Discussion
  Emma M. Wines and Marjory W. Card
  Odyssey, 1941

A quick introduction to parliamentary procedure.

How to Talk Well
  James F. Bender
  McGraw-Hill, 1949

Plainly written advice to the would-be speaker.

How to Write and Deliver a Speech
  John Ott
  Trident, 1970

From an idea to a finished speech, this text deals with research, organization, and delivery.

Podium Humor; a Raconteur's Treasury of Witty and Humorous Stories
  James C. Humes
  Harper & Row, 1975

A collection of humor suitable for public speaking, arranged and indexed by topic.

Speech and Man
  Charles T. Brown and Charles Van Riper
  Prentice-Hall, 1966

Interesting sidelights about speech and speakers.

A Treasury of the World's Great Speeches
  Houston Peterson (editor)
  Simon and Schuster, 1965

A collection of some magnificent examples of dynamic use of language. These are not only models for public speakers but a treasury of human thinking.

SCIENCE—GENERAL

Asimov's Guide to Science
  Isaac Asimov
  Basic Books, 1972

A clear and interesting introduction to the entire field of scientific knowledge.

Atlantic Beaches

See social studies—geography

A Closer Look
  Michael A. Godfrey
  Sierra Club, 1975

Observations we can make about the world of nature that is within easy reach.

The Closing Circle; Nature, Man, and Technology
  Barry Commoner
  Knopf, 1971

The ecological systems and how man is poisoning his environment.

Earth: Our Crowded Spaceship

See home economics—family life

Energy: Resource, Slave, Pollutant
  Robert S. Rouse and Robert O. Smith
  Macmillan, 1975

Energy is the central theme that pulls together all the physical sciences.

The Everglades
  Archie Carr
  Time-Life Books, 1973

Illustrations and text portraying this land of mystery.

Golden Nature Guides
  Golden Press

A series of paperbacks, nicely illustrated, showing the splendid variety of natural species.

Hawaii: A Natural History

See social studies—geography

How and Why Wonder Books
  Grosset

A series of simply written, beautifully illustrated books on a variety of scientific subjects, including *Ecology, Weather,* and many others.

Hunger Fighters

See home economics—foods

Inherit the Wind

See social studies—sociology

Investigating in Science Series
  American Book Company

Such easy-reading titles as *Energy from the Sun, Exploring the Universe,* and *Light and Heat* bring science within reach of the reading disabled student.

John Muir's Wild America
  Tom Melham
  National Geographic, 1976

Traces the route of this famous explorer and naturalist.

Life and Energy
  Issac Asimov
  Avon, 1962

For advanced students, this explanation of the relationship between life and energy, by the dean of science as well as science fiction writers, makes slow but illuminating reading.

Madame Curie, A Biography
  Marie Curie
  Doubleday, 1949

The struggle of a great woman scientist, as told by her loving and admiring daughter.

Microbe Hunters
  Paul de Kruif
  Pocket, 1926

Miniature biographies of great researchers in medicine, many of whom risked their reputations and even their lives in the battle against disease.

Nature Through the Seasons
  Richard Adams
  Simon and Schuster, 1975

Explanations for seasonal changes in plants and animals.

Of Matters Great and Small
  Isaac Asimov
  Doubleday, 1975

Essays on astronomy, energy, life, and many other topics. See also other Doubleday books in this series by the same author.

The Ozarks
  Richard Rhodes
  Time-Life, 1974

Plants and animals of this mountain region.

Plants, Life, and LGM
  Ben Bova
  Addison-Wesley

The search for life (Little Green Men) on other planets.

The Question and Answer Book of Everyday Science
  Ruth A. Sonneborn
  Random House

Very simple answers to simple questions, such as *Why is the sky blue?*, *What makes the wind blow?* and *How does a scab form when you cut yourself?*

Science Projects Handbook
  Shirley Moore (editor)
  Ballantine, 1960

The systematic approach to exploration explained, with suggested projects in many different areas of scientific inquiry.

The UFO Experience; a Scientific Inquiry
  J. Allen Hynek
  Regnery, 1972

An Air Force consultant gathers evidence concerning UFO's.

The Voyage of the Beagle
  Charles Darwin
  Harper, 1959

A shortened, edited version of this classic statement of the theory of evolution.

Water: The Web of Life
  Cynthia A. Hunt

Water around the world—its cycles and uses, and what can happen if we continue to abuse it.

The White Caps

See social studies—geography.

Wild Alaska
  Dale Brown
  Time-Life, 1972

Geology and plant and animal life of our largest state.

SCIENCE—BIOLOGICAL

Born Free
  Joy Adamson
  Pantheon, 1960

A lion cub is raised as a pet and then "taught" to live in the wild. See also *Living Free* by same author.

A Fine and Peaceful Kingdom
  Kent Durden
  Simon and Schuster, 1975

Dealing in personal experiences with skunks and owls and other animals, this book gives the reader a feeling of warm and satisfying interaction with the environment.

The Great Chain of Life
  Joseph Wood Krutch
  Houghton, 1957

A warm and loving look at animal behavior, with spill-offs into human behavior.

Learning About Nature Through Crafts
  Virginia W. Musselman
  Stackpole Books, 1969

Crafts projects that teach ecology.

Life and Death in a Coral Sea
  Jacques-Yves Cousteau
  Doubleday, 1971

This beautifully illustrated volume describes a world few people have ever seen—an undersea world filled with structures of greater beauty, complexity, and vastness than anything ever built on land. This famed explorer tells of adventure and discovery among the life forms of the great coral areas of the Red Sea and the Indian Ocean. See also other works by Cousteau.

Living Plants of the World
  Lorus and Margery Milne
  Random House, 1975

A guide to identifying many species of plant life.

Man's Most Dangerous Myth: The Fallacy of Race

See social studies—sociology.

Pond Life
  George K. Reid
  Golden, 1967

The world of plants, animals, insects, fish, reptiles, and birds that inhabit the quiet waters.

The Rainbow Book of Nature
  Donald Culross Peattie
  World, 1957

Easy-reading, beautifully illustrated introduction to biology.

The Shark; Splendid Savage of the Sea
  Jacques-Yves and Philippe
  Cousteau
  Doubleday, 1970

Photographs and text of research on this ocean predator.

Snakes of the World
  Raymond L. Ditmars
  Pyramid, 1931

Descriptions of several hundred varieties of snakes—their characteristics and habitats.

Wizard of the Dome; R. Buckminister Fuller, Designer for the Future
  Sidney Rosen

The life of ecologist, philosopher, and inventor of the geodesic dome.

SCIENCE—PHYSICAL

Albert Einstein, Creator and Rebel

See math.

Colonizing the Planets
  Eric Bergaust
  Putnam, 1975

The author speculates that Venus will be first to be colonized. Many problems are described, including alterations of the atmosphere.

The Coming Age of Solar Energy

See industrial arts.

Cup and Saucer Chemistry
  Nathan Shalit
  Grosset, 1972

Easy-reading chemistry experiments.

Galileo and the Scientific Revolution

See math.

How and Why Wonder Book of Weather

See science—general.

Kon-tiki
  Thor Heyerdahl
  Pocket, 1950

A small band of explorers set out on a raft of balsa logs to sail from the west coast of South America to the South Pacific. In addition to proving a theory, they have a fascinating time exploring the ocean from a particularly close vantage point.

The Laser; The Light That Never Was Before
  Ben Patrusky
  Dodd, 1966

History, description, and uses of the laser.

Life of the Past
  George Gaylord Simpson
  Bantam, 1954

Introduction to Paleontology.

A Physics Lab of Your own
  Steven J. Mark
  Houghton, 1964

Easy-reading, simple physics experiments.

Pictorial Guide to the Planets
  Joseph H. Jackson
  Crowell, 1973

Introduction to astronomy, with speculation concerning possibility of life on other planets.

The Rockhound's Manual
  Gordon S. Fay
  Harper, 1972

Introduction to gem and mineral collecting—finding material, lapidary work, ultraviolet light exhibiting, and many other facets of this popular hobby.

The Science of Chemistry
  Ira M. Freeman and A. Rae Patton
  Random House, 1968

Easy-reading introduction to chemistry.

Seesaws to Cosmic Rays
  Mitchell Wilson
  Lothrop, 1967

Easy-reading introduction to physics.

Turned-on; A Look at Electricity
  A. Harris Stone

Easy-reading experiments with magnetism and electricity.

Understanding Electricity and Electronics

See industrial arts.

The Voyages of Apollo; The Exploration of the Moon
  Richard S. Lewis
  New York Times Book, 1974

Scientific account of an historical event, and philosophical speculations concerning its significance.

Weather
  Armand N. Spitz
  Bantam

Introduction to why weather happens and how we observe and predict it.

Weather
  Philip D. Thompson and Robert O'Brien
  Time-Life, 1973

Why the weather changes, what causes such phenomena as hail and storms.

SEX EDUCATION

A good source of information is the Sex Information and Education Council of the United States. See directory of publishers at end of this section.

The Art of Loving

See psychology.

Facts About Sex for Today's Youth
  Sol Gordon
  Day, 1973

A straightforward book on the anatomy and psychology of sex. Information without moralizing.

Pairing; How to Achieve Genuine Intimacy

See psychology.

Sex and Birth Control; A Guide for the Young
  E. James Lieberman
  Crowell, 1973

A comprehensive, objective coverage of V.D., pregnancy, and other phases of sex.

SOCIAL STUDIES—
AMERICAN HISTORY

Abe Lincoln Grows Up
The Prairie Years
The Prairie Years and the War Years
  Carl Sandburg
  Harcourt, 1928, 1929, 1954

This three volume story of the life of one of our greatest presidents by one of America's greatest poets is a classic of biography and American history.

Adventures of Huckleberry Finn
  Mark Twain

Huck, Tom Sawyer, and his friends are involved in lots of adventures, including an idyllic raft ride and the freeing of a slave. An interesting glimpse of an American era.

America on Stage
  Stanley Richards (editor)
  Doubleday, 1976

Ten plays based on American history.

The Autobiography of Miss Jane Pittman

See social studies—ethnic studies

The Big Sky
  A. B. Guthrie

Historical novel debunks the myth of the noble pioneer, tells a pathetic tale of the degradation of the land, its people, and its resources.

Black Like Me

See social studies—ethnic studies.

Caddie Woodlawn
  Carol Ryrie Brink
  Macmillan, 1973

Story of a girl on the Wisconsin frontier in the 1860's.

Cannery Row
  John Steinbeck
  Viking, 1945

Once more Monterey, California comes to life as we see it in the days of fishing fleets and canneries, along with the colorful derelicts who inhabited Cannery Row.

Cimarron
  Edna Ferber
  Doubleday, 1930

A novel of Oklahoma from Indian Territory days to the oil strike and its consequences.

Crazy Horse and Custer; The Parallel Lives of Two American Warriors

See social studies—ethnic studies.

The Deerslayer
The Last of the Mohicans
The Pathfinder
The Pioneers
The Prairie
  James Fenimore Cooper

A series of novels about life among the Delaware, the Huron, and the Iroquois Indians.

Disasters That Made History
  Webb Garrison
  Abingdon, 1973

Accounts of floods, fires, earthquakes, and other tragedies of epic proportions.

The Four Days of Mayaguez
  Roy Rowan
  Norton, 1975

This account of the capture of an American ship tells us something about war and American foreign policy at the time.

Freedom Road
  Howard Fast
  Crown, 1964

Gideon Jackson rises from illiteracy to congressman. His dream of cooperation between Blacks and Whites in the South almost becomes a reality, then is wiped out. A vivid picture of the Reconstruction.

Giants in the Earth; A Saga of the Prairie
  O. E. Rølvaag
  Harper, 1927

A Norwegian immigrant couple pioneers in Dakota.

Gone With the Wind
    Margaret Mitchell
    Macmillan

A saga of love and life in the Old South during the Civil War era.

The Grapes of Wrath
    John Steinbeck
    Viking, 1939

Disillusion and despair are the fate of an Oklahoma family who are forced by drought to move to California.

The Great Chiefs

See social studies—ethnic studies.

Hard Times; An Oral History of the Great Depression
    Studs Terkel
    Pantheon, 1970

Life during the Great Depression, as told by those who lived it.

Jed
    Peter Burchard
    Coward McCann, 1960

The meeting of a union soldier and a southern boy who hates Yankees produces a tender and sensitive story.

Johnny Tremain
    Esther Forbes
    Dell, 1943

From the highest heights to the lowest depths falls Johnny, young apprentice to a Boston silversmith, when an accident disfigures him. Only by getting lost in a cause does Johnny regain himself. That cause is the American revolution.

Kit Carson's Autobiography
    Kit Carson
    University of Nebraska Press, 1966

Adventures of an American frontiersman, as told by the man who lived them.

A Lantern in Her Hand
    Bess Streeter Aldrich
    Scholastic, 1928

The moving story of Abbie Deal, pioneer woman, is a must, especially for girls, with its graphic picture of the hardships faced by pioneers in Nebraska at the end of the nineteenth century. It is also a beautifully drawn picture of people. Each pioneer has his own values—and spends his life in quest for whatever he considers important.

The Nickel-Plated Beauty
    Patricia Beatty
    Morrow, 1964

Story of young people in Washington Territory a century ago.

Northwest Passage
    Kenneth Roberts
    Doubleday, 1959

A portion of the life of Robert Rogers, who dreamed of finding a "Northwest Passage" to the West. Told by one of his followers.

The Octopus; A Story of California
    Frank Norris

The epic struggle between the wheat growers of California and a railroad which reached out its tentacles like an octopus to grab and engulf.

Profiles in Courage
John F. Kennedy
Harper, 1964

Biographical sketches of Americans who showed courage in moments of crisis.

The Promised Land
Mary Antin
Houghton, 1969

A young Jewess immigrates to a Boston slum from Russia and develops a deep love for America.

The Red Badge of Courage
Stephen Crane

Henry Fleming conquers fear, achieves manhood as a soldier in the Civil War.

Red Rock over the River
Patricia Beatty
Morrow, 1973

Two girls in the Arizona territory set out on a campaign. The story reveals much about the harsh realities of life in this primitive environment.

The Robber Barons

See business subjects.

1776
Peter Stone
Penguin, 1976

Comedy, drama, and music come together in this play about the Declaration of Independence.

The Spirit of Saint Louis
Charles A. Lindbergh
Scribner, 1975

An exciting account of the first solo transatlantic flight—from New York to Paris. Reissue of 1953 edition.

Walk the World's Rim
Betty Baker
Harper, 1965

An Indian boy travels with Cabeza de Vaca and Esteban the slave in their exploration of the New World. The book says much about human dignity and freedom.

Why We Can't Wait

See social studies—ethnic studies.

Witchcraft at Salem
Chadwick Hansen
Braziller, 1969

Story of a tragic and shameful period of history.

SOCIAL STUDIES—ANTHROPOLOGY

Beast or Angel? Choices That Make Us Human
René Dubos
Scribner, 1974

The unique qualities, good and not-so-good, of man.

Chariots of the Gods?
Erich von Däniken
Putnam, 1970

The author shows evidence that the earth was visited in ancient times by interplanetary creatures who interbred with early man.

Everyday Life in Prehistoric Times   See social studies—world history.

Kon-tiki   See science—physical

Primitive Worlds; People Lost in Time   Reports on six tribes still living in primi-
National Geographic Society, 1973   tive conditions.

SOCIAL STUDIES—
ETHNIC STUDIES

Aaron   See physical education.

Actor   Short plays and skits depicting Chicano
Luis Valdez and El Teatro   life.
Campesino
Cucaracha Press, 1971

African Rhythm—American Dance   See physical education.

Amanda's Choice   Cuban-American relationship portrayed
Isabelle Holland   through a friendship.
Lippincott, 1960

And Now Miguel   A boy working as a sheepherder in New
Joseph Krumgold   Mexico proves himself a man.
Crowell, 1953

Angela Davis, an Autobiography   A fiery black woman tells of her fight for
Angela Davis   justice.
Random House, 1974

Autobiography of Malcolm X As told to   A panorama of black life in America.
Alex Haley   From Lansing, Michigan to Harlem,
Grove, 1965   Malcolm ran the gamut from hustler to
drug pusher to burglar. After landing in
prison he began to read, learned about
the Black Muslims, became prominent in
the movement, and finally broke away in
disillusion.

The Autobiography of Miss Jane Pittman   An elderly black woman tells her story
Ernest J. Gaines   (fiction), a cavalcade of black life from
slavery to a dramatic walk for black free-
dom.

Aztecas Del Norte   The story of the Chicano in the United
The Chicanos of Aztlán   States, with emphasis on Native Ameri-
Jack D. Forbes   can roots. A study of the causes of many
Fawcett, 1973   social problems, as seen by one who
lived through many of them.

Barrio Boy
  Ernesto Galarza
  Ballantine

Autobiography of a boy who emigrates from a Mexican mountain village to a Barrio in Sacramento, California.

The Big Wave

See social studies—geography.

Bimby
  Peter Burchard
  Coward-McCann, 1968

A Georgia slave risks all in a dash for freedom.

Black Elk Speaks
  John G. Neihardt
  (Flaming Rainbow)
  University of Nebraska, 1961

The life story of a holy man of the Oglala Sioux, culminating with the massacre at Wounded Knee.

Black Like Me
  John Howard Griffin
  Signet, 1960

A white man darkens his skin and sets out to discover by personal experience what it is like to be black in America.

Black Out Loud; An Anthology of Modern Poems by Black Americans
  Arnold Adoff (editor)
  Macmillan, 1970

From Langston Hughes and LeRoi Jones to less well-known poets, this volume deals with black identity, black life, and other subjects.
  See also other books by this author.

The Book of Negro Folklore
  Edited by Langston Hughes and Arna Bontemps
  Dodd, 1950

A collection of black folklore from pre-civil war to the present.

The Book of Negro Humor
  Langston Hughes (editor)
  Dodd, 1966

Laugh with Jackie Robinson, Booker T. Washington, Jelly Roll Morton, and many others.

Bury My Heart at Wounded Knee
  Dee Brown
  Bantam

History of Indians of the West, terminating with the massacre by American soldiers of about 300 Indians at Wounded Knee.

Cesar Chavez; Autobiography of La Causa

See agriculture.

The Children of Ham
  Claude Brown
  Stein and Day, 1976

A group of Blacks in one of the worst sections of Harlem leave the world of hustling, crime, and dope and opt for cooperative living.

Crazy Horse and Custer; The Parallel Lives of Two American Warriors
  Stephen E. Ambrose
  Doubleday, 1975

The lives of an Oglala Sioux and a U.S. Army general, culminating in the battle of Little Big Horn, in which Custer was killed.

Ebony Pictorial History of Black America
  Johnson, 1971 (four volumes)

The American Black from African roots
to 1973.

Escape from Freedom

See social studies—sociology.

Eskimo Songs and Stories
  Edward Field (compiler and translator)
  Delacorte, 1973

A collection of Netsilik songs and stories.

Famous Mexican-Americans
  Clarke Newlon
  Dodd, 1972

Cesar Chavez, Anthony Quinn, and
others who have achieved fame.

The Fire Next Time
No Name in the Street
Nobody Knows My Name
Notes of a Native Son
  James Baldwin
  Dial Press

James Baldwin is a prolific and fiery
spokesman for black people's rage in
America.

Five Plays
  Langston Hughes
  Indiana University Press, 1963

Interesting folk plays for all-black casts.

The Flower Drum Song
  Lee Chin-Yang
  Farrar, 1957

A Chinese immigrant resists becoming
Americanized.

The Greatest, My Own Story

See physical education.

From Satchmo to Miles

See music.

The Great Chiefs
  Benjamin Capps
  Time-Life, 1975

Lives of great Indian chiefs—their positions in their tribes and their battles with
the Whites.

Great Negroes, Past and Present
  Russell L. Adams
  Afro-American Publishing Company

Biographies of 175 great Blacks in many
areas. Also contains charts showing
achievements of others not given biographical treatment.

Growing Up Puerto Rican
  Paulette Cooper
  Arbor House

Seventeen young Puerto Ricans tell their
stories, some incredible, some
heartbreaking.

House Made of Dawn
  M. Scott Momaday
  Harper, 1968

A young Indian finds his reservation
life-style in conflict with the life he lives
in Los Angeles.

I Know Why the Caged Bird Sings

See physical education.

*Indian Legends from the Northern Roc-
kies*
  Ella E. Clark
  University of Oklahoma Press

Myths and stories of 12 Indian tribes.

Island of the Blue Dolphins
  Scott O'Dell
  Houghton, 1960

An Indian girl lives on an island off the coast of California.

Jackie Robinson

See physical education.

Jenny Kimura
  Betty Cavanna
  Morrow, 1964

A Japanese girl comes to visit her grandmother in the United States, has conflicting feelings between her two cultures.

Journey to Topaz
  Yoshiko Uchida
  Scribner's, 1971

The fears and resentments, and the economic losses suffered by Japanese-Americans in a World War II evacuation camp.

The Lilies of the Field
  William E. Barrett
  Doubleday, 1962

A black man helps a group of nuns build a church—without knowing why.

Manchild in the Promised Land
  Claude Brown
  Signet, 1965

An American black man, raised in the ghetto, tells the dramatic story of his life—a life that experienced deprivation, hustling, crime, dope, sex, and all the frustrations of ghetto living.

My Lord, What a Morning

See music.

Nigger; An Autobiography
  Dick Gregory
  Dutton, 1964

The anger and frustration of a people are contained in this story of the life of a black man and his struggle for his own and his people's liberation.

Nuyorican Poetry; An Anthology of Puerto Rican Words and Feelings
  Miguel Algarin (editor)
  Morrow, 1975

From politics to love, this book expresses feelings of Americans of Puerto Rican ancestry. Written in the popular dialect that blends English with Spanish.

Our Citizens from the Caribbean
  Clarence Senior
  McGraw-Hill, 1965

The Cuban Revolution, with the resultant immigration to the United States. Also discusses some aspects of Cuban culture.

Pocho
  José Antonio Villareal
  Doubleday, 1970

The story of the deterioration of a Chicano family under Anglo influence, and the emergence of a new breed of Mexican-American. In this beautifully told story we see a proud man unable to maintain his self-respect as the family becomes increasingly Americanized.

The Portable North American Indian Reader
  Fredrick W. Turner
  Viking, 1974

Myths, poetry, and stories from American Indian tribes.

Power and Innocence; A Search for the Sources of Violence
  Rollo May
  Norton, 1972

May does not believe that the acquisition of power always leads to violence, as is frequently assumed. Part of the book deals with methods of coping with violence.

A Raisin in the Sun
  Lorraine Hansberry
  Random House

A drama about a black family's attempt to live in peace with their neighbors.

Ralph Bunche: UN Peacemaker

See social studies—government.

Ramona
  Helen Hunt Jackson

Classic romance of love and culture conflict in early California.

San Francisco Boy
  Lois Lenski
  Lippincott, 1955

Two youngsters from San Francisco's Chinatown have very different views of life.

Soul on Ice
  Eldridge Cleaver
  Delta, 1968

A hard-hitting, take-off-the-gloves comment on race relations in America.

The Tenacity of Prejudice; Anti-Semitism in Contemporary America
  Gertrude J. Selznick and Stephen Steinberg
  Harper, 1969

An inquiry into why certain people are affected by antisemitism.

To Kill a Mockingbird
  Harper Lee

Novel about a girl who grows up in a small town in Alabama. She and her family are forced to deal with race prejudice and fear of the unknown.

The Two Uncles of Pablo
  Harry Behn
  Harcourt, 1959

A little Chicano boy has something to teach two grown men.

Walk the World's Rim

See social studies—American history.

Waterless Mountain
  Laura Adams Armer and Sidney Armer
  McKay, 1931

A story of Navajo Indian life, beautifully illustrated.

West Side Story

See music.

The Whispering Wind; Poetry by Young American Indians
  Terry Allen (editor)
  Doubleday, 1972

Poetry of students at the Institute of American Indian Arts.

Why We Can't Wait
  Martin Luther King, Jr.
  Signet, 1963

The struggles of this great leader to get the Civil Rights movement off the ground.

Wilt

See physical education.

The Prince and the Pauper
Mark Twain

A young beggar is placed by mistake on the throne of England, while the real prince is forced to live as a beggar. This fine classic contains much commentary about living conditions in sixteenth century England.

SOCIAL STUDIES—GEOGRAPHY

See your local travel agent for free, beautifully illustrated travel brochures. Also see travel guides available in book stores, such as the $10—$15 dollar a Day Series, and Fodor's.

Atlantic Beaches
Jonathan Norton Leonard
Time-Life, 1972

The formation and decline of beaches and the types of beaches found along the Atlantic coast.

The Bermuda Triangle
Charles Berlitz

The mysterious disappearance of ships and planes in an area of the Caribbean. The author discusses possible reasons for these tragedies—some based on known scientific phenomena, some quite far-out.

The Big Wave
Pearl S. Buck
Day, 1973

A Japanese boy's family and home are swept away by a tidal wave, and he is taken in by the family of his friend.

The Everglades

See science—general.

The Good Earth
Pearl S. Buck

The story of Wang Lung, from wedding day to death-bed, encompasses every strata of precommunist Chinese society, as he ascends from poverty to riches. The first of a trilogy, including *Sons* and *A House Divided*.

Hawaii
James Michener
Random House, 1959

A long but epic novel of the fiftieth state, from its volcanic origin, through successive waves of immigration, to the Hawaii we know today. Told with major focus on a group of missionaries who went to preach and their descendents who remained to colonize.

Hawaii: A Natural History
Sherwin Carlquist and Jeanne R. Janish
Natural History Press, 1970

Origin, geology, climate, scenery, and plant and animal life.

John Muir's Wild America

See science—general.

The Ozarks

See science—general.

Papa Is All
Patterson Greene
Samuel French

Comedy-drama about life among the Mennonite in Pennsylvania.

Primitive Worlds; People Lost in Time

See social studies—anthropology.

Richard Halliburton's Complete Book of Marvels
Richard Halliburton
Bobbs, 1960

The great wonders of the world, some natural, some man-made. Includes the Grand Canyon, Yosemite Falls, the Taj Mahal, and the Egyptian pyramids.

The Search for Big Foot; Monster, Myth, or Man?
Peter Byrne
Acropolis Books, 1975

Fascinating collection of evidence that there really is a Big Foot in the North Pacific states.

In Search of Lake Monsters
Peter Costello
Coward, McCann

World-wide search for lake dwelling animals, with concentration on famous Loch Ness.

Shinega's Village
Shale Sellassie
Translated from Chaha by Wolf Leslau
UC Press, 1966

Conflict between twentieth century urban life and ancient village patterns is seen in this fictionalized memoir of village life in Ethiopia.

Teahouse of the August Moon
Vern Sneider
Signet, 1951

An American military officer, assigned to the occupation of Okinawa during World War II learns about geisha girls, tea houses, and a great new drink made from sweet potatoes.

The White Caps
Jacques Cousteau
World Publishing, 1974

Life at the North and South Poles photographed and described by a famous scientist-explorer.

Wild Alaska

See science—general.

SOCIAL STUDIES—GOVERNMENT

All the President's Men
Carl Bernstein and Bob Woodward
Simon and Schuster, 1974

True story of how two highpowered journalists went about investigating the Watergate story.

Animal Farm
  George Orwell
  Harcourt, 1954

The animals rebel, throw off their human masters, and establish a government where "all animals are equal." But soon they find that "some are more equal than others." Soon the pigs, who come to rule, are consorting with the hated enemy, man, and you can't tell the pigs from the people.

The C.I.A. and the Cult of Intelligence
  Victor Marchetti and John D. Marks
  Knopf, 1974

Inside story of the C.I.A.—how it developed from an intelligence-gathering institution to one of clandestine operations.

Deschooling Society
  Ivan Illich
  Harper, 1971

The author claims that schools as we know them are not conducive to education. He suggests alternative approaches.

Looking Backward
  Edward Bellamy

Julian West falls into a hypnotic sleep and awakens over a century later to find a beautiful world of cooperation, sharing, and love. When he sees the world he left again, he is appalled.

Nineteen Eighty-four; A Novel
  George Orwell
  Harcourt, 1949

A terrifying look at Orwell's vision of the near future. He sees a totalitarian state, with control of thought, of our everyday activities, and even our love lives.

Planet of the Apes
  Pierre Boulle
  Vanguard, 1963

Interplanetary explorers discover a place where apes act like men and men act like apes, with many implications about our social system.

Ralph Bunche: UN Peacemaker
  Peggy Mann
  Coward, McCann, 1975

Under-Secretary-General of the United Nations, he is credited with a major contribution towards peacekeeping, particularly in the Middle East.

The Rights of Students
  Alan Levine
  Dutton, 1974

Guide to teenage rights, largely in relation to school.

Teenagers and the Law
  John Paul Hanna
  Ginn, 1975

The legal rights and responsibilities of youth. Also deals with juvenile offenders.

Watership Down
  Richard Adams
  Macmillan, 1974

Although this is the story of a group of rabbits who set out to form a new warren, it has much to say about love, loyalty, cooperation, and fascism.

SOCIAL STUDIES—PHILOSOPHY

The Book: On the Taboo Against Knowing Who You Are
  Alan W. Watts
  Collier, 1966

A student of Eastern philosophy explains his belief in the unity of all things.

The Book of Prophecy
  Edward Edelson
  Doubleday, 1974

Tarot, I Ching, palmestry, and other forms of divination are discussed.

How the Great Religions Began
  Joseph Gaer
  Signet, 1929

Ten major world religions and the Reformation discussed and explained.

Siddhartha
  Hermann Hesse
  New Directions, 1951

An East Indian sets out to achieve wisdom and purity. His life-long wandering brings him in contact with the Buddha, with a courtesan, with the world of commerce, and finally with an ancient ferryman from whom he learns patience.

The Story of Philosophy
  Will Durant
  Simon and Schuster, 1933

A summary of the major contributions of the most important philosophers of Western civilization.

The World's Great Religions
  by the Editorial Staff of Life
  Golden, 1958

Hinduism, Islam, Judaism, Christianity, and other religions are examined, their major teachings, customs, and holidays explained. Beautifully illustrated.

Zen and the Art of Motorcycle Maintenance
  Robert M. Pirsig
  Morrow, 1974

The motorcycle becomes the focus of mental health and a way of looking at life, as Pirsig and his son tour the country. A convincing appeal to keep all our "motorcycles" in tune.

SOCIAL STUDIES—SOCIOLOGY

The Affluent Society
  John Kenneth Galbraith
  Houghton

The author points out that our social and economic thinking has not changed to meet current conditions.

After the Goat Man
  Betsy Byars
  Viking, 1974

An old man battles to save his home from the freeway wreckers.

Aria Da Capo
  Edna St. Vincent Millay
  Walter H. Baker Company

Poetic drama about friendship and hatred and war.

Aztecas Del Norte	See social studies—ethnic studies.
Barrio Boy	See social studies—ethnic studies.
Black Like Me	See social studies—ethnic studies.
Brave New World Aldous Huxley	A depressing view of where the author believes civilization is headed, with babies born in test tubes, lack of moral choice, and much of the population drugged into submission.
Brave New World Revisited Aldous Huxley Harper, 1958	The author of *Brave New World* points out that his predictions are coming true at a faster rate than he had anticipated.
Cities on the Move Arnold Toynbee Oxford, 1970	Housing and other urban problems of yesterday and today.
The Closing Circle	See science—general.
A Connecticut Yankee in King Arthur's Court	See social studies—European history.
The Consumer and Corporate Accountability	See home economics—consumer education.
Crime in America Ramsey Clark Pocket, 1970	Observations on the nature, causes, prevention, and control of crime by a former Attorney General of the United States.
Death of a Salesman Arthur Miller Viking, 1949	Dramatization of the destruction of a human being who is unable to experience success.
Don Camillo's Dilemma *The Little World of Don Camillo* Giovanni Guareschi Pocket	Adventures of a lovable Italian priest and his struggles with the Communists. Warm-hearted and humorous stories.
Earth: Our Crowded Spaceship	See home economics—family life.
Escape from Freedom Erich Fromm Holt, 1976	Commentary on the nature of human freedom and the inability of some people to cope with it. An analysis of Nazism.
Fail-safe Eugene Burdick and Harvey Wheeler McGraw-Hill, 1962	Chilling tale of what can happen if, by mistake, someone sets off an atomic war.
Future Shock Alvin Toffler Random House, 1970	In which directions is society changing, and what happens to us as the pace of change accelerates?
Go Ask Alice	See psychology.

The Great Gatsby
  F. Scott Fitzgerald
  Scribner, 1958

The gentle, well-mannered aristocracy of this country are unmasked to show the rotten, violent, self-seeking animals that reside within. In its dealings with a hedonistic, irresponsible society, this novel has much to say that is timely.

How and Why Wonder Book of Ecology

See science—general.

How to Be a Survivor
  Paul R. Ehrlich and Richard L. Harriman
  Ballantine, 1971

A look at population control, overdevelopment of industry and underdevelopment, agriculture, government, and other issues that must be faced if Spaceship Earth is to survive.

In Common Cause
  John W. Gardner
  Norton, 1973

The founder of the citizens' lobby *Common Cause* explains why he founded it and what he hopes it will accomplish.

Inherit the Wind (a play)
  Jerome Lawrence and Robert E. Lee
  Bantam, 1955

Courtroom drama loosely based on the famous Scopes "monkey trail" of 1925, in which the issue of scientific inquiry was defended and attacked by two brilliant legal minds.

Life and Death in a Coral Sea

See science—biology.

Man's Most Dangerous Myth; The Fallacy of Race
  Ashley Montagu
  Oxford, 1974

The author explains that differences between races are either insignificant in terms of social interaction or nonexistent.

Maple Street
  Nan Hayden Agle
  Pocket

A black girl finds a peach tree struggling to survive in a vacant lot. That sets off a series of events that ends with the building of a play-ground.

The Mouse That Roared
  Leonard Wibberley
  Little, 1955

Would you believe the tiny Duchy of Grand Fenwick, with twenty-three hearty archers, can defeat the United States in war and bring the world to its knees? It all happens in this hilarious spoof.

On Being Human
  Ashley Montagu
  Hawthorn, 1967

A convincing case is made for cooperation rather than competition in human affairs.

The Pearl
  John Steinbeck
  Bantam, 1945

Kino, a poor Indian, finds a valuable pearl and decides to use it to improve the opportunities for his son. But all the forces of society close in on him to keep

The Peter Principle
Laurence J. Peter and Rymond Hull
Morrow, 1969

him in his place, and good fortune turns to tragedy.

In this delightful spoof of bureaucracy, business, and industry, the authors expound on how everyone rises to his "level of incompetence."

The Night Is Dark and I Am Far from Home

See social studies—government.

On the Beach
Nevil Shute

A nuclear war has been fought, and a handful of survivors know they are doomed. How does one act, knowing that death will come soon?

The Prince and the Pauper

See social studies—European history.

The Pyramid Climbers
Vance Packard
Crest, 1962

Packard tells about life in a modern corporation, who makes it and who doesn't—and how a person knows when he or she has made it.

R. U R. (Rossum's Universal Robots)
Karel Capek

Science fiction drama about Robots taking over the world, as man delegates more and more work to the machine.

Self-renewal
John W. Gardner
Harper & Row, 1963

The founder of *Common Causes* speaks his mind on an important social issue—the need to be continually renewing and freshening our outlook and our institutions.

Silent Spring

See agriculture.

Small is Beautiful: Economics as if People Mattered
E. F. Schumacher
Harper and Row, 1973

The father of "appropriate technology" explains why he believes we need to conserve Earth's limited resources and convert from massive to smaller-scale industry.

So Human an Animal
René Dubos
Scribner, 1968

The author discusses the dangers of over-industrialization, recommends conservation and careful planning, living in harmony with nature.

Stranger in a Strange Land
Robert A. Heinlein
Putnam, 1961

A man of Earthan parentage, raised in a Martian culture, comes to Earth and, as founder of the Church of All Worlds, demonstrates that some of our most unquestioned beliefs—ranging from economics to sex—are in need of redefining.

Twenty Years at Hull House
  Jane Adams
  Macmillan, 1966

In this reissue of the original 1910 work, one of the pioneers of social work tells of her struggles.

Unsafe at any Speed
  Ralph Nader
  Grossman, 1972

An exposé of the inadequacies of private and federal safety controls on automobiles.

The Voyages of Apollo; The Exploration of the Moon

See science—physical

A Walden Two Experiment

See home economics—family life.

The Waste Makers
  Vance Packard
  Pocket, 1963

Exposé of practices in industry that rip off the consumer.
      See also other books by this author.

Water: The Web of Life

See science—general.

West Side Story

See music.

Why We Can't Wait

See social studies—ethnic studies.

SOCIAL STUDIES— WORLD HISTORY

Alexander the Great
  Peter Green
  Praeger, 1970

Interesting biography of a man driven by an insatiable thirst for conquest.

All Quiet on the Western Front
  Erich Maria Remarque
  Little, 1929

A German soldier tells of his horrible experiences in World War I. A classic of anti-war sentiment.

The Ancient Romans; How They Lived and Worked
  O. A. W. Dilke
  Dufour, 1975

The average Roman citizen comes to life as his living habits are described.

Anna and the King of Siam
  Margaret Landon
  John Day, 1944

A beautiful and moving story of an English schoolteacher hired by the King of Siam to instruct his many children.

Anne Frank: The Diary of a Young Girl
  Pocket, 1952

A warm, amusing, lovable true story of a group of people hiding out from the Nazis during World War II.

The Ark
  Margot Benary-Isbert
  Harcourt, 1953

A family starts over after World War II forces them into refugee camps.

B-G: Fighter of Goliaths; The Story of David Ben Gurion
  Gertrude Samuels
  Crowell, 1974

The story of the great statesman of Israel.

Caesar Michael Grant Follett, 1975	The life of the greatest of the Romans.
The Cherry Orchard Anton Chekhov	Chekhov brings to the stage the breakup of the aristocracy in Czarist Russia. This play foreshadows the coming of communism, as the people gain economic power and the beautiful, old, useless cherry orchard must be sold for tract houses.
A Connecticut Yankee in King Arthur's Court Mark Twain	This lampoon on knights and knighthood is not without its serious, even beautiful moments.
Cry, the Beloved Country Alan Paton	Current tensions in South Africa make this story of suffering and hate particularly potent.
Everyday Life in Prehistoric Times Marjorie Quennell Putnam, 1959	Describes the life style, as we know it, of those who lived before recorded history.
Exodus Leon Uris Doubleday, 1958	The exuberant story of the beginnings of the State of Israel, as seen through the eyes of a Christian nurse.
Fiddler on the Roof Joseph Stein Crown, 1964	Delightful musical play about life among Jews in Czarist Russia.
For Whom the Bell Tolls Ernest Hemingway Scribner, 1940	A novel about an incident in the Spanish Civil War depicts love and courage and the stupidity of war.
A Kind of Secret Weapon Elliot Arnold Scribner, 1969	A story of the underground resistance in Denmark during World War II.
Lawrence of Arabia Anthony Nutting Signet, 1961	An Englishman becomes deeply enmeshed in the wars and rivalries of the Arab world.
Life in Anglo-Saxon England R. I. Page Putnam, 1970	A glimpse at the British Isles of many centuries ago.
A Man for all Seasons Robert Balt Random House, 1962	The conflict between Sir Thomas Moore and Henry VIII.
Les Miserables Victor Hugo	Life in the lower depths of nineteenth century France. The nobility of man is contrasted with the cruelty of society.

The Riddle of the Pyramids
  Kurt Mendelssohn
  Praeger, 1974

The author has an interesting theory concerning why the pyramids of Egypt and Mexico were built.

Riders to the Sea
  John Millington Synge

The Irish revolution, a subject made timely by the current unrest in Ireland, portrayed in this very dramatic stage play.

Saint Joan
  Bernard Shaw

The trial of Joan of Arc.

A Tale of Two Cities
  Charles Dickens

The more terrifying consequences of the French revolution.

Twenty and Ten
  Claire Huchet Bishop
  Viking, 1952

Jewish refugee children are hidden from the Nazis during World War II.

Watch on the Rhine
Lillian Hellman

Stirring drama of spies and counterspies, of the Hitler movement, and the effect of Nazism on one family.

WOMEN'S STUDIES

A Doll's House
  Henrik Ibsen

Ibsen wrote this drama about the male attitude towards women long before the women's movement became popular.

Against Our Will
  Susan Brownmiller
  Simon and Schuster

A moving, although somewhat simplistic, explanation of the psychology of rape.

Angela Davis, An Autobiography

See social studies—ethnic studies.

Enterprising Women
  Caroline Bird
  Norton, 1976

Short biographies of successful American women.

The Feminine Mystique
  Betty Friedan
  Norton, 1974

The loss of identity of the American woman, as she is forced into the stereotyped wife and mother role.

Girls are Equal to; The Women's Movement for Teenagers
  Dale Carlson
  Atheneum, 1973

How teenage girls can organize study groups to improve their status.

Hail Columbia
  Patricia Beatty
  Morrow, 1970

Set in turn-of-the-century Oregon, this story involves the adventures of an early crusader for women's rights.

Madame Curie; A Biography

See science—general.

Men and Masculinity Joseph H. Pleck Prentice-Hall, 1974	The stereotyped male role and how it suppresses some of the most important aspects of a man's personality.
The Natural Superiority of Women Ashley Montagu Collier, 1974	Despite its title, this book discusses the social equality of women and the need for male-female love and understanding.
The New Feminism Lucy Komisar Watts, 1971	Traditional roles of women and how the woman's movement is changing them.
The Twelve Pound Look James Barrie	Twelve British pounds is all it took to liberate the "lucky" wife of a great man.
Women in Modern America; A Brief History Lois W. Banner Harcourt, 1974	Twentieth century trends in the changing status of women. Effects of the women's movement.
Women Who Win Francene Sabin Random House, 1975	Fourteen women athletes, their careers and the difficulties they have had because they were women in athletics.

DIRECTORY OF PUBLISHERS

Abingdon Press, 201 8th Ave. South, Nashville, Tenn. 37202.

Acropolis Bks., Ltd., Colortone Bldg., 2400 17th St. N.W., Washington, D.C. 20009.

Addison-Wesley Publishing Company, Inc., Reading, Mass. 01867.

Afro-American Publishing Company, Inc., 1727 South Indiana Ave., Chicago, Ill. 60616.

American Book Company, 450 West 33rd St., New York, N. Y. 10003.

American Youth Hostels, Inc., 20 West 17th St., New York, N.Y. 10011.

Arbor House Publishing Company, Inc., 641 Lexington Ave., New York, N.Y. 10022.

Atheneum Publishers, 122 East 42nd St., New York, N.Y. 10017.

Avon Books, 959 8th Ave., New York, N.Y. 10019.

Walter H. Baker, 100 Chauncy St., Boston, Mass. 02111.

Ballantine Books, Inc., 201 East 50th St., New York, N.Y. 10022.

Bantam Books, Inc., 666 5th Ave., New York, N.Y. 10019.

Basic Books, Inc., Publishers, 10 East 53rd St., New York, N.Y. 10022.

Berkley Publishing Corporation, 200 Madison Ave., New York, N.Y. 10016.

The Bobbs-Merrill Company, Inc., 4300 West 62nd St., Indianapolis, Ind. 46206.

Bradbury Press, Inc., 2 Overhill Rd., Scarsdale, N.Y. 10583.

George Braziller, Inc., 1 Park Ave., New York, N.Y. 10016.

Chilton Book Company, Chilton Way, Radnor, Penn. 19089.

Collier Books. See Macmillan Publishing Company.

William Collins & World Publishing Company, Inc., 2080 West 117th St., Cleveland, Ohio 44111.

Columbia University Press, 562 West 113th St., New York, N.Y. 10025.

Coward, McCann & Geoghegan, Inc., 200 Madison Ave., New York, N.Y. 10016.

Crest. See Fawcett.

Thomas Y. Crowell Company Inc., 666 5th Ave., New York, N.Y. 10019

Crown Publishers, Inc., 1 Park Ave., New York, N.Y. 10016.

The John Day Company, 666 5th Ave., New York, N.Y. 10019.

Delacorte Press, 1 Dag Hammarskjold Plaza, New York, N.Y. 10017.

Dell Publishing Company, Inc., 1 Dag Hammarskjold Plaza, 245 East 47th St., New York, N.Y. 10017.

Delta. See Dell.

The Dial Press, 1 Dag Hammarskjold Plaza, 245 East 47th St., New York, N.Y. 10017.

Dodd, Mead & Company, 79 Madison Ave., New York, N.Y. 10016.

Doubleday & Company, Inc., 245 Park Ave., New York, N.Y. 10017.

Drake Publishers, Inc., 801 2nd Ave., New York, N.Y. 10017.

Drama Book Specialists/Publishers, 150 West 52nd St., New York, N.Y. 10019.

Dramatists Play Service, Inc., 440 Park Ave. South, New York, N.Y. 10016.

Dufour Editions, Inc., Chester Springs, Penn. 19425.

E. P. Dutton & Company, Inc., 201 Park Ave. South, New York, N.Y. 10003.

M. Evans & Company, Inc., 216 East 49th St., New York, N.Y. 10017.

Farrar, Straus & Giroux, Inc., 19 Union Square West, New York, N.Y. 10003.

Fawcett Publications, Inc., Fawcett Bldg., Fawcett Place, Greenwich, Conn. 06830.

Follett Corporation, 1010 West Washington Blvd., Chicago, Ill. 60607.

Samuel French, 25 West 45th St., New York, N.Y. 10036.

Funk & Wagnalls Publishing Company, Inc., 666 5th Ave., New York, N.Y. 10019.

Garrard Publishing Company, 1607 North Market St., Champaign, Ill. 61820.

Ginn & Company, 191 Spring St., Lexington, Mass. 02173.

Glencoe Press, 17337 Ventura Blvd., Encino, Calif. 91316.

Golden Press, Publishers, 850 3rd Ave., New York, N.Y. 10022.

Grosset & Dunlap, Inc., 51 Madison Ave., New York, N.Y. 10010.

Grossman Publishers, 625 Madison Ave., New York, N.Y. 10022.

Grove Press, Inc., 196 West Houston St., New York, N.Y. 10014.

Harcourt Brace Jovanovich, Inc., 757 3rd Ave., New York, N.Y. 10017.

Harmony Books, 419 Park Ave. South, New York, N.Y. 10016.

Harper & Row, Publishers, 10 East 53rd St., New York, N.Y. 10022.

Hawthorn Books, Inc., 260 Madison Ave., New York, N.Y. 10016.

Holt, Rinehart and Winston, Inc., 383 Madison Ave., New York, N.Y. 10017.

Houghton Mifflin Company, 1 Beacon St., Boston, Mass. 02107.

Indiana University Press, 10th & Morton Sts., Bloomington, Ind. 47401.

Jalmar Press, Inc., 391 Munro St., Sacramento, Calif. 95825.

Johnson Publishing Company, Inc., Book Division, 820 South Michigan Ave., Chicago, Ill. 60605.

Alfred A. Knopf, Inc., 201 East 50th St., New York, N.Y. 10022.

Lane Publishing Company, Willow & Middlefield Roads, Menlo Park, Calif. 94025.

Larousse & Company, Inc., 572 5th Ave., New York, N.Y. 10036.

J. B. Lippincott Company, East Washington Square, Philadelphia, Penn. 19105.

Little, Brown & Company, 34 Beacon St., Boston, Mass. 02106.

Lothrop, Lee & Shepard Company, 105 Madison Ave., New York, N.Y. 10016.

McGraw-Hill Book Company, 1221 Ave. of the Americas, New York, N.Y. 10020.

David McKay Company, Inc., 750 3rd Ave., New York, N.Y. 10017.

Macmillan Publishing Co. Inc., 866 3rd Ave., New York, N.Y. 10022.

Meredith Corporation, 1716 Locust St., Des Moines, Iowa 50336.

Julian Messner, The Simon & Schuster Bldg., 1230 Ave. of the Americas, New York, N.Y. 10020.

William Morrow & Company, Inc., 105 Madison Ave., New York, N.Y. 10016.

New York Times Company, Book Division, 330 Madison Ave., New York, N.Y. 10017.

National Geographic Society, 17th & M Sts. N. W., Washington, D.C. 20036.

Natural History Press, 501 Franklin Ave., Garden City, N.Y. 11530.

The New American Library, Inc., 1301 Ave. of the Americas, New York, N.Y. 10019.

New Directions Publishing Corporation, 333 Ave. of the Americas, New York, N.Y. 10014.

The New Republic Book Company, Inc., 1220 19th St. N. W., Washington, D.C. 20036.

W. W. Norton & Company, Inc., 500 5th Ave., New York, N.Y. 10036.

Odyssey Press, 4300 West 62nd St., Indianapolis, Ind. 46268.

Oxford University Press, Inc., 200 Madison Ave., New York, N.Y. 10016.

Pantheon Books, Inc., 201 East 50th St., New York, N.Y. 10022.

Penguin Books, 625 Madison Ave., New York, N.Y. 10022.

Petersen Publishing Company, 8490 Sunset Blvd., Los Angeles, Calif. 90069

Pitman Publishing Corporation, 6 Davis Dr., Belmont, Calif. 94002.

Plays, Inc., 8 Arlington So., Boston, Mass. 02116

Pocket Books. See Simon & Schuster.

Praeger Publishers, Inc., 200 Park Ave., New York, N.Y. 10017.

Prentice-Hall, Inc., Route 9W, Englewood Cliffs, N.J. 07632.

G. P. Putnam's Sons, 200 Madison Ave., New York, N.Y. 10016.

Pyramid Press Publishing Company, 1686 Marshall St., Benwood, West Virginia 26031.

Rand McNally & Company, 8255 Central Park Ave., Skokie, Ill. 60076.

Random House, Inc., 201 East 50th St., New York, N.Y. 10022.

Henry Regnery Company, 180 North Michigan Ave., Chicago, Ill. 60601.

Reston Publishing Company, 11480 Sunset Hills Road, Reston, Virginia 22090.

Richards Rosen Press, Inc., 29 East 21st St., New York, N.Y. 10010.

Row Peterson. See Harper & Row.

Russell & Russell, Publishers, 122 East 42nd St., New York, N.Y. 10017.

Howard W. Sams & Company, Inc., Publishers, 4300 West 62nd St., Indianapolis, Ind. 46268.

Scholastic Books, 906 Sylvan Ave., Englewood Cliffs, N.J. 07632.

Charles Scribner's Sons, 597 5th Ave., New York, N.Y. 10017.

Sex Information and Education Council of the United States, 137–155 North Franklin, Hempstead, L.I. 11550.

Sierra Club Books, 1050 Mills Tower, San Francisco, Calif. 94104.

Signet Classics. See New American Library.

Silver Burdett Co., 250 James Street, Morristown, N.J., 07960.

Simon & Schuster, Inc., The Simon & Schuster Bldg., 1230 Ave. of the Americas, New York, N.Y. 10020.

Stackpole Books, Cameron & Kelker Sts., Box 1831, Harrisburg, Penn. 17105.

Stein & Day, Publishers, Scarborough House, Briarcliff Manor, N.Y. 10510.

Theatre Arts Books, 333 Ave. of the Americas, New York, N.Y. 10014.

Time-Life Books, 777 Duke St., Alexandria, Virginia 22314 (Unless otherwise noted Time-Life Books are also available to schools and libraries from Silver Burdett).

Trident Press, 630 5th Ave., New York, N.Y. 10020.

University of California Press, 2223 Fulton St., Berkeley, Calif. 94720.

University of Nebraska Press, 901 North 17th St., Lincoln, Neb. 68588.

University of Oklahoma Press, 1005 Asp Ave., Norman, Okla. 73069.

University of Wisconsin Press, Box 1379, Madison, Wis. 53701.

Vanguard Press, Inc., 424 Madison Ave., New York, N.Y. 10017.

Van Nostrand-Reinhold Company, 450 West 33rd St., New York, N.Y. 10001.

The Viking Press, 625 Madison Ave., New York, N.Y. 10022.

Vintage. See Random House.

Warner Books, Inc., 75 Rockefeller Plaza, New York, N.Y. 10019.

Washington Square Press, 630 5th Ave., New York, N.Y. 10020.

Watson-Guptill Publications, 1 Astor Plaza, New York, N.Y. 10036.

Franklin Watts, Inc., 730 5th Ave., New York, N.Y. 10019.

Willow House Publishers, P.O. Box 129, Stockton, Calif. 95201.

Winchester Press, 205 East 42nd St., New York, N.Y. 10017.

World Publishing. See Collins & World.

Writer's Digest, 9933 Alliance Road, Cincinnati, Ohio 45242.

INDEX

Additional bibliographic information is available in the appendices.